SANCTIONS IN EU COMPETITION LAW

In the early decades of European integration, the enforcement of EU competition law was highly centralised. Virtually all enforcement actions under Articles 101 and 102 TFEU were initiated by the European Commission. More recently, the enforcement of EU competition law has become less centralised – many would say even decentralised. In 2004, essentially in an effort to increase enforcement capacity in the wake of EU enlargement, the involvement of Member State competition authorities was significantly reinforced by national authorities being given the power to pursue infringements of EU competition law largely on the basis of their domestic enforcement regimes.

This combination of decentralisation and enforcement autonomy raises questions about the relationship between EU law and national law, as well as about the costs of enforcement. This book links these questions by analysing how competences in the area of sanctions are distributed between EU and national law, and how this influences the costs of enforcement. The author's conclusions, which highlight the economic implications of the choices made by competition authorities, courts and legislators, will be of use to all the above in further developing EU competition policy.

The thesis on which this book is based was declared runner-up in the 2013 Concurrences Awards.

Volume 6 in the series Hart Studies in Competition Law

Hart Studies in Competition Law

Volume 1: *Intellectual Property, Antitrust and Cumulative Innovation in the EU and the US*
Thorsten Käseberg

Volume 2: *State Aid and the European Economic Constitution*
Francesco de Cecco

Volume 3: *The Private Enforcement of Competition Law in Ireland*
David McFadden

Volume 4: *Cross-Border EU Competition Law Actions*
Edited by Mihail Danov, Florian Becker and Paul Beaumont

Volume 5: *European Merger Remedies: Law and Policy*
Dorte Hoeg

Sanctions in EU Competition Law

Principles and Practice

Michael J Frese

·HART·
PUBLISHING
OXFORD AND PORTLAND, OREGON
2016

Published in the United Kingdom by Hart Publishing Ltd
16C Worcester Place, Oxford, OX1 2JW
Telephone: +44 (0)1865 517530
Fax: +44 (0)1865 510710
E-mail: mail@hartpub.co.uk
Website: http://www.hartpub.co.uk

Published in North America (US and Canada) by
Hart Publishing
c/o International Specialized Book Services
920 NE 58th Avenue, Suite 300
Portland, OR 97213-3786
USA
Tel: +1 503 287 3093 or toll-free: (1) 800 944 6190
Fax: +1 503 280 8832
E-mail: orders@isbs.com
Website: http://www.isbs.com

First published in hardback 2014
Paperback edition, 2016

Hart Publishing is an imprint of Bloomsbury Publishing plc

British Library Cataloguing in Publication Data
Data Available

ISBN: HB: 978-1-84946-518-2
PB: 978-1-50990-703-8

Typeset by Hope Services, Abingdon
Printed and bound in Great Britain by
Lightning Source UK Ltd

ACKNOWLEDGEMENTS

This book is an edited version of the PhD thesis I defended on 22 November 2012 at the University of Amsterdam. The introductory and concluding chapters have been adapted and developments in legislation and case law have been accounted for up until 1 July 2013. Later developments have been included incidentally. For the rest, the original manuscript has remained largely intact.

Writing this book often felt like a lonely journey. As I was considering who to thank for their help, I was surprised by the long list of people who in some way or other contributed to the thesis and ultimately this book. In retrospect, the journey was not as lonely as it sometimes appeared. Some of the people who have helped me along the way should be mentioned.

First of all, I am very grateful to my supervisors Floris Vogelaar, Rein Wesseling and Kati Cseres. Without their commitment, this journey could not have been undertaken. Moreover, their comments prevented me from getting hopelessly lost along the way and their precision has contributed significantly to the structure and reader-friendliness of this book.

Apart from my supervisors, two other colleagues have performed a key role in this project. Ronald van Ooik agreed to read various drafts and has shared with me his unparalleled knowledge of European law. Thanks to him, I could make some last-minute improvements. I am also very grateful to René Smits. Apart from the useful discussions he and I regularly had, René introduced me to many interesting people within the *Nederlandse Mededingingsautoriteit*, invited me to seminars here and abroad, and arranged for me internships at the Office of Fair Trading (OFT) in London and the *Bundeskartellamt* in Bonn.

I should also thank the members of my reading committee. Adrienne de Moor-van Vugt, Saskia Lavrijssen, Petra Pohlmann, Barry Rodger and Wouter Wils were so kind to accept the invitation. It is both an honour and a privilege that these five experts were willing to read and comment on my work.

As already mentioned, I undertook various research internships in the preparation of this book. These were crucial in terms of understanding some of the domestic legal issues I had to grapple with. I would like to thank the OFT and in particular Ali Nikpay, Andrea Appella, Terry Butler and all other members of the OFT's executive office for offering me an internship and for making it such a valuable and pleasant stay. The fact that I was offered a desk next to the Chairman of the Board definitely contributed to the whole experience. I was lucky enough to be offered a similar internship at the *Bundeskartellamt*, where I worked for one of the cartel units. This brought me to the frontline of competition law enforcement.

I would like to thank the *Bundeskartellamt* and in particular Dr Wagemann and all other members of the *11. Beschlussabteilung* for this unique opportunity. Thanks to Cleary Gottlieb Steen & Hamilton LLP, I also had the opportunity to study the enforcement of competition law from the perspective of a defence counsel. I am grateful to the entire Cologne office and in particular to Dirk Schroeder, Romina Polley and Roman Zagrosek for their hospitality.

The largest part of this book was written at the Law School of the University of Amsterdam. I would like to thank all my colleagues at the Amsterdam Centre for European Law and Governance and the Department of International and European Public Law for creating such an inspiring and pleasant working environment, in particular Gerrit Jan Pulles, Erik Kok, Thomas Beukers, Herman van Harten, Aart Loubert and Jeremy Bierbach, with whom I shared offices. Furthermore, I would like to thank all my colleagues at the Amsterdam Center for Law & Economics for inspiring me through their dedication for research, in particular Maarten Pieter Schinkel, whose enthusiasm for research and antitrust policy has proven highly contagious. I should not forget my colleagues at the Department of Administrative Law either, in particular Arnout Klap, for offering me a position right after graduation and for making me enthusiastic for academia.

This book has profited from the feedback I received at the annual workshops of the Competition Law & Economics European Network (CLEEN). I should therefore thank the organisors and participants of the CLEEN workshops in Norwich, Amsterdam, Florence and Mannheim for providing a forum to present and discuss some of the ideas in this book.

Also on a more personal level, acknowledgements are fully justified. Ahmet Kilinç and Floris ten Have: thank you for being such great friends and paranymphs. Each of you played an important role in the development of this book. Ahmet, because of you I was in no hurry to leave the Law School after graduation. Floris, you were an excellent sparring partner and I enjoyed our 'SCI trips'. Family and friends, you have meant so much to me during these last couple of years. I am grateful to share my life with so many wonderful and loving people. My *hayati* Amira Fatima, you have joined me on the last and most difficult stages of this journey. Thank you for your love, care and patience. This journey has come to an end, but ours is just beginning.

My dear mother, thank you for supporting me in all my endeavours, for making me aim high and for always having made sure that I never needed to miss out on anything in life. I dedicate this book to you.

TABLE OF CONTENTS

ABBREVIATIONS

ABRvS	Afdeling Bestuursrechtspraak Raad van State
ACM	Autoriteit Consument en Markt
Awb	Algemene wet bestuursrecht
BGH	Bundesgerichtshof
BIS	Department for Business, Innovation & Skills
BKartA	Bundeskartellamt
BMWi	Bundesministerium für Wirtschaft und Technologie
BT-Drucksache	Drucksache des Deutschen Bundestages (Wahlperiode/Nummer)
CAA	Civil Aviation Authority
CA98	Competition Act 1998
CAT	Competition Appeal Tribunal
CBb	College van Beroep voor het bedrijfsleven
CDDA86	Company Directors Disqualification Act 1986
CMA	Competition and Markets Authority
EA02	Enterprise Act 2002
ECA	European Competition Authorities
ECHR	European Convention for the Protection of Human Rights and Fundamental Freedoms
ECN	European Competition Network
ECR	European Court Reports
ECtHR	European Court of Human Rights
EFTA	European Free Trade Agreement
ERRA 2013	Enterprise and Regulatory Reform Act 2013
GG	Grundgesetz
GWB	Gesetz gegen Wettbewerbsbeschränkungen
HR	Hoge Raad
ICN	International Competition Network
JB	Jurisprudentie Bestuursrecht
LG	Landesgericht
LJN	Landelijk Jurisprudentie Nummer
LKartB	Landeskartellbehörde
Mw	Mededingingswet
NCA	National Competition Authority
NJ	Nederlandse Jurisprudentie
NMa	Nederlandse Mededingingsautoriteit
OECD	Organisation for Economic Co-operation and Development

Ofcom	Office of Communications
Ofgem	Gas and Electricity Markets Authority
OFREG NI	Northern Ireland Authority for Utility Regulation
OFT	Office of Fair Trading
OFWAT	Water Services Regulation Authority
OLG	Oberlandesgericht
ORR	Office of Rail Regulation
OWiG	Gesetz über Ordnungswidrigkeiten
Rb	Rechtbank
SFO	Serious Fraud Office
Stb	Staatsblad
Stcr	Staatscourant
StGB	Strafgesetzbuch
StPO	Strafprozeßordnung
TEU	Treaty on European Union
TFEU	Treaty on the Functioning of the European Union
TK	Tweede Kamer
UNCTAD	United Nations Conference on Trade and Development
WODC	Wetenschappelijk Onderzoek- en Documentatiecentrum
WuW	Wirtschaft und Wettbewerb
WvSr	Wetboek van Strafrecht

TABLE OF CASES

European Court of Human Rights

Court of Justice of the European Union

General Court of the European Union

European Commission Decisions

Germany

Court Cases

BKartA Cases

Netherlands

Court Cases

NMa Cases

United Kingdom

Court Cases

TABLE OF LEGISLATION

International Conventions and Agreements

European Union

Treaties and other Primary Sources of EU Law

Germany

Laws

BKartA Guidance

Netherlands

Laws

OFT Guidance

Other

1

General Introduction

The competitiveness of the European market has been one of the key drivers of European integration and is probably one of the biggest attributes of the EU. Competitiveness and competition are part of the EU's DNA. In its founding Treaty texts, it can be read that the EU aims for a 'highly competitive social market economy'[1] and that it will conduct its economic policy in accordance with the principles of an open market economy with free competition.[2] One of the EU's core policy instruments for a competitive internal market is the operation of a legal regime that prohibits companies from distorting competition. More precisely, 'undertakings' may in principle not restrict competition through any form of cooperation or coordination and 'undertakings with a dominant position' are prohibited from excluding competitors and exploiting trading partners. These two prohibitions are laid down in Articles 101 and 102 of the Treaty on the Functioning of the European Union (TFEU).[3]

In the first decades of European integration, the enforcement of EU competition law was highly centralised. Virtually all enforcement actions under Articles 101 and 102 TFEU were initiated by the European Commission (hereinafter 'the Commission'). Meanwhile, the enforcement of EU competition law has become less centralised – many would even say decentralised. In 2004, essentially in an effort to increase enforcement capacity in the wake of the enlargement of the EU, the involvement of the Member States in the enforcement of EU competition law has been reinforced significantly. This change was brought about by the adoption of Council Regulation (EC) No 1/2003 (hereinafter 'Regulation 1/2003').[4] To date, undertakings engaging in anti-competitive behaviour can be chased by a whole network of competition authorities. The Commission and the national competition authorities combine forces (and resources) to guard the competitiveness of the European market.

Instead of harmonising national enforcement procedures, Regulation 1/2003 recognises the wide variation of public enforcement systems existing in the Member States.[5] Accordingly, national competition authorities prosecute infringements of

[1] Article 3(3) Consolidated Version of the Treaty on European Union [2008] OJ C115/13.

[2] Article 119 Consolidated Version of the Treaty on the Functioning of the European Union [2008] OJ C115/47.

[3] [2008] OJ C115/47.

[4] Council Regulation (EC) No 1/2003 of 16 December 2002 on the implementation of the rules on competition laid down in Articles 81 and 82 of the Treaty [2003] OJ L1/1.

[5] Recital 35 of the preamble to Regulation 1/2003.

EU competition law largely on the basis of domestic enforcement regimes. The combination of decentralisation and enforcement autonomy raises questions in relation to the relationship between EU law and national law. For instance, to what extent are the Member States subject to rules and principles of EU law in the enforcement of Articles 101 and 102 TFEU? Increasingly, this is becoming a topic of debate. The scope of the autonomy of the Member States has been tested in several recent cases before the Court of Justice of the European Union (hereinafter 'the Court of Justice'),[6] has been the subject of policy debates within the Commission[7] and has already featured in a number of academic publications.[8]

Apart from these legal questions, the decentralisation of enforcement competences also raises questions of an economic nature. The enforcement of EU competition law is a big industry. It provides work to many lawyers and economists, whether active in commercial practice or government positions (or even academia).[9] The clients of these services are generally undertakings and government agencies. For them, the enforcement of EU competition law therefore comes with certain costs.[10] Ultimately, these costs are borne by consumers and taxpayers.[11] Certainly for

[6] Case C-8/08 *T-Mobile Netherlands* [2009] ECR I-4529; Case C-439/08 *VEBIC* [2010] ECR I-12471; Case C-375/09 *Tele2 Polska* [2011] ECR I-3055; Case C-17/10 *Toshiba Corporation* [2012] OJ C98/3-4; Case C-681/11 *Bundeswettbewerbsbehörde v Schenker* [2012] OJ C89/11.

[7] Communication from the Commission to the European Parliament and the Council: Report on the functioning of Regulation 1/2003 [2009] COM 206 final.

[8] Without making any claim of providing an exhaustive overview, the enforcement autonomy of the Member States has featured in the following publications: J Bourgeois and T Baumé, 'Decentralisation of EC Competition Law Enforcement and General Principles of Community law' (2004) College of Europe Research Paper 4/2004 <www.coleurope.be> accessed 1 July 2013; P Oliver, 'Le Règlement 1/2003 et les Principes D'Efficacité et D'Équivalence' (2005) 41 *Cahiers de droit européen* 351; SACM Lavrijssen-Heijmans, *Onafhankelijke mededingingstoezichthouders, regulerende bevoegdheden en de waarborgen voor good governance* (Boom Juridische uitgevers 2006); FOW Vogelaar, 'Interface: EC and Dutch Competition Law – In Which Fields or Areas Would the Netherlands Still Have Autonomous Regulating Powers? And Would It Be Wise to Use Those Powers?' in D Obradovic and N Lavranos (eds), *Interface between EU law and National Law* (Europa Law Publishing, 2007) 187–202; Ch Lemaire and J Gstalter, 'The Silent Revolution Beyond Regulation 1/2003' (2008) 2 *GCP Online Magazine for Global Competition Policy* <www.competitionpolicyinternational.com> accessed 1 July 2013; M de Visser, *Network-Based Governance in EC Law: The Example of EC Competition and EC Communications Law* (Hart Publishing, 2009); A Gerbrandy, *Convergentie in het Mededingingsrecht: De Invloed van het EG-Recht op Materiële Toepassing, Toegang, Bewijs en Toetsing bij de Nederlandse Mededingingsbestuursrechter, Bezien in het Licht van Effectieve Rechtsbescherming* (Boom Juridische uitgevers, 2009); A Gerbrandy, 'Procedural Convergence in Competition Law: Towards a Spontaneous *Ius Commune*?' (2009) 2 *Review of European Administrative Law* 105; I Simonsson, *Legitimacy in EU Cartel Control* (Hart Publishing, 2010); L Parret, *Side Effects of the Modernisation of EU Competition Law* (Wolf Legal Publishers, 2011).

[9] *cf* Ch Harding, 'The Anti-Cartel Enforcement Industry: Criminological Perspectives on Cartel Criminalisation' in C Beaton-Wells and A Ezrachi (eds), *Criminalising Cartels: Critical Studies of an International Regulatory Movement* (Hart Publishing, 2011) 359

[10] See also K Hüschelrath, 'The Costs and Benefits of Antitrust Enforcement: Identification and Measurement' (2012) 35 *World Competition* 121.

[11] Provided that the enforcement of EU competition law has net welfare gains, the costs of enforcement can be wholly justifiable. It will be assumed that this is indeed the case, *cf* JB Baker, 'The Case for Antitrust Enforcement' (2003) 17 *Journal of Economic Perspectives* 27; Hüschelrath (n 10). Some competition authorities have started making outcome assessments to measure the welfare effects of their intervention. See NMa, 'Outcome van NMa-optreden: Een Beschrijving van de Berekeningsmethode' (2010) 1 NMa Working Papers <www.acm.nl/nl/publicaties/publicatie/7121/NMa-Working-Paper---Outcome-van-NMa-optreden-Een-beschrijving-van-de-berekeningsmethode/> accessed 1 July 2013;

an area such as EU competition law, which aims, among other things, to protect the interests of consumers,[12] these costs should be considered in designing an enforcement system. In this respect, it should be noted that a centralised enforcement system and a decentralised enforcement system have different cost structures. This should already be clear from the fact that a decentralised enforcement system requires several authorities. In addition, the existence of several enforcement regimes, each with its own powers and procedures, could have repercussions for the size of the 'enforcement industry' and the concomitant costs for consumers and taxpayers. For example, undertakings might have to consult several lawyers with expertise in various national regimes in relation to a single infringement. This example also makes clear that the economic implications of decentralisation are dependent on the relationship between EU law and national law – the larger the body of EU law that governs the national enforcement regimes, the less need there is for undertakings to consult specialist domestic counsel.

THE OBJECTIVES OF THIS BOOK

The combination of decentralisation and enforcement autonomy that characterises the current framework for EU competition law thus raises questions of both a legal and an economic nature. The above examples are just the tip of the iceberg and there are still many unclarities with regard to the relationship between EU law and national law, and the costs and benefits of decentralisation. Understanding these issues, both jointly and in isolation, is crucial for the enforcement of Articles 101 and 102 TFEU in individual cases, as well as for policy debates more generally. On the basis of these legal and economic insights, competition authorities may develop policy and practice, courts may render judgments, and legislators may evaluate and reconsider current legislation. Against this background, this book aims to clarify some of the legal and economic implications of the decentralisation of enforcement competences in the area of EU competition law. More specifically, it aims to clarify the relationship between EU law and national law for the decentralised enforcement of Articles 101 and 102 TFEU, and to explain how this relationship influences the costs of enforcing these competition law prohibitions.[13]As this development has brought the enforcement of EU competition law into line with the enforcement of

OFT, *Annual Report and Accounts 2011–12* < www.oft.gov.uk/shared_oft/annual_report/2012/OFT_Annual_Report_and_Resou1.pdf > accessed 1 July 2013.

[12] EU competition law aims to protect the interests of competitors, consumers and the structure of the market, *cf* Joined Cases C-501, C-513, C-515 and C-519/06 P *GlaxoSmithKline Services Unlimited* [2009] ECR I-9291 [63].

[13] It should be stressed that economic considerations alone need not be decisive in dividing enforcement competences between the EU level and the national level. Issues like these also have important implications for the legitimacy of EU competition policy. On the issue of decentralisation and legitimacy in the area of EU competition law, see Simonsson (n 8).

EU law more generally,[14] the discussion in this book may provide useful insights for the division of enforcement competences in other areas of EU law as well.[15]

The enforcement of Articles 101 and 102 TFEU relies on a variety of powers and procedures (sanctioning powers, investigatory powers, burden of proof, rights of defence etc). Irrespective of the enforcement authority, these powers and procedures can be provided by EU law or national law. It is beyond debate that EU law and national law jointly contribute to the current enforcement framework: some issues are subject to the 'centralisation effects' of EU law, while other issues remain within the autonomy of the Member States. One does not need to engage in a detailed analysis of the totality of enforcement powers and procedures to identify the legal and economic implications of decentralisation. This book will therefore focus on a single (but arguably the most important) aspect in the enforcement process: the availability and conditions of measures to terminate and penalise (putative and/or prima facie) infringements of Articles 101 and 102 TFEU. These measures will be referred to as 'sanctions'. It will be determined how the competences in the area of sanctions are distributed over the EU level and the national level, and how this may influence the costs of enforcement.

The enforcement actions of the Commission and the national competition authorities are generally referred to as 'public enforcement'. Public enforcement is at the centre of this book. In order to avoid any confusion about the term 'sanction', it is appropriate to explicitly exclude 'private enforcement' from the scope of study. Private enforcement refers to the actions initiated by private parties before national courts and tribunals. The prohibitions laid down in Articles 101 and 102 TFEU not only impose obligations, they also confer rights.[16] Anyone whose rights under Articles 101 and 102 TFEU have been breached may apply to the national courts for injunctive relief and/or full compensation of the damage suffered.[17] These responses too could be conceived as 'sanctions' for a breach of EU competition law. However, as national courts may apply Articles 101 and 102 TFEU in private disputes irrespective of how public enforcement is organised, private enforcement is of little import to the topic of this book.

[14] EU institutions are often not even equipped with powers to enforce EU law directly and the administration of EU law therefore primarily takes place at the Member State level. See JH Jans et al, *Europeanisation of Public Law* (Europa Law Publishing, 2007) 200.

[15] For example, it may provide food for thought for the centralisation tendencies in the regulated industries, where the EU is gradually expanding its enforcement powers. *cf* S Lavrijssen and L Hancher, 'Networks on Track: From European Regulatory Networks to European Regulatory "Network Agencies"' (2008) 34 *Legal Issues of Economic Integration* 23.

[16] Case 48/72 *Brasserie de Haecht* [1973] ECR 77; Case 127/73 *BRT v SABAM* [1972] ECR 51; Case C-234/89 *Delimitis* [1991] ECR I-935.

[17] Case C-453/99 *Courage v Crehan* [2001] ECR I-6297; Case C-253/00 *Muñoz* [2002] ECR I-7289; Joined Cases C-295/04–98/04 *Manfredi* [2006] ECR I-6619.

THE STRUCTURE OF THE BOOK

This book is structured as follows. After this general introduction, chapter two will describe how the enforcement of EU competition law has developed from a highly centralised system operated by the Commission into a system of decentralised enforcement. Chapter three then provides a theoretical framework for the examination of this and further legal developments by setting out the relevant economic considerations in allocating sanctioning competences. Chapters four and five detail the legal developments in the area of sanctions to which decentralisation gave rise. More specifically, chapter four identifies and analyses EU sanctioning principles. These principles are capable of limiting the sanctioning autonomy of the Member States and therefore effectively centralise parts of the sanctioning regime applicable to infringements of Articles 101 and 102 TFEU. In chapter five, the development of domestic sanctioning powers is analysed for a subset of jurisdictions. This subset includes Germany, the Netherlands and the UK. This provides an impression of the development of domestic sanctioning powers more widely. Jointly, chapters four and five describe the relationship between EU law and national law in terminating and penalising (putative and/or prima facie) infringements of Articles 101 and 102 TFEU. Chapter six then applies the theoretical framework of chapter three to the conclusions of chapters four and five with the aim of clarifying the economic implications of the current division of sanctioning competences. More specifically, the costs and benefits of the developments at the EU and the national level will be identified and discussed. Chapter seven provides an overview of the study's main findings in terms of legal and economic implications and offers some reflections and recommendations. Throughout this book, grey text boxes are used to elaborate on issues that are relevant to the discussion, but that are not crucial for understanding the main line of argument.

2

The Decentralisation of EU Competition Law

2.1 INTRODUCTION

In 2004, the enforcement of EU competition law has gone from a highly centralised system operated by the European Commission to a system of decentralised application in which the Commission and the national authorities work side by side. While this change has successfully increased enforcement capacity, its implications in terms of costs and benefits are less certain. The costs and benefits of decentralisation are dependent on a number of factors. For instance, on the costs side, it is important to consider to what extent decentralisation results in the duplication of enforcement infrastructure and procedures. On the benefits side, one of the aspects that needs to be taken into account is whether national authorities have a competitive advantage over the Commission in the enforcement of Articles 101 and 102 TFEU. Whereas chapter three will elaborate on these and other contingencies, this chapter does the groundwork by detailing the EU framework for decentralised enforcement. This framework determines to what extent costs and benefits of decentralisation can materialise. Against this background, this chapter clarifies the system of shared administration (section 2.2), the autonomy of the Member States with regard to sanctioning powers (section 2.3), and the mechanisms for cooperation and coordination between the Commission and the national authorities (section 2.4). The concluding section (2.5) already highlights some of the costs to which the decentralisation process has given rise.

2.2 SHARED ADMINISTRATION

The enforcement of EU competition law has been a shared responsibility of the Commission and the Member States from the very beginning. Part of the TFEU's earliest predecessor, Articles 103–05 TFEU provide a solid Treaty basis for the tasks of the Commission and the Member States in the enforcement of EU competition law. However, already by 1962, the Commission's role in the enforcement process was significantly consolidated and reinforced to the detriment of the national authorities. The adoption by the Council of 'Regulation 17',[1] the first procedural regulation for the application of Articles 101 and 102 TFEU (then Articles 85 and 86 of the Treaty establishing the European Economic Community), secured for the Commission a pivotal role in the enforcement process.[2] This Regulation gave the Commission the exclusive power to apply Article 101(3) TFEU and to exempt anti-competitive agreements from the prohibition of Article 101(1) TFEU.[3] Under the third paragraph of Article 101(3) TFEU, anti-competitive agreements that improve production or distribution or that bring about economic or technical progress may be exempted from the prohibition of the first paragraph. To benefit from this exemption, undertakings first had to notify their agreement to the Commission. During the notification procedure, parties to the agreement could not be penalised under Article 101 TFEU.[4]

This system of notification and exemption significantly frustrated the enforcement of Article 101 TFEU by the national authorities. Undertakings could still notify their agreement pending the proceedings before the national authorities, who would then have to await final judgment by the Commission or eventually the Court of Justice. This prospective may have been a disincentive for the national authorities to spend their scarce resources on the enforcement of Article 101(1) TFEU. In practice, neither Article 101 nor 102 TFEU was often applied in national procedures. In fact, some Member States had not even designated an authority with the power to apply these provisions. In sum, during the first decades of EU competition policy, the enforcement of Articles 101 and 102 TFEU found little resonance in the Member States and this may have been partly due to the prevailing legal framework.[5]

This all changed on 1 May 2004, when Regulation 17 was replaced by Regulation 1/2003.[6] With the adoption of this Regulation, the centralised system of notification and exemption has been abolished. By virtue of Article 1(3) of Regulation 1/2003, the Council has effectively recharacterised Article 101(3) TFEU from a ground for exemption into a directly applicable legal exception. Nowadays, undertakings operate their agreements at their own risk and peril without any notification thereof to any competition authority being required or even possible. A direct consequence of this is that infringements of Articles 101 and 102 TFEU can be pursued by the national authorities without any legal obstacles.

[1] Council Regulation (EEC) No 17 First Regulation implementing Articles 85 and 86 of the Treaty [1962] OJ 204/62.

[2] Wesseling has summarised the institutional and procedural features of Regulation 17 as follows: 'The Regulation generated a *centralised* system through *administrative* procedures with extensive *supranational* powers for the European Commission' (emphasis in original). R Wesseling, *The Modernisation of EC Antitrust Law* (Hart Publishing, 2000) 21.

[3] Article 101(3) TFEU in conjunction with Article 9(1) of Regulation 17.

[4] Article 15(5) of Regulation 17.

[5] See also Wesseling (n 2) 197; WPJ Wils, *The Optimal Enforcement of EC Antitrust Law: Essays in Law & Economics* (Kluwer Law International, 2002) 140.

[6] In fact, earlier unsuccessful attempts had been made by the Commission to stimulate the decentralised enforcement of Articles 101 and 102 TFEU, notably through the adoption of a Notice on cooperation between national competition authorities and the Commission [1997] OJ C313/3. See Wesseling (n 2) 203–07.

The recharacterisation of Article 101(3) TFEU was meant to promote decentralised application and to relieve the Commission's administrative services from the workload caused by the system of notification and exemption.[7] The former objective is in accordance with the EU principle of subsidiarity, requiring the EU, in areas which do not fall within its exclusive competence,[8] to act only if and insofar as the objectives of the proposed action cannot be achieved sufficiently by the Member States, but can rather be better achieved at the EU level.[9] This principle, which became a part of EU law with the adoption of the Treaty of Maastricht in 1992, essentially gives priority to decentralised application over centralised application. While considerations of subsidiarity will certainly have played a role in the recharacterisation of Article 101(3) TFEU and the process of decentralisation that it engendered, all this was mainly motivated by the objective to relieve the overburdened administrative services of the Commission. Ehlermann has put it even stronger. Commenting on the Commission proposal for Regulation 1/2003, he noted:

> In fact, the Commission only pursues *one* main goal, i.e., to increase the efficiency of the EC antitrust policy. In order to achieve this objective, the Commission proposes to adopt a system of radical decentralization. Decentralization is a tool, not an objective.[10]

By exchanging the exemption procedure for a legal exception, the Commission could shift resources from scrutinising notified agreements to investigating covert and more harmful forms of anti-competitive behaviour. Moreover, the enforcement burden from then on would be borne by the Commission and the national authorities jointly. In the light of the EU enlargement with 10 new Member States that took effect on 1 May 2004, these were urgent matters at the time that Regulation 1/2003 was drafted.[11]

The removal of legal obstacles alone could of course not forge the commitment of the Member States to enforce Articles 101 and 102 TFEU. Regulation 1/2003 therefore makes various other contributions to the decentralised enforcement of EU competition law. Pursuant to Article 35 of Regulation 1/2003, Member States have to designate an authority with the power to apply Articles 101 and 102 TFEU (national competition authority (NCA)). This authority then becomes responsible for the enforcement of Articles 101 and 102 TFEU and is subject to various

[7] *cf* Commission, 'White Paper on the Modernisation of the Rules Implementing Articles 85 and 86 of the EC Treaty' COM (1999) 101, executive summary, paras 6 and 10.

[8] The exclusive competences of the EU can be found in Article 3 TFEU and include 'the establishing of the *competition rules* necessary for the functioning of the internal market' (emphasis added). It is submitted herewith that this provision refers to the substantive competition rules ('what is prohibited?') and not to the enforcement of these competition rules ('what are the public law consequences of an infringement?'). This implies that the enforcement of Articles 101 and 102 TFEU is subject to the EU principle of subsidiarity.

[9] Article 5 TEU.

[10] CD Ehlermann, 'The Modernization of EC Antitrust Policy: A Legal and Cultural Revolution' (2000) 37 *Common Market Law Review* 537, 560.

[11] On the close connection between enlargement and decentralisation, see KJ Cseres, 'The Impact of Regulation 1/2003 in the New Member States' (2010) 6 *Competition Law Review* 145.

duties under Regulation 1/2003, eg, the obligation of professional secrecy.[12] Moreover, by virtue of Article 3(1) of Regulation 1/2003, NCAs and national courts have to assess any restriction of competition or abuse of dominance that 'affects trade between Member States' under Articles 101 and 102 TFEU.[13] In practice, this means that national authorities will often have to apply EU competition law if they want to end certain forms of anti-competitive behaviour in their home markets.

Decentralisation or Centralisation?

By virtue of Article 3(1) of Regulation 1/2003, NCAs will often have to apply EU competition law if they want to terminate certain anti-competitive behaviour in their home markets. The application of Articles 101 and 102 TFEU by the NCAs in turn triggers certain supervisory powers of the Commission, including a power to take over cases. Against this background, it has been argued that Regulation 1/2003 is more a centralising measure than a decentralising measure.[14] While it is appropriate to say that Regulation 1/2003 has harmonised competition law within the EU, any scepticism about whether NCAs would actually enforce Articles 101 and 102 TFEU has proved to be unwarranted. Regulation 1/2003 has thus led to developments in relation to both decentralisation and harmonisation. On the one hand, the Commission has divested enforcement competences to the NCAs. Cases that otherwise would have been handled by the Commission are now handled by one or more NCAs. On the other hand, some NCAs have simply continued their enforcement activities, albeit under a different flag. This book focuses on enforcement competences and reserves the terms 'centralisation' and 'decentralisation' to the allocation of these competences.

[12] Article 28 Regulation 1/2003.

[13] Articles 101 and 102 TFEU regard restrictive practices and abuses of dominance in the light of their impact on trade between Member States. The purpose of the effect on trade criterion is to define, within the context of competition law, the boundary between EU law and national law. EU law covers practices capable of affecting trade between Member States in a manner which might harm the attainment of the objectives of the internal market. To fulfil the effect on trade condition, it must be possible to foresee with a sufficient degree of probability, on the basis of objective factors of law or fact, that the restrictive practices may have an appreciable influence, whether direct or indirect, actual or potential, on the pattern of trade between Member States in such a way as to cause concern that they might hinder the attainment of a single market. Practices that seal off national markets or affect the structure of competition would be especially problematic in the light of this objective. See Commission Notice laying down Guidelines on the effect on trade concept contained in Articles 81 and 82 of Treaty [2004] OJ C101/81.

[14] See, eg, A Riley, 'EC Antitrust Modernisation: The Commission Does Very Nicely – Thank You! Part 2: Between the Idea and the Reality: Decentralisation under Regulation 1' (2003) 12 *European Competition Law Review* 657, 664. The conclusion that Regulation 1/2003 is more a centralising measure than a decentralising measure was also based on scepticism, back in 2003, that NCAs would actually apply Articles 101 and 102 TFEU (663).

Where national competition law is applied in parallel to EU competition law, this may not lead to the prohibition of practices that do not form an appreciable restriction of competition in the sense of Article 101 TFEU.[15] This creates a level playing field for (anti-competitive) agreements with an effect on trade and limits the chances of agreements being enforceable in one jurisdiction and not in another.[16] Member States remain free to apply stricter national rules in relation to *unilateral* conduct of undertakings. In other words, Member States may prohibit conduct that is exonerated under Article 102 TFEU.

Another contribution to the decentralised enforcement of Articles 101 and 102 TFEU is that Regulation 1/2003 has created a system of parallel competences. Regulation 1/2003 delimits neither the jurisdiction of the NCAs to apply Articles 101 and 102 TFEU nor the scope of their sanctioning powers.[17] With respect to the latter point, it should be noted that Article 5 of Regulation 1/2003 provides, without restrictions:

> The competition authorities of the Member States shall have the power to apply Articles 81 and 82 of the Treaty [now Articles 101 and 102 TFEU] in individual cases.

NCAs only lose their competence to apply Articles 101 and 102 TFEU in a particular case when proceedings have been initiated by the Commission.[18] Any further delimitation is solely a matter of national law or public international law.[19] Accordingly, cases can be dealt with either by the Commission, a single NCA or several NCAs. The authorities themselves are responsible for an efficient division of work (see below, section 2.4). The adoption of Regulation 1/2003 has thus enhanced the role and responsibility of the NCAs in the enforcement of Articles 101 and 102 TFEU. In practice, EU competition law is actually applied at a

[15] Article 3(2) of Regulation 1/2003. Practices that do not affect trade between Member States are not governed by this 'convergence clause'.

[16] See also KJ Cseres, 'Comparing Laws in the Enforcement of EU and National Competition Laws' (2010) 3 *European Journal of Legal Studies* 7, 15.

[17] See also S Brammer, 'Concurrent Jurisdiction under Regulation 1/2003 and the Issue of Case Allocation' (2005) 42 *Common Market Law Review* 1383, 1385, who argues that the power of NCAs to apply Articles 101 and 102 TFEU is not geographically restricted. The opposite position has also been taken. See R Smits, 'The European Competition Network: Selected Aspects' (2005) 32 *Legal Issues of Economic Integration* 175, 184, who argues that: 'Regulation 1/2003, although it contains a mechanism for apportioning the competence to act in the enforcement of Community competition law, does not provide for a single sanctioning system. Rather, it relies on nationally diverse systems without even granting a competence to sanction behaviour beyond the confines of State borders. Thus, in a case where one NCA acts to end and sanction an infringement, which affects the markets in several other Member States as well, the NCA's power to sanction seems restricted to the effect within the first State.'

[18] Article 11(6) of Regulation 1/2003.

[19] See in this respect also M de Visser, *Network-Based Governance in EC Law: The Example of EC Competition and EC Communications Law* (Hart Publishing, 2009) 297: 'Many competition laws require a causal link between alleged infringements and the territory for which the competition authority bears responsibility. This effects doctrine is in fact an extension of the Network Notice's allocation criteria. It will be a rare occurrence indeed if an authority with no connection whatsoever to the alleged infringement were to become responsible for its investigation' (footnote omitted). See further S Brammer, *Co-operation between National Competition Agencies in the Enforcement of EC Competition Law* (Hart Publishing, 2009) 484–85, who argues that public international law is of limited importance for the decentralised enforcement of Articles 101 and 102 TFEU.

Member State level and, reportedly, this has contributed to 'a significant increase of enforcement activities in the EU since 2004'.[20]

2.3 SANCTIONING AUTONOMY

With the decentralisation of EU competition law, not only has the number of enforcement authorities increased, but it has also resulted in a multiplication of sanctioning regimes. The decision to involve the Member States in the enforcement of Articles 101 and 102 TFEU has not been matched by the large-scale harmonisation of national sanctioning powers and procedures. Regulation 1/2003 recognises the wide variation of public enforcement systems existing in the Member States and therefore leaves intact the sanctioning autonomy of the Member States. As a result, NCAs may enforce Articles 101 and 102 TFEU, using different procedural frameworks and imposing different sanctions.[21] There are only relatively few issues with regard to sanctions that are dictated by Regulation 1/2003.[22] Nonetheless, these issues should be clarified before the scope of the sanctioning autonomy can be determined.

In accordance with Article 35 of Regulation 1/2003, Member States have to allocate enforcement competences in such a way that the provisions of the Regulation are effectively complied with. In *VEBIC*, the Court of Justice interpreted this provision as requiring Member States to ensure the effective enforcement of Articles 101 and 102 TFEU.[23] This conclusion has not attracted much attention, but there is of course a difference. While the *VEBIC* ruling was rendered in relation to an institutional peculiarity of the Belgian enforcement regime – the Belgian NCA could not defend its own decision on appeal – the Court's interpretation of Article 35 of Regulation 1/2003 extends beyond the narrow confines of this case. This general requirement of the effective enforcement of Articles 101 and 102 TFEU is broad enough to cover the allocation of sanctioning powers along with all other national enforcement powers and procedures.[24]

[20] Commission Staff Working Paper accompanying the Communication from the Commission to the European Parliament and the Council: Report on the functioning of Regulation 1/2003 [2009] COM 206 final, para 184.

[21] Cseres, 'The Impact of Regulation 1/2003' (n 11) 155.

[22] Also outside the area of 'sanctions', Regulation 1/2003 leaves the Member States with considerable autonomy in designing their enforcement regime. Probably the most clear exception to this rule is Article 2 of Regulation 1/2003, which 'centralises' the burden of proof for infringements of Articles 101 and 102 TFEU by providing: 'In any national or Community proceedings for the application of Articles 81 and 82 of the Treaty [now Articles 101 and 102 TFEU], the burden of proving an infringement of Article 81(1) or of Article 82 of the Treaty shall rest on the party or the authority alleging the infringement. The undertaking or association of undertakings claiming the benefit of Article 81(3) of the Treaty shall bear the burden of proving that the conditions of that paragraph are fulfilled.'

[23] Case C-439/08 *VEBIC* [2010] ECR I-12471.

[24] This point has earlier been made in MJ Frese, 'Case C-439/08, Vlaamse federatie van verenigingen van Brood- en Banketbakkers, IJsbereiders en Chocoladebewerkers (VEBIC), Judgment of the Court (Grand Chamber) of 7 December 2010' (2011) 48 *Common Market Law Review* 893.

Arguably more important from the perspective of the sanctioning autonomy of the Member States is Article 5 of Regulation 1/2003. This provision reads:

> The competition authorities of the Member States shall have the power to apply Articles 81 and 82 of the Treaty [now Articles 101 and 102 TFEU] in individual cases. For this purpose, acting on their own initiative or on a complaint, they may take the following decisions:
>
> – requiring that an infringement be brought to an end,
> – ordering interim measures,
> – accepting commitments,
> – imposing fines, periodic penalty payments or any other penalty provided for in their national law.
>
> Where on the basis of the information in their possession the conditions for prohibition are not met they may likewise decide that there are no grounds for action on their part.

The legal literature has been divided on the interpretation of Article 5 of Regulation 1/2003. Some commentators have concluded that it remains within the authority of the Member States to allocate specific enforcement powers to their NCAs,[25] whereas others have argued that NCAs can directly use the instruments listed in Article 5 of Regulation 1/2003.[26] This difference in opinion is also recognised in the Commission Staff Working Paper accompanying the Report on the functioning of Regulation 1/2003.[27] More recently, Advocate General Mazák has joined this debate through his opinion in *Tele2 Polska*, arguing in favour of the 'directly use' camp.[28] Mazák could even support his argument by referring to several NCAs that had already adopted enforcement measures directly on the basis of Article 5 of Regulation 1/2003.[29] Whatever could be said about these national practices, in *Tele2 Polska*, the Court of Justice seems to have sided with the 'no direct use' camp. In the latter case, the referring court asked explicitly whether on the basis of Article 5 of Regulation 1/2003, an NCA may bring to an end the procedure by taking a decision which states that there are *no grounds for action* on its part, even though national law provides in such circumstances only for the possibility of taking a negative decision on the merits, ie, a decision that the behaviour does not qualify as an infringement. The Court only censured the latter type of decision by holding:

> [S]ince . . . Article 5 of the Regulation is directly applicable in all the Member States, Article 5 precludes the application of a rule of national law which would require a procedure relating to the application of Article 102 TFEU to be brought to an end by a decision stating that there has been no breach of that article.[30]

25 P Oliver, 'Le Règlement 1/2003 et les Principes D'Efficacité et D'Équivalence' (2005) 41 *Cahiers de droit européen* 351, 367; J Faull and A Nikpay (eds), *The EC Law of Competition* 2nd edn (Oxford University Press, 2007) 2.78–2.80.

26 R Nazzini, *Concurrent Proceedings in Competition Law: Procedure, Evidence and Remedies* (Oxford University Press, 2004) 3.52; Smits (n 17) 184.

27 Commission Staff Working Paper (n 20) para 197.

28 Case C-375/09 *Tele2 Polska* [2011] ECR I-3055, Opinion of AG Mazák [53].

29 ibid.

30 C-375/09 *Tele2 Polska* [2011] ECR I-3055 [34].

This is significant as Article 5 of Regulation 1/2003 explicitly mentions that NCAs may decide that there are no grounds for actions on their part. The Court thus stopped short of interpreting Article 5 of Regulation 1/2003 as allocating powers to the NCAs directly.[31] This approach is in accordance with earlier case law dealing with similar issues.[32] It should therefore be concluded that the competences listed in Article 5 of Regulation 1/2003 are not directly available for the NCAs. In principle, a legal basis in national law is required before the latter may adopt any of the measures listed in this provision.

Pursuant to Article 5 of Regulation 1/2003, Member States may grant their NCAs the power to adopt cease-and-desist orders, to order interim measures, to accept commitments, to impose fines and periodic penalty payments, and to decide that there are no grounds for further action on their part. Furthermore, NCAs may impose any other penalty provided for in their national law. This could include penalties for natural persons.[33] Conversely, Member States are not required to provide for all these sanctions.[34] Not listed in Article 5 of Regulation 1/2003, and excluded from the NCAs' scope of competences, is the power to make findings of *in*applicability. By virtue of Article 10 of Regulation 1/2003, this power falls within the exclusive purview of the Commission. Whereas the NCAs may conclude that 'there are no grounds for action on their part', only the Commission may reach a finding that Articles 101 and 102 TFEU are *inapplicable* to a particular practice. This follows from *Tele2 Polska* (see above). In a later judgment, the Court has clarified that this means that national competition authorities cannot cause undertakings to entertain a legitimate expectation that their conduct does not infringe Article 101 or 102 TFEU.[35]

While not explicitly mentioned in Article 5 of Regulation 1/2003 either, NCAs do not seem barred from requiring undertakings to make specific changes in their commercial behaviour or their organisational structure in order to ensure compliance with Articles 101 and 102 TFEU, or from terminating investigations with a settlement, or from adopting declaratory findings of past infringements.[36]

[31] For a different interpretation, see P Pohlmann, 'Anmerkung zu EuGH, Urteil v 3.5.2011 – C-375/09 – Tele2 Polska' in *Lindenmaier-Möhring Kommentierte BGH-Rechtsprechung* 2011, 320463 (Beck-Online) <http://beck-online.beck.de/> accessed 1 July 2013: '*Ermächtigungsgrundlage für kartellbehördliche Verfügungen ist danach direkt Art. 5 VO 1/2003 i. V. mit der nationalen Zuständigkeitsregelung*' and '*Das nationale Recht hat nur noch die Aufgabe, eine bestimmte Behörde zu diesen Maßnahmen zu ermächtigen*'.

[32] Joined Cases C-383/06–C-385/06 *Europees Sociaal Fonds* [2008] ECR I-1561. See more generally on the issue of legality in the decentralised application of EU law JH Jans et al, *Europeanisation of Public Law* (Europa Law Publishing, 2007) 23–29.

[33] *cf* Article 12(3) of Regulation 1/2003.

[34] Oliver (n 25).

[35] Case C-681/11 *Bundeswettbewerbsbehörde v Schenker* [2012] OJ C89/11 [42].

[36] The Commission's administrative services seem less certain that NCAs may adopt decisions not explicitly mentioned in Article 5 Regulation 1/2003. *cf* Commission Staff Working Paper (n 20) para 198: 'the question has come up whether national competition authorities may adopt declaratory decisions in relation to past infringements. Given that Article 5 does not contain a provision equivalent to the last paragraph of Article 7(1) of Regulation 1/2003, there remains a question mark about whether the lack of an express provision may prevent national competition authorities from taking a decision on the basis of Articles 81 and 82 EC [now Articles 101 and 102 TFEU] in relation to past infringements where they do not intend to impose a fine'.

Decisions of this type cannot be equated with findings of inapplicability, as only the latter exonerate anti-competitive practices from public intervention. This interpretation is confirmed by *Bundeswettbewerbsbehörde v Schenker*, where the Court concluded:

> Article 5 of Regulation No 1/2003 admittedly does not provide expressly that the national competition authorities have the power to find an infringement of Article 101 TFEU without imposing a fine, but it does not exclude that power either.[37]

This was not the only interpretational question that the Court had to answer in *Bundeswettbewerbsbehörde v Schenker*. The referring Austrian court also wished to obtain clarification on the intention-related or negligence-related conditions regarding the imposition of a fine on a person who has infringed Articles 101 and 102 TFEU. In an important ruling, the Court concluded:

> It is not apparent from the wording of Article 5 of the regulation that conditions relating to intention or negligence have to be met in order for the measures of application which are provided for by the regulation to be adopted. However, if, in the general interest of uniform application of Articles 101 TFEU and 102 TFEU in the European Union, the Member States establish conditions relating to intention or negligence in the context of application of Article 5 of Regulation No 1/2003, those conditions should be at least as stringent as the condition laid down in Article 23 of Regulation No 1/2003 [governing the penalty powers of the Commission] so as not to jeopardise the effectiveness of European Union law.[38]

While the first part of this ruling indicates that EU enforcement obligations should not be read into Article 5 of Regulation 1/2003, the second part suggests that Member States which decide to draw inspiration from the Commission enforcement powers cannot stop halfway. What is puzzling is that the conditions of intent and negligence are facultative, but once adopted need to be 'at least as stringent as the condition laid down in Article 23 of Regulation No 1/2003'. One would have expected the Court to require Member States not to adopt conditions more stringent than the condition laid down in Article 23 of Regulation No 1/2003. Indeed, this is what the Court seemed to have had in mind, judging from the Court's subsequent application of this requirement.[39] Although the exact scope remains to be determined by the Court of Justice, it can safely be concluded that Regulation 1/2003 leaves the Member States with a considerable degree of sanctioning autonomy.

[37] Case C-681/11 *Bundeswettbewerbsbehörde v Schenker* [2012] OJ C89/11 [45].

[38] ibid [35]–[36].

[39] ibid [37]–[38]: 'In relation to the question whether an infringement has been committed intentionally or negligently and is, therefore, liable to be punished by a fine in accordance with the first subparagraph of Article 23(2) of Regulation No 1/2003, it follows from the case-law of the Court that that condition is satisfied where the undertaking concerned cannot be unaware of the anti-competitive nature of its conduct, whether or not it is aware that it is infringing the competition rules of the Treaty . . . Therefore, the fact that the undertaking concerned has characterised wrongly in law its conduct upon which the finding of the infringement is based cannot have the effect of exempting it from imposition of a fine in so far as it could not be unaware of the anti-competitive nature of that conduct.'

2.4 COOPERATION AND COORDINATION

Infringements of Articles 101 and 102 TFEU typically extend beyond national borders. Indeed, in the absence of an effect on trade between Member States, these prohibitions do not even apply. As a result, Member States cannot properly enforce the prohibitions of Articles 101 and 102 TFEU without the help of each other. The decentralisation of EU competition law has therefore called for coordination and cooperation in individual cases and with regard to enforcement policy. This has resulted in the creation of a European Competition Network (ECN). The ECN is based on the Joint Statement of the Council and the Commission on the Functioning of the Network of Competition Authorities[40] and has been worked out in the Commission Notice on cooperation within the Network of Competition Authorities (hereinafter 'Network Notice'),[41] as acknowledged and declared binding by NCAs from all the Member States.[42] The ECN provides a forum for the Commission and NCAs to meet and discuss cases and policy. Secretarial functions are organised by the administrative services of the Commission, which exemplifies the central position of the latter within the ECN.[43] Cooperation and coordination in individual cases is further facilitated by Regulation 1/2003, providing mutual duties for the Commission and the NCAs in the enforcement of Articles 101 and 102 TFEU.

2.4.1 Cooperation in Individual Cases: Case Allocation, Investigative Assistance and Consultation

As already mentioned, the enforcement system introduced by Regulation 1/2003 is based on the principle of parallel competences. All ECN members have the power to apply Articles 101 and 102 TFEU and they are jointly responsible for an efficient division of work. The objective of this system is that cases are handled by a single authority as often as possible.[44] For this purpose, Article 13 of Regulation 1/2003 provides a ground to suspend or terminate enforcement proceedings. In accordance with the Network Notice, parallel action by two or three NCAs is appropriate only where an agreement or practice has substantial effects on

[40] See <http://ec.europa.eu/competition/ecn/joint_statement_en.pdf > accessed 1 July 2013.

[41] [2004] OJ C101/03.

[42] Network Notice, para 42. The list of national authorities that have signed the Statement regarding the Commission Notice on Co-operation within the Network of Competition Authorities is available at <http://ec.europa.eu/competition/antitrust/legislation/list_of_authorities_joint_statement.pdf> accessed 1 July 2013. It should be noted that not all NCAs have signed the Statement. For example, none of the German state authorities has signed, although they have been designated as NCAs (see below, section 5.2.2).

[43] *cf* Cseres, 'Comparing Laws' (n 16) 25.

[44] Recital 18 of the preamble to Regulation 1/2003.

competition in their respective territories and the action of a single NCA would be insufficient to end or penalise the entire infringement adequately.[45] Where more than three Member States are affected by the agreement or practice, or where effective enforcement or other EU interests so require, the Commission is likely to deal with the case.[46] In all other cases, enforcement action will in principle be undertaken by a single NCA.[47] This will be the NCA that has a material link with the infringement and that is able to gather the necessary evidence to prove the infringement and to end, and penalise the entire infringement effectively.[48] For the purpose of case allocation, the Commission and the NCAs inform each other before or without delay after commencing the first investigative measures.[49] Dekeyser and Jaspers have described the practicalities of this mechanism as follows:

> An authority who is well placed and willing to investigate and sanction an infringement informs the Network of its intentions at an early stage of the investigation by inserting some basic information in a common case management system. This allows other authorities to signal their interest to also act in the case, either in parallel with the first authority (in the case of national competition authorities) or solely (in the case of the Commission). In the rare case that authorities disagree on the most suitable allocation of the case, bilateral discussions take place between the concerned authorities.[50]

Case allocation therefore remains somewhat informal and the ECN does not decide which authority or authorities will undertake the investigation.[51]

The ECN members also help each other in the investigation of cases. In accordance with Regulation 1/2003, the officials of the NCAs may assist the Commission in its inspections. NCAs will provide assistance either on their own request or on the request of the Commission.[52] In these cases, the officials of the NCAs will dispose of the same powers as the Commission officials.[53] NCAs may also carry out investigations on behalf of another ECN member in accordance with their domestic investigatory powers.[54] Investigative assistance is further facilitated by the information-exchange mechanism provided for in Article 12 of Regulation 1/2003. In accordance with this provision, ECN members have the power to provide one another with and use in evidence any matter of fact or law for the purpose of applying Articles 101 and 102 TFEU.[55] Where national competition law is applied in the same case and in parallel to EU competition law and does not lead to a different

[45] Network Notice, para 12.
[46] ibid, paras 14–15.
[47] ibid, para 11.
[48] ibid, para 8.
[49] Article 11(2) and (3) of Regulation 1/2003.
[50] K Dekeyser and M Jaspers, 'A New Era of ECN Cooperation: Achievements and Challenges with Special Focus on Work in the Leniency Field' (2007) 30 *World Competition* 3, 5–6.
[51] ibid.
[52] Article 20(5) of Regulation 1/2003.
[53] Articles 20(5) and 21(4) of Regulation 1/2003.
[54] Article 22 of Regulation 1/2003.
[55] Article 12(1) and (2) of Regulation 1/2003.

outcome, information exchanged under Article 12 of Regulation 1/2003 may also be used for the application of national competition law. Information that has been exchanged by ECN members may only be used in evidence to *impose sanctions on natural persons* where: (1) the law of the transmitting authority foresees sanctions of a similar kind; or (2) the information has been collected in a way which respects the same level of protection of the rights of defence of the natural persons.[56] However, information that has been exchanged may only be used to impose *custodial sanctions* if the first condition is fulfilled, ie where the law of the transmitting authority foresees custodial sanctions too.[57] Notwithstanding these limitations with regard to the use of exchanged information *in evidence*, Article 12(1) of Regulation 1/2003 authorises ECN members to exchange information *as intelligence* irrespective of the type of sanctions,[58] provided it is used for competition law purposes. Meanwhile, the Commission's administrative services report of 'a discussion' on whether the limitation on the use of information in evidence for the imposition of custodial sanctions is too far-reaching and constitutes an obstacle to effective enforcement.[59] If this discussion were to result in legislative amendments, this could mean that the 'level of protection' criterion becomes generally applicable. This would not necessarily remove all the obstacles to effective enforcement, however. Brammer has already indicated:

> It can hardly be expected for an NCA to be familiar with the procedural rules of its 26 colleague agencies. Moreover, comparing the two systems and making a well-founded judgement on the equivalence of protection afforded by both is a complex exercise. Each national law will consist of an elaborate, coherent system of detailed rules and principles which may be similar between Member States, but will hardly ever be identical.[60]

In other words, the mere existence of distinct sanctioning regimes could limit the possibilities for information-exchange and therefore hamper the enforcement of Articles 101 and 102 TFEU.

Finally, Network cooperation consists of mandatory consultation and other means to guarantee the uniform application of Articles 101 and 102 TFEU. The Commission has to consult with all ECN members before imposing any sanction.[61] More specifically, it needs to consult the so-called Advisory Committee on Restrictive Practices and Dominant Positions. This Advisory Committee is composed of representatives of the NCAs. With regard to the more general (enforcement) issues, Member States may appoint an additional representative with competence over competition matters (eg, an official working directly under the responsible minister). The Commission needs to take 'the utmost account' of the opinion delivered by the Advisory Committee.[62] Where the Advisory Committee

[56] Article 12(3) of Regulation 1/2003.
[57] ibid.
[58] Commission Staff Working Paper (n 20) para 239.
[59] ibid, para 245.
[60] Brammer (n 19) 476.
[61] Article 14 of Regulation 1/2003.
[62] Article 14(5) of Regulation 1/2003.

so recommends, the Commission publishes the opinion.[63] The NCAs, in turn, have to consult with the Commission before imposing sanctions for infringements of Articles 101 and 102 TFEU.[64] More precisely, the NCAs need to inform the Commission 'No later than 30 days before the adoption of a decision requiring that an infringement be brought to an end, accepting commitments or withdrawing the benefits of a block exemption Regulation'.[65] The uniform application of Articles 101 and 102 TFEU is further reinforced by the power of the Commission to relieve the NCAs of their enforcement competences by initiating proceedings itself.[66] Where the Commission has adopted an enforcement decision, NCAs cannot take decisions running counter to the decision of the Commission.[67] As soon as the actions of the NCAs enter the appeal stage, further mechanisms have been put in place to ensure the uniform application of Articles 101 and 102 TFEU. In addition to the possibility to refer questions to the Court of Justice for a preliminary ruling,[68] national courts may ask the Commission to transmit to them information in its possession or its opinion on questions concerning the application of EU competition law.[69] The Commission may also intervene as amicus curiae on its own initiative.[70] In any case, national courts may not take a decision running counter to a decision adopted or contemplated by the Commission.[71]

2.4.2 Coordination of Enforcement Policy

Further to its role in individual cases, the ECN provides a forum for a continuous dialogue between the Commission and the NCAs to discuss competition policy. For this purpose, it organises meetings for its members, conducts evaluations, adopts policy guidelines and publishes newsletters. Within this context, competition authorities discuss and share experiences with particular sectors of the economy or means of enforcement.[72] One of the ECN's more notable activities is that it has drawn up a model leniency programme (the ECN Model Leniency Programme), as

[63] Article 14(6) of Regulation 1/2003.
[64] Article 11(4) of Regulation 1/2003.
[65] ibid. Interpreted literally, this implies that NCAs need not communicate draft decisions punishing past infringements. In reality, this concerns the bulk of the decisions. As it is highly unlikely that the Council intended to exclude these decisions, it is suggested that Article 11(4) of Regulation 1/2003 should be interpreted broadly so as to include decisions on past infringements.
[66] Article 11(6) of Regulation 1/2003.
[67] Article 16(2) of Regulation 1/2003.
[68] Article 267 TFEU.
[69] Article 15(1) of Regulation 1/2003.
[70] Article 15(3) of Regulation 1/2003.
[71] Article 16(1) of Regulation 1/2003.
[72] Commission Staff Working Paper (n 20) para 248: 'Currently [in 2009], policy work is organised at four different levels of organisation: the yearly meetings of the Directors General of the European Competition Authorities, the Plenary meetings, the horizontal working groups and the sector-specific subgroups.' Discussions with relevance to sanctioning powers take place in the Director General's meetings, the Plenary meetings and various horizontal working groups.

revised in November 2012.[73] This document contains suggestions as to how the authorities should deal with cartel members that confess their wrongdoings. A leniency programme functions as a proverbial carrot for cartel members to break ranks and inform the authority. The ECN Model Leniency Programme aims to align key aspects of the leniency programmes of the Commission and NCAs. However, the Model is not binding on the Member States[74] and explicitly excludes the possibility of creating legitimate expectations. Notwithstanding its voluntary nature, the fact that this Model has been drafted by the Commission and the NCAs jointly suggests that it will be reflected in domestic penalty regimes.[75]

These activities of the ECN add to the discussions between the competition authorities taking place outside the EU framework, such as the discussions in the context of the European Competition Authorities (ECA),[76] the Organisation for Economic Co-operation and Development (OECD),[77] the International Competition Network (ICN)[78] and the United Nations Conference on Trade and Development (UNCTAD).[79] Perhaps with the exception of the latter, these organisations have contributed to the sharing of experiences and the drafting of best

[73] Available at <http://ec.europa.eu/competition/ecn/mlp_revised_2012_en.pdf> accessed 1 July 2013.

[74] *cf* Case C-360/09 *Pfleiderer* [2011] ECR I-5161 [21]–[22].

[75] ibid [23].

[76] The ECA was founded in April 2001 as a discussion forum for competition authorities in the European Economic Area (EEA). This forum consists of the Commission, the NCAs, the competition authorities of Norway, Iceland and Liechtenstein (all states that have signed the European Free Trade Agreement (EFTA)) and the EFTA Surveillance Authority. The ECA operates outside the public sphere; it has no office and does not manage a website either. The little information that is publicly available can be found on websites of the Commission and the NCAs. It appears that the ECA supports various working groups, including a working group on sanctions.

[77] The OECD was founded in December 1960 through a Convention signed by 20 states and has gradually expanded. Its origins date back to 1947, when its forerunner, the Organisation for European Economic Co-operation, was formed to administer the Marshall Plan for the reconstruction of Europe after the Second World War. In order to pursue its aim of economic growth, the OECD members promote the efficient use of economic resources, pursue policies for economic growth and efforts to reduce trade barriers and to liberalise markets. For this purpose, the OECD members can carry out joint studies and projects and, by unanimity, adopt binding decisions and recommendations. The OECD has a Secretariat consisting of several Directorates. The Directorate for Financial and Enterprise affairs supports various committees and working groups, amongst others the Competition Committee. In the field of competition law enforcement, the OECD has adopted various recommendations and policy briefs, and there are various Committee Reports, most notably in the field of sanctioning, leniency, cartel enforcement and inter-authority cooperation.

[78] The Commission and the NCAs are all members of the ICN. This global competition law network was launched by the competition law officials of 14 different jurisdictions, with the endorsement of the International Bar Association and after the impetus given by the United States' Assistant Attorney General for Antitrust and the EU's Commissioner for Competition. This network groups together competition authorities from around 100 jurisdictions and operates on the basis of a Memorandum on the Establishment and Operation of the International Competition Network. The ICN has a steering group and various working groups. The working groups undertake studies and adopt recommended practices in various fields of competition law, including enforcement and most notably institutional design and cartel enforcement.

[79] UNCTAD, established in 1964, promotes the economic development and integration in the world economy of developing countries. For this purpose, it operates a programme on International Trade and Commodities, which includes a programme on Competition and Consumer Policies. In this capacity, it functions mainly as a forum for discussion, peer review and technical assistance. For the decentralised enforcement of EU competition law, UNCTAD activities are hardly relevant.

practices in the field of competition law enforcement. For instance, in the context of the ECA working group on sanctions, the participating competition authorities have agreed on *Principles for convergence of pecuniary sanctions imposed on undertakings for infringements of antitrust law* (hereinafter 'the ECA Fining Principles').[80] This document is not binding, but does contain shared principles for the determination of fines in relation to infringements of competition law.

It can be concluded that the Commission and the NCAs have tried to limit the differences between their sanctioning regimes by coordinating some of their discretionary sanctioning powers in the context of the ECN or other international networks.

2.5 CONCLUSION

The EU framework for the enforcement of Articles 101 and 102 TFEU is based on a system of shared administration, sanctioning autonomy for the Member States, and mechanisms for cooperation and coordination. Shared administration implies that each Member State needs to designate an NCA and that infringements of Articles 101 and 102 TFEU can be prosecuted in parallel procedures. This inevitably leads to 'duplication costs'. In this respect, decentralisation can be seen as a rather inefficient way to increase enforcement capacity. Enforcement capacity could have been increased without any duplication costs simply by allocating additional resources to the Commission. Those Member States that already had fully operative authorities could have transferred some or all of those enforcement resources to Brussels. This alternative would also have saved on the 'coordination costs' needed to ensure the uniform and effective application of Articles 101 and 102 TFEU. Due to the mechanisms for consultation and uniform application, there should be no discrepancies in terms of what is prohibited and what is not. With these mechanisms in place, undertakings will not have to waste additional resources in complying with national variations of EU competition law and to incur potentially large 'transaction costs'. The convergence initiatives undertaken by the ECN and other international organisations will further limit these transaction costs, while ensuring that the effectiveness of EU competition law is not eroded by disparities in sanctioning regimes. However, all these mechanisms and initiatives will come at the expense of enforcement resources.[81] Also in this respect, decentralisation has been a rather costly venture. Furthermore, prevailing differences between the various sanctioning regimes, whether in terms of sanctioning powers or legal safeguards, could frustrate the exchange of information between the authorities and therefore the effectiveness of EU competition

[80] Available at <www.bundeskartellamt.de/wDeutsch/download/pdf/ECA/ECA_principles_for_convergence.pdf> accessed 1 July 2013.

[81] See also R Wesseling, 'The Draft-Regulation Modernising the Competition Rules: The Commission is Married to One Idea' (2001) 26 *European Law Review* 357, 377; Brammer (n 19) 21.

policy. This too could be seen as a 'coordination cost'. All of these costs could have been avoided if only there had been sufficient political support to improve the former centralised enforcement system. However, intended or not, this alternative would have prevented more than duplication costs and coordination costs alone – it would have ignored the potential benefits of decentralisation. To a large extent, these benefits can be explained precisely because several authorities can claim jurisdiction over a single case and because every Member State can design its sanctioning regime in accordance with domestic preferences. In order to shed more light on the implications of decentralisation, the economic contingencies need to be studied in more detail. This will be done in the following chapter.

3

The Economics of Decentralisation

3.1 INTRODUCTION

The decentralisation of EU competition law was mainly driven by the objective of increasing enforcement capacity. While the underlying problem of an under-staffed central authority could have been addressed more easily by increasing the European Commission's budget[1] (or by limiting the scope of the Commission's competences),[2] decentralisation was probably the only alternative that was politically feasible at that time.[3] Other implications of decentralisation were either taken for granted (eg, costs) or were of secondary importance in the decision to involve the Member States in the enforcement process (eg, subsidiarity). As a result, EU citizens are stuck with 28 or more NCAs[4] and various coordination efforts. To the extent that NCAs have actually taken over work from the Commission, EU citizens now also have to bear the costs of parallel procedures. Furthermore, the level of uniformity in the treatment of undertakings has been reduced.[5] Some undertakings will be exposed to more severe sanctions than others, depending on the authority that prosecutes the infringement. The other side of this coin is that EU citizens have been given more influence on 'their' sanctioning regime via the national parliaments. In this respect, any disparities in the

[1] *cf* WPJ Wils, 'The Modernisation of the Enforcement of Articles 81 and 82 EC: A Legal and Economic Analysis of the Commission's Proposal for a New Council Regulation Replacing Regulation No. 17' in B Hawk (ed), *Annual Proceedings of the Fordham Corporate Law Institute on International Antitrust Law and Policy* 2000 (Juris Publishing, 2001) 345; WPJ Wils, *The Optimal Enforcement of EC Antitrust Law: Essays in Law & Economics* (Kluwer Law International, 2002) 142.

[2] *cf* BJ Rodger and SR Wylie, 'Taking the Community Interest Line: Decentralisation and Subsidiarity in Competition Law Enforcement' (1997) 8 *European Competition Law Review* 485.

[3] *cf* PB Marsden, 'Inducing Member State Enforcement of European Competition Law: A Competition Policy Approach to "Antitrust Federalism"' (1997) 4 *European Competition Law Review* 234, 237.

[4] Since the accession of Croatia to the EU, there are now 28 Member States. Currently, there are already more than 28 NCAs, as some of the Member States have designated more than one authority for the enforcement of Articles 101 and 102 TFEU. It should be noted that many of the old and current Member States did not have a (well-staffed) authority at the time that Regulation 1/2003 was drafted; see A Riley, 'EC Antitrust Modernisation: The Commission Does Very Nicely – Thank You! Part 2: Between the Idea and the Reality: Decentralisation under Regulation 1' (2003) 12 *European Competition Law Review* 657, 658.

[5] To the extent that NCAs have continued their enforcement activities, albeit under an EU flag, Regulation 1/2003 has created more uniformity. However, this type of uniformity is not contingent on the sharing of enforcement competences and could have been realised through an improved centralised enforcement regime.

treatment of undertakings should simply be seen as a reflection of the wishes of these citizens. A priori, the decentralisation of EU competition law can thus be said to have had the following consequences. On the one hand, it has come with certain diseconomies, as it requires multiple authorities and coordination efforts, and may increase the number of parallel procedures. On the other hand, it has allowed Member States to provide for sanctioning powers that satisfy domestic demand, thereby using their resources in a more efficient manner. The decentralisation of EU competition law may also have implications for the *development* of sanctioning powers and procedures. More than ever, the pace of innovation in the area of competition law enforcement has become dependent on the Member States. Experiments by each Member State could accelerate 'regulatory innovation', but Member States may also insulate their jurisdictions from innovation by the Commission.

The economic implications of the decentralisation process are thus not self-evident. This chapter aims to clarify what economic theory predicts, given the legal framework established in chapter two. After first providing an overview of the various economic considerations in the allocation of regulatory competences more generally, we will zoom in on these considerations and apply them to the enforcement of EU competition law in separate paragraphs. For analytical purposes, this chapter contrasts the current system of decentralised enforcement with a hypothetical system of centralised enforcement. It is recognised that the pre-2004 enforcement system cannot be equated with a system of centralised enforcement, as several Member States already had a domestic competition authority and as the activities of some of these authorities may not have markedly changed. Nonetheless, this approach is useful because it identifies the advantages and disadvantages of decentralisation relative to other, conceivable enforcement regimes.

3.2 ECONOMIC CONSIDERATIONS IN THE ALLOCATION OF COMPETENCES

It is widely recognised in the economic literature on federalism that the devolution of competences from a central authority to local authorities (decentralisation) can have various implications for the costs of operating a legal system.[6] The devolution of competences may lead both to efficiencies and inefficiencies in the provision and administration of laws ('regulation'). Within this context, efficiency essentially refers to a situation in which tax money is not wasted.

The efficiencies of decentralisation can be static and dynamic in nature. Static efficiency refers to a situation in which citizens do not overpay for a given set of regulatory products. In many areas, the provision and administration of laws can

[6] For a brief account of the theory of federalism in the context of business regulation, see RP Inman and DL Rubinfeld, 'Making Sense of the Antitrust State-Action Doctrine: Balancing Political Participation and Economic Efficiency in Regulatory Federalism' (1996–97) 75 *Texas Law Review* 1203.

be organised more efficiently by decentralised authorities than a single centralised authority. This claim is especially true for areas of the law for which there exist strong 'heterogeneous preferences' within society. Heterogeneous preferences will arise when some people value particular regulatory products differently than others do. Decentralisation allows for the existence of a variety of legal regimes and this may accommodate these heterogeneous preferences. Fewer people will end up with either a government that in their eyes underperforms or paying for regulatory products they do not want.[7] However, in areas of the law where preferences are relatively homogeneous, decentralisation may still result in efficiency gains. This will be the case where decentralised authorities have an interest to perform well in the eyes of their 'customers' for reasons that are missing in a system of centralised rule making. One such reason could be that decentralised authorities compete with each other over mobile taxpayers. Any such 'regulatory competition' could improve regulatory outcomes relative to a situation in which rules are provided by a 'monopolist' central authority. Decentralisation could also enhance the possibilities for regulatory innovation. Regulatory innovation refers to a process of experimentation and learning by states or authorities which ultimately elevates the state of the art in a specific area of the law to a higher level. The possibilities for regulatory innovation increase with the number of regulatory authorities. Several authorities simply have more possibilities to experiment than one. Any form of regulatory competition could even stimulate these authorities to engage in innovative experiments. By perpetually improving the quality of regulation, regulatory innovation generates dynamic efficiencies.

Notwithstanding the above observations, decentralisation will not be efficient for every type of regulation. In areas of the law where the costs and benefits of regulation spill over into other jurisdictions, a decentralised authority could be tempted to 'underprovide' or 'overprovide'. For example, if the actions by one authority also benefit other jurisdictions, then there is a free-riding problem which can result in insufficient regulation. This will particularly be the case where authorities engage in regulatory competition. In these situations, centralisation (or coordination) could be more efficient.[8] From an economic perspective, centralisation could also be warranted where a diversity of legal regimes would hamper interjurisdictional trade. This may arise when undertakings need to comply with different, potentially conflicting rules. In such a case, decentralisation will result in 'transaction costs' for the undertakings concerned. Finally, centralisation may lead to 'economies of scale'. For some areas of regulation, it can be more

[7] In this respect, it should be noted that regulatory products, whether provided centrally or at a decentralised level, are generally indivisible and non-excludable. See R van den Bergh and P Camesasca, *European Competition Law and Economics: A Comparative Perspective* 2nd edn (Sweet & Maxwell, 2006) 407–08.

[8] However, in the words of Inman and Rubinfeld, 'centralization is no all-purpose cure for the efficiency ills of decentralization'. Under specific circumstances, centralised action upon so-called negative externality problems (where there is a tendency to overprovide) could be even more costly. In these circumstances, the central authority could best constrain the use of the good/regulation that causes the problem. See Inman and Rubinfeld (n 6) 1225–29.

efficient to maintain a single set of rules with a wide scope of application than having various authorities 'reinvent the wheel' over and over again. In these areas, decentralisation may lead to diseconomies of scale.

Within the context of EU competition law, these efficiencies and inefficiencies may arise in relation to the provision of enforcement powers and procedures. The decentralisation of enforcement competences may result in efficient 'preference matching', regulatory competition and regulatory innovation, but it may also lead to interjurisdictional spill-overs, transaction costs and diseconomies of scale. In fact, the coordination costs and duplication costs that have been mentioned earlier can be seen as examples of the latter. From an economic perspective, the decentralisation of EU competition law may thus have various advantages and disadvantages. While the promises and perils of decentralisation appeal to reason, it has been widely accepted that their accuracy and predictive value crucially depend on the object of regulation. To paraphrase Bratton and McCahery, concrete conclusions about the strengths and weaknesses of decentralisation must be delayed pending an enquiry of the regulatory domain.[9] The following sections will therefore analyse the current EU framework in light of the abovementioned economic considerations.

3.3 TRANSACTION COSTS AND DISECONOMIES OF SCALE

As has been suggested above, the decentralisation of EU competition law has come with some inherent economic losses. These losses are linked to transaction costs and diseconomies of scale. Transaction costs can arise when undertakings need to invest resources in complying with various legal regimes. The risk of increased compliance costs is mainly relevant with regard to discrepancies between behavioural norms. If the interpretation of the competition law prohibitions would differ across the Member States, undertakings would have to invest in information and would possibly be unable to implement a single business strategy throughout the EU. This would lead to significant transaction costs.[10] However, these costs have been avoided by including mechanisms for the uniform application of Articles 101 and 102 TFEU in Regulation 1/2003.[11] What remain are transaction costs due to disparities in

[9] WW Bratton and JA McCahery, 'The New Economics of Jurisdictional Competition: Devolutionary Federalism in a Second-Best World' (1997) 86 *Georgetown Law Journal* 201, 205.

[10] *cf* KJ Cseres, 'Comparing Laws in the Enforcement of EU and National Competition Laws' (2010) 3 *European Journal of Legal Studies* 7, 36, who nuances the issue of transaction costs: 'However, these costs can be especially relevant for large firms operating in interstate commerce, the same might not hold for small and medium sized undertakings operating mainly in national markets.'

[11] It should be noted that Member States are allowed to maintain national competition laws. Within the limits of Article 3 of Regulation 1/2003, these national competition laws may deviate from EU competition law (see above, section 2.2). This could lead to transaction costs after all. See P Pohlmann, 'Auf dem Weg zur Europäisierung nationalen Kartellrechts' in CJH Jansen et al (eds), *Europäische Dimensionen des Vertragsrechts und des Wettbewerbsrechts* (Münsterische Juristische Vorträge, Band 15, LIT Verlag 2005) 75. As this study is concerned with the enforcement of EU competition law alone, these costs will not be considered any further.

enforcement regimes.[12] Costs of this kind may be relatively modest. These disparities will 'only' amount to additional information costs, ie, legal advice. More importantly, these costs are only borne (or only need to be borne) if undertakings decide *not* to comply with Articles 101 and 102 TFEU.

Arguably a more serious drawback of the decentralisation of EU competition law are the diseconomies of scale. Decentralisation has led to duplication costs and coordination costs. Many of these costs are conditional on the fact that NCAs take over work that could have been done by the Commission. Coordination costs refer to the resources that have to be spent on making sure that differences in sanctioning regimes do not jeopardise the uniform and effective application of Articles 101 and 102 TFEU.[13] Brammer has noted in this respect:

> In view of the increased amount of information transmitted and the elevated complexity of information and information flows, the burden on the NCAs to properly administer the information circulating in the ECN has certainly become heavier. The general workload of the NCAs is further augmented by the fact that they may have to deal with a large number of different languages, which means that all officials have to be trained to understand (more) foreign languages and/or translations will have to be made by a separate translation service. It is thus safe to assume that the NCAs will have to make available additional resources (compared to the situation before 2004) in order to meet this new challenge. As concerns the Commission, its overall administrative burden will probably not have increased. However, it is submitted that many, if not all, of the resources that the Commission intended to free by abolishing the notification/authorisation system and shifting part of the workload to the NCAs will actually be absorbed by new tasks it has to assume as a result of the increased information exchange, the need to monitor NCAs and national courts and, possibly, the need to intervene in the proceedings before NCAs or national courts in order to safeguard the uniformity of EC competition law (eg as *amicus curiae*).[14]

Most of these resources could have been saved with a centralised enforcement system. Moreover, a centralised enforcement system would not suffer from enforcement disadvantages caused by restrictions to the use of information that has been exchanged between domestic authorities (see above, section 2.4). The current system of decentralised enforcement does suffer from these restrictions and this could also be seen as a cost of coordination.

Decentralisation has further led to duplication costs in terms of infrastructure.[15] A decentralised enforcement system requires several authorities and courts

[12] *cf* M de Visser, *Network-Based Governance in EC Law: The Example of EC Competition and EC Communications Law* (Hart Publishing, 2009) 351; L Parret, *Side Effects of the Modernisation of EU Competition Law* (Wolf Legal Publishers, 2011) 177.

[13] See also R Wesseling, 'The Draft-Regulation Modernising the Competition Rules: The Commission is Married to One Idea' (2001) 26 *European Law Review* 357, 377; S Brammer, *Co-operation between National Competition Agencies in the Enforcement of EC Competition Law* (Hart Publishing, 2009) 21.

[14] Brammer (n 13) 470 (footnotes omitted).

[15] See also D Geradin, 'Competition between Rules and Rules of Competition: A Legal and Economic Analysis of the Proposed Modernization of the Enforcement of EC Competition Law' (2002–03) 9 *Columbia Journal of European Law* 1, 22–25, who uses somewhat different terminology, naming some of these losses 'transaction costs'.

with several buildings, libraries, press offices, domain names etc and each with its own need for specialised staff.[16] To illustrate the costs of decentralisation, the recent merger of three regulatory authorities in the Netherlands (the competition authority, the telecom authority and the consumer authority) has reportedly resulted in cost savings of €3.38 million.[17] The decentralisation of Articles 101 and 102 TFEU has also led to duplication costs in terms of procedures. First, the Network Notice foresees parallel actions by two or three NCAs. This will necessarily result in duplication costs.[18] Second, the decentralisation of EU competition law, with its deference to national sanctioning regimes, has increased the possibility and need for litigation, with all the associated costs that go with this. This is the result of what could be termed the 'precedent deflation'. Legal precedents are welfare enhancing by reducing legal uncertainty and limiting the scope for future litigation.[19] A court ruling on the conditions under which a sanction may be imposed in one case can be relied upon by the authorities and the undertakings in subsequent cases. This could limit the number of disputes and court procedures. From this perspective, it would be most efficient if legal precedents in the context of EU competition law would apply throughout the EU.[20] Cases litigated before the Court of Justice on the basis of EU law, whether in the context of a direct action against a Commission decision or a reference for a preliminary ruling by a national court, will benefit the entire EU and allow for the intervention of the Commission and all the Member States.[21] These precedents are relatively easy to keep track of. The precedent value of cases litigated before national courts *on the basis of domestic procedural law* will of course be more limited. This loss is compounded by the fact that even if parties and ultimately courts would want to draw

[16] Duplication costs of this kind may seem relatively modest, as some Member States will have been able to 'piggyback' on existing infrastructure for domestic competition law. However, the ability to piggyback on existing infrastructure should not be overestimated. Around the turn of the new millennium, when Regulation 1/2003 was drafted, many of the old and current Member States did not have a (well-staffed) authority; see Riley (n 4) 658. More importantly, the ability to piggyback says relatively little about the costs of an enforcement system. After all, the maintenance of domestic infrastructure may be seen as a cost in and of itself.

[17] TK 2012–13, 33622, nr 3.

[18] I Simonsson, *Legitimacy in EU Cartel Control* (Hart Publishing, 2010) 341; WPJ Wils, 'The Principle of *Ne Bis in Idem* in EC Antitrust Enforcement: A Legal and Economic Analysis' (2003) 26 *World Competition* 131, 137. *cf* Wils, *The Optimal Enforcement of EC Antitrust Law* (n 1) 144: 'It may also make sense for a second authority to take up a case abandoned by a first authority, if the second authority has reasons to believe that it can do a better job than the first.'

[19] On the interplay between uncertainty and litigation, see G Dari-Mattiacci and B Deffains, 'Uncertainty of Law and Legal Process' (2007) 163 *Journal of Institutional and Theoretical Economics* 627, 627–56. See also WPJ Wils, 'The European Commission's 2006 Guidelines on Antitrust Fines: A Legal and Economic Analysis' (2007) 30 *World Competition* 197, 204: '[The Guidelines on the method for setting fines make] it easier for the addressees of fining decisions to understand why the fine was set at the level it was, thus possibly reducing the number of appeals.'

[20] *cf* European Commission, 'White Paper on Damages actions for breach of the EC antitrust rules' COM (2008) 165 final, where considerations of procedural economy has prompted the Commission to suggest that final decisions of the NCAs should have binding effect in actions for damages by private parties before the national courts.

[21] Article 40 of Protocol (No 3) on the statute of the Court of Justice of the European Union [2010] OJ C83/01.

inspiration from foreign precedents, language barriers alone make these cases more difficult to digest. In any case – and this is crucial – foreign precedents will not effectively limit the possibility for domestic precedents. If the stakes are high (which will typically be the case in relation to competition law disputes), the mere possibility of a domestic precedent could be enough to trigger litigation. The deflation of legal precedents can be seen as a diseconomy of scale which may result in significant duplication costs for the undertakings concerned and society as a whole.[22] However, there is also another side to this issue. The decentralised enforcement of Articles 101 and 102 TFEU will not take place in legal no man's land. Therefore, the costs associated with the deflation of legal precedents will in practice be offset, at least partially, by the existence of domestic precedents in other areas of the law. After all, general administrative law precedents could also reduce legal uncertainty and limit the scope for legal disputes in the context of Articles 101 and 102 TFEU.

In sum, the decentralisation of EU competition law can be associated with transaction costs for the undertakings involved, coordination costs for the competition authorities and duplication costs for undertakings, authorities and courts alike. Ultimately, all these costs are borne by taxpayers and consumers. While some of the costs could remain relatively modest, they would have been saved in a centralised enforcement system.

3.4 INFORMATION ADVANTAGES

One argument in favour of decentralisation is that NCAs have a competitive advantage over the Commission. This advantage consists in having better access to salient information. In this respect, it should be pointed out that competition authorities have a natural information disadvantage vis-a-vis the undertakings they have to monitor and that it is more difficult for the latter to hide information from local authorities than it would be from a more remote central authority.[23] In other words, decentralisation ameliorates some problems of asymmetric information. The NCAs will have better insight in domestic market conditions than the Commission. The people they employ read regional newspapers, may have personal shopping experiences, are familiar with the regulatory framework etc.

[22] A similar issue has been raised by Simonsson (n 18) 336, who argues: 'If there is no uniform standard, each and every Member State must make a similar journey, as have the Community courts in defining applicable procedure. Existing national procedure may not be sufficient in all respects. Adjustments in each Member State would include duplication of resources by legislators and courts.' See further Pohlmann (n 11) 73–74, who makes a similar point with regard to substantive competition law.

[23] R van den Bergh, 'Economic Criteria for Applying the Subsidiarity Principle in the European Community: The Case of Competition Policy' (1996) 16 *International Review of Law and Economics* 363, 365; van den Bergh and Camesasca (n 7) 422–24; Wils, 'The Modernisation of the Enforcement of Articles 81 and 82 EC' (n 1) 345; Wils, *The Optimal Enforcement of EC Antitrust Law* (n 1) 142; Geradin (n 15) 5, 19–20.

Decentralisation could thus enhance the effectiveness with which Articles 101 and 102 TFEU are enforced and thereby generate welfare gains.

While this information advantage provides a strong argument in favour of involving the Member States in the enforcement of EU competition law, it does not necessarily argue in favour of the prevailing sanctioning autonomy. This advantage would not have been jeopardised by a uniform sanctioning regime for all authorities.[24] In fact, the information advantage could have been obtained by setting up Commission field offices in the Member States. These are important considerations precisely because some of the costs associated with the EU framework for decentralised enforcement are due to the sanctioning autonomy of the Member States.

3.5 ACCOMMODATING DOMESTIC PREFERENCES

One of the more profound economic justifications for the current EU framework is that it accommodates domestic preferences. The decentralisation of EU competition law allows each Member State to design its own sanctioning regime for the enforcement of Articles 101 and 102 TFEU. As a result, more EU citizens will end up with the sanctioning regime they desire and this economises the allocation of government resources. This can be explained as follows.

First, decentralised decision makers are generally more responsive to the preferences of their citizens than a centralised decision maker. The smaller a given population, the more political influence each voter can exert. Votes get more clout, access to politicians will become easier and information about politicians will become more readily available.[25] Decentralisation also increases the number of enforcement alternatives, which makes it easier for citizens to monitor the performance of their government. Within the context of EU competition law, voters can rank the performance of their Member State against the performance of other Member States and the Commission. This may limit information asymmetries between government and voters and may therefore enhance the possibilities that voters' preferences will be satisfied even further.

Second, sanctioning preferences may very well differ between Member States.[26] For example, some Member States may wish to criminalise competition law and introduce custodial sanctions in the expectation that this will deter individuals from engaging in infringements, while other Member States may wish to rely on pecuniary sanctions for the undertakings involved. Domestic preferences may also differ in additional respects. Some Member States may wish to implement a deterring sanctioning regime by increasing the severity of the penalty. Other Member

[24] It should be noted that the harmonisation of sanctioning powers comes with costs of its own, eg, implementation costs.

[25] *cf* Inman and Rubinfeld (n 6) 1215.

[26] See also Cseres, 'Comparing Laws' (n 10) 36–37.

States could pursue the same objective by relying on a more moderate penalty, but increasing the chances of getting caught. Policy choices of this type are highly dependent on the political and moral views prevailing within society. These views may differ according to Member State. Some Member States may prefer a penalty that is cheap to administer, such as pecuniary sanctions, which are essentially transfer payments and impose few costs on society. Conversely, other Member States may prefer custodial sanctions. This type of sanction is more expensive to administer, but could send out stronger signals to society. Also, the interplay between the severity of the penalty and the chances of getting caught in designing a deterring sanctioning regime could lead to different outcomes depending on Member States. Some Member States may want to cut enforcement costs and let a small number of offenders pay hefty fines, while other Member States may think it more appropriate to invest in detection and spread out (higher) enforcement costs more evenly over society. Both approaches could deter as many infringements.

What all these examples are meant to illustrate is, first, that decisions as to how a sanctioning regime is designed have a bearing on enforcement expenditures and accompanying tax rates and, second, that sanctioning preferences could very well differ depending on the Member State. A decentralised enforcement system that is premised on sanctioning autonomy can accommodate heterogeneous preferences and may economise the allocation of government resources. Therefore, the current EU framework promises sanctioning regimes that are more efficient than the one-size-fits-all regime that comes with a centralised enforcement system.

Decentralisation could thus create disparities in enforcement expenditures between Member States. Geradin has argued that this could lead to the asymmetric application of EU competition law and eventually market fragmentation.[27] It is submitted herewith that this potential downside of decentralisation should not be overestimated. First, even if such fragmentation were to occur, this could be solved in a number of ways. The Commission could focus its attention on markets where decentralised enforcement is lacking and it could bring Member States with insufficient enforcement capacity before the Court of Justice for breach of Treaty obligations.[28] Second, and as a more important point, it is highly unlikely that Member States will reduce their enforcement expenditures to levels that are harmful to the EU as a whole. After all, the Member States will experience various disciplining effects in operating a sanctioning regime. This point will be clarified directly below.

[27] Geradin (n 15) 19–20. A similar concern has found its way into the Commission Staff Working Paper accompanying the Communication from the Commission to the European Parliament and the Council: Report on the functioning of Regulation 1/2003 [2009] COM 206 final, para 194: 'Certain criticism has been expressed in the course of the public consultation for this Report as to the limited resources of some national competition authorities and its possible impact on competition proceedings, e.g. limited capacity for investigations, longer duration of proceedings.'

[28] Geradin has noted the possibility of Commission intervention, but has rejected it as it would be 'contrary to the philosophy of the new system that the Commission replace failing national agencies': Geradin (n 15) 27. The fact that the Commission has been granted the power to replace failing national agencies (Article 11(6) of Regulation 1/2003) would seem to disprove this point.

3.6 REGULATORY COMPETITION

Decentralisation not only caters for different preferences between citizens of the various Member States, it also allows these citizens to form more homogeneous sub-societies by migrating to the Member State that best satisfies their preferences. Member States can implement a regulatory regime and attract people from abroad who relocate themselves in their jurisdiction. This process requires that citizens are mobile and will take locational decisions on the basis of regulatory preferences. Were this to happen, regulatory preferences can be satisfied at a reduced cost. Whether such sub-societies will emerge and whether this results in efficiency gains is dependent on various factors. This is predominantly the domain of the theory of regulatory competition. While the decentralisation of EU competition law is unlikely to trigger an efficiency-enhancing migration stream, Member States may still 'compete on the market for enforcement'. This section will explain the disciplining effects of this market, as well as their economic implications.

3.6.1 The Theory of Regulatory Competition

The theory of regulatory competition derives from the seminal article by Charles Tiebout on the provision of public goods.[29] With this article, Tiebout aimed to show that under particular circumstances, public goods can be provided more efficiently at a local level than at a national level. The basic idea behind Tiebout's model is that individuals can relocate themselves on the basis of preferences for public goods and corresponding levels of taxation.[30] This could trigger a competition between jurisdictions for taxpayers. This 'jurisdictional competition' guarantees the same efficiency in the provision of local public goods as competition among firms assures in the market for private goods. Jurisdictional competition is premised on the perception that a variety of goods and tax levels will better satisfy heterogeneous preferences and relies on a market mechanism to reach an equilibrium in which no consumer-voter would prefer any other outcome (Pareto-efficient).[31] In this equilibrium, the sum of consumer-voters' marginal rate of substitution of income for

[29] CM Tiebout, 'A Pure Theory of Local Expenditures' (1956) 64 *Journal of Political Economy* 416.

[30] This issue has been described very clearly by Bratton and McCahery: 'With *private* goods, market competition exerts downward pressure on producers' marginal costs, and market prices provide concrete information about consumers' rates of substitution. With *public* goods, in contrast, no obvious market exerts downward pressure on government producers' marginal costs. Nor does an obvious mechanism force taxpaying citizen-consumers truthfully to reveal their rates of substitution.' The authors then describe the attributes of Tiebout's model of jurisdiction competition: 'the Tiebout model links citizen mobility with preference revelation and predicts that locational decisions will reveal individual preferences for public goods and levels of taxation . . . The model goes on to predict that this preference revelation process leads to a market equilibrium'. See Bratton and McCahery (n 9) 207–09.

[31] Bratton and McCahery (n 9) 204.

the good equals the marginal costs of an additional unit of the good.[32] Under a working system of jurisdictional competition, periodic elections would no longer be needed; citizens would vote with their feet. While the model's assumptions are too unrealistic ever to be satisfied,[33] the disciplining effect and the potential efficiency gains of jurisdictional competition are broadly accepted and appeal to reason.

The same logic can be extended to the provision and administration of laws. Preferences for regulation too may differ and market mechanisms could drive decentralised decision makers to efficient outcomes.[34] Analogous to firms in a market for private goods competing for various targets (sales, revenue, profits etc), jurisdictions may compete for various benefits (tax income, economic productivity, political support etc). The greater the regulatory autonomy of each jurisdiction, the greater the scope for competition. Whether regulatory competition indeed results in efficient outcomes is dependent on various factors, most notably the absence of interjurisdictional spill-overs, transaction costs and diseconomies of scale.

The theory of regulatory competition could be extended to the enforcement of EU competition law. By enhancing the role of the Member States and by allowing each Member State to design its own sanctioning regime, Regulation 1/2003 has provided the basic conditions for regulatory competition. Economic benefits are to be expected if Member States are indeed disciplined in designing their enforcement regimes *and* this leads to a situation in which the preferences of consumer-voters are better satisfied compared to a system of centralised enforcement. Both factors will be considered in turn.

3.6.2 Competition in the Enforcement of EU Competition Law

The conditions under which the enforcement of EU competition law takes place and the interests at stake make it plausible that Member States will experience at least some market discipline in designing their enforcement regimes. This is the

[32] ibid 207.

[33] The assumptions underlying Tiebout's model are the following: (1) consumer-voters are fully mobile and will move to the jurisdiction that satisfies their preferences best; (2) consumer-voters have full knowledge about the conditions in each jurisdiction; (3) there are a large number of jurisdictions; (4) restrictions due to employment opportunities are not considered; (5) there are no interjurisdictional spillovers; (6) for every pattern of goods, there is an optimal jurisdiction size, which is defined in terms of the number of residents for which this bundle of goods can be produced at the lowest average cost; (7) jurisdictions below the optimum size seek to attract new residents to lower average costs. However, the model already breaks down when it is applied to a situation in which there are fixed jurisdictional boundaries. As demonstrated by Epple and Zelenitz, in such a situation, competition among local jurisdictions is not sufficient to prevent local governments from exercising monopoly power and usurp some (immobile) land rents. See D Epple and A Zelenitz, 'The Implications of Competition among Jurisdictions: Does Tiebout Need Politics?' (1981) 89 *Journal of Political Economy* 1197.

[34] FH Easterbrook, 'Antitrust and the Economics of Federalism' (1983) 26 *Journal of Law & Economics* 23, 34.

effect of what could be conceived as competition for *fine proceeds* and *reputation gains*. Competition for fine proceeds is induced by the 'all-or-nothing' characteristics of the EU legal framework, which delimits neither the jurisdiction of the NCAs to apply Articles 101 and 102 TFEU nor the scope of their sanctioning powers, while providing for: (1) the principle of single authority action as often as possible; (2) case allocation on the basis of enforcement possibilities;[35] and (3) the principle of *ne bis in idem* – no person may be found guilty or can be made the subject of proceedings a second time on the grounds of conduct in respect of which he or she has already been penalised or acquitted.[36] In other words, once the infringement has been penalised by one authority, other authorities may remain empty-handed. The multi-million euro fines that may be levied for infringements of Articles 101 and 102 TFEU will provide Member States with an incentive to furnish their authorities with strong enforcement powers and to assume jurisdiction over cases with domestic implications. This point has also been taken up by Simonsson, who details the Commission's lucrative enforcement business in 2004.[37]

Anecdotal evidence for this disciplining effect can be found in the parliamentary deliberations preceding the 2005 reform of the German fining regime. With this reform, the German competition authorities saw their fining powers being strengthened. As is clear from the report of the parliamentary committee responsible for competition matters, this amendment was considered to be especially urgent in light of the power of the Commission to take over cases pursuant to Article 11(6) of Regulation 1/2003 and the desire to secure fine proceeds for German citizens:

> Im zukünftigen Netzwerk der europäischen Wettbewerbsbehörden müssen alle Behörden über im Wesentlichen gleichwertige Sanktionsbefugnisse verfügen. Ist dies nicht der Fall, so steht der Europäischen Kommission die Möglichkeit zur Verfügung, einen Kartellfall an sich zu ziehen . . . mit der Folge, dass die umsatzbezogene Bußgeldbemessung nach Maßgabe von Artikel 23 Abs. 2 Satz 2 der Verordnung (EG) Nr. 1/2003 zur Anwendung kommt. Um der dezentralen Anwendung des europäischen Wettbewerbsrechts praktische Wirksamkeit ("effet utile") zu verschaffen, wird die Bußgeldbemessung nach deutschem Recht der europäischen Regelung angepasst. Damit wird eine effektive Bußgeldbemessung durch die deutschen Kartellbehörden

[35] In addition, NCAs that dispose of better sanctioning powers might receive more complaints. Lenaerts has suggested that NCAs that are severe and efficient in the enforcement of Articles 101 and 102 TFEU are likely to receive more complaints than colleagues performing less well. See K Lenaerts, 'Modernisation of the Application and Enforcement of European Competition Law – An Introductory Overview' in J Stuyck and H Gilliams (eds), *Modernisation of European Competition Law* (Intersentia Antwerp, 2002) 31. See also M Drahos, *Convergence of Competition Laws and Policies in the European Community. Germany, Austria, and the Netherlands* (Kluwer Law International, 2001) 436.

[36] Article 50 of the Charter of Fundamental Rights of the European Union [2007] OJ C 303/1; Article 4(1) of Protocol No 7 to the Convention for the Protection of Human Rights and Fundamental Freedoms, CETS No 117; Joined Cases C-238, C-244, C-245, C-247, C-250–252 and C-254/99 P *LVM* [2002] ECR I-8375; Case C-397/03 P *Archer Daniels Midland* [2006] ECR I-4429.

[37] Simonsson (n 18) 341–42.

sichergestellt. Dies dient auch dazu, dass die volkswirtschaftlichen Schäden durch den Kartellrechtsverstoβ in Deutschland kompensiert werden.[38]

Similar concerns prompted parliamentarians in the Netherlands to enquire what would happen with a fine that was collected by the Commission in relation to an infringement of Article 101 TFEU on the Dutch beer market.[39] These parliamentarians were of the opinion that as Dutch consumers suffered from the infringement, Dutch taxpayers were to benefit from the fine.[40] They also questioned why this case was prosecuted by the Commission instead of the domestic authority. In addition, this example illustrates the disciplining effect of fine proceeds, albeit indirectly and *ex post*.

Where fine proceeds alone are insufficient to rally a competition for cases (for instance, in cases where the imposition of a fine is not warranted), reputation gains will add to the equation. Member States may try to reinforce their status within the ECN and other international forums in order to increase their influence in policy making and/or to export their enforcement regimes to foreign jurisdictions.[41] International reputation could thus work as another disciplining factor in designing a domestic enforcement regime.[42] To grasp the importance of reputation in the field of competition law enforcement, it is only necesssary to refer to a 2011 consultation document by the UK Department for Business, Innovation & Skills, which boasts:

> The UK competition regime is highly regarded internationally. In 2010 the Global Competition Review awarded the Competition Commission (CC) its highest rating of 5 stars and the Office of Fair Trading (OFT) 4.5 stars, both appearing in the top 5 agencies in the world. In addition, an independent review of competition regimes by KPMG ranked the UK's competition regime third, behind the US and Germany. The National Audit Office (NAO) has also concluded that the competition regime (including as

[38] Deutscher Bundestag, *Beschlussempfelung und Bericht des Auschusses für Wirtschaft und Arbeit (9. Ausschuss) zu dem Gesetzentwurf der Bundesregierung – Drucksache 15/3640 – Entwurf eines Siebten Gesetzes zür Änderung des Gesetzes gegen Wettbewerbsbeschränkungen* (BT-Drucksache 15/5049) 50 <www.bundestag.de/dokumente/drucksachen/index.html> accessed 1 July 2013. The quoted text could be translated as follows: 'In the future Network of European competition authorities, all authorities should have substantially equivalent sanctioning powers. If this is not the case, the European Commission has the possibility to take over a cartel case . . . with the effect that the turnover-based fine calculation pursuant to Article 23(2), second sentence, of Regulation (EG) No 1/2003 becomes applicable. In order to provide useful effect ("effet utile") to the decentralised application of European competition law, the German rules relating to fine calculation will be brought into line with European rules. This will ensure the effective fine calculation by German competition authorities. In addition, this is also meant to ensure that the economic harm caused by the cartel infringement will be compensated in Germany.'

[39] TK 2006-2007, Aanhangsel 1586. See also M van der Woude, 'Redactionele signalen' (2007) 55 *SEW Tijdschrift voor Europees en economisch recht* 176.

[40] Where the Commission imposes a fine, in principle this fine becomes part of the Commission's annual budget. Excess amounts are distributed among the Member States. See TK 2006–07, Aanhangsel 1586.

[41] Member States could have an interest in exporting their enforcement regimes to foreign jurisdictions in an effort to reduce the transaction costs for national businesses dealing abroad.

[42] See also KJ Cseres, 'The Impact of Regulation 1/2003 in the New Member States' (2010) 6 *Competition Law Review* 145, 162–63.

> enforced by the sector regulators) is generally effective in meeting its aims and is well regarded internationally.[43]

In the same document it can be read that: 'The Government is committed to ensuring the UK's competition regime remains among the best in the world.'[44] The UK will certainly not be the only contender on the market for reputation. It may be assumed that reputation gains will accrue to Member States that handle infringements of Articles 101 and 102 TFEU efficiently.[45]

This disciplining effect of reputation gains is corroborated by the discourse on 'rank-order competition'.[46] Rank-order competition is premised on the dual presumption that voters will demand that their government provides for regulation of at least equal quality as regulation in other jurisdictions *and* that the government wants to be re-elected. Rank-order competition enhances the possibilities that consumer-voters' preferences will be satisfied.[47] The term 'competition' should not obscure the fact that this is not a contest between jurisdictions for a group of (potential) taxpayers or other (financial) advantages, but a contest between politicians within a single jurisdiction.[48] Within the context of EU competition law, voters can rank the performance of their Member State against the performance of other Member States (horizontal competition) and the Commission (vertical competition).[49]

In sum, it is plausible that Member States are disciplined in designing their enforcement regimes, whether through fine proceeds or (external or internal) reputation gains.

In theory, Member States could also compete for *tax-paying consumers* and *growth-creating producers*. However, upon closer inspection, it is implausible that there is a market for either one, at least in the context of EU competition law. It should be admitted that an effective enforcement regime for Articles 101 and 102 TFEU will enhance consumer welfare and could potentially attract tax-paying

[43] Department for Business, Innovation & Skills, *A Competition Regime for Growth: A Consultation on Options for Reform* (2011), para 1.4 (footnotes omitted) <www.bis.gov.uk/Consultations/competition-regime-for-growth> accessed 1 July 2013.

[44] ibid para 1.8.

[45] See also Simonsson (n 18) 342.

[46] P Salmon, 'Decentralisation as an Incentive Scheme' (1987) 3 *Oxford Review of Economic Policy* 24. This phenomenon is also referred to as 'yardstick competition'; see Bratton and McCahery (n 9) 256–59.

[47] Rank-order competition due to decentralisation makes another powerful prediction: it limits information assymmetries between government and vote-casting consumers. This gives decentralised government units yet another efficiency advantage over central government. *cf* Salmon (n 46); Bratton and McCahery (n 9) 258; Inman and Rubinfeld (n 6) 1246–47.

[48] Inman and Rubinfeld use the terms 'intergovernmental economic competition' and 'intragovernmental political competition' to make a similar distinction; see Inman and Rubinfeld (n 6) 1241ff. In their article, Inman and Rubinfeld argue that in case of: (1) open access to reform; (2) full information about policy consequences; and (3) the ability to mobilise support for reform, 'policies that make a majority of citizens better off will be on the agenda, known and understood by the voters, and chosen either directly by referendum or through elected representatives'. The conditions for this intragovernmental political competition would be more realistic than Tiebout's conditions for intergovernmental economic competition (at 1245–46).

[49] See also de Visser (n 12) 242.

consumers. However, 'bundling and mobility problems' dampen the disciplining potential of tax-paying consumers significantly, if not entirely. Even if disgruntled consumers would act rationally, relocating to a different Member State would still be unlikely. This is due to, on the one hand, consumers' bundled regulatory preferences and the limited number of jurisdictional alternatives and, on the other hand, the costs of mobility.[50] It should be noted that as there is no convincing narrative for competition for tax-paying consumers, Member States cannot get caught in a prisoner's dilemma either. This is important as the decentralised enforcement of Articles 101 and 102 TFEU has positive interjurisdictional spillovers; the enforcement actions by one Member State have benefits for other Member States.[51] Under market conditions, these positive interjurisdictional spillovers could give rise to inefficient underprovision.

Competition for growth-creating producers is equally unrealistic. Granted, a competition policy aimed at increasing consumer welfare will not necessarily be desired by every producer.[52] At the margins, therefore, producers with finite investment resources will leave jurisdictions/markets with severe enforcement regimes and enter jurisdictions/markets whose enforcement regimes are more relaxed. These costs in foregone trade and employment could discipline Member States and provide them with incentives to shirk on their enforcement efforts. This process is compounded by the fact that the costs of enforcement will rise with the severity of the sanctions. Moreover, in cases where the anti-competitive effects are partially exported and the monopoly profits are spent at home, Member States could have a further reason to be soft on business.[53] Thus, in theory, Member States could compete for a producer-friendly environment by softening

[50] Bratton and McCahery (n 9) 223, 234 and 260. See further Inman and Rubinfeld (n 6) 1241–44.

[51] The broad jurisdiction of the NCAs to apply Articles 101 and 102 TFEU and to punish infringements means that there are 'deterrence spillovers'. If tax-paying consumers would be mobile and sensitive to competition law enforcement regimes, they would move away from the jurisdiction that bears the full costs of enforcement without reaping the full benefit. This prisoner's dilemma would be particularly relevant with regard to a jurisdiction's choice to implement costly enforcement measures (eg, custodial sanctions). A similar point has also been made by Teichman in the context of US criminal law: 'Apprehending and prosecuting a criminal who commits crimes in several jurisdictions lowers the crime rate in all those jurisdictions if it deters the apprehended individual from committing future crimes. Similarly, incapacitating a criminal through incarceration lowers the crime rate in all jurisdictions victimized by the criminal at hand. Viewed from this perspective, jurisdictions might have *insufficient* incentives to invest in crime prevention since they will try to free-ride on the efforts of neighboring jurisdictions' (footnote omitted). D Teichman, 'The Market for Criminal Justice: Federalism, Crime Control, and Jurisdictional Competition' (2004–05) 103 *Michigan Law Review* 1831, 1861–62. See further A Ezrachi and J Kindl, 'Cartels as Criminal? The Long Road from Unilateral Enforcement to International Consensus' in C Beaton-Wells and A Ezrachi (eds), *Criminalising Cartels: Critical Studies of an International Regulatory Movement* (Hart Publishing, 2011) 419, 424.

[52] *cf* Drahos (n 35) 228, who puts it even more strongly: 'It is generally easier for firms to calculate the costs of a strict competition law, flowing from opportunity costs and administrative costs, than any possible gains, like protection from dominant firms or restrictive distribution contracts and increasing economic growth. It is much more insecure whether the firm will profit in the future from the decisions of the competition authority. The consequences of competition policy on growth and welfare depend even more on subjective beliefs. Thus I argue that it is probable that a large majority of firms will have a preference for a weak competition law.'

[53] See also van den Bergh (n 23) 372–73.

the consumer-friendly competition policy. In practice, though, this type of competition is unlikely. First, Member States and undertakings may have more confidence in the long-term benefits of technological leadership than the short-term benefits of an industrial policy favouring big enterprises.[54] Second, if the costs in terms of foregone consumer welfare are mainly borne by the consumers/voters of the producer-friendly jurisdiction, any such policy would be difficult to sell and would probably lead to domestic welfare losses.[55] Third, if anti-competitive effects are in large part exported to other jurisdictions, these jurisdictions, as well as the Commission, may start proceedings themselves.[56] Indeed, the Network Notice allocates cases to the Commission where effective enforcement so requires. While this prospect alone might not lead Member States to toughen up against 'national champions', it does reduce the disciplining effect of growth-creating producers and the risk of a 'race to the bottom' in terms of enforcement.

In sum, the threat of exit and the promise of entry do not appear credible enough to discipline Member States in satisfying consumer/producer preferences in the field of competition law enforcement. But even if there would be a market for tax-paying consumers and growth-creating producers, competition in this market would still be frustrated by the 'universal jurisdiction' of the Commission and the failure to delimit the jurisdictions of the NCAs. What remains, therefore, is a plausible case for some 'competition' between (and within) Member States for fine proceeds and reputation gains.

3.6.3 A Race to the Top?

The next question is whether competition between Member States leads to a situation in which the preferences of consumer-voters are better satisfied. It may be assumed that competition for fine proceeds and reputation gains will enhance the enforcement efforts of domestic authorities. The more effective the enforcement of Articles 101 and 102 TFEU, the lower the magnitude of anti-competitive behaviour. In principle, consumer-voters will thus benefit from this competition between Member States.[57] This claim is based on the assumption that decentralised

[54] ibid, 377: 'A decision to move to "cartel paradises" will be made primarily for commercial reasons and not because of the prospect of a lax antitrust jurisdiction . . . Successes in international trade are achieved through technological leadership, which is not necessarily due to monopoly power but may be the consequence of strong competitive pressures on the home market. Hence, competition policy may improve international competitiveness, contrary to the arguments in favor of an industrial policy favoring big enterprises through lax merger control. Nevertheless, it may not totally be excluded that considerations relating to the stringency of competition laws matter at the margin.'

[55] See also EM Fox, 'Antitrust Law on a Global Scale: Races Up, Down, and Sideways' in DC Esty and D Geradin (eds), *Regulatory Competition and Economic Integration: Comparative Perspectives* (Oxford University Press, 2001) 348–63; Geradin (n 15) 7.

[56] See also Geradin (n 15) 26.

[57] *cf* Lenaerts (n 35): 'National competition authorities which will prove to be severe and efficient in the enforcement of Articles 81 and 82 EC [now Articles 101 and 102 TFEU] are indeed likely to receive more complaints than others. It is submitted that this kind of *forum shopping* should not be discouraged since it will enhance the protection of competition.'

enforcement is not a zero-sum game in which effective enforcement in one jurisdiction merely displaces infringements to another jurisdiction.[58] While some displacement of infringements of Articles 101 and 102 TFEU may occur, increased enforcement throughout the EU will change the calculus of at least some rational operating undertakings in whether or not to comply with the law.

Nevertheless, there is an enforcement level beyond which the 'race to the top' will change into a 'race to the bottom' in terms of social welfare. This will be the case where the administrative costs of enforcement start outweighing the benefits. For example, a Member State that wants to root out every single infringement will probably be faced with excessive costs. A race to the bottom of such a kind seems unlikely, however, as Member States would incur all losses themselves and no one therefore has an interest in entering such a race. Yet, there may be a race to the bottom of a different kind – one resulting in 'overdeterrence'. Such a race could be triggered by a competition for fine proceeds. Where the expected fine for the undertakings concerned exceeds the social costs of the infringement, there will be a situation of 'inefficient overdeterrence'.[59] This could lead to at least four types of inefficiencies: (1) deterring socially valuable behaviour falling within the scope of the prohibition; (2) deterring socially valuable behaviour falling outside the scope of the prohibition as a result of legal ambivalence or error; (3) excessive monitoring costs by addressees of the prohibition – the private gains of monitoring exceed the social gains of compliance; (4) excessive litigation costs for all parties involved in the proceedings – the higher the stakes, the higher the investments in litigation.[60] When these costs are not fully borne by the prosecuting Member State, a market for fine proceeds may have perverse incentives. Each Member State could gain by inflicting greater welfare losses on society. This could stimulate Member States to impose excessive fines or to lower legal safeguards so as to raise the expected fine. To the extent that market forces indeed trigger such a race to the bottom, this race will in any case be slowed down, if not completely arrested, by the competition for reputation gains. Reputation gains are unlikely to accrue to Member States whose enforcement regimes would create welfare losses. It is therefore concluded that race to the bottom scenarios are unlikely.

However, this does not mean that a competition for fine proceeds is without its downsides. This competition may not only strengthen national fining powers, it

[58] For a different approach towards regulatory competition and crime displacement, see Teichman (n 51), who concludes that a decentralised criminal justice system could result in a dynamic process of inefficiently harsh punishments.

[59] AM Polinsky and S Shavell, 'Punitive Damages: An Economic Analysis' (1997–98) 111 *Harvard Law Review* 869, 886ff. The notion of overdeterrence implies that the optimal level of violations, in terms of social costs, can be above zero. While this might not be socially acceptable for breach of any law, for EU competition law, this seems a point for consideration.

[60] Polinsky and Shavell (n 59) 879–86; DR Fischel and AO Sykes, 'Corporate Crime' (1996) 25 *Journal of Legal Studies* 319, 321 and 324; MK Block and JG Sidak, 'The Cost of Antitrust Deterrence: Why Not Hang a Price Fixer Now and Then?' (1979–80) 68 *Georgetown Law Journal* 1131; WM Landes, 'Optimal Sanctions for Antitrust Violations' (1983) 50 *University Chicago Law Review* 652, 655; RA Posner, *Antitrust Law* 2nd edn (University of Chicago Press, 2001) 267.

could also frustrate efficient case allocation within the ECN.[61] In this respect, it should be recalled that the rules for case allocation remain somewhat informal (see above, section 2.4). The desire to collect a fine could frustrate the ECN objective of single authority action and could lead to an increased number of parallel procedures by the NCAs. As soon as one NCA starts an investigation, other NCAs may follow suit in order to secure their piece of the pie. This scenario is particularly likely for cases involving two or three Member States – cases involving more than three Member States will generally be picked up by the Commission. In other words, the competition for fine proceeds may increase the number of procedures (see above, section 3.3).

Taking into account all the above considerations, it is plausible that the regulatory framework of Regulation 1/2003 fosters a market mechanism through which Articles 101 and 102 TFEU are enforced more effectively and the interests of consumer-voters are better served. This suggests that the decentralisation of EU competition law brings with it certain economic benefits. Notwithstanding these benefits, it should not be forgotten that the decentralisation of EU competition law has also led to duplication costs and that these costs are partially due to this market mechanism. Against this background, it is important to consider one final benefit of decentralisation: regulatory innovation.

3.7 REGULATORY INNOVATION

By increasing the possibilities for experimentation and learning, decentralisation can also be beneficial for regulatory innovation. Regulatory innovation refers to the expansion of the storehouse of knowledge with regard to regulatory design. It thus refers to an ongoing process rather than to an end state. Experiments can be considered 'innovative' provided they add to earlier experiences and have the potential to solve a particular social problem. Decentralisation creates 'legal laboratories' in which experiments can be carried out without risk to the greater polity.[62] Justice Brandeis of the US Supreme Court has called this 'one of the happy incidents of the federal system'.[63] The same could be said for the constitutional

[61] See also Wils, 'The Principle of *Ne Bis in Idem* in EC Antitrust Enforcement' (n 18) 139.

[62] See also A Arcuri and G Dari-Mattiacci, 'Centralisation versus Decentralisation as a Risk-Return Trade-Off' (2010) 53 *Journal of Law and Economics* 359. These authors conclude, amongst other things, that 'decentralization is a desirable solution for decisions that are important to society, that are affected by serious scientific uncertainty, and for which society is risk averse' (at 374).

[63] *New State Ice Co v Liebmann* 285 US 262, 311 (1932) (dissenting opinion). Justice Brandeis further concluded: 'The discoveries in physical science, the triumphs in invention, attest to the value of the process of trial and error. In large measure, these advances have been due to experimentation. In those fields experimentation has, for two centuries, been not only free but encouraged. Some people assert that our present plight is due, in part, to the limitations set by courts upon experimentation in the fields of social and economic science; and to the discouragement to which proposals for betterment there have been subjected otherwise. There must be power in the states and the nation to remould, through experimentation, our economic practices and institutions to meet changing social and economic needs' (at 311–12).

system of the EU.[64] One need not have to see decentralised governments as laboratories in order to admit that independent efforts by various jurisdictions will provide more information about what does or does not work. Where jurisdictions engage in regulatory competition, innovative regulatory solutions are particularly likely to emerge.[65] The value of regulatory innovation is especially strong in areas of the law that are characterised by their complexity and technical difficulty. However, in any setting of imperfect information and learning-by-doing, there are potential gains to be had from experimentation.[66] This could include the area of competition law enforcement.[67] In this respect, reference could be made to a 2012 consultation report of the UK's Office of Fair Trading:

> Effective enforcement of competition law is vital for efficient markets and as a driver for economic growth, delivering benefits for consumers and the economy. It is important that the Office of Fair Trading . . . like other competition authorities, keeps innovating and constantly improving the conduct of effective and efficient competition enforcement.[68]

By allowing for experimentation and learning among the Member States in terminating and punishing infringements of EU competition law, decentralisation could elevate the state of the art in competition law enforcement to a higher level. For instance, if a Member State were to experiment with custodial sanctions, other Member States could learn from these experiences and make an informed choice as to whether or not to follow this example. The learning effects of this experiment should be sought in the achievements in terms of deterrence ('will the number of infringements decrease?') and in the technical aspects of introducing this criminal law penalty (eg, 'how will criminal courts deal with this new type of offence?'). More generally, it can be argued that the potential for regulatory innovation is greatest if Member States would experiment with sanctioning powers for which there is no Commission equivalent whatsoever.

Member States can learn from successful regulatory experiments elsewhere – and this immediately confronts the idea of regulatory innovation with a theoretical problem. The possibility to learn from experiments abroad creates a free-riding problem and a prisoner's dilemma, in which there will be less innovation than is socially preferable.[69] However, in the context of EU competition law, any such

[64] Geradin (n 15) 5–6.

[65] Van den Bergh, 'Economic Criteria for Applying the Subsidiarity Principle in the European Community' (n 23) 366; R van den Bergh, 'Towards an Institutional Legal Framework for Regulatory Competition in Europe' (2000) 53 *KYKLOS* 435, 438–39. See further Inman and Rubinfeld (n 6) 1248–49.

[66] WE Oates, 'An Essay on Fiscal Federalism' (1999) 37 *Journal of Economic Literature* 1120, 1132.

[67] Van den Bergh, 'Towards an Institutional Legal Framework for Regulatory Competition in Europe' (n 65) 455; Wils, 'The Modernisation of the Enforcement of Articles 81 and 82 EC' (n 1) 345; Wils, *The Optimal Enforcement of EC Antitrust Law* (n 1) 142; WPJ Wils, 'Leniency in Antitrust Enforcement: Theory and Practice' (2007) 30 *World Competition* 25, 36; Geradin (n 15) 17–18.

[68] Office of Fair Trading, *Review of the OFT's Investigation Procedures in Competition Cases* (OFT 1263con2 2012), para 1.1 <www.oft.gov.uk/shared_oft/policy/OFT1263con2> accessed 1 July 2013.

[69] S Rose-Ackerman, 'Risk Taking and Reelection: Does Federalism Promote Innovation?' (1980) 9 *Journal of Legal Studies* 593. Through a simple model in which the elected official only cares about re-election, a single elected official controls government policy and bureaucracies play a passive role,

free-riding problem will be seriously mitigated by the reputation gains that accrue to first-movers. Moreover, the ECN awards a 'prize' to innovative Member States.[70] As enforcement possibilities are part of the ECN's case allocation criteria, innovative Member States have better chances in collecting fines for infringements of Articles 101 and 102 TFEU.

The EU enforcement framework even facilitates interjurisdictional learning. First of all, the Commission needs to consult the Advisory Committee composed of representatives of the NCAs before imposing any sanction for infringements of Articles 101 and 102 TFEU. The NCAs in turn have to consult the Commission before sanctions can be imposed. These consultation mechanisms have created a structural dialogue between the various authorities. As a consequence of this consultation process, competition authorities learn about the sanctioning possibilities and methods elsewhere, and this may feed back into domestic policy.[71] In addition to these consultation requirements with regard to individual cases, the ECN provides a forum for policy discussions. This too may contribute to interjurisdictional learning.[72] Within the context of the ECN, competition authorities can discuss and share experiences with sanctioning powers for the enforcement of Articles 101 and 102 TFEU. The Commission's administrative services have noted in this respect:

> This constant dialogue between the network members on all levels over the last years has significantly contributed to a coherent approach and coherent application of the EC competition rules. The permanent exchange of experiences and views, very often in an informal manner, has established confidence and trust between network members, increased the expertise and promoted convergence. It has led to the creation of a space to think that allows fruitful discussions in a spirit of close cooperation and with the final objective of promoting a common competition culture in Europe.[73]

As a result of these discussions, the ECN has already drawn up guidelines for effective domestic leniency programmes. In addition to the activities within the ECN, the Commission and the NCAs regularly discuss enforcement policy with colleagues from outside the EU. In light of the cooperation between the authorities within the ECN, the governance structure created by Regulation 1/2003 has been described in terms of 'regulatory co-opetition', pulling together competition

Rose-Ackerman has established that due to the re-election motive, the lack of sorting by risk preferences, external effects and the impact of migration, there will be few useful experiments among local governments. See also Oates (n 66) 1133.

[70] The use of 'prizes' to encourage innovation by decentralised government units has been proposed by Rose-Ackerman as a (second-best) solution to solve the free-rider problem with regulatory innovation; see Rose-Ackerman (n 69) 615–16.

[71] See also Drahos (n 35) 434.

[72] *cf* Cseres (n 10) 27, who is less enthusiastic: 'the possibility to function as a melting pot of national laboratories is limited by the dominance of the Commission and its clear intention to push EU law as the benchmark of harmonisation'.

[73] Commission Staff Working Paper accompanying the Communication from the Commission to the European Parliament and the Council: Report on the functioning of Regulation 1/2003 [2009] COM 206 final, para 249.

and cooperation and indicating that the enforcement of Articles 101 and 102 TFEU relies on a combination of these two opposing approaches.[74]

Regulatory innovation could also take place in the national courts and with regard to legal safeguards for undertakings and individuals. As a result of decentralisation, EU law will be applied more frequently in the national courts. These courts will need to review the legality of domestic decisions adopted on the basis of Articles 101 and 102 TFEU.[75] In this capacity, national courts will not only apply domestic procedural law, they will also have to apply EU legal safeguards, for example, EU fundamental rights (see chapter four). In the context of these procedures, national courts may refer questions to the Court of Justice for a preliminary ruling. Whether or not with the help of the Court of Justice, the application of these EU legal safeguards in national procedures could create important precedents.[76] In addition, this may elevate the state of the art in competition law enforcement to a higher level.

It follows from the above discussion that the EU framework for competition law enforcement is conducive to regulatory innovation. Also in this respect, decentralisation has clear economic benefits compared to a system of centralised enforcement.

3.8 CONCLUSION

This chapter has provided a theoretical account of the costs and benefits of the current decentralised enforcement system relative to a system of centralised enforcement. On the costs side, the decentralisation of EU competition law has resulted in (or has at least maintained) transaction costs for the undertakings involved, coordination costs for the competition authorities and duplication costs for undertakings, authorities and courts alike. To some extent, these costs derive from the fact that multiple authorities need to be funded and some cases will be prosecuted by two or more authorities. Other costs are due to the fact that sanctioning regimes may differ between Member States. Arguably one of the most costly features of this second category is what has been termed precedent deflation. The precedent value of cases litigated before national courts *on the basis of domestic procedural law* will be more limited than cases litigated before the Court of Justice. This deflation of legal precedents can be seen as a diseconomy of scale which may result in significant duplication costs. The larger the sanctioning

[74] DC Esty and D Geradin, 'Regulatory Co-opetition' in DC Esty and D Geradin (eds), *Regulatory Competition and Economic Integration: Comparative Perspectives* (Oxford University Press, 2001) 40–43.

[75] National courts may also apply Articles 101 and 102 TFEU in the context of private enforcement.

[76] For a more extensive discussion of national precedents on EU law, see HJ van Harten, *Autonomie van de Nationale Rechter in het Europees Recht: Een Verkenning van de Praktijk Aan de Hand van de Nederlandse Europeesrechtelijke Rechtspraak Over de Vestigingsvrijheid en het Vrijedienstenverkeer* (Boom Juridische uitgevers, 2011) 177ff.

autonomy for the Member States, the larger the transaction costs, coordination costs and duplication costs will be.

On the benefits side, decentralisation has reduced the problem of asymmetric information that confronts any competition authority. National authorities can be assumed to have superior knowledge over domestic market circumstances. By involving the Member States in the enforcement of Articles 101 and 102 TFEU, more infringements can be uncovered. However, this benefit justifies only part of the current EU framework. Costs that are associated with the sanctioning autonomy of the Member States cannot be justified by the information advantages of decentralisation. These costs could have been avoided by harmonising the national sanctioning regimes. However, not only would this have created costs of its own (eg, the costs of implementation), it would also have ignored various benefits associated with sanctioning autonomy. First, a decentralised enforcement system that is premised on sanctioning autonomy can accommodate heterogeneous preferences between Member States and may economise the allocation of government resources. Second, sanctioning autonomy fosters regulatory innovation. In this respect, it can be concluded that the larger the sanctioning autonomy for the Member States, the larger the potential benefits in terms of preference matching and regulatory innovation.

It follows from the above that some costs and benefits are more or less given with the decision to involve the Member States in the enforcement of EU competition law. This is the case, for instance, with respect to the costs associated with having multiple authorities and the benefits of having knowledge on domestic market circumstances. But the economic implications of decentralisation are also dependent on the scope of the sanctioning autonomy and the development of the domestic sanctioning regimes. The larger the sanctioning autonomy of the Member States, the better the possibilities for preference matching and regulatory innovation, but also the larger the losses in terms of transaction costs, coordination costs and duplication costs. The economies and diseconomies of the current EU framework are therefore ultimately dependent on the heterogeneity of sanctioning preferences in the Member States (reflected in the disparities in sanctioning regimes) and the level of 'decentralisation-induced' innovation (eg, domestic sanctioning powers with no Commission precedent).[77]

In the light of these considerations, chapter four will revisit the sanctioning autonomy of the Member States. More specifically, it will analyse the extent to which national sanctioning powers for infringements of Articles 101 and 102

[77] The economic implications of the decentralised enforcement system are of course not limited to the costs and benefits associated with sanctioning powers. Other enforcement powers and procedures may be at least as important (eg, investigatory powers). Moreover, the learning effects of decentralisation are not limited to the *enforcement* of Articles 101 and 102 TFEU ('what are the public law consequences of an infringement?'). Just as important, if not more important, are the learning effects with regard to the *application* of Articles 101 and 102 TFEU ('what type of commercial practices fall within the scope of the prohibitions?'). However, it should be noted that as these costs and benefits are not linked to sanctioning powers, they are not linked to the sanctioning autonomy of the Member States either.

TFEU are subject to EU rules and principles other than Regulation 1/2003. Chapter five will then detail the development of a number of national sanctioning regimes within these EU boundaries. By establishing the scope of the sanctioning autonomy and the development of the national sanctioning regimes, conclusions can be drawn as to the economies and diseconomies of the current enforcement system. This will be covered in chapter six.

4

Uncovering EU Sanctioning Principles

4.1 INTRODUCTION

It was concluded in chapter two that Regulation 1/2003 leaves the Member States with a sizeable level of discretion in allocating sanctioning powers to their NCAs. However, Regulation 1/2003 is not the only source of EU law that is able to limit the sanctioning autonomy of the Member States. This should already be clear from the analysis of *Bundeswettbewerbsbehörde v Schenker* (see above, section 2.3). In fact, the EU has a grip on the decentralised enforcement of Articles 101 and 102 TFEU through various strings of influence. Where the Member States act as 'agents' of EU law, enforcing Articles 101 and 102 TFEU, the domestic sanctioning powers are subject to EU rules and principles (hereinafter simply referred to as 'principles')[1] of a more general nature.[2] These principles form a legal framework for the Member States, narrowing down the sanctioning autonomy that has been left by Regulation 1/2003. The applicability of these EU principles in the Member States can be seen as a form of centralisation, in the sense that the terms and conditions for the enforcement of Articles 101 and 102 TFEU are dictated by EU law.

It follows from chapter three that the applicability of EU sanctioning principles can have economic implications. The more the sanctioning autonomy of the Member States is narrowed down, the fewer the possibilities for preference matching and regulatory innovation, but also the smaller the losses in terms of transaction costs, coordination costs and duplication costs. In order to examine the economies and diseconomies of the current division of sanctioning competences between the EU and its Member States, the nature of these sanctioning principles will be studied below. This analysis will also explain many of the legal implications of decentralisation.

[1] The use of the term 'principles' and all derivatory terms are used as a shorthand for every norm of EU law, whether rule or principle. For the purposes of this study, a distinction between rules and principles is less important than the fact that both types of EU legal norms may penetrate the national legal order.

[2] See also JH Jans et al, *Europeanisation of Public Law* (Europa Law Publishing, 2007) 201; WPJ Wils, 'EU Anti-trust Enforcement Powers and Procedural Rights and Guarantees: The Interplay between EU Law, National Law, the Charter of Fundamental Rights of the EU and the European Convention on Human Rights' (2011) 34 *World Competition* 189; A de Moor-van Vugt, *Maten en Gewichten: Het evenredigheidsbeginsel in Europees perspectief* (PhD dissertation, Schoordijk Instituut/Centrum voor wetgevingsvraagstukken, 1995).

In anticipation of the findings in this chapter, it should be mentioned that the EU sanctioning principles derive from four different sources of law, namely:

(1) Articles 101 and 102 TFEU;
(2) the free movement rights;
(3) the fundamental rights; and
(4) the duty of sincere cooperation.[3]

The sanctioning principles deriving from Articles 101 and 102 TFEU are obviously limited in scope, but all other principles govern the enforcement of EU law more generally.[4] After having clarified in section 4.2 how the EU sanctioning principles penetrate the national legal orders, the subsequent four sections provide a detailed analysis of the relevant sources of EU law. This analysis aims to identify and clarify the various sanctioning principles. The concluding section (4.7) discusses the level of centralisation to which these sanctioning principles give rise.

4.2 EU PRINCIPLES IN THE NATIONAL LEGAL ORDER

How do *EU* sanctioning principles penetrate the *national* legal orders? Before identifying and analysing the EU sanctioning principles, this question should be addressed. By enforcing Articles 101 and 102 TFEU, the NCAs enter the realm of EU law and essentially become agents of the EU. This is relevant, as the 'centralisation effect' of EU principles is limited to the actions of the Member States within the scope of EU law.[5] Accordingly, the EU sanctioning principles have no direct implications for the enforcement of *national* competition law.[6] Moreover, as will become clear below, the EU sanctioning principles mainly derive from Treaty provisions and general principles of EU law. The working of these primary sources of EU law extends to the decentralised enforcement of Articles 101 and 102 TFEU.

[3] While this study focuses on 'sanctions', the above legal sources influence the entire enforcement process in the Member States, from the earliest inspection to the ultimate stage of judicial review. See MJ Frese, 'De Doorwerking van Europese Rechtsbeginselen bij de Decentrale Handhaving van het EU Mededingingsrecht' (2012) 61 *Ars Aequi* 108.

[4] Jans et al (n 2) 206–20.

[5] Case C-249/96 *Grant v South-West Trains Ltd* [1998] ECR I-621. See further Case C-617/10 *Akerberg* [2013] OJ C114/7, where the scope of application of EU law seems to have been widened: 'where a court of a Member State is called upon to review whether fundamental rights are complied with by a national provision or measure which, in a situation where action of the Member States is not entirely determined by European Union law, implements the latter for the purposes of Article 51(1) of the Charter, national authorities and courts remain free to apply national standards of protection of fundamental rights, provided that the level of protection provided for by the Charter, as interpreted by the Court, and the primacy, unity and effectiveness of European Union law are not thereby compromised' ([29]).

[6] Most if not all Member States operate a system of domestic competition law for anti-competitive practices without an 'effect on trade'. This study is not concerned with the enforcement of these national laws.

Finally, any *conflict* between EU principles and national law is settled in favour of the former.[7] This follows from the EU principle of priority.[8]

The principle of priority guarantees the penetration of EU law in the national legal orders. On the basis of this principle, EU law has priority over national law. In *Costa v ENEL*, the Court of Justice found that by creating the EU (or rather its predecessor, the European Economic Community), the Member States have limited their sovereign rights and have created a body of law which binds both their nationals and themselves.[9] At the same time, the Court held that the terms and spirit of the EU make it impossible for the Member States to accord priority to national law. Meanwhile, it has become clear that any principle of EU law has and retains priority over any rule or principle of national law.[10] Pursuant to the principle of priority, NCAs and national courts therefore have to disregard any rule or principle of national law that conflicts with any principle of EU law. While there can be disagreement about the legal basis of the principle of priority,[11] Member States agree on the existence of this principle.[12]

Within the context of EU competition law, the priority of EU law over national law manifests itself in various ways. First, *EU competition law has priority over national law*. Accordingly, the prohibitions of Articles 101 and 102 TFEU cannot be overruled by national law.[13] These prohibitions apply to all undertakings active in the EU[14] and must be fully and uniformly applied in all Member States.[15] Moreover, Member States may not adopt or keep in force any measure that would deprive Articles 101 and 102 TFEU of their useful effect.[16] Further, the application of national competition law parallel to EU competition law is allowed only insofar as the uniform application of the latter and the full effect of the implementing measures are not prejudiced.[17] Finally, national institutions should have the power to set aside national law that might prevent Articles 101 and 102 TFEU

[7] Not every disparity between EU and national law necessarily results in conflict. For instance, where an EU principle sets a minimum legal safeguard and a principle of national law provides further protection, there might be a disparity, but no conflict.

[8] Case 6/64 *Costa v ENEL* [1964] ECR 585. See also Declaration 17 concerning primacy annexed to the Final Act of the Intergovernmental Conference which adopted the Treaty of Lisbon [2010] OJ C83/335. Other words used to denote the priority or primacy of EU law over national law are 'precedence' or 'supremacy'. This book uses the term 'priority', as it is felt that priority has a less hierarchical connotation than some of the other terms and is therefore more responsive to sentiments and constitutional traditions in some of the Member States.

[9] *Costa v ENEL* (n 8).

[10] Case 11/70 *Internationale Handelsgesellschaft* [1970] ECR 1125; Case C-224/97 *Ciola* [1999] ECR I-2517.

[11] For a more extensive discussion of this issue, see P Craig and G de Búrca, *EU Law: Text, Cases, and Materials* 5th edn (Oxford University Press, 2011) 267–96.

[12] *cf* Declaration 17 (n 8).

[13] *Costa v ENEL* (n 8).

[14] Case 14/68 *Wilhelm* [1969] ECR 1.

[15] Case 106/77 *Simmenthal* [1978] ECR 629.

[16] Case 13/77 *INNO v ATAB* [1977] ECR 2115.

[17] *Wilhelm* (n 14); Joined Cases 253/78 and 1–3/79 *Giry and Guerlain* [1980] ECR 2327.

from having full effect.[18] Second, *the priority of EU law influences the terms and conditions of the decentralised enforcement of EU competition law*. Where the Member States enforce Articles 101 and 102 TFEU, the domestic enforcement powers are governed by EU principles. These principles function as a legal framework and govern the enforcement actions of the Member States.

Before starting with the analysis of the EU sanctioning principles, one further point needs to be clarified, ie, the 'identification process'. As was mentioned earlier, most of the EU sanctioning principles are not readily cognisable. The development of these principles is to a considerable extent the achievement of the Court of Justice. In a process that can be referred to as 'judicial harmonisation'[19] or, as in this study, 'centralisation', the Court has formulated specific sanctioning principles on the basis of more general sources of EU law. In this respect, it should be noted that rulings of the Court of Justice extend beyond the narrow confines of the case at hand.[20] While the opportunity for the Court to elaborate on the requirements for the decentralised enforcement of EU competition law has been limited so far, there exists a vast body of case law on the legality of the Commission's enforcement decisions and on the administration of EU law more generally. For two reasons, many of these cases and the principles developed therein are equally valid for the decentralised enforcement of EU competition law. First, to the extent that these principles derive from primary sources of EU law, there can be no strict distinction with regard to the application of these principles between the centralised and decentralised enforcement of Articles 101 and 102 TFEU or between the enforcement of EU competition law and other EU law. Second, the procedures of the Commission in the context of Articles 101 and 102 TFEU are a benchmark for the procedures of the NCAs.

This benchmarking entails that the adequacy of national procedures for the enforcement of EU law may be evaluated against the EU's internal legal system.[21] This conclusion follows from the case *Upjohn* case,[22] where the question arose as to whether the limited scope of review for UK courts to revoke marketing authorisations for medical products was in conformity with EU law. The Court of Justice considered first that where an EU authority has to make complex assessments, it enjoys a wide margin of discretion, the exercise of which is subject to limited judicial review.[23] It continued:

[18] *Simmenthal* (n 15); Case 103/88 *Fratelli Costanzo* [1989] ECR 1839; Case C-198/01 *Consorzio Industrie Fiammiferi* [2003] ECR I-8055.

[19] L Parret, *Side Effects of the Modernisation of EU Competition Law* (Wolf Legal Publishers, 2011) 166.

[20] See, in this respect, the discussion on the binding effect of rulings of the Court of Justice for future legal disputes in J Schwarze in Schwarze (Hrsg), *EU-Kommentar* (3. Auflage Nomos 2012) AEUV Artikel 267 Rdnr 71 and Ch Gaitanides in Von der Groeben/Schwarze, *Kommentar zum Vertrag über die Europäische Union und zur Gründung der Europäischen Gemeinschaft* (6. Auflage Nomos 2004) Artikel 234 EG Rdnr 92. Both authors conclude that preliminary rulings on the interpretation of EU law have, in any case, de facto binding effect for future legal disputes ('*tatsächlich rechtsbildende Kraft*').

[21] P Oliver, 'Le Règlement 1/2003 et les Principes D'Efficacité et D'Équivalence' (2005) 41 *Cahiers de droit européen* 351, 374–75; T Tridimas, *The General Principles of EU Law* 2nd edn (Oxford University Press, 2006) 416.

[22] Case C-120/97 *Upjohn* [1999] ECR I-223.

[23] ibid [34].

> Consequently, Community law does not require the Member States to establish a procedure for judicial review . . . which involves a more extensive review than that carried out by the Court in similar cases.[24]

Similar reasoning stood on the basis of *i-21 Germany*, where the Court concluded that EU law does not, in principle, require national authorities to reopen decisions which have become final upon the expiry of reasonable time limits for legal remedies or by exhaustion of those remedies.[25] The Court based this conclusion on its earlier *AssiDomän Kraft Products* judgment,[26] where the Commission was not required to reopen an earlier decision either. Both *Upjohn* and *i-21 Germany* strongly suggest that enforcement principles applicable to the procedures of the Commission are a benchmark for the procedures of the national authorities.[27] This applies a fortiori to the enforcement of Articles 101 and 102 TFEU, where the close cooperation between the various authorities has resulted in highly integrated legal orders. The recent ruling in *Bundeswettbewerbsbehörde v Schenker* suggests that benchmarking may even impose positive obligations onto the Member States (see above, section 2.3).[28] In sum, the terms and conditions under which the Commission executes its enforcement mandate with regard to Articles 101 and 102 TFEU are highly relevant for the Member States.[29]

However, a word of caution should be noted here. The wholesale transposition of the often highly specific rules and principles formulated in the context of Commission procedures to the level of the NCAs, whether by virtue of priority or through benchmarking, is not without risks. These rules and principles will be a reflection of the overall enforcement regime of the Commission. Their transposition to the national legal orders means that these rules and principles are abstracted

[24] ibid [35].

[25] Joined Cases C-392/04 and C-422/04 *i-21 Germany and Arcor* [2006] ECR I-8559 [51].

[26] Case C-310/97 P *AssiDomän Kraft Products* [1999] ECR I-5363.

[27] Gerbrandy seems to hold a different opinion. She argues that Court rulings on direct actions against Commission decisions have no precedent value *by virtue of EU law*. See A Gerbrandy, *Convergentie in het Mededingingsrecht: De Invloed van het EG-Recht op Materiële Toepassing, Toegang, Bewijs en Toetsing bij de Nederlandse Mededingingsbestuursrechter, Bezien in het Licht van Effectieve Rechtsbescherming* (Boom Juridische uitgevers, 2009) 450.

[28] In *Bundeswettbewerbsbehörde v Schenker*, the referring Austrian court wished to obtain clarification with respect to intention-related or negligence-related conditions regarding the imposition of a fine on a person who has infringed Articles 101 and 102 TFEU. The Court first concluded that it is not apparent from the wording of Article 5 of the regulation that conditions relating to intention or negligence have to be met in order for the measures provided for by the regulation to be adopted. It then held: 'However, if, in the general interest of uniform application of Articles 101 TFEU and 102 TFEU in the European Union, the Member States establish conditions relating to intention or negligence in the context of application of Article 5 of Regulation No 1/2003, those conditions should be at least as stringent as the condition laid down in Article 23 of Regulation No 1/2003 [governing the penalty powers of the Commission] so as not to jeopardise the effectiveness of European Union law.' Case C-681/11 *Bundeswettbewerbsbehörde v Schenker* [2012] OJ C89/11 [36].

[29] While the terms and conditions under which the Commission executes its enforcement mandate with regard to Articles 101 and 102 TFEU are 'highly relevant' for the Member States, they do not necessarily ban domestic alternatives. For example, in Case T-38/02 *Groupe Danone* [2005] ECR II-4407 [362]–[363], the General Court accepted that an EU definition of recidivism ('a finding of infringement has been made in the past') could exist alongside domestic definitions of recidivism ('a fine has been imposed in the past').

away from their original context and purpose and, subsequently, are then applied to a situation for which they have not been drawn up. This could disturb national checks and balances with regard to enforcement powers. For example, Commission standards for rights of defence could be inappropriate for national enforcement regimes with more severe sanctions. As rights of defence are generally a reflection of the severity of the available sanctions, both these elements of a sanctioning regime should preferably be applied in tandem. This transposition issue essentially applies to any rule or principle applicable to Commission procedures. While this does not detract from the above findings on the identification of EU sanctioning principles, it does warrant flexibility in translating Commission standards for national purposes.

With the 'centralisation effect' and the 'identification process' having been clarified, the following sections will provide a detailed analysis of each of the relevant sources of EU law. This analysis is meant to uncover the EU sanctioning principles and to establish the prevailing sanctioning autonomy of the Member States. The approach for each of these principles is the same: first, their content and meaning is clarified, then, the centralisation effect of these principles is established.

4.3 SANCTIONING PRINCIPLES IN ARTICLES 101 AND 102 TFEU

4.3.1 Introduction

Articles 101 and 102 TFEU contain the competition law prohibitions. By virtue of these provisions, anti-competitive behaviour in the European market is prohibited. However, more than just proscribing particular conduct, Articles 101 and 102 TFEU also determine *who* should ultimately bear responsibility for this conduct. The Court of Justice has read various 'liability principles' into Articles 101 and 102 TFEU. These principles, in turn, have an impact on the sanctioning powers of the competition authorities.

The liability principles have been formulated mainly in the context of Commission procedures, but they extend to the enforcement actions of the Member States. As will be established below, all these principles are based directly on the text of Articles 101 and 102 TFEU, making a distinction between centralised and decentralised enforcement at best artificial and at worst in conflict with fundamental conceptions of EU law.[30] The conditions for the application of Articles 101 and 102 TFEU are EU law concepts. The interpretation of these concepts is the sole task of the Court of

[30] Another question is which principles are actually based directly on the text of Articles 101 and 102 TFEU. Case C-8/08 *T-Mobile Netherlands* [2009] ECR I-4529 shows that the Court of Justice takes an 'all-inclusive approach' by even including in this category legal presumptions for proving infringements of Article 101 TFEU. This point has been criticised in MJ Frese, 'Tightening the Grip on the Application of Article 81 EC Treaty: The European Court of Justice Guards its Province' (2011) 37 *Legal Issues of Economic Integration* 87.

Justice.[31] Once the Court has rendered an interpretation of one of these conditions, this interpretation applies throughout the EU. In this respect, the Court has held in *Eco Swiss* that there can be no differences of interpretation between the various institutions that apply these provisions,[32] be that the Commission, an NCA or a national court. More recently, this requirement has been reiterated in *T-Mobile Netherlands*.[33]

In *T-Mobile Netherlands*, the Court of Justice required the referring court to use a legal presumption in the application of Article 101 TFEU. The legal presumption itself was formulated several years earlier in the context of Commission procedures.[34] The Court extended the scope of application of this presumption of causality between concertation and practice – necessary for establishing a 'concerted practice' in the sense of Article 101 TFEU – to the decentralised enforcement of Article 101 TFEU. To this effect, it first concluded that this presumption is a matter of Treaty interpretation and that the nature of Article 101 TFEU demands that this interpretation is also binding on the Member States.[35] It then held:

> In applying Article 81 EC [now Article 101 TFEU], any interpretation that is provided by the Court is therefore binding on all the national courts and tribunals of the Member States.[36]

This conclusion, which logically extends to NCAs,[37] requires Member States to apply a presumption of causality between contact and market conduct in the application of Article 101 TFEU. More generally, *T-Mobile Netherlands* suggests that *any* rule or principle which the Court infers from Articles 101 and 102 TFEU is binding for the Member States. This point has been confirmed in later case law.[38] Against this background, it should be concluded that the principles for the attribution of liability in relation to infringements of Articles 101 and 102 TFEU are binding as well.[39] Member States cannot disregard the liability principles without endangering the uniform application of Articles 101 and 102 TFEU. As a result, the sanctioning autonomy of the Member States is narrowed down. The following three sections will study the various liability principles.

[31] Articles 19 Consolidated Version of the Treaty on European Union [2008] OJ C115/13 (TEU), 263 TFEU and 267 TFEU.

[32] Case C-126/97 *Eco Swiss* [1999] ECR I-3055 [40].

[33] *T-Mobile Netherlands* (n 30) [49]–[50].

[34] Case C-49/92 P *Anic* [1999] ECR I-4125.

[35] *T-Mobile Netherlands* (n 30) [49].

[36] ibid [50].

[37] *cf Fratelli Costanzo* (n 18).

[38] Joined Cases T-141, T-142, T-145 and T-146/07 *Otis* [2011] ECR II-4977 [77]: 'By virtue of that principle [the principle that penalties must be specific to the offender], which applies *in any administrative procedure that may lead to the imposition of penalties under EU competition law*, an undertaking may be penalised only for acts imputed to it individually' (emphasis added).

[39] Frese (n 30).

4.3.2 Liability and the Concept of 'Undertaking'

Articles 101 and 102 TFEU prohibit 'undertakings' from engaging in anti-competitive conduct. The Court of Justice has interpreted these prohibitions as applying solely to conduct engaged in by undertakings on their own initiative.[40] In addition, the notion of undertaking has prompted the Court to adopt detailed principles on the attribution of liability. These principles have a direct influence on the conditions under which fines can be imposed. As yet, the Court has only had the chance to apply these principles in the context of Commission procedures. However, as the notion of undertaking needs to be applied uniformly throughout the EU, the liability principles that are part of this notion are capable of limiting the sanctioning autonomy of the Member States.

The Principle of Personal Responsibility

An undertaking in the sense of Articles 101 and 102 TFEU is an entity engaged in an economic activity, irrespective of its legal status and the way in which it is financed.[41] This entity may or may not have legal personality itself[42] and it may consist of several legal and/or natural persons.[43] The mere fact that the share capital of two separate commercial companies is held by the same person or the same family is insufficient in itself to establish that those two companies form an economic unit.[44] Conversely, the possibility that within a group of companies various majorities are formed within each of the respective shareholders' meetings does not in itself exclude the possibility of a single economic unit.[45] As long as there is a unitary organisation of personnel and tangible and intangible elements which pursues a specific economic aim on a long-term basis and can contribute to a restriction of competition or an abuse of dominance, it qualifies as an undertaking for the purposes of Articles 101 and 102 TFEU.[46]

Lacking the capacity to carry rights and obligations, these economic entities cannot bear responsibility for their own actions. Liability for infringements of Articles 101 and 102 TFEU should therefore be allocated to the legal or natural person that is ultimately in charge. The Court of Justice has allocated liability on

[40] Anti-competitive behaviour attributable wholly to a Member State falls outside the scope of Articles 101 and 102 TFEU. See Case T-271/03 *Deutsche Telekom* [2008] ECR II-477 [85]; Case C-280/08 P *Deutsche Telekom* [2010] ECR I-9555 [80] et seq.

[41] Case C-41/90 *Höfner and Elser* [1991] ECR I-1979 [21]; Case C-280/06 *Ente tabacchi italiani* [2007] ECR I-10893 [38]; Case T-386/06 *Pegler* [2011] ECR II-1267 [42] et seq.

[42] Joined Cases C-189, C-202, C-205–08 and C-213/02 P *Dansk Rørindustri* [2005] ECR I-5425 [113].

[43] Case 170/83 *Hydrotherm* [1984] ECR 2999 [11]; Case C-97/08 P *Akzo Nobel* [2009] ECR I-8237 [55]; Case C-90/09 P *General Química* [2011] ECR I-1 [35]; Case T-321/05 *AstraZeneca* [2010] ECR II-2805 [818]–[820].

[44] Case C-196/99 P *Aristrain* [2003] ECR I-11005 [99].

[45] Case C-407/08 P *Knauf Gips* [2010] ECR I-6375 [73].

[46] Case T-9/99 *HFB* [2002] ECR II-1487 [54].

the basis of the principle of personal responsibility.[47] In *Bolloré II*, the General Court has concluded that this principle of personal responsibility is a part of EU competition law.[48] Pursuant to this principle, it falls to the legal or natural person actually managing the undertaking when the infringement was committed to answer for that infringement.[49] Where the infringement is committed by an economic entity consisting of several natural and/or legal persons but without a person bearing overall responsibility, the various natural and/or legal persons may be held liable jointly and severally.[50] In *Siemens AG Österreich*, the General Court even found that the issue of joint and several liability is a legal effect which follows as a matter of law from Article 101 TFEU.[51] It then continued:

> [W]here several persons may be held personally liable for the participation in an infringement of one and the same undertaking . . . they must be regarded as jointly and severally liable for that infringement.[52]

In the view of the General Court, the issue of joint and several liability cannot be freely decided upon by the competition authority. It should be noted that this limitation of the authority's discretion is in marked contrast with various other doctrines under the principle of personal responsibility (see below). This issue is currently pending before the Court of Justice.[53]

The Court of Justice has thus far granted the Commission considerable flexibility in applying the principle of personal responsibility. This flexibility follows most clearly from the doctrines of 'parent liability' and 'economic continuity'. The Commission may stretch the principle of personal responsibility if the conditions for parent liability or economic continuity apply. This allows the Commission to impose higher fines.

Parent Liability

In most cases, infringements of Articles 101 and 102 TFEU are committed by incorporated entities and liability can be attributed to a legal person, ie a company. This company may own the undertaking directly or indirectly through a shareholding.[54] In the latter case, the shareholding may even be through an interposed company.[55] Companies may be liable for the anti-competitive behaviour of an undertaking they indirectly own. This 'parent liability' does not require full ownership. In fact, even a 50 per cent shareholding may be sufficient to establish

[47] *cf Anic* (n 34) [145]; *Ente tabacchi italiani* (n 41) 39; Case C-352/09 P *ThyssenKrupp Nirosta* [2011] ECR I-2359 [143].

[48] Case T-372/10 *Bolloré II* [2012] OJ C235/13 [52].

[49] Case C-279/98 P *Cascades* [2000] ECR I-9693 [78]; *HFB* (n 46) [103]; Joined Cases C-201/09 P and C-216/09 P *ArchelorMittal* [2011] ECR I-2239 [101].

[50] *HFB* (n 46) 66.

[51] Joined Cases T-122–24/07 *Siemens AG Österreich* [2011] ECR II-793 [149] and [155].

[52] ibid [150].

[53] Case C-231/11 P *Commission v Siemens AG Österreich* [2011] OJ C204/17.

[54] *cf* Case 48/69 *ICI* [1972] ECR 619.

[55] *General Química* (n 43) [84]–[89].

parent liability.[56] Parent liability is based directly on the notion of undertaking. To this effect, the Court of Justice concluded in *Akzo Nobel*:

> 58. [T]hat the conduct of a subsidiary may be imputed to the parent company in particular where, although having a separate legal personality, that subsidiary does not decide independently upon its own conduct on the market, but carries out, in all material respects, the instructions given to it by the parent company . . .
>
> 59. That is the case because, in such a situation, the parent company and its subsidiary form a single economic unit and therefore form a single undertaking . . . Thus, the fact that a parent company and its subsidiary constitute a single undertaking within the meaning of Article 81 EC [now Article 101 TFEU] enables the Commission to address a decision imposing fines to the parent company, without having to establish the personal involvement of the latter in the infringement.[57]

The legal basis and scope of parent liability thus follow directly from the text of Articles 101 and 102 TFEU. The practical relevance of this 'parent liability' is that the parent company may have deeper pockets than its subsidiaries and is therefore able to pay a higher fine. The decision to go after the parent company instead of the subsidiary and to impose a higher fine is a discretionary power of the authority.[58] Thus, the doctrine of parent liability does not exonerate subsidiaries. Similarly, the authority may impute full liability to the parent company even if the subsidiary has been sold to a third party in the period between infringement and penalisation.[59] It follows from *Bolloré II* that the decision to attribute liability to the parent or subsidiary can be based on considerations of effectiveness and dissuasiveness.[60]

In principle, the anti-competitive behaviour of an undertaking may be attributed to the parent company, ie, the indirect owner, only where the latter *exercises* decisive influence over this behaviour.[61] The mere possibility of exercising decisive influence is not enough; influence should actually have been exercised.[62] In this respect, the doctrine of parent liability can be seen as a hallmark of the principle of personal reponsibility. However, this influence may be 'inferred' from the economic and legal links between the parent company and its subsidiaries.[63] Moreover, it follows from a consistent line of cases that an (almost)[64] 100 per cent

[56] Case T-341/01 *Avebe* [2006] ECR II-3085; Case T-76/08 *EI du Pont de Nemours and Company* [2012] OJ C80/15.

[57] *Akzo Nobel* (n 43).

[58] Joined Cases T-236, 239, 244, 246, 251 and 252/01 *Tokai Carbon (Graphite Electrodes)* [2004] ECR II-1181 [279] and [282]; Joined Cases T-259–64 and T-271/02 *Raiffeisen Zentralbank Österreich (Lombard Club)* [2006] ECR II-5169 [330] et seq; Case T-24/05 *Alliance One International* [2010] ECR II-5329 [155]–[157]; *Pegler* (n 41) [103]–[105]; *General Química* (n 43) [85]–[86]; Case C-499/11 P *Dow Chemical* [2011] OJ C355/11 [49].

[59] *cf* Case C-511/11 P *Versalis* [2011] OJ C340/13 [52].

[60] *Bolloré II* (n 48) [91]–[92].

[61] *ArchelorMittal* (n 49) [96].

[62] *Alliance One International* (n 58) [128]; *EI du Pont de Nemours and Company* (n 56) [60].

[63] *EI du Pont de Nemours and Company* (n 56) [62].

[64] Case C-508/11 P *Eni* [2011] OJ C340/12 [47].

shareholding, whether direct or through an interposed company,[65] constitutes a 'rebuttable' presumption that the parent company has indeed exercised decisive influence.[66] In any case, there is no need for the parent to be implicated or even to have been aware of the infringement in order to be held liable.[67] In fact, the condition of influencing the subsidiary's conduct does not even require the parent's influence to relate to the activities which are directly linked to the infringement.[68] It follows from *Eni* that to rebut the presumption, it has to be shown that the subsidiary can act with complete autonomy not only at the operational level but also at the financial level.[69] Corporate reality is such that this will rarely be the case.[70] In this respect, the doctrine of parent liability can be seen as a relaxation of the principle of personal responsibility.

Economic Continuity

The doctrine of economic continuity constitutes a further relaxation of the principle of personal responsibility. In accordance with the economic continuity doctrine, liability may be attributed to a legal person other than the one that managed the undertaking at the time that the infringement was committed. This may take place after a change in the legal form or name of the undertaking.[71] Such changes do not create a new undertaking free of liability for the anti-competitive behaviour of its predecessor, when, from an economic point of view, the two are identical.[72]

This economic continuity doctrine may also apply to transfers of undertakings. This is the case when the effectiveness of EU competition law so requires.[73] The effectiveness of EU competition law calls for the reliance on economic continuity either when the legal person responsible for running the undertaking has ceased to exist in law after the infringement has been committed,[74] the transferring legal person remains nothing but an empty shell,[75] there exist clear structural links between

[65] ibid [63]; *Alliance One International* (n 58) [132].

[66] *ArchelorMittal* (n 49) [97]–[98].

[67] Case T-376/06 *Legris Industries* [2011] OJ C145/19 [54] and [58]; *General Química* (n 43) [102]–[103].

[68] *Alliance One International* (n 58) [170].

[69] *Eni* (n 64) [68].

[70] The Court of Justice has suggested that if it can be demonstrated that contacts between subsidiary and parent were limited to the former's financial results in the context of the group's consolidated accounts, this would rebut the presumption: *General Química* (n 43) [108]. On the other hand, the exchange of sales figures between companies within a group is indicative for the existence of a single economic unit; *cf Knauf Gips* (n 45) [78].

[71] Similarly, acquiring the business name of an entity that engaged in anti-competitive practices is not sufficient to constitute liability; *cf Pegler* (n 41).

[72] Joined Cases 29/83 and 30/83 *CRAM and Rheinzink* [1984] ECR 1679 [9].

[73] Case T-134/94 *NMH Stahlwerke* [1999] ECR II-239 [46]; *HFB* (n 46) [106]; *Raiffeisen Zentralbank Österreich (Lombard Club)* (n 58) 325; Joined Cases T-117/07 and T-121/07 *Areva and Alstom* [2011] ECR II-633 [66].

[74] *Anic* (n 34) [145].

[75] *NMH Stahlwerke* (n 73) [48]; Joined Cases C-204, C-205, C-211, C-213, C-217 and C-219/00 P *Aalborg Portland* [2004] ECR I-123 [359].

the legal persons (eg, intra-group transactions)[76] or the acquiring undertaking has explicitly assumed liability.[77] In all other circumstances, liability remains with the transferor.

The rationale underlying the economic continuity doctrine is twofold. First, a penalty imposed on an undertaking that continues to exist in law but has ceased economic activity is not likely to have a deterrent effect.[78] Second, if no possibility were foreseen to impose a penalty on an entity other than the one which committed the infringement, undertakings could escape penalties simply by changing their identity through restructurings, sales or other legal or organisational changes.[79]

Centralisation Effects

The following conclusions can be drawn in relation to the sanctioning autonomy of the Member States. While ultimately a matter for future litigation, it is plausible that *Member States* should impute liability in accordance with the EU principle of personal responsibility and – for this purpose – should recognise the doctrines of parent liability and economic continuity. After all, the principle and its progeny follow directly from Articles 101 and 102 TFEU. However, just like the Commission, the *NCAs* are also in principle allowed to refrain from seeking parent liability or from applying the doctrine of economic continuity in individual cases. This means that the EU doctrines of parent liability and economic continuity only bind the *national courts* before which appeals can be brought against administrative decisions. If an NCA decides to apply the EU doctrines and does so correctly, the national court cannot invalidate this approach on the basis of national law.

4.3.3 Liability and the Concept of 'Agreement'

The 'agreement' or 'concerted practice' is the means through which undertakings should restrict competition in order to fall within the scope of Article 101 TFEU.[80] These concepts translate the objective of EU competition law to have economic operators determine their commercial policy independently.[81] In accordance with this objective, the Court of Justice has interpreted these concepts widely so as to cover any form of cooperation and coordination.[82] Patterns of conduct by several undertakings may be a manifestation of a single and complex infringement or a

[76] *Aalborg Portland* (n 75) [359]; Case T-43/02 *Jungbunzlauer* [2006] ECR II-3435 [131]–[133]; *Pegler* (n 41) [55].

[77] *ThyssenKrupp Nirosta* (n 47) [143]–[153].

[78] *Ente tabacchi italiani* (n 41) [40].

[79] ibid [41].

[80] Associations of undertakings can fall within the scope of Article 101 TFEU through the adoption of anti-competitive decisions.

[81] *Anic* (n 34) [116].

[82] *cf* Case 48/69 *ICI* [1972] ECR 619 [64]; *Anic* (n 34) [112]; Case T-99/04 *AC-Treuhand* [2008] ECR II-1501 [118].

single and continuous infringement (SCI).[83] Even if one or several elements of such a pattern qualify as infringements in their own right, these elements may still qualify jointly as a single infringement. Better yet, even if none of the different elements, considered separately, constitutes an agreement or concerted practice prohibited by Article 101(1) TFEU, these elements, considered together, may qualify as such.[84] The complementarity of elements seems to have become the decisive criterion.[85]

The SCI concept has various implications for the liability of undertakings. The characterisation of 'various instances of conduct' as constituting one and the same infringement may directly affect the penalty that can be imposed. The existence of an SCI prevents the competition authorities from prosecuting 'various instances of conduct' separately[86] and also prevents the imposition of several distinct fines.[87] At the same time, this characterisation effectively extends the statute of limitation of the SCI's earliest manifestations. The limitation period for the 'single infringement' starts running with the last instance of conduct.[88]

The SCI concept also affects the penalty more indirectly. Participation in an SCI makes the undertaking responsible for the entire, but single, infringement committed during its participation. An undertaking that takes part in an SCI through conduct of its own which itself qualifies as an agreement or concerted practice contrary to Article 101 TFEU and which was intended to help bring about the infringement as a whole is also responsible, for the duration of its participation in the infringement, for conduct put into effect by other undertakings in the context of the same infringement. This is the case if the undertaking was aware of the offending conduct of the other participants or could reasonably have foreseen it and was prepared to take the risk.[89] Even passive forms of participation (eg, tacit approval) are capable of rendering an undertaking liable in the context of a single infringement, as the effect of this complicity is thought to encourage the continuation of the infringement and to compromise its discovery.[90] However, the fact that an undertaking has not taken part in all aspects of an anti-competitive scheme or that it played only a minor role in the aspects in which it did participate must be taken into consideration when the gravity of the infringement is assessed and if and when it comes to determining the fine.[91]

[83] *Anic* (n 34) [114]. The SCI concept also applies to decisions of associations of undertakings (Joined Cases T-101/05 and T-110/05 *BASF and UCB* [2007] ECR II-4949 [159]) and even to infringements of Article 102 TFEU (*AstraZeneca* (n 43) [892]).

[84] *Knauf Gips* (n 45) [48].

[85] Case T-385/06 *Aalberts Industries* [2011] ECR II-1223 [88].

[86] Joined Cases T-71, T-74, T-87 and T-91/03 *Tokai Carbon (Speciality Graphite)* [2005] ECR II-10 [118].

[87] *BASF and UCB* (n 83) [158].

[88] Case C-235/92 P *Montecatini* [1999] ECR I-4539 [196]–[197].

[89] *Anic* (n 34) [83]; *Aalborg Portland* (n 75) [83]; *AC-Treuhand* (n 82) [130]. See also *Aalberts Industries* (n 85), where the General Court annulled the respective Commission Decision for failure to establish the applicant's awareness with the offending conduct of the other participants.

[90] *Aalborg Portland* (n 75) [84]; *Dansk Rørindustri* (n 42) [142]; *AC-Treuhand* (n 82) [130].

[91] *Anic* (n 34) [90].

Centralisation Effects

The following conclusions can be drawn in relation to the sanctioning autonomy of the Member States. As the SCI concept derives from the text of Article 101 TFEU,[92] *Member States* need to recognise this concept in all its manifestations. This is all the more pertinent as the SCI concept not only facilitates the penalisation of cartels but also offers legal safeguards to the undertakings involved.[93] It can further be concluded that while *NCAs* may decide not to include certain patterns of conduct within their SCI finding, they cannot prosecute complementary anti-competitive instances separately under Article 101 TFEU. Also, *national courts* are bound by the SCI concept. If an NCA decides to include certain patterns of conduct within its SCI finding and does do correctly, the national court cannot invalidate this approach on the basis of national law. Conversely, national courts should annul administrative decisions punishing manifestations of an SCI that could have been included in an earlier decision.

4.3.4 Liability and the Concept of 'Restriction of Competition'

An infringement of Article 101 TFEU demands a 'restriction of competition'. In *AC-Treuhand*, the applicant claimed that perpetrating an infringement of Article 101 TFEU implies that an undertaking restricts its own commercial autonomy vis-a-vis its competitors. For the applicant, a consultancy firm, this was not the case; it 'only' administrated the anti-competitive agreements between producers of organic peroxides. The General Court gave this claim short shrift. It considered that the 'contextual notion of restriction of competition' does not rule out the possibility that an undertaking may participate in the implementation of such a restriction even if it does not restrict its own freedom of action on the market on which it is primarily active.[94] More precisely:

> [I]t is only by making all 'undertakings' within the meaning of Article 81(1) EC [now Article 101(1) TFEU] subject to liability that that useful effect can be fully guaranteed, since that makes it possible to penalise and to prevent the creation of new forms of collusion with the assistance of undertakings which are not active on the markets concerned by the restriction of competition, with the aim of circumventing the prohibition laid down in Article 81(1) EC.[95]

It follows that the prohibition of Article 101 TFEU is addressed to all undertakings that contribute to the infringement, irrespective of their role in the infringement.

[92] The SCI concept also applies to infringements of Article 102 TFEU; *cf AstraZeneca* (n 43) [892]. However, since infringements of Article 102 TFEU are typically committed by a single undertaking, the implications of this concept for the undertaking's liability are more straightforward.

[93] Practice shows that undertakings generally dispute a finding of an SCI, which suggests that these findings are normally experienced as an extension of liability.

[94] *AC-Treuhand* (n 82) 127. See also Case T-29/05 *Deltafina* [2010] ECR II-4077 [47]–[49].

[95] ibid.

Article 101 TFEU therefore renders all participating undertakings liable as co-perpetrators. However, the Court has insisted that the limited importance of the undertaking's role in the infringement should influence the severity of the penalty.[96]

Centralisation Effects

While this is ultimately a matter for the Court of Justice to decide, the legal basis of this 'co-perpetrator doctrine' suggests that *Member States* cannot exclude accessory forms of participation from the scope of Article 101 TFEU. The fact that national law indeed provides for a single form of liability for all participants is useful, but strictly speaking entirely irrelevant.[97] This does of course not mean that *NCAs* have to prosecute every co-perpetrator for its involvement in the infringement; they could decide to proceed only against some of the perpetrators.[98] Where an NCA decides to apply the 'co-perpetrator doctrine', it should not forget to account for the degree of participation in the severity of the penalty. The co-perpetrator doctrine narrows down the sanctioning autonomy of the Member States most strongly in the appeal stage of the enforcement procedure. The *national court* cannot invalidate administrative decisions rendered under this EU doctrine on the basis of national law.

4.4 SANCTIONING PRINCIPLES IN THE FREE MOVEMENT RIGHTS

The decentralised enforcement of Articles 101 and 102 TFEU is also subject to EU principles of a more general nature. The prohibitions laid down in Articles 101 and 102 TFEU do not operate in isolation – they form part of the EU's more comprehensive internal market policy[99] and operate alongside other policy areas, notably EU citizenship. Maintaining the internal market and forging EU citizenship are core objectives of the EU.[100] These areas of EU law are closely related and create free movement rights for economic operators and EU citizens. Accordingly, discrimination on the grounds of nationality and unjustified restrictions of the free movement of goods, persons, services and capital are prohibited. On many occasions, all outside the realm of EU competition law, the Court of Justice has found national sanctions contrary to the free movement provisions, either for being discriminatory or excessive. This section establishes that Member States should also take account of the free movement rights in imposing sanctions for

[96] *Deltafina* (n 94) [61]. See also *AC-Treuhand* (n 82) [155].

[97] *cf* R Raum in Langen/Bunte, *Kommentar zum deutschen und europaïschen Kartellrecht* (Band 1: Deutsches Kartellrecht, 11. Auflage, Carl Heymanns Verlag / Luchterhand 2011) § 81 RdNr 71: 'Das Europäische Recht überlasst die Umsetzung einer Sanktionierung den Mittgliedstaaten . . . Mithin gilt der deutsche Einheitstäterbegriff.'

[98] *cf* Case T-24/90 *Automec II* [1992] ECR II-2223.

[99] Protocol (No 27) on the Internal Market and Competition [2010] OJ C83/309.

[100] Article 3 TEU.

infringements of Articles 101 and 102 TFEU and explains what this requirement precisely entails.

Discriminatory sanctions for infringements of EU competition law are prohibited. This already follows from Article 18 TFEU, which provides:

> Within the scope of application of the Treaties, and without prejudice to any special provisions contained therein, any discrimination on grounds of nationality shall be prohibited.

In the enforcement of Articles 101 and 102 TFEU, Member States may not discriminate on the grounds of nationality. Accordingly, Member States may not impose heavier or more severe sanctions for infringements of Articles 101 and 102 TFEU on non-nationals, whether natural or legal persons, than on their own nationals. The same applies to the Commission, which may not impose discriminatory sanctions either.

Article 18 TFEU can be relied upon only to the extent that the right to a non-discriminatory treatment is not already protected by 'any special provisions'.[101] For the NCAs, there could even be a more pertinent legal basis for the prohibition of discrimination in the enforcement of Articles 101 and 102 TFEU. Above and beyond Article 18 TFEU, national sanctioning powers are affected by the EU free movement rights, deriving from EU citizenship and the internal market. Pursuant to Article 20(2)(a) TFEU, EU citizens shall have the right to move and reside freely within the territory of the Member States. Pursuant to Article 26(2) TFEU, the internal market comprises an area without internal frontiers in which the free movement of goods, persons, services and capital is ensured. In particular situations, these free movement liberties could be threatened by competition law sanctions and demand priority over the latter.

The free movement rights and the competition law prohibitions jointly protect the internal market from being recompartmentalised.[102] In this respect, there is no conflict between these two policy areas. However, national sanctions for infringements of EU competition law could limit EU citizens and undertakings from making use of their free movement rights. For example, someone who is locked away in prison for having committed an infringement of Article 101 or 102 TFEU is obviously unable to make use of its free movement rights. Contrary to some of its Advocates General,[103] the Court of Justice has not been willing to exclude national criminal law or other means of enforcement from the scope of the free movement rights.[104] This means that any conflict between the free movement rights and national sanctioning regimes should be reconciled *within* the specific legal framework of the free movement rights.

[101] *cf* Case C-379/92 *Peralta* [1994] ECR I-3453 [18]; Case C-100/01 *Olazabal* [2002] ECR I-10981 [25]; Case C-341/05 *Laval* [2007] ECR I-11767 [54].

[102] Protocol (No 27) on the Internal Market and Competition (n 99). See also *Eco Swiss* (n 32) [36].

[103] Case 175/78 *Saunders* [1979] ECR 1129, Opinion of AG Warner; Case C-299/95 *Kremzow* [1997] ECR I-2629, Opinion of AG La Pergola.

[104] Case 175/78 *Saunders* [1979] ECR 1129; Case C-299/95 *Kremzow* [1997] ECR I-2629.

The effect of the free movement rights on national sanctions can be illustrated by the cases *Sjöberg and Gerdin*[105] and *Calfa*,[106] both of which deal with the free movement of services. Sjöberg and Gerdin were prosecuted under Swedish law for the promotion of gambling organised outside Sweden. In the proceedings before the national court, the question arose as to whether Swedish law was contrary to the free movement of services for subjecting the promotion of gambling organised outside Sweden to more severe treatment than the promotion of gambling organised in Sweden. The Court of Justice effectively concluded that Swedish law was contrary to the free movement of services by holding that:

> [I]f the persons carrying out the promotion of gambling organised in Sweden without a licence incur penalties which are less strict than those imposed on the persons who advertise gambling organised in other Member States, then it must be stated that those arrangements are discriminatory and that the [domestic legal provisions] are contrary to Article 49 EC [now Article 56 TFEU] and, consequently, unenforceable against the persons being prosecuted in the main actions.[107]

In *Calfa*, the Court of Justice had to consider the compatibility with EU law of the Greek expulsion order imposed on the Italian Ms Calfa for using soft drugs during her holiday on Crete. Within this context, the Court concluded:

> Although in principle criminal legislation is a matter for which the Member States are responsible, the Court has consistently held that Community law sets certain limits to their power, and such legislation may not restrict the fundamental freedoms guaranteed by Community law.[108]

The Court found the ruling of expulsion for life to constitute a clear obstacle to the freedom to provide services: Ms Calfa could no longer receive touristic services in Greece.[109] These cases thus provide clear examples of how free movement rights may affect the sanctioning powers of Member States.

The free movement rights prohibit any restrictions, either as a result of (indirect) discrimination on nationality or resulting from other impediments.[110] Such restrictions may be the result of (lacking)[111] administrative or judicial measures for law enforcement.[112] On numerous occasions, the Court of Justice has considered that national sanctions were liable to deter individuals from making use of

[105] Joined Cases C-447/08 and C-448/08 *Sjöberg and Gerdin* [2010] ECR I-6921.
[106] Case C-348/96 *Calfa* [1999] ECR I-11.
[107] *Sjöberg and Gerdin* (n 105) [56].
[108] *Calfa* (n 106) [17].
[109] ibid [18].
[110] For the wide scope of application of the four economic freedoms, reference could be made to Articles 30, 34 and 35 TFEU and Case 8/74 *Dassonville* [1974] ECR 837 (for goods); Articles 45 and 49 TFEU and Case C-415/93 *Bosman* [1995] ECR I-4921 (for persons); Article 56 TFEU and Case C-76/90 *Säger* [1991] ECR I-4221 (for services); Article 63 TFEU and Case C-222/97 *Trummer and Mayer* [1999] ECR I-1661 (for capital).
[111] Case C-265/95 *Commission v French Republic (Spanish Strawberries)* [1997] ECR I-6959.
[112] *cf Calfa* (n 106); Case 299/86 *Drexl* [1988] ECR 1213.

their free movement rights, whether in relation to goods,[113] workers,[114] establishment,[115] services[116] or capital.[117] Often this took place in the context of sanctions for breaches of formalities;[118] sometimes the administrative rules in question were even specifically meant to enhance free movement. In those cases, expulsion orders and detention, but also significant pecuniary sanctions were considered too severe a sanction. However, there have also been various cases in which the Court considered the restrictive effect of national sanctions for breaches of substantive rules: breaching professional codes,[119] travelling without a ticket,[120] drug abuse,[121] illegal waste dumping,[122] theft,[123] murder[124] and *anti-competitive behaviour by an undertaking with market power.*[125]

In *Milk Marque*,[126] the Court of Justice had to assess competition law sanctions from the perspective of the free movement rights. This case dealt with the compatibility of a reparatory sanction imposed within the context of UK competition law with the free movement of goods. The UK authorities prohibited a dairy cooperative with market power from entering into contracts with undertakings (including undertakings established in other Member States) for the processing on its behalf of milk produced by its members. The Court concluded that this measure did *not* have an equivalent effect as quantitative export restrictions, as prohibited by Article 35 TFEU. To this effect, it held:

> 118. [T]hat provision [Article 35 TFEU] concerns national measures which have as their specific object or effect the restriction of patterns of exports and thereby the establishment of a difference in treatment between the domestic trade of a Member State and its export trade, in such a way as to provide a particular advantage for national production or for the domestic market of the State in question . . .
>
> 119. However, that is not the case with regard to measures . . . which come within national competition policy, are designed to limit anti-competitive practices engaged in by just one agricultural cooperative and apply indistinctly to processing contracts entered into with undertakings established in the United Kingdom and those entered into with undertakings established in other Member States.[127]

[113] Case 41/76 *Donckerwolcke* [1976] ECR 1921; Case C-262/99 *Louloudakis* [2001] ECR I-5547.

[114] Case 48/75 *Royer* [1976] ECR 497; Case 118/75 *Watson and Belmann* [1976] ECR 1185; Case 8/77 *Sagulo* [1977] ECR 1495.

[115] Case C-193/94 *Skanavi* [1996] ECR I-929; Case C-81/09 *Idrima Tipou* [2010] ECR I-10161.

[116] *Calfa* (n 106).

[117] Case 203/80 *Casati* [1981] ECR 2595; *Idrima Tipou* (n 115).

[118] *cf* Case C-378/97 *Wijsenbeek* [1999] ECR I-6207; *Skanavi* (n 115); Case C-210/91 *Commission v Greece (Travellers' Personal Effects)* [1992] ECR I-6735; Case 118/75 *Watson and Belmann* [1976] ECR 1185.

[119] *Idrima Tipou* (n 115).

[120] Case 298/84 *Iorio* [1986] ECR 247.

[121] *Calfa* (n 106).

[122] *Peralta* (n 101).

[123] *Saunders* (n 104).

[124] *Kremzow* (n 104).

[125] Case C-137/00 *Milk Marque* [2003] ECR I-7975.

[126] ibid.

[127] ibid.

Significantly, the Court concluded that the measures in *Milk Marque* could not lead to a restriction in patterns of export as they were limited in scope (addressed to a single undertaking) and did not discriminate. These points suggest that national sanctions for competition law infringements are not excluded from the free movement regime altogether. Moreover, with respect to the second point – that the measures did not discriminate – it should be noted that *Milk Marque* concerned potential *export* restrictions. In accordance with established case law on export restrictions, the Court applied a 'discrimination test': only discriminatory export limitations are prohibited under the free movement regime.[128] Yet, in relation to *import* restrictions and restrictions to the free movement of persons, services and capital, a wider 'restriction test' is applicable. Any restriction is prohibited, not just discriminatory restrictions (see above). Under such a test, even non-discriminatory trade-restrictive sanctions could be prohibited. Therefore, *Milk Marque* cannot be read as an exoneration of competition law sanctions from the free movement regime.

Centralisation Effects

For the purposes of the decentralised enforcement of Articles 101 and 102 TFEU, it can be concluded, first, that discriminatory sanctions are prohibited. Further, it can be argued that excessive sanctions for commercial practices that barely have anti-competitive effects and sanctions that directly limit trade flows both risk being found to be contrary to the EU free movement regime. The latter conclusion is subject to one important *caveat*, however. The free movement limitations on national sanctioning regimes, which are quite subtle already, will be even more delicate where the decentralised enforcement of EU competition law is concerned. First, proving that enforcement measures actually hinder cross-border trade will be a challenging task.[129] Second, free movement does not necessarily trump competition. In this respect, it should be noted that both the free movement rights and the competition law prohibitions are primary sources of EU law, forming part of the EU's internal market policy and having a fundamental status within the EU.[130] Indeed, the Court of Justice has referred to Articles 101 and 102 TFEU

[128] Case 15/79 *Groenveld* [1979] ECR 3409. More recently, the Court of Justice seems to apply a wider test. See Case C-205/07 *Gysbrechts* [2008] ECR I-9947 [43]: 'even if a prohibition such as that at issue in the main proceedings is applicable to all traders active in the national territory, its actual effect is none the less greater on goods leaving the market of the exporting Member State than on the marketing of goods in the domestic market of that Member State'.

[129] *cf* Case C-412/97 *Italo Fenocchio* [1999] ECR I-3845, where the Court of Justice held that the possibility that nationals would hesitate to sell goods to purchasers in another Member States as a result of the unavailability of an order for summary payment against a debtor established outside Italy (as opposed to debtors within the jurisdiction of the Italian courts) was too uncertain and indirect.

[130] The fundamental status of EU competition law has been confirmed in *Eco Swiss* (n 32) [36]. The fundamental status of the free movement provisions has been confirmed in Case 186/87 *Cowan* [1989] ECR 195 [19]. With the adoption of the Treaty of Lisbon in 2007, there have been debates on the status of EU competition policy. The EU Treaties no longer explicitly mention EU competition policy as an instrument for the attainment of the EU objectives; *cf* Articles 2 and 3 TEU. The system

as fundamental and essential to the internal market.[131] Greater internal market considerations could thus legitimise sanctions with chilling side-effects on cross-border trade – all the more so as Member States act as 'agents' of EU competition law. It should further be noted that restrictions to the free movement rights can be justified on various public interest grounds. These include restrictions necessary for reasons of 'public policy' and 'public security'.[132] It can be concluded from *Van den Bergh Foods* that the interest of EU competition law is a public interest worthy of protection.[133] Even if national sanctions for infringements of EU competition law were found to restrict inter-state trade, they may therefore still be justifiable provided they are proportionate[134] and in accordance with fundamental rights.[135] In sum, while the free movement rights narrow down the sanctioning autonomy of the Member States, this is unlikely to have a significant influence on the domestic regimes. The type of sanctions that are ultimately prohibited under the free movement rights will generally not be contemplated by the Member States anyway.

4.5 SANCTIONING PRINCIPLES IN THE FUNDAMENTAL RIGHTS

4.5.1 Introduction

The EU is based on the rule of law and therefore upholds certain fundamental rights.[136] These rights qualify as primary sources of EU law and have priority over

of undistorted competition, as a means for the EU's social market economy, has been 'demoted' to a Treaty Protocol, Protocol (No 27) on the Internal Market and Competition (n 99), where it is considered to form an intricate part of the EU's broader internal market policy. This cosmetic operation has changed little to the status of EU competition policy, whose normative provisions remain a primary source of EU law.

[131] *Eco Swiss* (n 32) [36]; Joined Cases T-217/03 and T-245/03 *FNCBV* [2006] ECR II-4987 [97]; Case C-52/09 *TeliaSonera* [2011] ECR I-527 [21].

[132] Articles 36, 45, 52, 62 and 65 TFEU and Article 27 of Directive 2004/38/EC on the rights of citizens of the Union and their family members to move and reside freely within the territory of the Member States [2004] OJ L158/77 (as corrected subsequently).

[133] *cf* Case T-65/98 *Van den Bergh Foods* [2003] ECR II-4653 [170].

[134] Were such a justification to be necessary, the trade restrictive sanction would be subject to a proportionality test. Disproportionate sanctions for a legitimate cause may still be contrary to the free movement rights. It follows from *Louloudakis*, first, that the severity of sanctions cannot simply be raised to excessive levels and, second, that a sanction might be considered to be disproportionate either when multiple sanctions are imposed or the amount of a pecuniary sanction constitutes a multiple of the illegal gains: *Louloudakis* (n 113) [67].

[135] Case C-260/89 *ERT* [1991] ECR I-2925; Case C-368/95 *Familiapress* [1997] ECR I-3689. In the words of Tridimas (n 21) 326: 'The effect of *ERT* and *Familiapress* is that compatibility with human rights is part of the enquiry which the Court performs in order to assess whether a national measure which interferes with the fundamental freedoms is permitted under Community law.'

[136] Preamble of the Charter of Fundamental Rights of the European Union [2007] OJ C303/1.

any other rule of EU law.[137] Accordingly, in *Schmidberger*, the Court of Justice gave priority to fundamental rights over Treaty provisions by holding that:

> [S]ince both the [EU] and its Member States are required to respect fundamental rights, the protection of those rights is a legitimate interest which, in principle, justifies a restriction of the obligations imposed by [EU] law.[138]

This means that the enforcement of Articles 101 and 102 TFEU can only take place within the boundaries of the EU fundamental rights. Regulation 1/2003 even makes specific reference to this obligation by stating in recital 37 of its preamble that:

> This Regulation respects the fundamental rights and observes the principles recognised in particular by the Charter of Fundamental Rights of the European Union. Accordingly, this Regulation should be interpreted and applied with respect to those rights and principles.

It follows from the priority of EU law over national law that the decentralised enforcement of EU competition law should take place in accordance with these fundamental rights.[139] Many of the EU fundamental rights will apply at a Member State level anyway. Most, if not all, EU fundamental rights originally derive from the constitutional traditions of the Member States. However, the EU nature of these rights strengthens their effect in the context of the decentralised enforcement of EU competition law and makes them enforceable against the failing Member State by the Commission and other Member States before the Court of Justice,[140] and by private parties before the national courts.[141] Moreover, EU fundamental rights may protect interests that have not been recognised under national law and may therefore supplement national legal safeguards. It is in this capacity that the EU fundamental rights are most relevant for this study. By protecting interests beyond those in the national legal system, the EU fundamental rights effectively centralise parts of the enforcement process. As was indicated in chapter three, this could have various economic implications for the enforcement system.

Limitation of the Centralisation Effects

The question could be raised as to whether NCAs may (or should!) content themselves with EU fundamental rights in disregard of more generous national rights. The answer to this question is crucial for the sanctioning autonomy of the Member States. If NCAs would have to apply the more sober EU legal safeguards,

[137] *cf* Case 117/83 *Könecke* [1984] ECR 3291; Case 80/86 *Kolpinghuis* [1987] ECR 3969; Case C-112/00 *Schmidberger* [2003] ECR I-5659; Case C-60/02 *Rolex* [2004] ECR I-651; Joined Cases C-387, C-391 and C-403/02 *Berlusconi* [2005] ECR I-3565.

[138] *Schmidberger* (n 137) [74].

[139] *Internationale Handelsgesellschaft* (n 10); Case 5/88 *Wachauf* [1989] ECR 2609.

[140] Articles 258 and 259 TFEU.

[141] Joined Cases C-6/90 and C-9/90 *Francovich and Bonifaci* [1991] ECR I-5357.

undertakings would be deprived of rights granted under national law. If NCAs could apply these national legal safeguards, the protection of fundamental rights in proceedings under Articles 101 and 102 TFEU could differ depending on the authority. It is submitted herewith that this latter point should in principle not be given any weight. The level of fundamental rights protection has significance only in relation to sanctioning powers. Without the uniformity of sanctioning powers, disparities in fundamental rights protection will not have any direct implications for the level playing field within the EU and will therefore not be to anyone's prejudice. In a similar vein, it should be noted that by applying fundamental rights more generously, national jurisdictions do not affect EU rights either. The legal interest affected by the application of generous national safeguards – the effectiveness of EU policy – is more abstract and uncertain. While considerations of effectiveness could incidentally reduce legal safeguards (see below, section 4.5.4), EU law seems ultimately more concerned with the rule of law than with the uniformity and effectiveness of EU competition law.[142] Therefore, EU law does not require NCAs to content themselves with EU fundamental rights in disregard of more generous national rights.[143] This is confirmed by Article 53 of the EU Charter, which provides that:

> Nothing in this Charter shall be interpreted as restricting or adversely affecting human rights and fundamental freedoms as recognised . . . by the Member States' constitutions.

Therefore, EU fundamental rights only provide a floor below which neither the Commission nor the NCAs may operate.

Sources of Fundamental Rights

EU fundamental rights derive from various sources of law. The most direct legal source for fundamental rights in the EU legal order is the EU Charter of Fundamental Rights (hereinafter 'the EU Charter').[144] Since the Treaty of Lisbon entered into force in 2009, the EU Charter has been given the status of a primary source of EU law.[145] In accordance with its preamble, the EU Charter 'reaffirms' in particular the rights as they result from the constitutional traditions of the Member

[142] Case C-17/10 *Toshiba Corporation* [2012] OJ C98/3-4, Opinion of AG Kokott [54]: 'However desirable a uniform and efficient interpretation and application of competition law within the European Union may be, it must not come at the price of infringing principles based on the rule of law.' See also Gerbrandy (n 27) 84.

[143] *cf* Tridimas (n 21) 321, who refers to Weiler and concludes that: (i) implementing legislation should be struck down where it violates the EU standard for the protection of fundamental rights even if it does not violate the said standard set by national law; and (ii) if the implementing measure clears the human rights protection standard set by EU law but fails to clear the higher standard set by national law, the national court is entitled to strike down the measure. In the latter case, the higher standard of protection provided by national law must, however, not prejudice the effective enforcement of EU law. See also Wils (n 2) 209.

[144] [2007] OJ C303/1.

[145] Article 6(1) TEU.

States and the European Convention for the Protection of Human Rights and Fundamental Freedoms (ECHR).[146] As a result, Charter rights that correspond to rights laid down in the ECHR or that derive from the constitutional traditions of the Member States should be interpreted accordingly.[147] Charter rights for which provision is made in the Treaty on European Union (TEU) or the TFEU are exercised under the conditions and within the limits defined by those Treaties.[148] Apart from the fundamental rights protection guaranteed by the EU Charter, Article 6(2) TEU requires the EU to seek accession to the ECHR. This will bring the EU and its dealings under the fundamental rights supervision of the European Court of Human Rights (ECtHR).[149] Prior to the coming into force of the Treaty of Lisbon, fundamental rights were protected as general principles of EU law.[150] The Court of Justice has recognised the existence and application of general principles of EU law on the basis of what is currently Article 19 TEU. In accordance with this provision, the Court is required to ensure that in the interpretation and application of the Treaties, *the law* is observed. This task allows the Court to draw inspiration outside the Treaty texts, notably from national legal systems.[151] Rules common to the Member States and essential in their legal systems as genuine general principles of law qualify as general principles of EU law. Accordingly, the ECHR and other international treaties to which the Member States are signatories should be respected *by virtue of EU law*.[152] The constitutional traditions common to the Member States are still protected as general principles of EU law.[153] With all these legal sources for fundamental rights protection in the EU, there can be little concern over their legal basis when these rights are relied upon in the context of EU competition law.[154]

[146] Convention for the Protection of Human Rights and Fundamental Freedoms, CETS No 005.

[147] Article 52(3) and (4) EU Charter. *cf* Case C-279/09 *DEB* [2010] ECR I-13849.

[148] Article 52(2) EU Charter.

[149] On 5 April 2013, negotiators for the 47 Council of Europe Member States and the EU finalised the draft accession agreement of the EU to the European Convention on Human Rights. The Court of Justice will now be asked to give its opinion on the text. See Council of Europe press release DC041 (2013) <https://wcd.coe.int> accessed 1 July 2013.

[150] *Kremzow* (n 104) [14]. See also *Internationale Handelsgesellschaft* (n 10) [4]; Joined Cases C-20/00 and C-64/00 *Booker Aquaculture* [2003] ECR I-7411 [65]; Case C-540/03 *Parliament v Council* [2006] ECR I-5769 [35].

[151] P Pescatore, 'Les Droits de L'Homme et L'Integration Europeenne' [1969] *Cahiers de droit européen* 629, 642; Tridimas (n 21) 19–20.

[152] *cf Kremzow* (n 104) [14]. See also *Internationale Handelsgesellschaft* (n 10) [4]; Case 4/73 *Nold* [1974] ECR 491 [13]; *Booker Aquaculture* (n 150) [65]; *Parliament v Council* (n 150) [35].

[153] Article 6(3) TEU.

[154] In this respect, it should be noted that the applicability of the EU Charter is qualified. By virtue of Protocol (No 30) on the application of the Charter of Fundamental Rights of the European Union to Poland and to the United Kingdom [2010] OJ C83/313, the scope of application of the EU Charter is limited in relation to Poland and the UK. In accordance with the Presidency Conclusions of the European Council of 29/30 October 2009, the Czech Republic will be included in Protocol (No 30) at the time of the next Accession Treaty; see <http://register.consilium.europa.eu/pdf/en/09/st15/st15265-re01.en09.pdf> accessed 1 July 2013. Most relevant for the decentralised enforcement of EU competition law is Article 1(1) of this Protocol, pursuant to which: 'The Charter does not extend the ability of the Court of Justice, or any court or tribunal of Poland or of the United Kingdom, to find that the laws, regulations or administrative provisions, practices or action of Poland or of the United

Of the multitude of fundamental rights applicable to the decentralised enforcement of Articles 101 and 102 TFEU, several have particular relevance for national *sanctioning powers*, ie, the stage of the enforcement process where the authority decides on the consequences of a (putative and/or prima facie) infringement. It appears uncontroversial that the enforcement of EU competition law should take place with respect to human dignity and all human rights related thereto,[155] and that no one may be deprived of his or her liberty by arbitrary arrest or detention.[156] Yet, the impact of other fundamental rights on national sanctioning powers may be less self-evident. To clarify the Member States' sanctioning autonomy, the following fundamental rights would require further analysis:

- the right to property (section 4.5.2);
- the right to economic engagement (section 4.5.3);
- the principle of legal certainty (section 4.5.4);
- the right to a reasoned decision (section 4.5.5);
- the principle of good administration (section 4.5.6);
- the protection against undue delays (section 4.5.7);
- the principle of retroactivity *in mitius* (section 4.5.8);
- the principle of *ne bis in idem* (section 4.5.9);
- the principle of *nulla poena sine culpa* (section 4.5.10);
- the principle of equal treatment (section 4.5.11);
- the proportionality between infringement and sanction.

These rights derive from the EU Charter, the ECHR and/or the general principles of EU law. Each of these fundamental rights has the ability to limit the sanctioning autonomy of the Member States with regard to Articles 101 and 102 TFEU and thus to centralise parts of the enforcement regime. Because of its close links to the principles deriving from Article 4(3) TEU, the principle of proportionality between infringement and sanction is dealt with in section 4.6.5.

Kingdom are inconsistent with the fundamental rights, freedoms and principles that it reaffirms.' Therefore, it seems that the enforcement actions of the competition authorities of Poland and the UK (and the Czech Republic) cannot be assessed against the rights and freedoms laid down in the EU Charter directly. While it is unclear how this provision will be applied in practice, it is also suggested that these Member States cannot disregard those Charter rights that have been recognised in the Court's case law as general principles of EU law.

[155] No civilised woman or man would ever contemplate the introduction of capital punishment or any other form of corporal punishment irrevocably leading to torture or inhuman or degrading treatment or punishment. Clearly, these types of sanctions could under no circumstances be used to address infringements of EU competition law, as this would be contrary to Articles 1–5 EU Charter, Article 3 ECHR, Article 1 Protocol No 6 to the ECHR (CETS No 114) and Article 1 Protocol No 13 to the ECHR (CETS No 187). The Court of Justice has recognised that the protection of human dignity may influence the Member States' implementation obligations: Case 29/69 *Stauder* [1969] ECR 419.

[156] Article 6 EU Charter and Article 5 ECHR.

4.5.2 The Right to Property

The fundamental right to property protects ownership and exploitation of assets.[157] This right is not absolute in nature; it has a social function and may be restricted to achieve other public interests recognised under EU law.[158] Any such restrictions should correspond to the objectives of this interest and may not constitute a disproportionate and intolerable interference, impairing the very substance of this right. To this effect, the General Court held in *Van den Bergh Foods*:

> [T]hat the application of Article 85 and 86 of the Treaty [now Article 101 and 102 TFEU] constitutes one of the aspects of public interest in the Community . . . Consequently, pursuant to those articles, restrictions may be applied on the exercise of the right to property, provided that they are not disproportionate and do not affect the substance of that right.[159]

The right to property is mainly relevant for the use of reparatory sanctions, eg, compulsory divestitures, compulsory licences or compulsory supplies. In *SGL Carbon*, the Court of Justice held that the right to property is not applicable in relation to fines.[160] Remarkably, in the more recent *Schindler* case, the General Court did entertain the applicant's argument that the fine was contrary to the right to property, but dismissed it on substantive grounds.[161] Irrespective of whether the approach in *Schindler* will be followed by the Court of Justice, this case demonstrates that, in any case, a fine will not easily run counter to this principle.

In practice, the property rights relied upon against reparatory sanctions mainly concern *intellectual* property rights. Under exceptional circumstances, the refusal by a dominant undertaking to license intellectual property rights to another undertaking may constitute an abuse prohibited by Article 102 TFEU.[162] This behaviour could attract a sanction ordering the dominant undertaking to license its intellectual property right.

It follows from *Microsoft* that in these 'refusal to license' cases, the assessment of the reparatory sanction in the light of the right to property is rendered virtually obsolete by the preceding question of whether the refusal to license indeed constitutes an infringement.[163] The legality of the restriction of the undertaking's property rights is then reduced to the consistency between the established infringement

[157] Article 17 EU Charter, Article 1 Protocol No 1 to the ECHR (CETS No 009) and Case 44/79 *Hauer* [1979] ECR 3727; *Booker Aquaculture* (n 150); Case C-491/01 *BAT* [2002] ECR I-11453.

[158] *Nold* (n 152) [14].

[159] *Van den Bergh Foods* (n 133) [170].

[160] Case C-308/04 P *SGL Carbon* [2006] ECR I-5977 [108].

[161] Case T-138/07 *Schindler* [2011] ECR II-4819 [185]–[196].

[162] Case 238/87 *Volvo* [1988] ECR 6211; Joined Cases C-241/91 P and C-242/91 P *Magill* [1995] ECR I-743; Case C-418/01 *IMS Health* [2004] ECR I-5039; Case T-201/04 *Microsoft* [2007] ECR II-3601. See more extensively FOW Vogelaar, 'The Compulsory Licence of Intellectual Property Rights under the EC Competition Rules: An Analysis of the Exception to the General Rule of Ownership Immunity from Competition Rules' (2009) 6 *Competition Law Review* 117.

[163] *Microsoft* (n 162) [691].

and the sanction.[164] However, in recognition of the undertaking's property rights, the licensor may demand payment of 'reasonable royalties' by the licensee.[165] The question of what this entails has been the subject matter of *Microsoft II*.[166] The General Court was not in a position to formulate general rules on reasonable royalties, but various criteria can be inferred from this case: first, these royalties can be more than 'token remuneration';[167] second, they may be calculated as a proportion of the revenue made with the licence;[168] third, the fact that some parties are willing to pay a certain amount for the royalties in question does not make them reasonable;[169] fourth, the remuneration rates may not reflect the strategic value of the property right, but should be limited to its intrinsic value (ie, the innovative character).[170]

Centralisation Effects

It follows from the foregoing that the EU fundamental right to property only has a modest impact on the sanctioning autonomy of the Member States.[171] Its effects are largely subsumed by the conditions for establishing the infringement and the EU principle of proportionality (see below, section 4.6.5). It should be noted, however, that the paucity of legal safeguards against incursions on the right to property in the context of EU competition law has been lamented in the legal literature. The prevailing safeguard of reasonable royalties would be insufficient from a human rights perspective.[172] In particular, the unclear rules on the royalties payable and the unsatisfying judicial protection have been considered problematic in this respect.[173] While *Microsoft II* might have clarified some issues, there remains considerable discretion on the part of the Commission to determine whether a certain rate is reasonable or not.[174]

[164] ibid [246]–[266].
[165] Case T-69/89 *RTE* [1991] ECR II-485 [98].
[166] Case T-167/08 *Microsoft II* [2012] OJ C243/13.
[167] ibid [160].
[168] ibid [120].
[169] ibid [119].
[170] ibid [141]–[143].
[171] This conclusion is in line with Tridimas' conclusions on the application of the right to property more generally. See Tridimas (n 21) 315–16.
[172] A Andreangeli, 'Between Economic Freedom and Effective Competition Enforcement: The Impact of the Antitrust Remedies Provided by the Modernisation Regulation on Investigated Parties' Freedom to Contract and to Enjoy Property' (2010) 6 *Competition Law Review* 225.
[173] ibid 250.
[174] *cf Microsoft II* (n 166) [95]: 'Microsoft is, on the other hand, right to maintain that several rates may be covered by the notion of "reasonable remuneration rates". Nevertheless, that finding confirms the merits of the Commission's argument that it is not for it to choose a particular rate of remuneration from among what are reasonable rates for the purpose of the 2004 decision and impose that rate upon Microsoft.'

4.5.3 The Right to Economic Engagement

The fundamental right to economic engagement consists of the right to engage in work and pursue a professional occupation and the freedom to conduct a business. These rights originate in the Court's case law[175] and meanwhile have found their way into Articles 15 and 16 of the EU Charter. The right to economic engagement is closely related to the right to property – more specifically the right to use one's property – and these rights are often relied upon together.[176] Similar to the right to property, the right to economic engagement is also not absolute in nature.[177] One could come up with various types of sanctions for infringements of Articles 101 and 102 TFEU that may affect the right to economic engagement. Disqualification orders for company officers or orders excluding undertakings from public tenders or licences may come to mind. Tridimas has suggested that extensive bans on taking up employment in the state and private sectors could indeed be contrary to the EU right to economic engagement.[178] Sanctions of this type immediately stress the relevance of the right to economic engagement alongside the protection offered by the right to property.

Centralisation Effects

The right to economic engagement seems capable of limiting the sanctioning autonomy of the Member States. However, at this stage, it is hard to predict how seriously national sanctions will be tested. Article 52 of the EU Charter is equivocal on this point. On the one hand, it seems very protective by providing that any limitation on the exercise of the rights and freedoms recognised by the EU Charter may be made only if they are necessary and genuinely meet objectives of general interest recognised by the EU or the need to protect the rights and freedoms of others.[179] On the other hand, the Charter accepts that the right to economic engagement can only be exercised under the conditions and within the limits defined by the EU Treaties.[180] This suggests that the right to economic engagement is subject to all the limitations that have been accepted in the context of the free movement rights, including limitations needed for the effective enforcement of EU competition law (see above, section 4.4). For the purposes of the decentralised enforcement of Articles 101 and 102

[175] *Nold* (n 152) [14]; *Hauer* (n 157) [32]; Case 240/83 *ADBHU* [1985] ECR 531; Case C-84/95 *Bosphorus* [1996] ECR I-3953 [21].

[176] *Hauer* (n 157) [16]; *Bosphorus* (n 175) [19].

[177] *Nold* (n 152) [14]; *Wachauf* (n 139) [18]. See also *Booker Aquaculture* (n 150) [68], which states that 'restrictions may be imposed on the exercise of [fundamental] rights, in particular in the context of a common organisation of the markets, provided that those restrictions in fact correspond to objectives of general interest pursued by the Community and do not constitute, with regard to the aim pursued, a disproportionate and intolerable interference imparing the very substance of those rights'.

[178] Tridimas (n 21) 315–16.

[179] Article 52(1) EU Charter.

[180] Article 52(2) EU Charter.

TFEU, the protection offered by the right to economic engagement would then add little to the EU free movement rights. The implications of the right to economic engagement will have to be clarified through future litigation. It can be concluded that, at this stage, the right to economic engagement imposes no clear limitations onto the Member States with regard to the type of sanctions that can be used against infringements of Articles 101 and 102 TFEU.

4.5.4 The Principle of Legal Certainty

The EU principle of legal certainty derives from various sources of law and limits the sanctioning autonomy of Member States in a number of ways.[181] It requires Member States to adopt limitation periods for the exercise of their sanctioning powers and to respect the principle of legality and the principle of non-retroactivity of penalties. All three of these will be discussed in turn.

Limitation Periods

The principle of legal certainty requires Member States not to leave undertakings in uncertainty as to their legal position indefinitely. This requirement follows from EU case law on Commission procedures.[182] There is no reason to expect any other interpretation when it comes to national procedures under Articles 101 and 102 TFEU. As a result, Member States cannot exercise their sanctioning powers excessively late. In fact, limitation periods will have to apply to any decision under Articles 101 and 102 TFEU, irrespective of whether a sanction is imposed.[183] In this respect, the principle of legal certainty supplements any statutory limitation periods, for instance, limitation periods that are limited to the imposition of penalties, such as Article 25 of Regulation 1/2003. In principle, the duration of the limitation periods, as well as other detailed rules, falls within the autonomy of the Member States.[184] Once the Member States have provided for a limitation period, the effects of this EU principle are exhausted.[185] Only if a Member State fails to provide for a limitation period do national courts need to censure enforcement actions that have been initiated excessively late.[186] Closely related to the requirement not to leave undertakings in uncertainty about their legal position indefinitely is the protection against undue delays. The latter principle derives from the

[181] Article 49 EU Charter, Article 7 ECHR and *Dansk Rørindustri* (n 42); *Jungbunzlauer* (n 76). See further *Könecke* (n 137); *Kolpinghuis* (n 137); *Berlusconi* (n 137).

[182] Case 51/69 *Bayer* [1972] ECR 745 [20]; Joined Cases T-22/02 and T-23/02 *Sumitomo* [2005] ECR II-4065 [81].

[183] *cf Sumitomo* (n 182) 84–87: 'the absence of legislative limitation does not preclude censure of the Commission's action, in a specific case, in the light of the principle of legal certainty' ([87]).

[184] *cf* ibid [83] and [87].

[185] *cf Bolloré II* (n 48) [114]–[117].

[186] *Sumitomo* (n 182) [88].

fundamental right of defence and has slightly different implications. This principle will be discussed in section 4.5.7.

The Principle of Legality

The principle of legal certainty further requires sanctions to rest on a clear and unambiguous legal basis.[187] This requirement, which is also known as the principle of legality, forms the second limitation on the sanctioning autonomy of Member States. The terms under which sanctions may be imposed for infringements of Articles 101 and 102 TFEU should allow natural and legal persons to make informed choices with regard to their behaviour.[188] These terms need not to be so precise that the consequences of an infringement of Article 101 or 102 TFEU are foreseeable with absolute certainty. What suffices is that the provision is accessible and the sanction foreseeable.[189] This accessibility and foreseeability may follow from a statutory provision, case law, policy documents and case practice.[190]

In accordance with the maxim *nullum crimen, nulla poena sine lege*, the principle of legality applies, first and foremost, to penalties.[191] However, the obligation of legality in principle also applies outside the field of punitive sanctions. This can be concluded from *Penycoed*,[192] where the Court of Justice applied the principle of legality to the imposition of a levy on the production of milk outside the allocated quota. In accordance with the applicable EU legislation, the *purchaser* of the milk was liable for the payment of the levy. The question was raised as to whether the competent national authorities could impose a levy on the *producer* of the milk when the levy could not be collected from the purchaser. The Court considered that without a legal basis defining the conditions and scope of the authority's power, the purchaser could not be substituted for the producer.[193] While this did not discharge the Member State in question from its obligation to recover the levies,[194] it demonstrates the applicability of the principle of legality with regard to reparatory sanctions. This approach to the principle of legality finds support in the case law of the ECtHR. In *Beyeler v Italy*, the ECtHR decided that reparatory sanctions may also be subject to a separate obligation of legality, namely when they encroach on the right to property.[195]

[187] *Könecke* (n 137); Case 137/85 *Maizena* [1987] ECR 4587.

[188] Case C-76/06 P *Britannia Alloys & Chemicals* [2007] ECR I-4405 [79]; *ArchelorMittal* (n 49) [68]; *ThyssenKrupp Nirosta* (n 47) [81].

[189] *Schindler* (n 161) [99].

[190] ibid [96].

[191] *ThyssenKrupp Nirosta* (n 47) [80]; *Jungbunzlauer* (n 76) [70]–[92]; *Areva and Alstom* (n 73) [210].

[192] Case C-230/01 *Penycoed* [2004] ECR I-937.

[193] ibid [32].

[194] ibid [34] et seq.

[195] *cf Beyeler v Italy* App No 33202/96 (ECtHR, 5 January 2000) [108]–[109]: 'that an essential condition for an interference to be deemed compatible with Article 1 of Protocol No. 1 is that it should be lawful' ([108]) and 'the principle of lawfulness also presupposes that the applicable provisions of domestic law be sufficiently accessible, precise and foreseeable' ([109]).

Legality v Effectiveness

Tensions could arise between the principle of legality and other EU principles, notably the principle of effective enforcement (see below, section 4.6.3). The absence of (adequate) sanctions at a national level could be detrimental to the effective enforcement of EU law. It follows from EU case law that in these situations of conflict, either effectiveness considerations or legality requirements prevail depending on the nature of the sanction. With regard to reparatory sanctions, there are clear precedents that effectiveness considerations should be given priority and that a Member State could (and should!) remedy an infringement even in the absence of an appropriate legal basis.[196] Applied to the context of EU competition law, this means that NCAs should be deemed competent to terminate an infringement, using any adequate reparatory sanction, even in the absence of a specific domestic legal basis. Punitive sanctions are treated differently, however. Effectiveness considerations alone cannot function as a legal basis for NCAs to impose an adequate *penalty*.[197] Even if this would mean that a severe infringement of Article 101 or 102 TFEU would go un(der)penalised, this would not overrule the requirement of legality.

Notwithstanding the above conclusion, the case law does suggest that Member States may allow their NCAs a certain margin of discretion with regard to the severity of the penalty in order to ensure effective enforcement. This can be concluded from *Jungbunzlauer*, where the General Court held that:

> [T]o avoid excessive prescriptive rigidity and to enable a rule of law to be adapted to the circumstances, a certain degree of unforeseeability as to the penalty which may be imposed for a given offence must be permitted. A fine subject to sufficiently circumscribed variation between the minimum and the maximum amounts which may be imposed for a given offence may therefore render the penalty more effective both from the viewpoint of its application and its deterrent effect.[198]

The Court then concluded that, in relation to fines, a margin of discretion ranging from €1,000 to 10 per cent of the undertaking's worldwide turnover constitutes a sufficient legal basis for adopting fining decisions.[199] What seems important, for the purposes of legality, is that there is a statutory maximum penalty.

The Principle of Non-retroactivity of Penalties

The principle of legality includes the principle of non-retroactivity of penalties. In accordance with the latter principle, the terms and conditions of penalties for infringements of Articles 101 and 102 TFEU should correspond with those laid down at the time when the infringement was committed.[200] Moreover, natural

[196] *Penycoed* (n 192); *Consorzio Industrie Fiammiferi* (n 18).
[197] *Könecke* (n 137) [16]; *Rolex* (n 137).
[198] *Jungbunzlauer* (n 76) [84].
[199] ibid [83]–[92].
[200] *Areva and Alstom* (n 73) [133].

and legal persons cannot be punished more severely than they were permitted to expect at the time of the offence.[201] The Court of Justice has created some uncertainty as to the scope of this principle by suggesting that it only applies to *criminal* penalties.[202] However, the subsequent application of this principle to fines imposed by the Commission under EU competition law suggests that this principle has a bearing on punitive sanctions more generally and competition law penalties in particular.[203]

The Court of Justice views the principle of non-retroactivity through the prism of effectiveness and essentially reduces its safeguards to the requirement of statutory certainty.[204] As long as the legal basis and conditions for the penalty are not altered, a change in administrative policy or practice will not easily be considered contrary to this principle.[205] For example, the competition authorities may change their fining guidelines without ever having to apply different guidelines to a single continuous infringement. Undertakings cannot legitimately expect sanctioning policy or practice to remain constant over time.[206] However, the EU principle of non-retroactivity does demand that infringements are penalised in accordance with the fining guidelines applicable at the time that the infringement came to an end. This could require the authorities to penalise an infringement of Article 101 or 102 TFEU in accordance with fining guidelines that have become outdated in the meantime.

Centralisation Effects

The EU principle of legal certainty has various implications for the decentralised enforcement of Articles 101 and 102 TFEU. First, Member States should draw up statutes of limitation, as they cannot delay the exercise of their sanctioning powers indefinitely. Further, they should ensure that sanctions for infringements of Articles 101 and 102 TFEU rest on a clear and unambiguous legal basis so that the consequences are foreseeable. This requirement applies to punitive sanctions and in principle also to reparatory sanctions that limit the undertakings' right to property. However, effectiveness considerations dictate that NCAs should be deemed competent to terminate any infringement, irrespective of its statutory powers. Finally, Member States may accord their NCAs with considerable discretion as to the level of a punitive sanction, as long as the maximum penalty is defined by law. All these requirements 'limit' the sanctioning autonomy of the Member States. These examples show what this limitation could entail: Member States may neither allow their NCAs to breach the EU principle of legal certainty nor curtail their NCAs in effectively enforcing Articles 101 and 102 TFEU. It should be noted

[201] Case 331/88 *FEDESA* [1990] ECR I-4023 [42].

[202] *Rolex* (n 137) [60]–[63].

[203] Case C-397/03 P *Archer Daniels Midland* [2006] ECR I-4429; *Areva and Alstom* (n 73) [131]–[132].

[204] *Archer Daniels Midland* (n 203) [20]–[24].

[205] *cf Schindler* (n 161) [117]–[130].

[206] *Dansk Rørindustri* (n 42) [191]–[193].

that the latter 'limitation' derives from the EU principle of effectiveness (see below, section 4.6.3) rather than the EU principle of legal certainty.

4.5.5 The Right to a Reasoned Decision

The right to a reasoned decision is the flipside of the authority's duty to state reasons. Under this duty, there is a requirement to explain the grounds for deciding on a particular sanction for an infringement of EU law. This duty, which is separate from stating the reasons for finding an infringement, follows from the general principle of effective judicial protection. The duty to state reasons for a particular sanction is an essential procedural requirement, which must also be distinguished from the question of whether the reasoning is well founded.[207] The fact that the reasoning might be erroneous cannot call into question the sufficiency of the reasoning for a decision.[208] The requirements to be satisfied by the statement of reasons depend on the circumstances of each case, in particular the content of the measure in question, the nature of the reasons given and the interest which the addressees of the measure, or other parties to whom it is of direct and individual concern, may have in obtaining explanations.[209] A breach of the right to a reasoned decision could affect the legality of the decision, but may also be remedied in other ways (eg, a reduction of the penalty).[210]

The specific requirements under the duty to state reasons can be grasped from case law on Article 296 TFEU, the Statute of the Court of Justice and the Rules of Procedure of the General Court. The statement of reasons must be appropriate to the sanction at issue and must disclose in a clear and unequivocal manner the reasoning followed by the institution which adopted that sanction in such a way as to enable the person concerned to ascertain the reasons for it and to enable the competent judicial body to exercise its power of review.[211] This duty covers in principle every aspect of the sanctioning decision, eg, the culpability of the offender,[212] the decision to impose a penalty,[213] the determination of the fine,[214] the method for calculating a 'deterrence multiplier'[215] and the reduction of the fine for reasons of cooperation.[216] Yet, in terms of actual explanation, the duty to

[207] Case C-280/08 P *Deutsche Telekom* (n 40) [130].

[208] Case T-378/06 *IMI* [2011] OJ C145/20 [68].

[209] Case C-280/08 P *Deutsche Telekom* (n 40) [131]; Case T-110/07 *Siemens* [2011] ECR II-477 [310]; *IMI* (n 208) [67].

[210] In accordance with Case T-148/89 *Tréfilunion* [1995] ECR II-1063 [42], the right to a reasoned decisions forms part of the EU principle of good administration. Breach of the principle of good administration could affect the legality of the administrative decision, but may also be remedied with a reduction of the penalty, cf Tridimas (n 21) 412–13.

[211] Case C-280/08 P *Deutsche Telekom* (n 40) [130] and [136].

[212] ibid [130].

[213] Case T-461/07 *Visa* [2011] ECR II-1729 [221].

[214] ibid [288].

[215] *Siemens* (n 209) [310].

[216] *IMI* (n 208) [66].

state reasons for a particular sanction is not extremely demanding. In *Deutsche Telekom*, the Court of Justice considered that the duty to state reasons in relation to the intentional or negligent nature of the infringement was fulfilled by the reference to Article 15(2) of Regulation 17 (now Article 23(2) of Regulation 1/2003), which referred to this condition, and by the detailed grounds for considering the appellant's pricing practices abusive and for considering him responsible for the infringement.[217] In *Siemens*, the General Court reviewed the sufficiency of reasons for the application of a certain deterrence multiplier.[218] It accepted that the Commission did not indicate the method adopted in arriving at the precise level of the multiplier. It also considered that the duty to state reasons was satisfied as the Commission had set out the factors which enabled it to measure the gravity and duration of the infringement, and was not required to set out a more detailed account of the figures relating to the method of calculating the fine.[219] It continued that:

> [I]t is desirable, but not a requirement of the obligation to state reasons, that the Commission indicate the figures which influenced the exercise of its discretion when setting the fines, especially in regard to the desired deterrent effect.[220]

The above cases suggest that the scope of the EU duty to state reasons for a particular sanction is limited to mentioning the elements that have been taken into account and does not extend to the actual assessment of these elements in the process of deliberation.

The Centralisation Effects

The duty of Member States under EU law to state reasons for administrative decisions has traditionally focused on the protection of (fundamental) EU rights.[221] The principle of effective judicial protection, from which this duty derives, has been formulated by the Court of Justice as a safeguard for Treaty rights. In the light of Article 47 of the EU Charter, which requires an effective remedy in relation to violations of 'rights and freedoms guaranteed by the law of the Union', there can be no doubt that the principle of effective judicial protection also applies to the decentralised enforcement of EU competition law. The rights and freedoms at stake are the rights granted under Articles 101 and 102 TFEU, notably Article 101(3) TFEU, and the fundamental rights and freedoms protected by the EU Charter and the general principles of EU law, eg, the right to property and the principle of legality. As a result, the sanctioning powers of the Member States are subject to an EU duty to state reasons. This duty is confirmed by the fact that the

[217] Case C-280/08 P *Deutsche Telekom* (n 40) [132]–[133].
[218] *Siemens* (n 209).
[219] ibid [311].
[220] ibid [312].
[221] Case 222/86 *Heylens* [1987] ECR 4097; Case C-467/01 *Eribrand* [2003] ECR I-6471; Case C-239/05 *BVBA Management, Training en Consultancy* [2007] ECR I-1455.

Commission is under an identical duty[222] and that these Commission procedures, in turn, are a benchmark for national procedures. This EU duty does not go beyond indicating the elements that have led to a particular sanction. Nonetheless, Member States remain in principle free to decide that sanctions for infringements of Articles 101 and 102 TFEU require a more elaborate explanation, for instance, by requiring their NCA to explain carefully the relative weight of each element in arriving at a certain sanction.

4.5.6 The Principle of Good Administration

The principle of good (or sound) administration has been recognised under EU law and is applicable to competition law procedures.[223] It is closely related to the principle of legal certainty and the rights of defence, and it applies to any aspect of the *administration* of EU competition law.[224] The principle of good administration manifests itself in various ways and includes, amongst other things, the right to a hearing, the right to access one's file, the right to hear reasons for the actions of the administration, the right of compensation for miscarriages in the administration of EU law and the principle of *res judicata*. The principle of good administration also influences the exercise of sanctioning powers. In *Tréfilunion*, the General Court held that it would be contrary to the principle of good administration if an undertaking that has been fined for an infringement of Articles 101 and 102 TFEU would have to bring court proceedings in order to determine in detail the method for calculating the fine.[225] Reportedly, the Commission adopted its first fining guidelines as a direct result of this judgment.[226] More generally, it could be argued that the principle of good administration requires authorities to clarify how they will exercise (and have exercised) their discretionary sanctioning powers. The principle of good administration also influences the exercise of sanctioning powers in other respects. In *BASF*, the General Court applied this principle to the Commission's leniency procedure and concluded that:

> If an undertaking makes contact with the Commission with a view to cooperating to an extent which may be rewarded under the Leniency Notice and a meeting is organised in that context between the institution and that undertaking, the minutes of such a meeting, recording the essential aspects of the assertions made at that meeting, must be drawn up or, at the very least, a sound recording must be made, pursuant to the principle of sound administration, if the undertaking in question so requests at the latest at the beginning of the meeting.[227]

[222] *cf* Case C-272/09 P *KME* [2012] OJ C32/4 [91]–[101].
[223] Case T-113/07 *Toshiba Corp (Gas Insulated Switchgear)* [2011] ECR II-3989 [75].
[224] *cf* Tridimas (n 21) 411.
[225] *Tréfilunion* (n 210) [142].
[226] WPJ Wils, 'The European Commission's 2006 Guidelines on Antitrust Fines: A Legal and Economic Analysis' (2007) 30 *World Competition* 197, 202–03.
[227] Case T-15/02 *BASF* [2006] ECR II-497 [502].

It follows that the handling of leniency applications is subject to the principle of good administration. Furthermore, the principle of good administration also has something to say about the treatment of recidivism. It can be concluded from *Lafarge* that the Commission may increase the amount of the fine for reasons of recidivism even if the decision finding the first infringement is still subject to review, provided, however, that the recidivism increment is undone if the first decision is annulled.[228] It seems that the principle of good administration is relied upon ever more often and in relation to a broad range of issues, albeit that it is often unsuccessful.[229] Future litigation will have to clarify the exact implication of this EU principle. Breach of the right to good administration could affect the legality of the administrative decision. It may also lead to a variety of remedies, one of which is the reduction of the penalty.[230]

Centralisation Effects

The principle of good administration has been codified in Article 41 of the EU Charter. This suggests that this principle has a fundamental status in the EU legal order. However, it can be debated whether the scope of this principle extends to the administration of EU law by national institutions. Article 41 of the EU Charter relates solely to institutions, bodies, offices and agencies *of the EU* and so do the majority of cases. In fact, very recently in *Cicala*, the Court adopted a literal interpretation of this provision and concluded that Article 41 of the EU Charter is *not* addressed to the Member States.[231] It should be noted that this ruling was made in a somewhat unusual context, in which the Court had to determine whether it was competent to render a preliminary ruling. It should further be noted that there have also been instances where the Court of Justice has interpreted EU *legislation* in accordance with the principle of good administration.[232] This could suggest that EU law includes a general principle of good administration that extends beyond the narrow confines of Article 41 of the EU Charter. It is submitted herewith that there are indeed good reasons to extend the action radius of this principle to the decentralised administration of EU law. In accordance with *Upjohn*[233]

[228] Case C-413/08 *Lafarge* [2010] ECR I-5361 [81]–[89].

[229] Case T-299/08 *Elf Aquitaine* [2011] ECR II-2149 (where the principle of good administration was relied upon in relation to the assessment of parent liability, the treatment of indicia in establishing the infringement and the suspension of the decision pending the review of another decision); Case T-343/08 *Arkema France* [2011] ECR II-2287 (where the principle of good administration was relied upon in relation to the increase in the amount of the fine for reasons of recidivism); *Microsoft II* (n 166) (where the principle of good administration was relied upon in relation to the imposition of a periodic penalty payment before having specified the obligations to the required degree); Case T-83/08 *Denki Kagaku Kogyo Kabushiki Kaisha* [2012] OJ C80/16 (where the principle of good administration was relied upon in relation to access to a non-confidential version of a transcript of the statement made by another party to the infringement at the *in camera* hearing by the Commission).

[230] Tridimas (n 21) 412–13.

[231] Case C-482/10 *Cicala* [2012] OJ 49/11 [28].

[232] Case C-428/05 *Laub* [2007] ECR I-5069 [25]; Case C-104/01 *Libertel* [2003] ECR I-3793.

[233] *Upjohn* (n 22).

and *i-21 Germany*,[234] rules and principles applicable to Commission procedures function as a benchmark for national procedures. Considering its fundamental status, this should apply a fortiori to the EU principle of good administration. A procedural safeguard that is so fundamental for the EU's internal legal order as to warrant its inclusion in the EU Charter should not be dependent on the level of administration. Although this is obviously a matter for the Court to decide, it is argued that the Member States should be considered to be bound by the EU principle of good administration in the enforcement of Articles 101 and 102 TFEU.[235]

4.5.7 The Protection Against Undue Delays

It was already concluded in section 4.5.4 that Member States cannot delay the exercise of their sanctioning powers indefinitely. As a consequence, Member States should provide for a limitation period beyond which decisions can no longer be adopted.[236] Closely related to this requirement is the protection against undue delays. Even within the boundaries of reasonable limitation periods, undue delays in enforcement proceedings should be avoided. This principle focuses on periods of inactivity during the various stages of the enforcement procedure rather than on the duration of the procedure as such.[237]

The protection against undue delays in administrative procedures constitutes a general principle of EU law.[238] This principle originally derives from the fundamental right of defence and has as an ultimate consequence that a decision establishing an infringement (and imposing sanctions) can no longer be adopted. This is the case if the delay prevents the undertaking from defending itself adequately against the objections of the competition authorities.[239] Yet, the protection against undue delays is also capable of reducing the penalty. In various cases, the Court of Justice has exercised its powers of review to reduce fines imposed by the Commission for reasons of undue delay.[240] This concerned cases where there were long periods of inactivity on the part of the Commission, but where rights of defence had not actually been breached. In these cases, the Court compensated the undertakings for the extended period of uncertainty. Initially, this resulted in modest reductions of €50,000 and €100,000.[241] More recently, the General Court

[234] *i-21 Germany and Arcor* (n 25).

[235] *cf* Tridimas (n 21) 449, who concluded that EU and national authorities can be viewed as part of a single constitutional structure, subject to the equivalent standards of accountability.

[236] See text at n 183.

[237] Case C-105/04 P *Nederlandse Federatieve Vereniging voor de Groothandel op Elektrotechnisch Gebied* [2006] ECR I-8725 [38]; *Bolloré II* (n 48) [115]–[116].

[238] *Nederlandse Federatieve Vereniging voor de Groothandel op Elektrotechnisch Gebied* (n 237) [35].

[239] ibid [42]–[43].

[240] Case C-185/95 P *Baustahlgewebe* [1998] ECR I-8417; Joined Cases T-5/00 and T-6/00 *Nederlandse Federatieve Vereniging voor de Groothandel op Elektrotechnisch Gebied and Technische Unie BV* [2003] ECR II-5761; Case T-240/07 *Heineken* [2011] ECR II-3355.

[241] *Baustahlgewebe* (n 240); *Nederlandse Federatieve Vereniging voor de Groothandel op Elektrotechnisch Gebied and Technische Unie BV* (n 240).

has become less patient with the Commission and reduced Heineken NV's €220 million fine for its participation in the *Dutch Beer* cartel by as much as five per cent.[242]

The issue of undue delays caused by periods of inactivity on the part of the Commission needs to be distinguished from unreasonably long proceedings. In *Bollore II*, the General Court concluded that a breach of reasonable periods does *not* affect the amount of the fine, as Regulation 1/2003 has provided a '*réglementation complète*'.[243] It should be noted that the long duration of the proceedings leading to the decision in *Bolloré II* was not caused by periods of inactivity on the part of the Commission.

Centralisation Effects

It is difficult to determine how exactly this protection against undue delays needs to be implemented at a national level. It would in any case not be warranted to conclude from current EU case law that every finding of undue delay should automatically lead to a five per cent reduction of the penalty. However, Member States cannot ignore the fact that the Court has taken a firm stance against delays caused by the Commission. The Court is no longer willing to accept that periods of inactivity on the part of the administrative authority come at the expense of the undertakings. A symbolic compensation will no longer do. National courts will have to follow suit and make sure that addressees of sanctioning decisions adopted under Article 101 or 102 TFEU are compensated for any undue delays. This development will limit the sanctioning autonomy of the Member States, in that it provides an additional ground for review and terminates situations of unlimited delay.

4.5.8 The Principle of Retroactivity *in Mitius*

Penalty powers should be used retroactively if this would result in a more lenient penalty. Retroactive application of the more lenient penalty (or retroactivity *in mitius*) is a general principle of EU law.[244] It is the opposite of the principle of non-retroactivity of penalties (see above, section 4.5.4). The latter derives from the principle of legal certainty. The principle of retroactivity *in mitius* derives from considerations of equity and proportionality.[245] While individuals cannot be punished more severely than they were allowed to expect at the time that the act was committed, they should benefit from penalty statutes that have been mitigated subsequent to their act. What seems decisive for this principle is that the newly

[242] *Heineken* (n 240).

[243] *Bolloré II* (n 48) [115]–[116].

[244] *Berlusconi* (n 137) [66]–[69]; Case C-45/06 *Campina* [2007] ECR I-2089; Case C-420/06 *Jager* [2008] ECR I-1315; Case C-17/10 *Toshiba Corporation* [2012] OJ C98/3-4, para 64.

[245] *Toshiba Corporation* (n 142), Opinion of AG Kokott [60].

introduced penalty reflects a revised assessment as to what reaction is commensurate with the gravity of the infringement.[246] This suggests that the scope of this principle extends to administrative guidelines for the exercise of penalty powers.

A revised assessment as to the appropriate penalty could of course mean that EU law is enforced less effectively than it used to be. It follows from *Berlusconi*[247] that in these cases the principle of retroactivity *in mitius* has priority over considerations of effective enforcement. *Berlusconi* dealt with the implementation of the First Company Law Directive. In accordance with this Directive, Italian law provided for penalties for a failure to respect corporate accounting rules. Domestic investigations had established an infringement of these accounting rules and the Italian government subsequently passed a bill that reduced the penalties for such infringements. Within this context, the Court of Justice had to give a preliminary ruling on the relation between effective enforcement and the principle of retroactivity *in mitius*. The Court gave priority to the latter. However, rather than weighing these principles against each other, the Court came to its conclusion on the ground that Member States may not rely on a Directive to aggravate the criminal liability of individuals. The Court therefore simply disregarded the requirement to provide for effective penalties laid down in the Directive. Nonetheless, this case does permit the conclusion that the principle of retroactivity *in mitius* has priority over considerations of effective enforcement. Any other conclusion would lead to the paradoxical situation that the general principle of effectiveness laid down in Article 4(3) TEU would be more demanding than the specific requirement of effective enforcement laid down in a Directive.[248]

Centralisation Effects

As the principle of retroactivity *in mitius* is a general principle of EU law, it governs the decentralised enforcement of EU competition law.[249] This means that the introduction of more lenient penalties for infringements of Articles 101 and 102 TFEU or the adoption of more lenient administrative guidelines for the exercise of penalty powers need to be applied retroactively. NCAs and national courts should apply this principle irrespective of the consequences for the effectiveness of EU competition policy.

4.5.9 The Principle of *Ne Bis in Idem*

The EU principle of *ne bis in idem* precludes any person from being found guilty or proceedings from being brought against it a second time on the grounds of conduct in respect of which he or she has been penalised or acquitted by a previ-

[246] *Jager* (n 244) [70]; *Toshiba Corporation* (n 142), Opinion of AG Kokott [60].
[247] *Berlusconi* (n 137).
[248] *cf* Tridimas (n 21) 264-265.
[249] *Toshiba Corporation* (n 142), Opinion of AG Kokott [57].

ous final decision.[250] *Ne bis in idem* is a general principle of EU law that derives from the constitutional traditions of the Member States, as inspired by the ECHR, and which has been codified in Article 50 of the EU Charter.[251] This principle rests on two pillars: legal certainty and equity.[252] The prohibition to commence a second proceeding does not require that the first proceeding has culminated in a judicial decision. In fact, the principle does not even require the involvement of a court or tribunal.[253] However, the application of this principle presupposes that a finding has already been made on the question of whether or not an offence has been committed.[254] The termination of proceedings for entirely procedural reasons therefore does not preclude the opening of proceedings a second time.[255]

The prohibition to commence a second proceeding has for a consequence that double punishment is prohibited as well. Indeed, the prohibition of double punishment should be seen as a mere corollary of the prohibition to commence a second proceeding.[256] Only by appreciating this subtle difference is one able to explain why the principle of *ne bis in idem* does not preclude authorities from taking into account recidivism in determining an appropriate penalty.[257]

In accordance with consistent EU case law in the field of anti-competitive practices, the principle of *ne bis in idem* is subject to the threefold condition of identity of the facts, unity of the offender and unity of the legal interest protected.[258] The principle of *ne bis in idem* has special relevance for the system of decentralised enforcement of EU competition law. While the Court of Justice has not yet ruled specifically on this issue, the principle of *ne bis in idem* would seem to apply to parallel or consecutive enforcement procedures under Articles 101 and 102 TFEU by different competition authorities. Whereas Regulation 1/2003 leaves open the possibility of parallel and/or consecutive enforcement proceedings by the Commission and NCAs,[259] the hierarchical superior legal principle of *ne bis in*

[250] *Toshiba Corporation* (n 244) [94].

[251] *cf* Joined Cases 18/65 and 35/65 *Gutmann* [1967] ECR 61; *Wilhelm* (n 14); Case 7/72 *Boehringer Mannheim* [1972] ECR 1281; *Maizena* (n 187); Joined Cases T-305–07, T-313–16, T-318, T-325, T-328, T-329 and T-335/94 *LVM* [1999] ECR II-931; Joined Cases C-187/01 and C-385/01 *Gözütok and Brügge* [2003] ECR I-1345; *Akerberg* (n 5).

[252] *Gözütok and Brügge* (n 251), Opinion of AG Colomer [49].

[253] *Gözütok and Brügge* (n 251) [31].

[254] Joined Cases C-238, C-244, C-245, C-247, C-250 to C-252 and C-254/99 P *LVM* [2002] ECR I-8375, para 60.

[255] *cf* Case C-469/03 *Miraglia* [2005] ECR I-2009.

[256] See B van Bockel, *The Ne Bis in Idem Principle in EU Law* (Wolters Kluwer, 2010) 122ff, who concludes that the EU principle of *ne bis in idem* prohibits double prosecution and that the prohibition of double punishment is simply the corollary of the former. See also WPJ Wils, 'The Principle of *Ne Bis in Idem* in EC Antitrust Enforcement: A Legal and Economic Analysis' (2003) 26 *World Competition* 131, 134 and 144.

[257] Case T-189/06 *Akema France* [2011] ECR II-5455, para 128.

[258] *Aalborg Portland* (n 75) [338]; *Toshiba Corporation* (n 244) [97].

[259] While parallel proceedings by the Commission and one or more NCAs are explicitly excluded (Article 11(6) of Regulation 1/2003), consecutive proceedings are not (Article 16(2) of Regulation 1/2003). See also *Toshiba Corporation* (n 244) [74] et seq. In addition, parallel and/or consecutive proceedings by various NCAs are possible (Article 16(1) of Regulation 1/2003). The likelihood of parallel and/or consecutive proceedings by various NCAs has been reduced as a result of case allocation rules (see above, section 2.4).

idem may prevent these authorities from opening a second proceeding.[260] This already follows implicitly from *Jungbunzlauer*, where the General Court held:

> The Community case-law has . . . held that an undertaking may be made defendant in two parallel sets of proceedings concerning the same infringement and, thus, incur concurrent sanctions, one imposed by the competent authority of the Member State in question, the other a Community sanction, to the extent that the two sets of proceedings pursue different ends and that the legal rules infringed are not the same.[261]

Subject to the threefold condition of identity of the facts, unity of the offender and unity of the legal interest protected, NCAs may not initiate proceedings under Articles 101 and 102 TFEU, let alone impose sanctions, for presumed infringements already decided on either by themselves, by the Commission or by another NCA.

Identity of the Facts

The principle of *ne bis in idem* is subject to the condition of 'identity of the facts'. It is submitted herewith that the principle of *ne bis in idem* should have consequences for the prosecution of infringements that are part of a pattern of conduct and qualify as an SCI (see above, section 4.3.3). After all, if the existence of an SCI prevents a competition authority from prosecuting 'various instances of conduct' separately and from imposing several distinct fines, why would it suddenly be allowed for two or more competition authorities to prosecute and penalise various manifestations of an SCI? If the principle of *ne bis in idem* and the SCI concept have to be taken seriously, then one cannot allow anti-competitive conduct that forms part of a pattern of conduct to be penalised in separate procedures. This limitation should also apply to parallel or consecutive enforcement proceedings that do not have any geographical overlap.[262] To make matters more concrete, in a market-sharing arrangement covering two Member States, the responsible NCAs should not be allowed to each prosecute both undertakings for anti-competitive conduct in their respective home markets. In order to have every aspect of such an infringement penalised, either a single authority would have to

[260] *cf* Case C-375/09 *Tele2 Polska* [2011] ECR I-3055, Opinion of AG Mazák [30]. See also S Brammer, *Co-operation between National Competition Agencies in the Enforcement of EC Competition Law* (Hart Publishing, 2009) 363–419.

[261] *Jungbunzlauer* (n 76) [286].

[262] *cf* Wils (n 256) 146; Brammer (n 260) 378–81. See also on this issue Commission Staff Working Paper accompanying the Communication from the Commission to the European Parliament and the Council: Report on the functioning of Regulation 1/2003 [2009] COM 206 final, para 223, which reported a rare instance of parallel actions by the German and Belgian authorities: 'The Belgian authority which imposed the second fine notably contemplated the issue of "*ne bis in idem*". It considered inter alia that it was able to impose a fine in regard of the effects of the cartel in the Belgian territory and based on the turnover in Belgium insofar as the first fine had been imposed by the German authority in view of the effects in the German territory only. The case might prima facie have presented the opportunity for the Community Courts (pursuant to an Article 234 EC reference [now Article 267 TFEU]) to clarify questions relating to the principle of *ne bis in idem* and in particular the definition of "*idem*". However, neither of the decisions was appealed.'

assume jurisdiction over the entire infringement[263] or each NCA would have to focus on one of the undertakings. However, while the principle of *ne bis in idem* is taken seriously, the same cannot be said for the SCI concept. In her recent opinion in *Toshiba Corporation*, AG Kokott concluded, first, that the principle of *ne bis in idem* covers cross-border infringements, but then found it perfectly acceptable for various authorities to prosecute and punish various manifestations of an SCI.[264] The Court of Justice sided with its Advocate General on this matter.[265] As *Toshiba Corporation* concerned the application of *national* competition law (for the period prior to the accession of the Czech Republic to the EU) subsequent to EU competition law, it is currently still unclear how the principle of *ne bis in idem* should be applied in relation to consecutive proceedings against a single and continuous infringement of Article 101 TFEU.

Unity of the Offender

In applying the condition of 'unity of the offender', the General Court has focused on the persons that are ultimately liable for the infringement.[266] The principle of *ne bis in idem* precludes:

> [P]enalising more than once, for the same infringement of [EU] competition law, the same conduct of the undertaking on the market through the persons which may be held personally liable for it.[267]

It is therefore not contrary to the principle of *ne bis in idem* to hold various persons, whether natural or legal, jointly and severally liable for the conduct of a single undertaking.[268] Similarly, this principle does not preclude competition authorities from penalising separate (associations of) undertakings owned by the same (legal) person or sharing the same members either.[269] It logically follows that the principle of *ne bis in idem* is not opposed to the penalisation of natural persons for an infringement for which the responsible legal person has already been penalised, or vice versa. It seems immaterial whether or not the legal person and natural person are penalised by a single authority or by separate authorities.[270] Accordingly, three businessmen could be sentenced to imprisonment and disqualified as directors in the UK for their role in the *Marine Hose Cartel*, while the companies involved had already been fined by the Commission.[271] However, what does not seem to be allowed is for the same natural or legal person to be punished

[263] It should be recalled that Regulation 1/2003 does not delimit the geographical scope of the sanctioning powers of the NCAs.

[264] *Toshiba Corporation* (n 142) [100] and [131].

[265] *Toshiba Corporation* (n 244) [98]–[103].

[266] *FNCBV* (n 131) [344].

[267] *Siemens AG Österreich* (n 51) [151].

[268] ibid.

[269] *FNCBV* (n 131) [340]–[346].

[270] *cf* Brammer (n 260) 384; van Bockel (n 256) 104, 219–21.

[271] WPJ Wils, 'The Relationship between Public Antitrust Enforcement and Private Actions for Damages' (2009) 32 *World Competition* 3, 4.

twice or more *under Article 101 or 102 TFEU*, for instance, in subsequent administrative and criminal proceedings.

Unity of the Legal Interest Protected

The 'legal interest-condition' of the *ne bis in idem* principle has been the object of growing criticism.[272] So far, this condition has been mainly relevant with regard to the parallel application of EU competition law and domestic or foreign competition law. In a recent opinion in *Toshiba Corporation*, AG Kokott has unsuccessfully invited the Court of Justice to change its case law and take account only of the material acts, thus abandoning the condition of 'unity of the legal interest protected'.[273] The Court of Justice maintains that EU competition law does not protect the same legal interests as the competition laws of the Member States and third countries. Articles 101 and 102 TFEU require the anti-competitive behaviour to be 'capable of affecting trade between Member States'. These provisions thus intend to safeguard competition *within the EU market*. National competition law would not take account of this dimension.[274] The actions by third country competition authorities would aim at the protection of competition within their territorial jurisdiction, on the basis of specific objectives and substantive rules, and through legal measures that may have a variety of legal consequences.[275] It is questionable whether this distinction according to the legal interest protected is still in conformity with the ECHR. The ECtHR seems to have abandoned this condition.[276] In any case, this distinction is not in conformity with the case law of the Court of Justice on the principle of *ne bis in idem* in the Convention implementing the Schengen Agreement.[277]

In any case, the EU principle of natural justice requires a reduction of the penalty for persons caught by EU competition law which have already been confronted with an earlier penalty under national competition law for identical facts.[278] This form of mitigation has been justified by the close interdependence between the internal market and the markets of the Member States, and by the (erstwhile applicable) special system for the division of jurisdiction between the

[272] Wils (n 256) 143.

[273] *Toshiba Corporation* (n 244).

[274] *Wilhelm* (n 14) [3].

[275] *cf SGL Carbon* (n 160) [29]; Case C-289/04 P *Showa Denko* [2006] ECR I-5859 [53].

[276] *Zolotukhin v Russia* App No 14939/03 (ECtHR, 10 February 2009) [82]–[84]: 'the Court takes the view that Article 4 of Protocol No. 7 must be understood as prohibiting the prosecution or trial of a second "offence" in so far as it arises from identical facts or facts which are substantially the same' ([82]) and 'The Court's inquiry should therefore focus on those facts which constitute a set of concrete factual circumstances involving the same defendant and inextricably linked together in time and space, the existence of which must be demonstrated in order to secure a conviction or institute criminal proceedings' ([84]).

[277] Convention implementing the Schengen Agreement of 14 June 1985 between the Governments of the States of the Benelux Economic Union, the Federal Republic of Germany and the French Republic on the gradual abolition of checks at their common borders [2000] OJ L239/19. See Case C-150/05 *Van Straaten* [2006] ECR I-9327.

[278] *Wilhelm* (n 14) [11]; *Boehringer Mannheim* (n 251) [3]; *Tokai Carbon (Graphite Electrodes)* (n 58) [132]; Case T-322/01 *Roquette Frères* [2006] ECR II-3137 [279].

EU and its Member States.[279] It is submitted herewith that Member States are also subject to the EU principle of natural justice, meaning that they need to mitigate the penalty for a breach of national competition law if the person in question has already been punished under EU competition law.[280] This requirement is relevant not only in relation to the application of *substantive* competition law (domestic equivalents to Articles 101 and 102 TFEU), but also in relation to *procedural* competition law (eg, law meant to bolster the effectiveness of competition rules, such as a criminal offence provision).

Centralisation Effects

The EU principle of *ne bis in idem* is capable of limiting the sanctioning autonomy of the Member States with regard to infringements of Articles 101 and 102 TFEU. While this principle is not concerned with the type and nature of sanctions, it may exclude sanctions altogether. In fact, the principle of *ne bis in idem* could prohibit the NCAs from initiating enforcement actions in the first place. In this respect, all domestic sanctioning regimes are subject to the same EU limitation and will necessarily converge towards a shared minimum standard. The EU principle of *ne bis in idem* prohibits NCAs from commencing proceedings under Articles 101 and 102 TFEU against any person already penalised or acquitted for certain material acts by a previous decision *under Articles 101 and 102 TFEU*. It is irrelevant which Network authority has taken this earlier decision. The EU principle of *ne bis in idem* does not seem to prohibit a situation in which various authorities start parallel or consecutive actions against distinct manifestations of an SCI. Similarly, the EU principle of *ne bis in idem* does not prohibit NCAs from commencing proceedings under Articles 101 and 102 TFEU against persons already penalised or acquitted for certain material acts by a previous decision under national competition law either, or vice versa. However, in these cases, the EU principle of natural justice does demand that the second penalty is reduced.

4.5.10 The Principle of *Nulla Poena Sine Culpa*

Under the principle of *nulla poena sine culpa*, there can be no punishment without fault.[281] Punishment is just and beneficial to society only if the offence was committed intentionally or negligently. Penalties are meant to punish the offender and to deter future offences rather than to restore a previous situation. For the

[279] *Tokai Carbon (Graphite Electrodes)* (n 58) [132] and [141]; *Roquette Frères* (n 278) [287]. This suggests that the EU principle of natural justice has no effect where enforcement procedures under Articles 101 and 102 TFEU have been preceded by enforcement procedures in third countries. This is indeed confirmed by the case law; see *Boehringer Mannheim* (n 251) [3]; *Showa Denko* (n 275) [60]; *SGL Carbon* (n 160) [36]; *Roquette Frères* (n 278) [284]–[292].

[280] *cf Wilhelm* (n 14) [11]. See also de Moor-van Vugt (n 2) 108.

[281] Article 7 ECHR and Case C-210/00 *KCH* [2002] ECR I-6453.

latter objective, fault would be an inappropriate requirement, which explains why reparatory sanctions are not subject to any such requirement.

The scope of application of the principle of *nulla poena sine culpa* is currently still unclear. What is certain is that this principle does not apply outside the field of penalties.[282] However, the Court of Justice has created some doubts as to whether every type of penalty is subject to this principle. In *Estel*, *Lucchini* and *Alfer*, the Court effectively applied the principle of *nulla poena sine culpa* to non-criminal penalties, notably fines.[283] However, in *Maizena* and more recently in *KCH*, application of this principle was reserved for criminal sanctions alone.[284] The latter cases dealt with punitive sanctions that were linked to aid schemes voluntarily entered into. The Court rejected the application of the principle of *nulla poena sine culpa* to these sanctions. To give a consistent narrative for the above cases, it should be concluded that this principle does not apply to punitive sanctions forming part of a legal regime voluntarily entered into.[285]

In any case, Regulation 1/2003 recognises the principle of *nulla poena sine culpa* by making Commission fines subject to intent or negligence.[286] The alternative requirement of intent or negligence can be fulfilled already when the undertaking played a subsidiary, accessory or passive role[287] and where the undertaking cannot have been unaware of the anti-competitive nature of its conduct.[288] Whether or not it is aware that this conduct is contrary to Article 101 or 102 TFEU is irrelevant. For the purposes of imposing fines, the Court of Justice considers negligent infringements of EU competition law to be as serious as intentional infringements.[289] Yet, the degree of fault may affect the severity of the penalty in other ways. In *Degussa*, the General Court concluded that the principle of *nulla poena sine culpa* requires the Commission, in fixing the amount of the fine, to determine the scale of and responsibility for the infringement on the basis of facts and circumstances prevailing *at the time of the infringement*, instead of any later period.[290]

Centralisation Effects

Apart from the questions that may arise in relation to the material scope of the principle of *nulla poena sine culpa* (see above), there can also be some doubt about

[282] Case 177/88 *Dekker* [1990] ECR I-3941; Case C-180/95 *Draehmpaehl* [1997] ECR I-2195.

[283] Case 83/83 *Estel* [1984] ECR 2195; Case 179/82 *Lucchini* [1983] ECR 3083; Case 2/83 *Alfer* [1984] ECR 799.

[284] *Maizena* (n 187) [12]–[13]; *KCH* (n 281) [35].

[285] In this respect, it should also be noted that the ECtHR has considered that the voluntary nature of a regulatory regime is a relevant aspect for the scope of fundamental rights; *cf O'Halloran and Francis v UK* App Nos 15809/02 and 25624/02 (ECtHR, 29 June 2007) [57].

[286] Article 23(2) of Regulation 1/2003.

[287] *cf Deltafina* (n 94) [55] et seq. At [61] the General Court reiterated: 'although the limited importance, as the case may be, of the participation of the undertaking concerned cannot therefore call into question its individual liability for the infringement as a whole, it none the less has an influence on the assessment of the extent of that liability and thus the severity of the penalty.'

[288] Joined Cases 96–102, 104, 105, 108 and 110/82 *IAZ International Belgium* [1983] ECR 3369 [45].

[289] Case C-137/95 P *SPO* [1996] ECR I-1611 [55].

[290] Case T-279/02 *Degussa* [2006] ECR II-897 [270]–[285].

the decentralised application of this principle. Its inclusion in Regulation 1/2003 with regard to Commission fines gives a strong indication that penalties for infringements of EU competition law cannot be imposed without any form of fault, irrespective of the level of administration. This view has recently been supported by Advocate General Kokott in her opinion in *Bundeswettbewerbsbehörde v Schenker*.[291] The Court did not address the issue specifically, but did suggest that the application of the principle of *nulla poena sine culpa* was *not* mandated by EU law.[292] Moreover, outside the field of EU competition law, the Court of Justice has implicitly rejected that there is an unqualified EU requirement for the Member States to apply the principle of *nulla poena sine culpa*. It has insisted on various occasions that a national system of strict criminal liability is not in itself contrary to EU law.[293] In the absence of specific EU legislation, Member States may provide for such a system on the condition that the penalties are similar to those imposed in the event of infringements of national law of a similar nature and importance and are proportionate to the seriousness of the infringement. In a system of strict criminal liability, fault is not a precondition for the offence and the person responsible for this offence cannot exonerate itself by disproving its intent or negligence. One cannot reconcile such a system of strict liability with the principle of *nulla poena sine culpa* without compromising this principle. It is therefore unclear whether and to what extent Member States are under an EU duty to apply conditions of intent or negligence in punishing infringements of Articles 101 and 102 TFEU. As a more fundamental point, one can debate over whether the principle of *nulla poena sine culpa* constitutes a general principle of EU law.

4.5.11 The Principle of Equal Treatment

The application of EU law is governed by the principle of equal treatment. In accordance with this principle, similar situations may not be treated differently and different situations may not be treated similarly, unless there would be an objective justification for such treatment.[294] This principle applies to different parties in a single case and across different cases.[295] When applying the principle of equal treatment to sanctions for infringements of Articles 101 and 102 TFEU, one should compare the treatment of every single element that has a bearing on the severity of the sanction (eg, the characteristics of the undertakings, the infringements and the markets, and the behaviour of the undertakings during and after the

[291] *Bundeswettbewerbsbehörde v Schenker* (n 28), Opinion of AG Kokott [41] et seq.

[292] *Bundeswettbewerbsbehörde v Schenker* (n 28) [35]–[36].

[293] Case 326/88 *Hansen* [1990] ECR I-2911 [11]–[20]; Case C-177/95 *Ebony Maritime* [1997] ECR I-1111 [35]–[37].

[294] *cf Tokai Carbon (Graphite Electrodes)* (n 58) [219]; *Britannia Alloys & Chemicals* (n 188) [40] and [44].

[295] The principle of equal treatment includes the prohibition of discrimination on the grounds of nationality: Article 21(2) of the EU Charter, Article 18 TFEU and Case C-29/95 *Pastoors* [1997] ECR I-285. Discrimination on the grounds of nationality that affects the free movement of goods, persons, services or capital is prohibited pursuant to the particular free movement provision (see above, section 4.4).

infringement). In *Bolloré*, for instance, the General Court made a detailed analysis of the relative usefulness of documents submitted in the context of leniency applications. In light of the principle of equal treatment, the Court concluded that the Commission committed a manifest error of assessment.[296] In *Bollore II*, the question arose as to whether the attribution of liability to only one of the undertakings' parent company amounted to unequal treatment.[297] The General Court concluded that it did not as the circumstances were sufficiently different. Yet, this case does indicate that the principle of equal treatment also applies to the attribution of liability within a group of companies. In *Toshiba Corp (Gas Insulated Switchgear)*, the General Court applied the principle of equal treatment to the reference year for determining the relevant turnover in calculating the amount of the fine. It concluded that the undertaking in question had not been treated equally in relation to the other undertakings and that there was no objective justification for this discrimination.[298] Consequently, the Court annulled part of the decision.

A Further Example

The implications of the principle of equal treatment can be further demonstrated in *JFE Engineering*.[299] In this case, the General Court found that the requirement of equal treatment had been breached as different situations were treated similarly. Both European and Japanese undertakings active in the market for seamless steel tubes were involved in an infringement of Article 101 TFEU. These undertakings agreed to respect each other's home markets. Yet, only the European undertakings were found to have been involved in anti-competitive supply contracts. In accordance with these contracts, one of the European undertakings closed its production activities and was supplied by the others in accordance with a fixed quota. This was meant to ring-fence the European market. The Japanese undertakings argued that the fines imposed on them for agreeing to refrain from selling their products in Europe was disproportionate in comparison with the level of the fines imposed on the European producers. This objection found resonance with the General Court, which concluded that the Commission was required to draw inferences from the European dimension of the cartel.[300]

[296] Joint Cases T-109, T-118, T-122, T-125, T-126, T-128, T-129, T-132 and T-136/02 *Bolloré* [2007] ECR I-947 [694]–[708]. See further Joined Cases T-45/98 and T-47/98 *Krupp Thyssen Stainless and Acciai Speciali Terni* [2001] ECR II-3757 [237]–[248], where the General Court applied the principle of equal treatment to the opportunities provided by the Commission to the undertakings to cooperate in exchange for a reduction of the fine.

[297] *Bolloré II* (n 48) [83] et seq.

[298] *Toshiba Corp (Gas Insulated Switchgear)* (n 223) [280] et seq. See also Case T-133/07 *Mitsubishi Electric Corp* [2011] ECR II-4219 [264] et seq.

[299] Joined Cases T-67, T-68, T-71 and T-78/00 *JFE Engineering* [2004] ECR II-2501.

[300] Another approach was taken in *Toshiba Corp (Gas Insulated Switchgear)* (n 223). In [261] of that judgment, the General Court rejected the objection of unequal treatment in determining the amount of the fine on the following grounds: 'given the nature of the applicant's commitment under the common understanding, the fact that it did not participate in the distribution of GIS projects in the EEA is

By omitting to take account of these anti-competitive supply contracts in determining the amount of the fine for the European producers, the Commission was found to have treated different situations similarly without objective justification. The Commission thereby infringed the requirement of equal treatment.[301] The Court remedied the inequality by mitigating the fine for the Japanese undertakings. It did so reluctantly, however. It considered that the most appropriate way of restoring a fair balance between the addressees of the contested decision would be to increase the amount of the fine imposed on each of the European producers. In fact, the unlimited jurisdiction conferred upon the Court allows it to increase penalties. However, it refrained from increasing the fines for the European producers as the latter did not have the opportunity to give their views on this matter.[302] Therefore, the Court decided that the most suitable way of remedying the unequal treatment was to reduce the fines for the Japanese applicants.[303]

Rather than mandating total equality, the EU principle of equal treatment requires that any difference in treatment is proportionate to the difference in circumstances. In reviewing the 'equality' of Commission fines, the General Court takes a practical approach and allows the Commission to categorise punishable circumstances and concomitant fines in various bands of severity.[304] Review of this division is limited to its coherence and objective justification.[305] In fact, the General Court seems to put more weight on the proportionality of a sanction than on the equality of sanctions.[306]

Total equality need not be ensured for yet another reason. The Court of Justice has held on numerous occasions that the Commission's practice in previous decisions cannot itself serve as a legal framework for the imposition of fines in competition matters. Decisions in other cases can only give an indication of (in)equality since the facts of those cases are not likely to be the same or sufficiently similar. More importantly, undertakings must take into account that within the statutory limits, fining levels may be increased at any time.[307] Even the application of different calculation methods to contemporaneous infringements as a consequence of

irrelevant, since it was not necessary for it to intervene. Thus, the fact referred to by the applicant was not the result of its choice, but a mere consequence of the nature of its participation in the agreement relating to the EEA market. On the other hand, that same participation was a prerequisite for ensuring that the allocation of GIS projects in the EEA could be carried out among the European producers in accordance with the rules agreed to that effect.'

301 *JFE Engineering* (n 299) [570]–[573].

302 ibid [578].

303 ibid [579].

304 *cf Tokai Carbon (Graphite Electrodes)* (n 58).

305 Case T-26/02 *Daiichi Pharmaceuticals* [2006] ECR II-713 [85].

306 Case T-303/02 *Westfalen Gassen* [2006] ECR II-4567 [174].

307 *cf Britannia Alloys & Chemicals* (n 188) [60]–[61]; Joined Cases 100–03/80 *Musique Diffusion française* [1983] ECR 1825.

the date of the decision has not been considered contrary to the EU principle of equal treatment.[308]

Undertakings cannot escape being punished on the ground that another trader, not subject to the proceedings, has not been punished either.[309] This limitation follows from *Peróxidos Orgánicos*,[310] where the General Court accorded priority to legality over equality. In the words of the General Court:

> A possible unlawful act committed with regard to another undertaking, which is not party to the present proceedings, cannot induce the Court to find that it is discriminatory and, therefore, unlawful with regard to the applicant. Such an approach would be tantamount to laying down a principle of 'equal treatment in illegality' and to requiring the Commission, in the present case, to disregard the evidence in its possession to sanction the undertaking which has committed a punishable infringement, solely on the ground that another undertaking which may find itself in a comparable situation has unlawfully escaped being penalised. In addition, as is clear from the case-law on the principle of equal treatment, where an undertaking has acted in breach of Article 81(1) EC [now Article 101(1) TFEU], it cannot escape being penalised altogether on the ground that other undertakings have not been fined, where, as in this case, those undertakings' circumstances are not the subject of proceedings before the Court.[311]

While the Court's line of reasoning raises some questions – why would it be unlawful for an undertaking to escape penalisation when the Commission's enforcement powers are discretionary? – it is clear that undertakings cannot rely on the principle of equality to dispute the legality of the sanction.

Centralisation Effects

Subject to the same relaxations as the Commission, the Member States should also have regard to the principle of equal treatment in the enforcement of EU competition law. They may not treat similar situations differently and different situations similarly unless there would be an objective justification for such treatment. In the enforcement of Articles 101 and 102 TFEU, NCAs should ensure equal treatment with regard to every single element that adds to the severity of the sanction. In this respect, the EU principle of equal treatment limits the Member States' sanctioning autonomy and contributes to a uniform body of procedural rules. However, just like the Commission, the NCAs may also apply the principle of equal treatment with a certain flexibility and categorise punishable circumstances and concomitant penalties in various bands of severity. Similarly, the EU principle of equal treatment does not prevent NCAs from raising the level of fines or from going after some undertakings while not bothering with others. Consistent with most of the sanctioning principles deriving from the EU fundamental rights,

[308] *Archer Daniels Midland* (n 203) [28]–[32]. *cf Musique Diffusion française* (n 307).

[309] Joined Cases C-89, C-104, C-116, C-117 and C-125–29/85 *Ahlström Osakeyhtiö* [1993] ECR I-1307 [197].

[310] Case T-120/04 *Peróxidos Orgánicos* [2006] ECR II-4441.

[311] ibid [77].

the principle of equal treatment leaves the Member States entirely free in terms of choosing the appropriate sanctioning powers.

4.6 SANCTIONING PRINCIPLES IN THE DUTY OF SINCERE COOPERATION

4.6.1 Introduction

To the extent that EU law does not provide specific rules for the enforcement of Articles 101 and 102 TFEU, Member States may rely on home-grown approaches.[312] Outside the realm of Regulation 1/2003 (see above, section 2.3) and the EU sanctioning principles detailed in the previous three sections, Member States may thus experiment and organise their sanctioning regime in accordance with domestic preferences. However, in enjoying this sanctioning autonomy, Member States cannot disregard their role and responsibility with regard to the administration of EU law. Member States therefore remain subject to the general EU duty of sincere cooperation.[313] In accordance with Article 4(3) TEU:

> [T]he Union and the Member States shall, in full mutual respect, assist each other in carrying out tasks which flow from the Treaties.
>
> The Member States shall take any appropriate measure, general or particular, to ensure fulfilment of the obligations arising out of the Treaties or resulting from the acts of the institutions of the Union.
>
> The Member States shall facilitate the achievement of the Union's tasks and refrain from any measure which could jeopardise the attainment of the Union's objectives.

This duty of sincere cooperation applies to all areas of EU activity and is the single most important rule in the relation between EU and national institutions. It applies to all national authorities, whether executive, legislative or judicial and whether central, regional or local.[314] The duty of sincere cooperation can be seen as a panacea for problems with the implementation of EU law in the national legal orders. It reconciles the EU principle of subsidiarity with the EU interests of uniform and effective application. The duties of the Member States under Article 4(3) TEU find their limits in the rule of law. This provision cannot create *de novo* obligations; it can only build upon and reinforce existing EU obligations.[315]

[312] *Tele2 Polska* (n 260) [33].

[313] Case 68/88 *Commission v Greece (Greek Maize)* [1989] ECR 2965 [23].

[314] J Temple Lang, 'Community Constitutional Law: Article 5 EEC Treaty' (1990) 27 *Common Market Law Review* 645.

[315] *cf* Case 229/86 *Brother Industries* [1987] ECR 3757. Although the duty of sincere cooperation cannot create de novo obligations, it can have far-reaching implications for the division of powers within the Member States; see *Penycoed* (n 192); *Consorzio Industrie Fiammiferi* (n 18).

A Variety of Duties

The requirements under Article 4(3) TEU are not readily cognisable. They have to be inferred from a vast body of case law, dealing with various policy areas and different implementation issues. EU case law on Article 4(3) TEU could be categorised in various ways.[316] With regard to the enforcement of EU competition law, it seems helpful to divide the cases into three categories.

First, the duty of sincere cooperation safeguards *rights* that have been granted by EU law. In the absence of specific EU rules, it is for the domestic legal system of each Member State to designate the courts and tribunals having jurisdiction and to lay down the detailed procedural rules governing actions for safeguarding rights that derive from EU law.[317] This principle of procedural autonomy is limited by the duty of sincere cooperation. As a result, the national procedural rules must neither be less favourable than those governing similar domestic actions (the principle of equivalence) nor render virtually impossible or excessively difficult the exercise of EU rights (the principle of effectiveness).[318]

Second, the duty of sincere cooperation reinforces *obligations* imposed by EU law. Insofar as EU obligations are not complemented by specific implementation requirements, it is for the Member States to ensure the implementation in accordance with the procedural and substantive rules of national law.[319] The duty of sincere cooperation places the Member States under a duty to take all appropriate measures, whether general or specific, to ensure the fulfilment of this obligation.[320] More specifically, this duty requires the adoption of effective, proportionate and – if needed – dissuasive measures that are no less favourable than those applicable to comparable situations wholly governed by national law.[321]

Third, the duty of sincere cooperation requires the Commission and the national institutions to work together in good faith with a view to overcoming implementation difficulties, ie, to facilitate institutional cooperation. This is a mutual obligation: the national institutions are required to assist the Commission[322] and the

[316] Temple Lang (n 314); J Temple Lang, 'The Development by the Court of Justice of the Duties of Cooperation of National Authorities and Community Institutions under Article 10 EC' (2007–08) 31 *Fordham International Law Journal* 1482.

[317] Case 120/73 *Lorenz* [1973] ECR 1471.

[318] Case 33/76 *Rewe* [1976] ECR 1989; Case 45/76 *Comet* [1976] ECR 2043; Joined Cases C-430/93 and C-431/93 *Van Schijndel and Van Veen* [1995] ECR I-4705. A national rule or practice which prevents the national courts from safeguarding rights deriving from the direct effect of EU law altogether (even temporarily) would prevent these provisions of EU law from having full force and effect and would be contrary to the EU principle of priority; *cf Simmenthal* (n 15); Case C-221/89 *Factortame II* [1990] ECR I-2433; Case C-453/99 *Courage v Crehan* [2001] ECR I-6297.

[319] Joined Cases 51–54/71 *International Fruit Company* [1971] ECR 1107.

[320] Case 3/73 *Hessische Mehlindustrie Karl Schöttler* [1973] ECR 745; *Royer* (n 114); Case 50/76 *Amsterdam Bulb* [1977] ECR 137; Joined Cases 205–15/82 *Deutsche Milchkontor* [1983] ECR 2633.

[321] *cf* Joined Cases 146, 192 and 193/81 *BayWa* [1982] ECR 1503; *Deutsche Milchkontor* (n 320); Case 14/83 *Von Colson and Kamann* [1984] ECR 1891; *Commission v Greece (Greek Maize)* (n 313).

[322] Case 94/87 *Commission v Germany (Illegal State Aid)* [1989] ECR 175; Case C-234/89 *Delimitis* [1991] ECR I-935; Case C-344/98 *Masterfoods* [2000] ECR I-11369; Case C-94/00 *Roquette Frères* [2002] ECR I-9011.

Commission is required to assist the national institutions in the implementation of EU law.[323]

Sincere Cooperation in Relation to EU Rights and EU Obligations: A Principled Distinction

The impact of Article 4(3) TEU on the autonomy of the Member States differs according to whether Member States need to enforce EU *obligations* or to facilitate the enforcement of EU *rights*. In the context of EU competition law, the enforcement of EU obligations relates to the duty of NCAs to proceed against infringements of Articles 101 and 102 TFEU. Facilitating the enforcement of EU rights relates to the private enforcement of EU competition law. While a principled distinction is not generally made in the legal literature,[324] various differences can be observed with regard to Member States' duties in relation to EU obligations and EU rights.[325] In this respect, it should be noted that the duty of sincere cooperation in the context of EU rights is closely linked to the concept of direct effect. Precisely this concept has left deep incursions in the division of competences at a national level.[326] Although the concept of direct effect is not irrelevant in the context of the enforcement of EU obligations either – private parties may rely on EU rights of a procedural nature (eg, fundamental rights) to fend off enforcement actions – it mainly serves to reinforce substantive EU rights (eg, the right to claim for damages under Article 101 TFEU). In any case, enforcement obligations resting on the Member States have no direct effect.[327]

[323] Case 2/88 *IMM Zwartveld* [1990] ECR 3365; Case T-353/94 *Postbank* [1996] ECR II-921.

[324] *cf* K Lenaerts, D Arts and I Maselis, *Procedural Law of the European Union* 2nd edn (Sweet & Maxwell, 2006) 3-003: 'Art.10 of the EC Treaty [now Article 4(3) TEU] places national courts and tribunals under a duty to ensure the "full effectiveness of Community law". The Court of Justice has defined this duty by means of a number of Community constraints with which national procedural law and law relating to sanctions must comply. Those constraints (the principles of equivalence and effectiveness) are a practical expression of the principles of the primacy and direct effect of Community law and aim at enabling individuals to claim before national courts the *full* enforcement and protection of the rights which they derive from Community law' (footnotes omitted). See also Temple Lang, 'The Development by the Court of Justice of the Duties of Cooperation' (n 316); S Prechal, 'EC Requirements for an Effective Remedy' in J Lonbay and A Biondi (eds), *Remedies for Breach of EC Law* (John Wiley & Sons, 1997) 3.

[325] One of the few authors who does make a principled distinction between the enforcement of EU obligations and EU rights for the purposes of the duty of sincere cooperation (or rather the principle of effectiveness) is Dougan. In fact, Dougan even makes a further distinction in relation to the enforcement of EU rights. The requirement of effectiveness would be different when an individual exercises EU-based claims against a public authority than when these claims are exercised against another individual. See M Dougan, *National Remedies Before the Court of Justice: Issues of Harmonisation and Differentation* (Hart Publishing, 2004) 26–52. In addition, AG Bot has made a principled distinction between the enforcement of EU obligations and EU rights for the purposes of the principle of effectiveness. See Case C-455/06 *Heemskerk and Schaap* [2008] ECR I-8763, Opinion of AG Bot [122] et seq.

[326] *cf Fratelli Costanzo* (n 18); Joined Cases 143/88 and 92/89 *Zuckerfabrik* [1991] ECR I-415; *Factortame II* (n 318).

[327] See also Oliver (n 21) 371.

The wording and working of the principles deriving from the duty of sincere cooperation are different, depending on whether domestic procedures foster the enforcement of EU rights or EU obligations. First, whereas the enforcement of EU obligations is governed by the principles of equivalence, effectiveness, proportionality and dissuasiveness, the enforcement of EU rights is governed by the principles of equivalence and effectiveness alone.[328] Second, the conditions under the principle of effectiveness are different for each of the two enforcement trajectories.[329] The Court of Justice seems more demanding of Member States when it comes to EU rights than when it comes to EU obligations.[330] Third, the implications of the principle of equivalence can be different. Where an EU right is at stake, the principle of equivalence may in very exceptional circumstances limit the enforcement actions of national authorities.[331]

For the purposes of this study, mainly the second category is relevant – the duty of sincere cooperation as a reinforcement of EU obligations. This means that the Court's elaborations in *Greek Maize*[332] are crucial in understanding the EU sanctioning principles deriving from the duty of sincere cooperation. In *Greek Maize*, the dispute centred on the measures to be taken by the Greek government against importers of maize fraudulently withholding import levies from the EU budget. The Court considered that Member States are bound under Article 4(3) TEU to give effect to the principles of equivalence, effectiveness, proportionality and dissuasiveness.[333] Later cases have clarified the scope of application of these prin-

[328] *cf* Joined Cases C-295–98/04 *Manfredi* [2006] ECR I-6619, where the Court of Justice limited its assessment on the necessity (and compatibility with EU law) of punitive *damages* for infringements of EU competition law to the principles of effectiveness and equivalence. The Court concluded that Member States are not under an inherent EU obligation to provide for punitive damages. If the enforcement of EU rights would have been subject to the principle of dissuasiveness, another outcome might have been expected.

[329] *cf Heemskerk and Schaap* (n 325), Opinion of AG Bot [122] et seq.

[330] For the enforcement of EU obligations, the principle of effectiveness is formulated positively, requiring Member States to penalise effectively. For the enforcement of EU rights, the Court of Justice requires Member States not to make the exercise of EU rights virtually impossible or excessively difficult. This suggests that the Court applies a negative test in relation to the latter. While the intensity with which the Court applies the principle of effectiveness indeed differs, the intensity of application does not track the phrasing of the principle. Notwithstanding the negatively formulated requirement in relation to EU rights, the Court has not shied away from superimposing private law remedies on the Member States. See Case C-213/89 *Factortame I* [1990] ECR I-2433; *Courage v Crehan* (n 318); Case C-253/00 *Muñoz* [2002] ECR I-7289. This somewhat activistic approach has often been motivated by the desire to ensure the direct effect of EU rights. Paradoxically, the Court has been rather reticent in superimposing sanctions onto the Member States for the enforcement of EU obligations. See Case C-265/95 *Commission v France (Spanish Strawberries)* [1997] ECR I-6959; Case C-36/94 *Siesse* [1995] ECR I-3573; Case C-213/99 *De Andrade* [2000] ECR I-11083.

[331] *cf* Case C-34/02 *Pasquini* [2003] ECR I-6515.

[332] *Commission v Greece (Greek Maize)* (n 313).

[333] ibid. See also *Siesse* (n 330); *De Andrade* (n 330); Case C-382/09 *Stils Met* [2010] ECR I-9315. In earlier cases the Court was less specific and required the Member States to provide for 'appropriate' penal-

ciples. First, the *Greek Maize* principles apply in situations where EU legislation does not mention enforcement at all or where EU legislation only leaves the Member States some discretion in the organisation of enforcement. Second, these principles apply in disputes over whether a Member State uses appropriate means to enforce EU law[334] and in disputes over whether a Member State has (un)lawfully extended the scope of EU legislation.[335] Considering the system of shared administration in the area of EU competition law, the *Greek Maize* principles apply a fortiori to the enforcement of Articles 101 and 102 TFEU.

A closer examination of the principles articulated in *Greek Maize* allows for the following categorisation:

(i) Member States must ensure that infringements of EU law are penalised under procedural conditions analogous to those that are applicable to infringements of national law of a similar nature and importance.
(ii) Member States must ensure that infringements of EU law are penalised under substantive conditions analogous to those that are applicable to infringements of national law of a similar nature and importance.
(iii) Member States must ensure that infringements of EU law are penalised under procedural conditions that make the penalty effective, proportionate and dissuasive.
(iv) Member States must ensure that infringements of EU law are penalised under substantive conditions that make the penalty effective, proportionate and dissuasive.

In subsequent cases, the Court has applied these principles to different types of sanctions, eg, fines,[336] confiscation orders,[337] surcharges[338] and compensatory payments.[339] This suggests that the *Greek Maize* principles extend beyond penalties and apply to sanctions for infringements of EU law more generally. For the purposes of this study, the terms 'procedural conditions' and 'substantive conditions', as used by the Court in *Greek Maize*, are understood as covering both sanctioning procedures and sanctioning powers.

The following four sections will detail the implications of the principles of equivalence, effectiveness, dissuasiveness and proportionality for the sanctioning autonomy of the Member States with regard to Articles 101 and 102 TFEU.

ties; *cf* Case 50/76 *Amsterdam Bulb* (n 320) [32]–[33]; Joined Cases 205–15/82 *Deutsche Milchkontor* (n 320) [18].

[334] *Commission v Greece (Greek Maize)* (n 313); Case C-7/90 *Vandevenne* [1991] ECR I-4371; Case C-354/99 *Commission v Ireland (Animal Protection)* [2001] ECR I-7657; Case C-382/92 *Commission v UK (Transfer of Undertaking)* [1994] ECR I-2435; Case C-383/92 *Commission v UK (Collective Redundancies)* [1994] ECR I-2479.

[335] *De Andrade* (n 330); *Siesse* (n 330); *Hansen* (n 293); *Ebony Maritime* (n 293).

[336] *Commission v Ireland (Animal Protection)* (n 334).

[337] *Ebony Maritime* (n 293).

[338] *Siesse* (n 330); *De Andrade* (n 330).

[339] *Commission v UK (Transfer of Undertaking)* (n 334); *Commission v UK (Collective Redundancies)* (n 334).

4.6.2 The Principle of Equivalence

The principle of equivalence essentially prohibits discrimination against EU law. Member States must ensure that infringements of EU law are terminated and penalised under conditions, both procedural and substantive, which are analogous to those applicable to infringements of national law of a similar nature and importance. The principle of equivalence is an autonomous legal principle that should be respected, irrespective of whether EU law is enforced effectively.[340]

The application of this principle raises the question as to what the domestic law equivalent should be against which to assess sanctions for infringements of EU competition law. As long as Member States operate a regime of national competition law, this question seems to have been resolved by the Court of Justice in *Manfredi*.[341] Applying the principle of equivalence in a private enforcement context, the Court considered:

> [I]t is for the domestic legal system of each Member State to designate the courts and tribunals having jurisdiction to hear actions for damages based on an infringement of the Community competition rules and to prescribe the detailed rules governing those actions, provided that the provisions concerned are not less favourable than those governing actions for damages based on an infringement of national competition rules.[342]

In a similar vein, it can be argued that sanctions for infringements of EU competition law should be equivalent to sanctions for infringements of national competition law.[343] This of course raises the question of what qualifies as national *competition* law and who should have the final say on this matter: the Court of Justice or the Member States? In practice, it is not always clear whether or not a particular sanction forms part of national competition law and therefore whether that sanction should be available for EU competition law. For example, the UK government has argued that the criminal cartel offence does not form part of national competition law.[344] This argument was made not so much to deprive EU competition law from particular sanctions, but rather to justify that criminal procedures under UK law may run alongside the administrative procedures of the Commission. However, this discussion does make clear that it is not always obvious what qualifies as national competition law. Issues of this kind have not yet reached the Court of Justice.

[340] Case C-326/96 *Levez v Jennings* [1998] ECR I-7835 [38].

[341] *Manfredi* (n 328).

[342] ibid [72].

[343] This interpretation is less obvious than it appears. It could be argued that the nature and importance of EU competition law cannot be equated with national competition law. First, unlike national competition law, EU competition law also has a market integration objective. Second, the importance of EU competition law for the EU legal order exceeds the importance normally accorded to national competition law; *cf Eco Swiss* (n 32). Therefore, it has been suggested in the legal literature that the maximum sanctions available for infringements of EU competition law might have to be even more severe than those available for national competition law; see Oliver (n 21) 367–68.

[344] Department for Business, Innovation & Skills, *Growth, Competition and the Competition Regime: Government Response to Consultation* (2012) para 7.30 <www.bis.gov.uk/Consultations/competition-regime-for-growth> accessed 1 July 2013.

Like all other principles deriving from the duty of sincere cooperation, the principle of equivalence only applies in the absence of specific EU legislation. As a result, this principle requires Member States to enforce EU competition law with measures equivalent to those prevailing in national competition law, provided that these measures are compatible with EU legislation. This caveat can be clarified with the help of *Tele2 Polska*.[345] In this case, the Court of Justice prohibited NCAs from using certain measures in the enforcement of EU competition law (the adoption of a negative decision on the merits) for being contrary to the wording, scheme and objectives of Regulation 1/2003, even though this measure was available for the enforcement of national competition law (see above, section 2.3). The more general conclusion may be drawn that the duty of sincere cooperation laid down in Article 4(3) TEU can only supplement existing requirements under EU legislation and cannot amend these.

Centralisation Effects

The principle of equivalence limits the sanctioning autonomy of the Member States. The latter may not reserve particular sanctioning powers (for instance, appropriate but costly sanctions) solely for infringements of national competition law. While this principle narrows down the autonomy of the Member States, it does *not* force a 'foreign' sanction onto the Member States and therefore does not lead to more uniformity throughout the EU. After all, it only requires the Member States to align their sanctioning powers and procedures for infringements of Articles 101 and 102 TFEU to those for infringements of national competition law.

4.6.3 The Principle of Effectiveness

The duty of sincere cooperation further contains a principle of effectiveness. This principle is capable of limiting the sanctioning autonomy of the Member States and it may even lead to more uniformity throughout the EU. The implications of this principle cannot be determined in the abstract. Effective sanctioning in one area of EU law could mean that as many infringements as possible should be terminated and punished, whereas in other areas, case prioritisation may take place without jeopardising the effectiveness of EU law. Effective sanctioning will therefore have a different meaning with regard to, for instance, the EU fisheries policy than with regard to EU competition law. Another important circumstance for the implications of the principle of effectiveness is that the EU is neither solely relying on the Member States nor on public enforcement to implement its competition policy. After all, the Commission may initiate enforcement actions too and private parties may always bring a case under Article 101 or 102 TFEU before the national courts. The competition authorities of the Member States therefore need

[345] *Tele2 Polska* (n 260).

not act upon every infringement in order to maintain an effective competition policy.[346] Such discretion may be less desirable in other fields of EU law, notably those where there is no private enforcement alternative. But even within the context of EU competition law, the implications of the principle of effectiveness are case-specific. Different types of anti-competitive behaviour warrant different types of sanctions.[347]

Flexibility

Before detailing the specific requirements in the area of competition law sanctions, it should be pointed out that the principle of effectiveness leaves the Member States with considerable flexibility. NCAs are not under any inherent EU obligation to terminate or penalise every (intentional or negligent) infringement.[348] Instead, they should be considered to enjoy the same margin of discretion as the Commission. In *Automec II*, it was decided that the Commission may prioritise cases and need not go after every potential infringement.[349] In addition, it follows from *Visa* that the Commission's margin of discretion in setting the amount of the fine 'extends, necessarily, to deciding whether or not it is appropriate to impose a fine'.[350] It is in the specific context of each case that the Commission decides whether it is appropriate to impose a fine in order to penalise the infringement and protect the effectiveness of competition law.[351] There is no reason to assume that the NCAs would be subject to stricter requirements than the Commission in this respect.

This flexibility under the principle of effectiveness extends to the type of sanctions that can be imposed for infringements of Articles 101 and 102 TFEU. This follows from *Nunes*, where the Court of Justice was asked to decide whether a Member State is empowered to impose criminal penalties for conduct which only attracts a sanction of a civil law nature under EU law.[352] It should be recalled that the *Greek Maize* principles not only apply in disputes over whether a Member State has used the appropriate means to enforce EU law, but also in disputes over whether a Member State has (un)lawfully extended the scope of EU law. Against this background, the Court concluded:

[346] *cf Automec II* (n 98).

[347] *cf* I Simonsson, *Legitimacy in EU Cartel Control* (Hart Publishing, 2010) 18, who even argues: 'it . . . seems unlikely that effectiveness means the same thing when referred to in various parts of the Regulation [1/2003]. Effectiveness of fines must be interpreted in relation to the case law on sanctions as developed by the Community Courts. When effectiveness is used as the legal basis for regulating burden of proof and fact-finding in Regulation 1[/2003], it must be understood in the light of the abundant case law on rights of defence'.

[348] Although NCAs are not under any inherent EU obligation to terminate or penalise every (intentional or negligent) infringement, their prosecutorial discretion is not unlimited. In fact, in *Bundeswettbewerbsbehörde v Schenker*, the Court concluded that 'the national competition authorities must proceed by way of exception only not to impose a fine where an undertaking has infringed that provision intentionally or negligently': *Bundeswettbewerbsbehörde v Schenker* (n 28) [46].

[349] *Automec II* (n 98).

[350] *Visa* (n 213) [212].

[351] Joined Cases T-213/95 and T-18/96 *SCK and FNK* [1997] ECR II-1739 [239]; *Visa* (n 213) [218].

[352] Case C-186/98 *Nunes and de Matos* [1999] ECR I-4883.

> [T]hat Article 5 of the Treaty [now Article 4(3) TEU] requires the Member States to take all effective measures to sanction conduct which affects the financial interests of the Community. Such measures may include criminal penalties even where the Community legislation only provides for civil sanctions. The sanction provided for must be analogous to those applicable to infringements of national law of similar nature and importance, and must be effective, proportionate and dissuasive.[353]

It follows that the mere fact that Regulation 1/2003 grants particular sanctioning powers to the Commission and qualifies these as non-criminal[354] does not circumscribe the sanctioning possibilities of the Member States. The latter may, for instance, decide to enforce Articles 101 and 102 TFEU by means of custodial sanctions. In fact, Regulation 1/2003 even anticipates that national sanctioning powers will deviate from the Commission's powers.[355] More generally, it can be concluded that considerations of effectiveness normally will not force specific sanctions onto the Member States.[356]

Notwithstanding the above conclusions, it should be noted that particular forms of liability may be superimposed on the Member States by the EU legislator precisely to ensure that EU law is fully effective and to take away potential distortions of competition. While the Court of Justice has excluded the harmonisation of penalties in the area of competition law on the basis of Article 103(2)(a) TFEU,[357] this seems nonetheless possible on the basis of Article 114 and/or Article 83(2) TFEU. On the basis of Article 114 TFEU, the EU legislator may adopt measures for the approximation of the provisions laid down by law, regulation or administrative action in Member States which have as their object the establishment and functioning of the *internal market*. In accordance with Protocol (No 27) on the Internal Market and Competition, the internal market includes a system ensuring that competition is not distorted. Accordingly, the harmonisation of penalties in the area of EU competition law on the basis of Article 114 TFEU is possible if this is needed to ensure that competition is not distorted. This interpretation is confirmed by *Tobacco Advertising*,[358] *Framework Decision Environmental Crimes*[359] and *Framework Decision Ship-Source Pollution*.[360] On the basis of Article 83(2) TFEU, the EU legislator may adopt directives with minimum rules with regard to the definition of criminal offences and sanctions, should this be necessary to ensure the effective implementation of an EU policy in any area which has been subject to harmonisation measures.

[353] ibid [14].
[354] Article 23(5) of Regulation 1/2003.
[355] Article 12 of Regulation 1/2003 contains specific rules for the transmission of information to jurisdictions that provide custodial sanctions for infringements of EU competition law (see above, section 2.4).
[356] *Vandevenne* (n 334).
[357] Case C-240/90 *Germany v Commission (Exclusion from Subsidy Schemes)* [1992] ECR I-5383 [23].
[358] *cf* Case C-376/98 *Germany v European Parliament and Council (Tobacco Advertising)* [2000] ECR I-2247.
[359] Case C-176/03 *Commission v Council (Framework Decision Environmental Crimes)* [2005] ECR I-7879.
[360] Case C-440/05 *Commission v Council (Framework Decision Ship-Source Pollution)* [2007] ECR I-9097.

It could be argued that Article 83(2) TFEU also provides a legal basis for the adoption of directives with minimum rules with regard to *criminal* sanctions in the area of EU competition law.

Sanctioning Principles

The principle of effectiveness requires Member States to terminate and penalise infringements of Articles 101 and 102 TFEU effectively. Both national legislators and NCAs should take note of this requirement. The former should provide for effective sanctioning powers, while the latter should use these powers effectively. What constitutes an effective sanction for the purposes of Article 4(3) TEU depends on the type of anti-competitive behaviour and the circumstances of the case. It is suggested that persisting infringements, whether as a consequence of the undertaking's behaviour or its very structure, require a remedy that effectively terminates the infringement. How this is achieved seems less important. A cease-and-desist order together with a sufficiently severe penalty payment and attached to a well-reasoned decision establishing the infringement may be as effective as an order stating positively what commercial changes are to be made (divestitures, compulsory licensing etc).

In any case, considerations of effectiveness would appear to require Member States to provide for interim measures where appropriate. In *Camera Care*,[361] the Court of Justice accepted that the Commission could adopt interim measures even though this power had not been granted explicitly. A decisive factor for the Court in reaching this conclusion was that this power had not been excluded explicitly and that it had to be avoided that the exercise of powers that had been granted explicitly to the Commission – powers to bring to an end any infringement – were rendered ineffectual or illusory.[362] Moreover, the Court found the possibility of adopting protective interim measures necessary in view of the efficacy of competition law and the protection of the legitimate interests of Member States and undertakings.[363] In light of these considerations, one may argue that Member States cannot make do without interim measures either.

It is further submitted that intentional and negligent infringements, whether persisting or terminated, require a penalty that punishes the offender and acts as an effective deterrent. Precisely for the enforcement of Articles 101 and 102 TFEU, the Court of Justice has underpinned the importance of penalties and notably fines.[364] Moreover, the conditions for liability may not be overly strict. In the context of Commission procedures, the Court of Justice has been keen to limit the thresholds for liability. The effectiveness of EU competition law would be com-

[361] Case 792/79 R *Camera Care* [1980] ECR 119.

[362] ibid [15]–[18].

[363] ibid.

[364] Case C-429/07 *Inspecteur van de Belastingdienst v X BV* [2009] ECR I-4833 [36]–[37]. Articles 101 and 102 TFEU would be ineffective if they were not accompanied by fines and the effectiveness of penalties is a condition for the coherent application of these prohibitions.

promised if these conditions were too demanding. Accordingly, in *Volkswagen*,[365] the Court accepted a rather low threshold for intent – an alternative condition for the Commission's penalty power and a variable for the amount of the fine. Intent can already be established without having to identify the persons who acted improperly within the undertaking or who ought to have been held responsible for any defective organisation of the undertaking.[366] In the light of *Volkswagen*, it can be argued that the need to penalise infringements of Articles 101 and 102 TFEU effectively prevents the Member States from applying overly demanding conditions.[367] Whether a penalty is imposed on a natural person or a legal person and whether this penalty is of an administrative or criminal law nature remains within the sanctioning autonomy of the Member States.

The Principle of Effectiveness and Leniency

It has been argued in the literature that whichever penalty a Member State ultimately imposes, the duty of sincere cooperation requires it to mitigate this penalty in relation to whistleblowing cartel participants. More precisely, Member States would have to mitigate their penalties in relation to undertakings that have successfully applied for leniency in another jurisdiction within the EU.[368] Undertakings would be dissuaded from breaking ranks and confess their cartel involvement to one authority if faced with full and hefty fines in other jurisdictions. This would seriously interfere with the EU objective of improving the effectiveness of EU competition law and could frustrate the Commission's leniency policy, as well as those of the NCAs. Therefore, the duty of sincere cooperation would require NCAs (and possibly also the Commission) to take into account successful leniency applications in other jurisdictions within the EU and to mitigate the penalty otherwise imposed.[369] As to the practical working of this obligation, Temple Lang has further suggested that:

> [I]t would have to be an obligation to reduce any national fine which would otherwise be imposed by a percentage corresponding to the reduction given by the Commission. No other obligation would make sense.[370]

This interpretation of the duty of sincere cooperation would introduce a one-stop-shop for leniency in the EU through the backdoor of the principle of effectiveness. It would also imply that Member States are required to operate a leniency programme of their own.[371] By way of background, it should be noted that the

[365] Case C-338/00 P *Volkswagen* [2003] ECR I-9189.
[366] ibid [98].
[367] See also Simonsson (n 347) 309; Oliver (n 21) 367.
[368] J Temple Lang, 'The Implications of the Commission's Leniency Policy for National Competition Authorities' (2003) 28 *European Law Review* 430; Simonsson (n 347) 274–75.
[369] Temple Lang (n 368) 431–32.
[370] ibid 432.
[371] Indeed, Simonsson has suggested that Member States have to operate a leniency programme of their own: Simonsson (n 347) 306.

Court of Justice has recognised that leniency programmes are useful tools and thus serve the objective of the effective application of Articles 101 TFEU and 102 TFEU.[372] In addition, the Commission and the NCAs have recognised the importance of leniency programmes throughout the entire EU and have drafted and published an ECN Model Leniency Programme. This model coordinates the various leniency programmes, but does not provide for a one-stop-shop.

It is debatable whether such an extensive interpretation of the duty of sincere cooperation is justified. First, it breaks with consistent EU case law that Article 4(3) TEU can only reinforce existing requirements. Second, it would be difficult to reconcile with the idea behind Regulation 1/2003, as it would effectively limit the competences of the NCAs in starting parallel proceedings. Third, it is entirely speculative that a one-stop-shop for leniency makes the programme substantially more effective – it would of course reduce costs for undertakings and taxpayers. More importantly, this extensive interpretation of the duty of sincere cooperation has not found resonance with the Court of Justice. Member States' requirements in relation to leniency have been touched upon in *Pfleiderer*, where the Court held:

> [W]hile the establishment and application of those rules [on leniency] falls within the competence of the Member States, the latter must none the less exercise that competence in accordance with European Union law . . . In particular, they may not render the implementation of European Union law impossible or excessively difficult . . . and, specifically, in the area of competition law, they must ensure that the rules which they establish or apply do not jeopardise the effective application of Articles 101 TFEU and 102 TFEU.[373]

While the Court has therefore accepted that leniency programmes are useful tools to uncover and bring to an end infringements of Articles 101 and 102 TFEU,[374] it has unmistakenly found that the Member States are entirely free in deciding whether or not to operate a leniency programme of their own. If anything, the Court has held that the principle of effectiveness requires Member States *not* to mitigate fines. In *Bundeswettbewerbsbehörde v Schenker*, the Court held that a decision not to impose a fine can be made under a national leniency programme only insofar as the programme is implemented in such a way as not to undermine the requirement of the effective and uniform application of Article 101 TFEU.[375] It then determined that 'immunity from or not imposing a fine . . . can be accorded in strictly exceptional situations only, such as where an undertaking's cooperation has been decisive in detecting and actually suppressing the cartel'.[376]

[372] Case C-536/11 *Bundeswettbewerbsbehörde v Donau Chemie* [2012] OJ C13/5 [42].
[373] Case C-360/09 *Pfleiderer* [2011] ECR I-5161 [24].
[374] ibid [25].
[375] *Bundeswettbewerbsbehörde v Schenker* (n 28) [47].
[376] ibid [49].

Centralisation Effects

It follows from the above that while the Member States retain considerable flexibility under the principle of effectiveness, their sanctioning autonomy is nonetheless reduced. NCAs should be able to terminate every type of infringement, whatever its causes. This means that they should even be able to terminate infringements that are the result of the undertaking's very structure. Whether they do so through a positive order for structural changes or a negative order with regard to 'structural infringements' seems less important. Furthermore, they should be able to adopt interim measures pending the investigation in order to ensure that the objective of the investigations is not compromised. Finally, they should be able to impose deterrent penalties under conditions that are not overly strict. This requirement to provide for deterrent penalties is subject to further EU conditions, which will be detailed directly below.

4.6.4 The Principle of Dissuasiveness

Member States must ensure that infringements of EU law are penalised under procedural and substantive conditions which make the penalty dissuasive. Occasionally, a Member State is criticised for failing this requirement.[377] This requirement, which could be referred to either as the principle of dissuasiveness or the principle of deterrence, also applies to infringements of EU competition law. Member States should ensure that undertakings are dissuaded from committing infringements of Articles 101 and 102 TFEU. Sanctions that are not able to change the undertakings' intent or to induce them to take the requisite precautionary measures do not dissuade. Logically, the requirement to provide for dissuasive sanctions applies solely to infringements committed intentionally or negligently. Undertakings acting contrary to EU competition law in good faith may be corrected by means of a sanction, but simply cannot be dissuaded. The Court of Justice has insisted that infringements that are harmful both to competition and to the attainment of the EU's greater internal market objectives (eg, market-sharing and boycotts) especially require a dissuasive sanction.[378]

Penalties for infringements of Articles 101 and 102 TFEU should dissuade both the offender and society at large.[379] These objectives are commonly referred to as special (or specific) deterrence and general deterrence. The adequate level of special deterrence should be determined on the basis of the undertaking's characteristics. This follows from *Microsoft*, where the General Court took into consideration Microsoft Corp's current and future economic capacity, its capabilities for engaging

[377] *Commission v Ireland (Animal Protection)* (n 334); *Commission v UK (Transfer of Undertaking)* (n 334); *Commission v UK (Collective Redundancies)* (n 334).

[378] *Musique Diffusion française* (n 307) [105]–[106].

[379] *Showa Denko* (n 275) [16].

in new infringements and its prior convictions in other jurisdictions.[380] Special deterrence further requires that the undertakings' characteristics are considered as they were at the end of the infringement rather than at any earlier point in time.[381] The objective of special deterrence further requires that any earlier infringement of EU competition law (recidivism) is taken into account.[382] The objective of general deterrence requires the severity of the penalty to be assessed not solely by reference to the particular situation of the undertaking.[383] This objective has the effect of raising the severity of the penalty as not every infringement will be penalised.[384] The undertakings that are caught bear the costs of this objective by having to sustain a more severe penalty than would have been needed to deter them from committing infringements in the future. Indeed, in the application of the principle of dissuasiveness, regard may be had to the frequency of infringements.[385]

The dual objective of special and general deterrence helps to clarify the apparently contradictory inferences by the Court of Justice and the General Court from the principle of dissuasiveness. It follows from EU case law that while penalties imposed in other jurisdictions cannot diminish the need to have dissuasive sanctions for infringements of EU competition law,[386] infringements of competition rules in other jurisdictions do warrant more severe sanctions for infringements of EU competition law.[387] Whereas the former inference can be explained by considerations of general deterrence, the latter may find its explanation in the need to ensure special deterrence. The General Court also seems to take account of the issue of 'marginal deterrence': an undertaking that already engages in one form of anti-competitive behaviour should be deterred from engaging in a second infringement. This would at least explain why the requisite deterrent effect of two penalties for two already terminated infringements of Article 101 TFEU is assessed separately.[388] Owing to the deterrence increment for both infringements, undertakings could be deterred from committing a second infringement.

The objective of general deterrence requires the details of the infringement and the penalty to be published.[389] Without publication, it would be difficult to send out a clear signal to society. In *Bank Austria Creditanstalt*, the General Court held that in order to guide undertakings in complying with Articles 101 and 102 TFEU:

[380] *Microsoft* (n 162).

[381] *Siemens AG Österreich* (n 51) [126].

[382] *Groupe Danone* (n 29) [348]; *Arkema France* (n 229) [66]. See also WPJ Wils, 'Recidivism in EU Antitrust Enforcement: A Legal and Economic Analysis' (2012) 35 *World Competition* 5, 12.

[383] *Showa Denko* (n 275) [23]; *Tokai Carbon (Graphite Electrodes)* (n 58) [147].

[384] *cf Commission v Ireland (Animal Protection)* (n 334).

[385] *Musique Diffusion française* (n 307) [108].

[386] *cf SGL Carbon* (n 160) [37]; *Showa Denko* (n 275) [61]; *Tokai Carbon (Graphite Electrodes)* (n 58) [147]–[148].

[387] *Microsoft* (n 162).

[388] *Tokai Carbon (Speciality Graphite)* (n 86) [334]–[336].

[389] *cf* Case T-198/03 *Bank Austria Creditanstalt* [2006] ECR II-1429 [57]; Case C-54/07 *Feryn* [2008] ECR I-5187 [39].

> [I]t is essential that economic operators be informed, through the publication of decisions finding infringements and imposing fines, of the conduct that has led the Commission to take punitive action.[390]

In the light of the shared responsibility of the NCAs with regard to the enforcement of Articles 101 and 102 TFEU and the principle of dissuasiveness, it is suggested that NCAs are also under an EU obligation to publish penalty decisions. The General Court has already confirmed that the publication of penalty decisions is fully warranted and cannot be blocked by considerations of professional secrecy or legality.[391] At the same time, EU case law also suggests that some flexibility for the competition authority in determining an appropriate penalty, and the corresponding uncertainty for the undertakings, results in more general deterrence.[392] The combination of publication and this uncertainty allows the competition authorities to send out clear signals to society, while limiting the possibility for undertakings to engage in infringements on the basis of cost-benefit analyses.[393]

Centralisation Effects

It can be concluded that NCAs have to penalise intentional and negligent infringements of Articles 101 and 102 TFEU in a way that deters both the offender and society at large. This has an effect on the severity of domestic sanctions. Member States should further publish the details of penalty decisions. Finally, the Member States are urged to leave their NCAs with sufficient flexibility in meting out an appropriate penalty. The first two requirements in particular limit the sanctioning autonomy of the Member States. Notwithstanding the above limitations, the Member States remain entirely free to decide on the appropriate type of penalties, as well as on the interplay between the severity of the penalties and the chances of getting caught in designing a deterring sanctioning regime. The latter point means that the Member States can either focus on detection rates or rely on severe penalties.

4.6.5 The Principle of Proportionality

As a final requirement under the duty of sincere cooperation, Member States should apply the principle of proportionality in terminating and penalising infringements of Articles 101 and 102 TFEU. The principle of proportionality is a general principle of EU law, the roots whereof are not limited to the duty of

390 *Bank Austria Creditanstalt* (n 389) [57].

391 Case T-474/04 *Pergan Hilfsstoffe für industrielle Prozesse* [2007] ECR II-4225 [72]; *Bank Austria Creditanstalt* (n 389) [68]–[78].

392 Case T-150/89 *Martinelli* [1995] ECR II-1165 [59]; *Groupe Danone* (n 29) [135].

393 Case T-1/89 *Rhône-Poulenc* [1991] ECR II-867, Opinion of AG Vesterdorf [III]. On the interplay between deterrence and (un)certainty, see further Wils (n 226) 204–06.

sincere cooperation. For the purposes of EU competition law, it constitutes a fundamental right for the legal and natural persons that are the subject of enforcement actions,[394] and it reinforces the implementation of Articles 101 and 102 TFEU and EU law more generally.[395] In its fundamental right capacity, the principle of proportionality directly influences the sanctioning powers of the Member States, whether as an obligation resting on the Member States by virtue of Article 4(3) TEU or as a subjective right under Article 49 of the EU Charter. In its other capacity, the principle of proportionality reinforces the EU free movement rights[396] and Articles 101 and 102 TFEU.[397] In this capacity, the principle of proportionality is, first, capable of limiting domestic sanctions for infringements of Articles 101 and 102 TFEU that hinder inter-state trade (see above, section 4.4). Second, it may also strengthen domestic sanctions in order to reinforce Articles 101 and 102 TFEU by ensuring that sanctions are proportionate 'enough'. The latter dimension is largely covered by the principles of effectiveness and dissuasiveness (see above, sections 4.6.3 and 4.6.4). It follows that the principle of proportionality has various identities and serves different masters. This section focuses on the principle of proportionality in its fundamental right capacity. In this respect, it should be noted that the scope of application of Article 4(3) TEU is much wider than that of Article 49 of the EU Charter. The latter provision is limited to criminal offences. While it cannot be excluded that the Court of Justice will give a wide interpretation to the term 'criminal offence', it is deemed unlikely that this will include reparatory sanctions.

Punitive Sanctions

In relation to punitive sanctions, the General Court applies a two-step proportionality test: the sanction must not be disproportionate for the objectives pursued and the application of a sanction must be proportionate to the gravity of the infringement. This test can be found in *Otis*, where the Court concluded:

> [That] fines must not be disproportionate to the aims pursued, that is to say, to compliance with the competition rules, and that the amount of the fine imposed on an undertaking for an infringement of competition law must be proportionate to the infringement, viewed as a whole, account being taken, in particular, of the gravity of the infringement.[398]

In the first step, the proportionality of a particular penalty can be considered by abstracting away from the concrete situation. For instance, are custodial sanctions disproportionate to the implemention of EU competition policy? In the second step, the circumstances of the case can enter the equation. For instance, is a fine equivalent to eight per cent of the undertaking's worldwide turnover proportion-

[394] Article 4(3) TEU and Article 49 EU Charter.
[395] Article 4(3) TEU.
[396] *cf Skanavi* (n 115); *Louloudakis* (n 113).
[397] Article 4(3) TEU.
[398] *Otis* (n 38) [384].

ate to its involvement in the cartel? Member States will in any case not be castigated easily at the first step.[399] The Court of Justice does not even require that a particular type of penalty is proportionate to every single group of potential addressees.[400]

The principle of proportionality requires that the severity of the penalty is determined on the basis of the established facts and circumstances, and that none of these factors is given disproportionate significance over the others.[401] In the event of an infringement committed by several undertakings, the relative gravity of the participation of each of them has to be taken into account.[402] More precisely, the roles played by each of them in the infringement for the duration of their participation should be established and accounted for in the severity of the sanction.[403] As a result, the ringleaders to an infringement should be punished more severely than other participants.[404] With regard to corporate fines, it seems appropriate to relate the penalty to the 'scale of the infringement' and the 'economic power' of the undertaking.[405] Regard should be had of the turnover to which the infringement relates; fines may not be a reflection of the total turnover of the undertaking if the turnover accounted for by products to which the infringement related was relatively low.[406]

The Court of Justice and the General Court have ruled out the necessity of taking into account particular facts and circumstances that could be deemed prima facie relevant in meting out a proportionate penalty. It should be noted that these rulings, of course, do not limit the sanctioning autonomy of the Member States. EU law does not require the penalty to be proportionate to the undertaking's size on the product market in respect of which the infringement was committed.[407] It further follows from EU case law that the Commission is not required in setting the amount of the fine to take into account the degree of culpability,[408] the harmful effects of the infringement[409] or the illegal gains of the offender.[410] This is especially noteworthy in relation to the prohibition laid down in Article 101 TFEU, which even has 'anti-competitive object' and 'anti-competitive effect' as alternative conditions and where

[399] *cf Nunes and de Matos* (n 352), where the Court was asked to decide whether a Member State is empowered to impose criminal penalties for conduct which only attracts a sanction of a civil law nature under EU law. The Court only mentioned the principle of proportionality and did not make a substantive evaluation.

[400] *cf* Case 5/73 *Balkan-Import-Export* [1973] ECR 1091 [22]–[23].

[401] *Arkema France* (n 229) [63].

[402] *AC-Treuhand* (n 82) [155].

[403] *Groupe Danone* (n 29) [277].

[404] Case T-410/03 *Hoechst* [2008] ECR II-881 [423]. Simonsson (n 347) 320 comes to a different conclusion: 'It is not possible to imply at present that Member States are required to impose higher fines on ringleaders and instigators' She bases this conclusion, mistakenly it is argued, on the assumption that the Court's case law is entirely based on the procedural framework governing the Commission's actions.

[405] *Musique Diffusion française* (n 307) [121]; Case T-77/92 *Parker Pen* [1994] ECR II-549 [94].

[406] *Parker Pen* (n 405) [94]–[95].

[407] *Archer Daniels Midland* (n 203) [101].

[408] *SPO* (n 289) [55]–[57].

[409] Case T-141/94 *Thyssen Stahl* [1999] ECR II-347, para 636.

[410] Case T-213/00 *CMA CGM* [2003] ECR II-913 [340]–[341]; *Bolloré* (n 296) [671].

one could have expected the degree of culpability and the size of the effect, respectively, to play a decisive role.[411] While the General Court has indicated that it will take into account the degree of culpability when punishing 'object-restrictions' and take into account the harmful effects of the infringement when punishing 'effect-restrictions',[412] it has only paid lip service to this intention.[413]

Reparatory Sanctions

The principle of proportionality also applies in relation to reparatory sanctions. Reparatory sanctions are meant to remedy the illegality rather than to punish the offender. Reparatory sanctions in the area of EU competition law regularly take the form of orders prohibiting (the continuation of) certain action or requiring certain action.[414] These orders are subject to the principle of proportionality. In accordance with *Magill*:

> [T]he principle of proportionality means that the burden imposed on undertakings in order to bring an infringement of competition law to an end must not exceed what is appropriate and necessary to attain the objective sought, namely re-establishment of compliance with the rules infringed.[415]

The practical implications of this requirement can be demonstrated with the help of *Sarrió*.[416] In *Sarrió*, the General Court had to review the legality of a Commission order prohibiting the exchange of information between undertakings found to have participated in a cartel on the market for cartonboard. More specifically, the Commission had prohibited Sarrió SA from exchanging aggregated statistical data and statistical information. The Court accepted that the Commission had the power to specify what the undertaking had to do to bring the infringement to an end.[417] However, such requirements could not exceed what is appropriate and necessary to attain the objective of restoring compliance with Article 101 TFEU.[418] The Court considered that the proportionality of the prohibition was dependent on whether the exchange itself was contrary to Article 101 TFEU.[419] It then concluded:

[411] *cf* Wils (n 226) 222–23, who favours a policy in accordance with which intentional infringements are penalised more harshly than negligent infringements.

[412] *Thyssen Stahl* (n 409).

[413] The General Court has *not* been criticised over this matter by the Court of Justice either. *cf KME* (n 222) [34]: 'the actual impact of cartels on the market is not a decisive factor for determining the level of fines'. However, these considerations have found resonance in Commission *policy*. In its *Guidelines on the matter of setting fines*, the Commission indicates that infringements that have not been implemented or that have been committed as a result of negligence warrant a reduced fine. See Commission Guidelines on the method of setting fines [2006] OJ C210/2 (paras 22 and 29).

[414] *cf* Joined Cases 6/73 and 7/73 *Commercial Solvents* [1974] ECR 223 [45]; Case T-334/94 *Sarrió* [1998] ECR II-1446 [266]; Joined Cases T-456/05 and T-457/05 *Gütermann* [2010] ECR II-1443 [63].

[415] *Magill* (n 162) [93].

[416] *Sarrió* (n 414).

[417] ibid [267].

[418] ibid.

[419] ibid [276].

> Such a prohibition exceeds what is necessary in order to bring the conduct in question into line with what is lawful because it seeks to prevent the exchange of purely statistical information which is not in, or capable of being put into, the form of individual information on the ground that the information exchanged might be used for anti-competitive purposes. First, it is not apparent from the Decision that the Commission considered the exchange of statistical data to be in itself an infringement of Article 85(1) of the Treaty [now Article 101(1) TFEU]. Second, the mere fact that a system for the exchange of statistical information might be used for anti-competitive purposes does not make it contrary to Article 85(1) of the Treaty, since in such circumstances it is necessary to establish its actual anti-competitive effect.[420]

The Court thus concluded that the prohibition to exchange statistical information was a disproportionate sanction.

It follows from *Sarrió* that the proportionality of orders prohibiting (the continuation of) certain action is dependent on this action itself being contrary to Article 101 or 102 TFEU. This conclusion works two ways. In *Gütermann*, it was decided that the proportionality of the remedy 'does not depend on the situation of the undertakings concerned at the time when the contested decision was adopted'.[421] As a result, the fact that one of the participants in the *Industrial Thread* cartel was no longer active in this sector did not affect the validity of a remedy requiring this undertaking to refrain from repeating the illegal behaviour.[422] A similar approach obviously cannot be transposed to orders requiring certain positive action. In these cases, the infringement results from the status quo. Yet, orders requiring certain action are also subject to the principle of proportionality.[423]

Negotiated Forms of Reparation

While the requirements of appropriateness and necessity apply to reparatory sanctions,[424] negotiated forms of reparation are subject to a more limited proportionality test. It follows from *Alrosa* that commitment decisions under Article 9 of Regulation 1/2003, with which the Commission terminates an investigation without a finding of infringement but after the undertaking has given commitments to make certain changes in its commercial activities, are not subject to a comprehensive appropriateness test:

> Application of the principle of proportionality by the Commission in the context of Article 9 of Regulation No 1/2003 is confined to verifying that the commitments in question address the concerns it expressed to the undertakings concerned and that they have not offered less onerous commitments that also address those concerns adequately. When carrying out that assessment, the Commission must, however, take into consideration the interests of third parties.[425]

420 ibid [280].
421 *Gütermann* (n 414) [66].
422 ibid [65]–[66].
423 *Van den Bergh Foods* (n 133) [170].
424 *Gütermann* (n 414) [63].
425 Case C-441/07 P *Alrosa* [2010] ECR I-5949 [41].

The Court of Justice concluded further that the Commission is not required to seek out less onerous or more moderate solutions than the commitments offered to it.[426] In so doing, it overturned the General Court's ruling on this matter. The approach of the Court of Justice in relation to the proportionality of commitment decisions is in stark contrast to the treatment of reparatory sanctions. The Court of Justice deliberately deviated from this approach simply by holding that as the characteristics of the power to terminate an infringement differ from the characteristics of the power to adopt a commitment decision, the requirements under the principle of proportionality also differ.[427] An explanation for this discrepancy could be that commitments should address *the concerns of the Commission* expressed in a *preliminary assessment*. This could require more onerous measures than what would be needed to address a *proven infringement*.[428]

Different Proportionality Standards

It follows from the foregoing that the proportionality requirements differ in relation to the type of sanction.[429] While punitive sanctions are essentially subject to a negative test, filtering out disproportionate sanctions, the Court applies a full-blown proportionality test ('appropriate and necessary') to reparatory sanctions. Conversely, negotiated forms of reparation are subject only to a very light proportionality test focusing mainly on the principle's reinforcing effects. The difference between punitive sanctions and reparatory sanctions is especially noteworthy. Only procedures resulting in the imposition of punitive sanctions are subject to the presumption of innocence.[430] The application of this principle requires courts to undertake a full review with regard to administrative penalties. One would therefore expect the Court to apply the principle of proportionality more thoroughly in relation to punitive sanctions than to reparatory sanctions. It should be noted in this respect that from the undertaking's perspective, reparatory sanctions could be far more costly than pecuniary penalties. Whereas the latter might be perceived as a tax on anti-competitive profits, the former actually prevent the continuation of certain, potentially very lucrative, commercial behaviour. Notwithstanding these considerations, the reason for the Court to adopt a different approach is probably one of pragmatism rather than principle. It will generally be easier for the Court to review the necessity of a reparatory sanction than the necessity of the level of a penalty.

[426] ibid [61].

[427] ibid [38].

[428] This point has been made earlier in MJ Frese, 'Het Toezeggingsbesluit; Kenmerken van een Nieuw Handhavingsinstrument' (2007) *Markt & Mededinging* 39, 43.

[429] This conclusion is in line with Tridimas' findings on the application of the principle of proportionality more generally: 'far from dictating a uniform test, proportionality is a flexible principle which is used in different contexts to protect different interests and entails varying degrees of judicial scrutiny'. Tridimas (n 21) 173.

[430] *Toshiba Corp (Gas Insulated Switchgear)* (n 223) [80]; *Mitsubishi Electric Corp* (n 298) [74].

Centralisation Effects

It can be concluded that the Member States should take into account the principle of proportionality in terminating and penalising infringements of Articles 101 and 102 TFEU. The requirements under this principle differ depending on the sanction. Punitive sanctions may not be disproportionate to the aim of compliance. This requirement still leaves the Member States with considerable leeway. In meting out a proportionate penalty, NCAs should pay attention to the role played by the undertakings in the infringement as well as to the scale of the infringement. Reparatory sanctions might arguably be subject to a stricter proportionality regime. These sanctions may not exceed what is appropriate and necessary to (re-)establish compliance with Articles 101 and 102 TFEU. Negotiated forms of resolution are virtually excluded from the principle of proportionality, at least from the principle's mitigating capacity. It follows that the EU principle of proportionality mainly limits the NCAs in imposing reparatory sanctions.

4.7 CONCLUSION

Contrary to what Regulation 1/2003 may suggest, national legislators are not entirely free in allocating sanctioning powers to their NCAs. The NCAs themselves are not entirely free in exercising their powers either. Where the Member States act as 'agents' of EU law, enforcing Articles 101 and 102 TFEU, the domestic sanctioning powers are governed by various EU principles. This chapter has aimed to clarify these principles. The EU sanctioning principles limit the autonomy of the Member States and may enhance the uniformity of enforcement procedures throughout the EU. In this respect, these principles can be seen as a form of centralisation. In accordance with what has been concluded in chapter three, these principles can have various economic implications. The more comprehensive the EU legal framework for domestic sanctioning powers, the fewer the possibilities for preference matching and regulatory innovation, but the larger the savings on transaction costs, duplication costs and coordination costs. This chapter has therefore provided relevant input for the discussion about the economies and diseconomies of the current EU framework for competition law enforcement (see chapter six). This concluding section summarises the above findings.

4.7.1 EU Principles in the National Legal Order

Section 4.2 paved the way for the analysis of EU sanctioning principles. The centralisation effect of these principles is due to the EU principle of priority. On the basis of this principle, EU law has priority over national law. Only outside the scope of EU law do the Member States remain free in their legislative activities.

While the opportunities for the Court to elaborate on the requirements for the decentralised enforcement of EU competition law have been limited so far, there exists a vast body of case law on the legality of the Commission's enforcement decisions and on the administration of EU law more generally. For two reasons, many of these cases and the principles developed therein are equally valid in relation to the decentralised enforcement of EU competition law. First, to the extent that these principles derive from primary sources of EU law, there can be no strict distinction with regard to the application of these principles between the centralised and decentralised enforcement of Articles 101 and 102 TFEU, or between the enforcement of EU competition law and other EU law. Second, the procedures of the Commission in the context of Articles 101 and 102 TFEU constitute a benchmark for the procedures of the NCAs. It follows that every EU principle with relevance to sanctions is capable of limiting the sanctioning autonomy of the Member States in the context of EU competition law. Apart from the specific rules laid down in Regulation 1/2003, the applicable principles for the sanctioning powers of the Member States derive from: (i) Articles 101 and 102 TFEU themselves; (ii) the EU free movement rights; (iii) the EU fundamental rights; and (iv) the duty of sincere cooperation laid down in Article 4(3) TEU.

4.7.2 Centralisation Effects of Articles 101 and 102 TFEU: Liability Principles

Section 4.3 has shown that some elements of Articles 101 and 102 TFEU have developed into detailed principles for the attribution of liability. This concerns the elements of 'undertaking', 'agreement' and 'restriction of competition'. The liability principles originating in the competition law prohibitions are motivated mainly by considerations of uniform and effective enforcement, but they occasionally also protect undertakings and their owners against spurious allegations by competition authorities.

It has been concluded that the Member States have to apply the EU principle of personal responsibility. In this context, Member States should also recognise the doctrines of parent liability and economic continuity. The latter obligation is especially relevant for national review courts. The NCAs may in principle always decide to refrain from seeking parent liability or from imputing liability on the economic successor of the culprit in individual cases.

It has further been concluded that NCAs should apply Article 101 TFEU in accordance with the doctrine of the 'single and complex infringement' or 'single and continuous infringement' (SCI) and that this also has implications for the liability of the undertakings involved. Again, national review courts need to sanction this approach. The SCI doctrine also limits the discretion of the NCAs. While NCAs may decide not to include certain anti-competitive manifestations of an SCI in their investigation, they cannot prosecute these manifestations separately. However, the latter safeguard seems limited to the actions by a single NCA and risks losing much of its meaning in situations of parallel actions by various NCAs.

As a final point in section 4.3, it has been argued that Member States cannot exclude any form of participation in a cartel from the scope of Article 101 TFEU. As with the earlier points, this issue is also most relevant in the review stage of the enforcement proceedings. National courts need to accept that any form of participation qualifies as co-perpetration, irrespective of the domestic procedural framework. This co-perpetrator doctrine is not without its obligations for the NCAs either. First, it seems inappropriate for NCAs to refrain from proceeding against particular participants systematically and solely on the basis of their marginal role in the infringement. More importantly, in applying the co-perpetrator doctrine, NCAs should take account of the degree of participation in deciding on the severity of the penalty.

4.7.3 Centralisation Effects of the Free Movement Rights

The implications of the free movement rights for the decentralised enforcement of EU competition law have been detailed in section 4.4. Several conclusions have been reached. First, domestic sanctions for infringements of Articles 101 and 102 TFEU are indeed conditioned by the free movement rights. Second, it follows from the applicability of the free movement rights (as supplemented by Article 18 TFEU) that discriminatory sanctions for infringements of Articles 101 and 102 TFEU are prohibited. Third, excessive sanctions for anti-competitive conduct with hardly any significance or – more problematic – sanctions that directly limit trade flows both risk being caught and overruled by the free movement rights.

4.7.4 Centralisation Effects of the Fundamental Rights

Section 4.5 has identified and analysed a whole range of fundamental rights with particular salience for domestic sanctioning powers. The following principles have been identified as relevant: the right to property, the right to economic engagement, the principle of legal certainty, the right to a reasoned decision, the principle of good administration, the protection against undue delays, the principle of retroactivity *in mitius*, the principle of *ne bis in idem*, the principle of *nulla poena sine culpa*, the principle of equal treatment and, finally, the principle of proportionality. The latter principle has been discussed in the context of the EU duty of sincere cooperation. It has been demonstrated that EU case law on the above rights is not always elaborate or even unequivocal. Still, numerous concrete conclusions have been drawn with regard to the sanctioning autonomy of the Member States and the centralisation of sanctioning powers and procedures.

In accordance with the right to property, any restriction of ownership or the exploitation of assets should correspond to the objectives of Articles 101 and 102 TFEU. In the case of compulsory licensing under Article 102 TFEU, for instance, this means that the licensor is entitled to reasonable compensation. Closely related to this is the right to economic engagement. While this right still needs to develop in the context of EU competition law, it seems capable of limiting Member States in administering sanctions that are aimed at the professional activities of the undertaking or its staff.

Under the principle of legal certainty, Member States have to draw up statutes of limitation, as they cannot delay the exercise of their powers to impose penalties for infringements of Articles 101 and 102 TFEU indefinitely. Furthermore, Member States should ensure that sanctions for infringements of Articles 101 and 102 TFEU rest on a clear and unambiguous legal basis so that the consequences of an infringement are foreseeable. Finally, Member States wishing to grant their NCAs a margin of discretion as to the level of the penalty should provide for an upper limit.

The right to a reasoned decision and the corresponding duty to state reasons require the Member States to ensure that the exercise of discretionary sanctioning powers remains verifiable. Pursuant to this duty, NCAs are required to explain the grounds for deciding on a particular sanction.

The principle of good administration is relied upon ever more frequently and in relation to a broad range of issues. Considering its fundamental nature and general principle status, it would appear to extend to the decentralised enforcement of Articles 101 and 102 TFEU. Based on case law in relation to Commission decisions, it can be concluded the principle of good administration requires competition authorities to clarify how they will exercise their discretionary penalty powers, to record the essential aspects of the assertions made at meetings in the context of a leniency application and to undo any increase of the fine for reasons of recidivism if the decision finding the first infringement is subsequently annulled. Further implications for the sanctioning powers of the competition authorities need to be clarified in future case law.

Another fundamental right that penetrates the national legal orders and that is capable of limiting the sanctioning autonomy of Member States is the protection against undue delays. This requires Member States to compensate undertakings for periods of inactivity in the enforcement process. This could be done by applying a rebate to the penalty otherwise imposed.

A reduction of the penalty could also be required by the principle of retroactivity *in mitius*. In accordance with this principle, the introduction by a Member State of more lenient penalties for infringements of Articles 101 and 102 TFEU demands immediate application to all running investigations. More lenient penalties thus need to be applied retroactively.

Some fundamental rights exclude domestic sanctions altogether. The principle of *ne bis in idem* prohibits NCAs from commencing proceedings under Articles 101 and 102 TFEU against any person that has already been penalised or acquitted for certain material acts by a previous decision under Articles 101 and 102 TFEU. As a result, double punishment is prohibited as well.

The analysis of the principle of *nulla poena sine culpa* has shown that it is highly uncertain whether this principle constitutes a general principle of EU law. Outside the field of EU competition law, the Court of Justice has implicitly denied the existence of this principle and there is no clear authority for the applicability of this principle in the context of the *decentralised* enforcement of Articles 101 and 102 TFEU. As a result, it is still unclear whether or not the principle of *nulla poena sine culpa* is capable of centralising parts of the sanctioning regime.

By virtue of the principle of equal treatment, Member States are precluded from treating similar situations differently and different situations similarly. With regard to sanctions, this requirement should be applied to every single element that ultimately decides the severity of the sanction (eg, involvement of the undertaking, size of the undertaking and cooperation by the undertaking). In terms of practical implications, this principle is mainly concerned with instances of manifest inequality.

As to the centralisation effects of all of these principles, it should be emphasised that they only provide a floor below which Member States may not operate. Therefore, centralisation only takes place to the extent that national laws are less generous. However, Member States may be precluded from adopting more generous legal safeguards where this would conflict with the duty of sincere cooperation, for instance, where this would limit the effectiveness of EU competition law.

4.7.5 Centralisation Effects of the Duty of Sincere Cooperation

Further to the sanctioning principles deriving from Regulation 1/2003, Articles 101 and 102 TFEU, the free movement rights and the fundamental rights, domestic sanctioning powers for EU competition law are subject to the duty of sincere cooperation laid down in Article 4(3) TEU. Section 4.6 detailed the requirements of the Member States under this duty, more specifically under the principles of equivalence, effectiveness, dissuasiveness and proportionality. With regard to the centralisation effects of these principles, it should be noted that they apply both in disputes over whether a Member State uses appropriate means to enforce EU law and in disputes over whether a Member State has unlawfully extended the scope of EU legislation.

Under the principle of equivalence, sanctions for infringements of EU competition law should at least be equal to sanctions for infringements of national competition law. This means that the national legislator should provide its NCA with a set of sanctioning powers for the purposes of Articles 101 and 102 TFEU that are at least equal to those for national competition law. NCAs, in turn, may not reserve particular useful (but perhaps costly) sanctioning powers for infringements of national competition law. While the principle of equivalence limits the sanctioning autonomy of the Member States, it does not lead to more uniformity throughout the EU.

Unlike the principle of equivalence, the principle of effectiveness leaves the Member States with considerable flexibility as to the sanctions they use for the enforcement of Articles 101 and 102 TFEU. Pursuant to the principle of effectiveness, NCAs should be able to terminate every type of infringement. How this is organised seems less important. However, this requirement does imply that NCAs should be able to order the termination of anti-competitive behaviour, even when this behaviour is caused by the very structure of the undertaking. As a further requirement under the principle of effectiveness, NCAs should be able to adopt interim measures pending the investigation. A final requirement under this principle is that NCAs are able to impose deterrent penalties under conditions that are not overly restrictive. This requirement is further supported by the principle of dissuasiveness.

The principle of dissuasiveness mandates that Member States punish intentional and negligent infringements of Articles 101 and 102 TFEU with penalties that deter both the offender and society at large. As a consequence of the latter objective, Member States need to publish the details of penalty decisions and should be able to punish undertakings more severely than they might personally deserve.

A final aspect of the Member States' duty of sincere cooperation is that they should ensure proportionality between infringement and sanction. This requirement not only derives from the duty of sincere cooperation, it also qualifies as a fundamental right on which undertakings and individuals may rely. The principle of proportionality requires that punitive sanctions may not be disproportionate 'to the aim of compliance'. This means that NCAs should pay attention to the role played by the undertakings in the infringement as well as to the scale of the infringement. Interestingly, reparatory sanctions seem subject to a stricter regime. These sanctions may not exceed what is appropriate and necessary for compliance with Articles 101 and 102 TFEU. Furthermore, negotiated forms of resolution are virtually excluded from the fundamental right of proportionality between 'infringement' and 'sanction'.

4.7.6 The Areas and the Degree of Centralisation

It can be concluded from the above that there exists an EU framework for decentralised sanctioning that consists of a variety of legal principles. While the principles deriving from Regulation 1/2003, Articles 101 and 102 TFEU and the duty of sincere cooperation are mainly concerned with the uniform and effective application of EU competition law, the free movement rights and the fundamental rights guarantee that the enforcement actions of the Member States do not impinge on core EU entitlements. Several observations can be made as to the areas and the degree of centralisation caused by these principles, as well as to their economic implications.

First, *the EU sanctioning principles are hardly concerned with the type of sanctions that Member States deploy in the enforcement of Articles 101 and 102 TFEU.* Apart from proscribing inhumane or degrading penalties and prescribing interim measures, none of the EU principles actually limits the autonomy of Member States with regard to the type of sanctions. For example, the EU principle of effectiveness, while expecting NCAs to be able to terminate and punish any type of infringement, seems incapable of superimposing particular, potentially very effective, sanctions onto the Member States. To make this point more concrete, Member States remain free to decide whether or not to provide for structural remedies (positive orders to divest shares/assets) and/or custodial sanctions. This is only different in cases where the Member State in question already provides for these sanctions in the context of national competition law and the principle of equivalence therefore demands that these sanctions are also available for EU competition law. Notwithstanding these conclusions as to the concrete EU requirements, the ubiquity of corporate fines in the context of EU competition law makes this type of sanction virtually unavoidable (see above, section 4.6.3). In any case, the Member States remain entirely free to decide whether or not to open an investigation and, once an infringement has been established, whether or not to impose a sanction.

Second, and in line with the first observation, *the EU sanctioning principles are mainly concerned with the conditions under which domestic sanctioning powers are exercised.* Examples of this form of centralisation are plentiful. Let us briefly revisit two. In section 4.3.2, it has been concluded that where an NCA imposes a fine for an infringement of Articles 101 and 102 TFEU, it should apply the EU principle of personal responsibility in determining who should bear the financial burden. Another example can be taken from section 4.5.6. Where a Member State grants its NCA discretionary fining powers, it has to ensure that the latter explains the methods for calculating the fine.

Third, *many of the EU sanctioning principles still leave the Member States with considerable discretion in determining the conditions for the domestic sanctioning powers.* For example, irrespective of the strong normative connotation of the EU principle of dissuasiveness or the EU principle of equal treatment, Member States will be castigated under these principles only in cases of manifest failure. With regard to the principle of dissuasiveness, for instance, it would seem rather exceptional that a Member State will need to adjust the severity of its penalties in order to reach deterrence levels that are current in other jurisdictions. As a consequence, the principle of dissuasiveness (like other principles) has only limited prescriptive value.

Fourth, *many of the more detailed EU sanctioning principles relate to the legal safeguards for the undertakings involved rather than to the performance standards for the authorities.* The more detailed sanctioning principles mainly derive from the EU fundamental rights and the EU free movement rights. These principles ensure that the authorities do not encroach upon core EU entitlements.

Fifth, *the detailed sanctioning principles deriving from the EU fundamental rights only provide a floor below which the Member States may not operate.* The Member States may choose to adopt higher legal standards, provided that this does not jeopardise the effectiveness of EU competition policy.

Considering the areas and degree of centralisation, it can be concluded that the EU sanctioning principles are currently not providing much uniformity when it comes to sanctions for EU competition law. Therefore, they do not limit to any significant extent the transaction costs, coordination costs and duplication costs associated with the system of decentralised enforcement. However, this also means that the Member States have retained the possibility of accommodating domestic sanctioning preferences and engaging in regulatory innovation, certainly in relation to the type of sanctions. The more heterogeneous the sanctioning preferences across the Member States and the more numerous the innovative experiments, the more likely it becomes that the benefits of decentralisation outweigh the costs. These issues will be examined in the following chapter, where we turn our attention to the development of a number of national sanctioning regimes.

5

The Development of Domestic Sanctioning Powers

5.1 INTRODUCTION

In addition to the centralisation effects detailed in chapter four, the sanctioning powers of the Member States are also subject to other forces. In its 2009 Report on the functioning of Regulation 1/2003, the European Commission observed a significant degree of voluntary convergence of national enforcement powers and procedures, and concluded that this process was due to Regulation 1/2003 and policy work in the ECN.[1] These findings are in line with observations in the academic literature.[2] In fact, earlier work in this area by Drahos has demonstrated that convergence tendencies long preceded the adoption of Regulation 1/2003.[3] The Commission's findings are based on a Staff Working Paper.[4] In this Working Paper, the Commission's administrative services refer to the 'consistent trend' towards deterrent fines and further note 'considerable convergence' with regard

[1] Communication from the Commission to the European Parliament and the Council: Report on the functioning of Regulation 1/2003 [2009] COM 206 final, para 31.

[2] H Vedder, 'Spontaneous Harmonisation of National (Competition) Laws in the Wake of the Modernisation of EC Competition Law' (2004) 1 *Competition Law Review* 5; Ch Lemaire and J Gstalter, 'The Silent Revolution Beyond Regulation 1/2003' (2008) 2 GCP Online Magazine for Global Competition Policy <www.competitionpolicyinternational.com> accessed 1 July 2013; M de Visser, *Network-Based Governance in EC Law: The Example of EC Competition and EC Communications Law* (Hart Publishing, 2009) 242; KJ Cseres, 'The Impact of Regulation 1/2003 in the New Member States' (2010) 6 *Competition Law Review* 145.

[3] M Drahos, *Convergence of Competition Laws and Policies in the European Community: Germany, Austria, and the Netherlands* (Kluwer Law International, 2001). In the context of her quest for tendencies of convergence and divergence, Drahos has compared similarities and differences in the enforcement of competition law by the Commission, the German authorities, the Dutch authorities and the Austrian authorities at two moments in time (1950 and 2000). Her focus was on enforcement institutions and the initiation of procedures and punitive sanctions, and was limited to a 'macro-level' comparison. She concluded first that while there was considerable variety in 1950 (at 165–66), this was less the case in 2000 (at 172–75), certainly with regard to the Commission and the German and Dutch authorities. Her second conclusion was that there had been strong convergence between the German and the Dutch authorities, some convergence between the Commission and the Dutch authorities, and no convergence between the Commission and the German authorities (at 205).

[4] Commission Staff Working Paper accompanying the Communication from the Commission to the European Parliament and the Council: Report on the functioning of Regulation 1/2003 [2009] COM 206 final.

to the power to adopt interim measures and commitment decisions.[5] The Working Paper also mentions '(micro-)divergence' of Member States' enforcement systems.[6] Amongst other things, this divergence would relate to the calculation methods for fines, the availability of criminal sanctions, the applicable prescription periods, the power to adopt structural remedies and the procedures leading to the adoption of commitment decisions.[7]

In accordance with what has been concluded in chapter three, a process of convergence testifies that there is an increasing degree of homogeneity with regard to sanctioning preferences between the Member States. Dependent on the drivers of this process, convergence could be the result of interjurisdictional learning. Convergence therefore has various economic implications. Against this background, this chapter examines the degree and drivers of convergence with regard to domestic sanctioning powers. For this purpose, sanctioning powers and their development will be analysed for a subset of jurisdictions. This subset includes Germany, the Netherlands and the UK. This selection has the benefit of comparing three jurisdictions that have an entirely different, yet long-standing history of competition policy.[8] Any convergence tendencies observable in these regimes could be significant for the existence of such tendencies more widely and could therefore be evidence for homogeneous preferences in terms of sanctioning powers. Moreover, these jurisdictions are generally perceived to perform well in the area of competition law enforcement.[9] The below analysis has two further objectives: first, to provide a critical analysis of four sanctioning regimes, highlighting some features of the domestic regimes that are difficult to reconcile with the EU sanctioning principles set out in chapters two and four; and, second, to contribute to the interjurisdictional learning process by detailing various sanctioning alternatives. All these objectives require an indepth analysis of the selected four sanctioning regimes.

What will follow is a comparative legal analysis in which different types of sanctioning powers are compared cross-jurisdictionally. This analysis will be preceded by a comparison of the institutional enforcement frameworks in which these sanctioning powers are situated. Accordingly, this chapter deals with:

[5] ibid paras 202 and 204.

[6] ibid para 205.

[7] ibid paras 203–05.

[8] For an extensive description of the competition law traditions in Germany and the Netherlands, as well as Austria, see Drahos (n 3). For a description of the competition law traditions in the UK, see BJ Rodger, 'The Competition Act and the Enterprise Act Reforms: Sanctions and Deterrence in UK Competition Law' in G Dannecker and O Jansen (eds), *Competition Law Sanctioning in the European Union: The EU-Law Influence on the National Law Systems of Sanctions in the European Area* (Kluwer Law International, 2004) 101.

[9] Germany, the Netherlands and the UK generally end up high in the yearly rankings of the *Global Competition Review*, which is a journal and news service owned by Law Business Research Ltd. It brings out yearly 'star ratings' of competition authorities from across the globe. The 'elite' authorities are awarded five stars, 'very good' authorities are awarded 4.5 or 4 stars, 'good' authorities are awarded 3.5 or 3 stars, and 'fair' authorities are awarded no more than 2.5 stars. In the period between 2005 and 2012, the German's *Bundeskartellamt* and the UK's Office of Fair Trading have been awarded four stars or more. The rankings of the Dutch competition authority fluctuate between 3.5 and 4 stars. On a European scale, it is fair to say that these authorities are among the high achievers.

- institutional enforcement frameworks (section 5.2);
- interim measures (section 5.3);
- early resolution measures (section 5.4);
- declaratory findings (section 5.5);
- reparatory sanctions (section 5.6);
- pecuniary sanctions (section 5.7);
- custodial sanctions (section 5.8);
- disqualification orders (section 5.9).

The following eight sections are all structured alike. Each section starts with an introduction to the particular element of the sanctioning framework, is then broken down in separate sections to study all four jurisdictions, and concludes with findings on the degree and drivers of convergence in that area. Section 5.10 summarises the findings.

5.2 INSTITUTIONAL ENFORCEMENT FRAMEWORKS

This section primarily has a preparatory function. It is meant to explain institutional features that have a bearing on the entire enforcement process and to help us to appreciate the intricacies of the various sanctioning powers that will be discussed in later sections. The term 'institution' refers to the public bodies (administrative authorities or courts) that have a role in the public enforcement of EU competition law. A basic understanding of the institutional framework in the selected jurisdictions is also necessary for an accurate perspective on these sanctioning powers. For example, the sanctioning powers of an administrative authority will be more or less severe depending on the review mandate (scope and intensity) of the appeal courts. Further to this introduction to the four sanctioning regimes, this section highlights some institutional differences (and similarities) as well as some tendencies of institutional convergence and divergence.

5.2.1 Enforcement Institutions at the EU Level

At the EU level, the enforcement of Articles 101 and 102 TFEU is in the hands of the Commission. The Commission derives its enforcement competence directly from the Treaties.[10] Regulation 1/2003 provides the Commission with the requisite powers. The Commission is a fully integrated enforcement authority. It decides on the initiation of proceedings, it conducts the investigations, it formulates the objections against the undertakings, it takes a decision on the legality of the behaviour and it imposes sanctions. In practice, all the preparatory activities

[10] Article 104 TFEU and Article 17 TEU.

are performed by the administrative services of the Commissioner in charge of competition policy. These administrative procedures are governed by Commission Regulation (EC) No 773/2004.[11] In accordance with this Regulation, the Commission should issue a statement of objections, informing the parties of the Commission's objections, prior to the adoption of any sanction.[12] Parties may then respond to the statement of objections in writing, setting out all facts relevant for their defence.[13] For this purpose, the Commission grants access to the administrative file.[14] Parties may also request a hearing before the Commission's administrative services[15] as well as an oral hearing before the Hearing Officer.[16] The position of the Hearing Officer has been established through a Decision of the President of the Commission.[17] The Hearing Officer safeguards the effective exercise of procedural rights.[18]

Decisions of the Commission can be appealed before the General Court,[19] with a further appeal on points of law to the Court of Justice.[20] The General Court has jurisdiction to review the legality of the decision. A decision can be annulled on the grounds of lack of competence, infringement of an essential procedural requirement, infringement of any rule of EU law, or misuse of powers.[21] In addition, the General Court has unlimited jurisdiction to review decisions whereby the Commission has fixed a fine or periodic penalty payment.[22] Accordingly, it may cancel, reduce or even increase these punitive sanctions as it deems appropriate. In practice, this difference in jurisdiction between punitive sanctions and all other decisions does not play a prominent role, and certainly not with regard to the intensity of review. The General Court increasingly scrutinises the Commission's finding of infringement while tending to follow the Commission's approach in determining the amount of the fine. The General Court reserves its powers to increase fines for exceptional cases only.

[11] Commission Regulation (EC) No 773/2004 relating to the conduct of proceedings by the Commission pursuant to Articles 81 and 82 of the EC Treaty [2004] OJ L123/18.

[12] Article 10(1) of Regulation 773/2004.

[13] Article 10(3) of Regulation 773/2004.

[14] Article 15 of Regulation 773/2004.

[15] Article 11 of Regulation 773/2004.

[16] Articles 12 and 14 of Regulation 773/2004.

[17] Decision on the function and terms of reference of the hearing officer in certain competition proceedings [2011] OJ L275/29.

[18] Article 4 of the Decision on the function and terms of reference of the hearing officer in certain competition proceedings.

[19] Article 256 TFEU, in conjunction with Article 263 TFEU.

[20] Article 256 TFEU.

[21] Article 263 TFEU.

[22] Article 31 Regulation 1/2003, in conjunction with Article 261 TFEU. See further Case C-386/10 P *Chalkor* [2012] OJ C32/9.

5.2.2 Enforcement Institutions in Germany

In Germany, the enforcement of Articles 101 and 102 TFEU is split into two trajectories, each with its own procedural framework. Articles 101 and 102 TFEU can be enforced through reparatory proceedings (*Verwaltungsverfahren*) and penalty proceedings (*Bußgeldverfahren*). Reparatory proceedings can only result in reparatory sanctions. In cases where a penalty could be warranted, investigations should take place in accordance with penalty proceedings. What starts out as reparatory proceedings could develop into penalty proceedings or vice versa. Infringements warranting both penalties and remedies formally require two (parallel) procedures. Whereas reparatory proceedings are directed at the undertakings that actually committed the infringement, penalty proceedings are directed first and foremost at the natural persons responsible for the infringement.

The basic legal text for competition law in Germany is the Act against Restrictions of Competition (*Gesetz gegen Wettbewerbsbeschränkungen* (GWB)). With regard to the enforcement of Articles 101 and 102 TFEU, this text supplements various framework laws. The GWB only deals with penalty proceedings summarily. Penalty proceedings are subject to the Act on Administrative Offences (*Gesetz über Ordnungswidrigkeiten* (OWiG)). Reparatory proceedings, on the other hand, are largely covered by the GWB.

The burden of enforcing Articles 101 and 102 TFEU is shared by various institutions. By virtue of § 50(1) GWB, enforcement competences have been granted to the Federal Cartel Authority (*Bundeskartellamt* (BKartA)) and the 16 designated state authorities (*Landeskartellbehörden* (LKartBs)). These authorities will be jointly referred to as 'German authorities', 'competition authorities' or 'authorities'. There is no hierarchical relationship between the BKartA and the LKartBs.[23] In addition to these 'first-line' enforcement authorities, the public prosecutor has a role in the enforcement of Articles 101 and 102 TFEU. As soon as penalty proceedings reach the appeal stage, the public prosecutor takes over the case from the BKartA/LKartB. The former makes an autonomous decision whether or not to pursue the case.[24] While the public prosecutor thus occupies a key position in the enforcement of Articles 101 and 102 TFEU, it has not been designated as an NCA. This sits oddly with Regulation 1/2003, especially because it means that an institution other than an NCA applies Articles 101 and 102 TFEU and because it circumvents the Regulation's professional secrecy safeguards (see above, section 2.2).[25]

[23] C Becker in Loewenheim/Meessen/Riesenkampff, *Kartellrecht* (Band 2: GWB, Verlag CH Beck, 2006) § 48 Rdnr 1.

[24] In practice, the public prosecutor will terminate the proceedings only in exception circumstances; see R Raum in Langen/Bunte, *Kommentar zum deutschen und europaïschen Kartellrecht* (Band 1: Deutsches Kartellrecht, 11. Auflage, Carl Heymanns Verlag/Luchterhand, 2011) § 81 Rdnr 67.

[25] The requirement of professional secrecy, laid down in Article 28 of Regulation 1/2003, does not extend to the public prosecutor. Yet, the competition authorities need to share highly confidential information every time a case is transferred to the public prosecutor.

The BKartA is a so-called independent federal authority (*selbständige Bundesbehörde*).[26] This notion derives from the German Constitution (*Grundgesetz* (GG)) and has various implications for the institutional position of the BKartA. By virtue of Article 87(3) GG, the federal legislator may create independent federal authorities for purposes falling within the former's scope of competences. Often, these authorities are subordinated to federal departments.[27] The term 'independent' refers to the authority's independence vis-a-vis the responsible minister. For 'organisational' and 'functional' purposes, the authority can operate independently of the minister.[28] However, the term 'independent' does not connote a lack of power for the minister to get involved in the authority's operations. The degree to which ministerial instructions can be given depends on the general powers of the responsible minister rather than on the characteristics of the particular authority.[29]

The BKartA is subordinated to the Federal Department of Economic Affairs and Technology (*Bundesministerium für Wirtschaft und Technologie* (BMWi)).[30] The BKartA is, in any case, independent from the BMWi in an organisational and functional fashion: it can take decisions in its own name and on its own initiative.[31] The question of whether BMWi has the power to give instructions to the BKartA is the subject of debate. Some commentators argue that a lack of legal grounds to the contrary suggest that the BMWi *does* have this power.[32] Others commentators refer to the system of the GWB and the type of the decisions that the BKartA takes to draw the opposite conclusion.[33] Still other commentators deny the BMWi powers of instruction for reasons of the authority's structure, with its specific units in charge of actual decision making (see below).[34] Although the issue remains unresolved, there can be no doubt that the BMWi should not[35] and is not likely to[36] exercise any power of instruction lightly.

The organisational structure of the BKartA shields the enforcement of Articles 101 and 102 TFEU from non-competition law considerations. The GWB has allocated decision-making powers in individual cases to special units within the BKartA (*Beschlussabteilungen*).[37] To date, 12 such units exist. Three units are solely respon-

[26] § 51(1) GWB.

[27] P Lerche in Maunz/Dürig, *Kommentar zum Grundgesetz* (Stand April 2009, Verlag CH Beck) Art 87 Rdnr 183–84.

[28] Lerche in Maunz/Dürig (n 27) Art 87 Rdnr 183–84.

[29] ibid Art 87 Rdnr 184.

[30] § 51(1) GWB.

[31] *cf* Lerche in Maunz/Dürig (n 27) Art 87 Rdnr 184, notes 77 and 78.

[32] R Bechtold, *Kartellgesetz* (Gesetz gegen Wettbewerbbeschränkungen, 5. Auflage, Verlag CH Beck, 2008) § 52 Rdnr 2–3. See also P Jung, 'National Report for Germany' in D Cahill (ed), *The Modernisation of EU Competition Law Enforcement in the EU: FIDE 2004 National Reports* (Cambridge University Press, 2004) 195.

[33] Becker in Loewenheim/Meessen/Riesenkampff (n 23) § 52 Rdnr 2.

[34] V Emmerich, *Kartellrecht* (Verlag CH Beck, 2008) 537.

[35] Bechtold (n 32) § 52 Rdnr 2.

[36] Becker in Loewenheim/Meessen/Riesenkampff (n 23) § 52 Rdnr 1, where the four times that the BMWi made use of its power to give general instructions (in 1972, 1976, 1978 and 1980) are listed.

[37] § 51(2) GWB.

sible for cartels, while the other nine units are structured according to sectors of the economy and have a broader agenda, dealing with both restrictive practices and merger control. In principle, these 12 units are exclusively competent for all enforcement decisions.[38] Decisions are taken in a three-member composition, consisting of a chair and two other members.[39] The members are government officials that have been appointed for life.[40] Eligible for membership are individuals suitable for a position as judge or senior civil servant.[41] Not only does this reinforce the arm's-length relation between the BKartA and the BMWi,[42] it also prevents the authority's superiors, notably the President of the BKartA, from influencing decisions.

In addition, the LKartBs may apply Articles 101 and 102 TFEU. LKartBs are established by their respective state legislators. The state legislator also determines the specific institutional structure of the LKartB and the procedures that it should follow in reparatory proceedings.[43] In practice, the state departments of economic affairs fulfil the role of LKartB, or better yet the state ministers or senators of economic affairs.[44] In contrast to the BKartA, LKartBs are not characterised by their organisational and functional independence, and proceedings for the enforcement of Articles 101 and 102 TFEU are integrated within the infrastructure of the state department. The resources devoted to competition law enforcement at the state level cannot be compared to the resources of the BKartA. Depending on the respective state administration, competition issues will be managed by anything ranging from a small team to a single part-time official. As a result, enforcement actions by the LKartBs under Articles 101 and 102 TFEU will remain rather exceptional. The allocation of enforcement competences to the LKartBs was mainly motivated by the objective of securing their role within the context of *national* competition law.[45]

[38] T Nägele in Jaeger/Pohlmann/Rieger/Schroeder, *Frankfurter Kommentar zum Kartellrecht* (Stand April 2009, Verlag Dr Otto Schmidt) § 51 Tz 13. Exceptions to this exclusive competence relate to investigatory powers, which in particular circumstances could also be exercised by officials of the BKartA. See § 59(3), (4) GWB.

[39] § 51(3) GWB. It is possible and common practice that a *Beschlussabteilung* consists of more than three members. This allows each *Beschlussabteilung* to deal with several cases simultaneously. A single *Beschlussabteilung* could thus render decisions in several compositions of three members.

[40] § 51(2) and (4) GWB.

[41] § 51(4) GWB. These decision-making units within the BKartA are not to be considered as courts in the sense of independent and impartial tribunals, but are '*unselbständige Untergliederungen*' of the BKartA. See Nägele (n 38) § 51 Tz 11–16.

[42] Bechtold argues that the BMWi could give instructions to the *Beschlussabteilungen*. See Bechtold (n 32) § 52 Rdnr 1.

[43] § 84 GG.

[44] Bechtold (n 32) § 48 Rdnr 3; H-J Bunte, *Kartellrecht* (Verlag CH Beck, 2008) 401.

[45] Due to Article 3(1) of Regulation 1/2003, national authorities need to apply EU competition law in parallel to national competition law. Without the power to apply Articles 101 and 102 TFEU, the role of the LKartBs with regard to national competition law would be rendered less meaningful. See Begründung zum Regierungsentwurf der 7. GWB-Novelle vom 26. Mai 2004, *WuW-Sonderheft* (Verlagsgruppe Handelsblatt, 2005) 141.

Case Allocation and Network Cooperation

Case allocation between the BKartA and the LKartBs takes place in accordance with § 48(2) GWB. Enforcement proceedings can be transferred from the BKartA to an LKartB and vice versa. Whenever the BKartA or the LKartBs initiate enforcement procedures, a duty exists to inform the relevant LKartB or the BKartA.[46] This mechanism applies to the initiation of both reparatory and penalty proceedings.[47] Enforcement competence is allocated on the basis of an effect principle (*Auswirkungsprinzip*).[48] Neither the seat of the undertakings involved nor the geographical markets in which they are active are relevant for case allocation purposes. The BKartA is the competent authority for all cases where the anti-competitive practice affects more than one German state. Anti-competitive practices the effects of which are limited to a single state are handled by the LKartB of this state.[49] Already limited cross-border effects suffice to prompt the BKartA's exclusive competence.[50] In accordance with § 49(3) and (4) GWB, the BKartA and the LKartBs can deviate from this mechanism in individual cases and agree on a case being transferred to a federal or state level, whatever the case may be.[51] Thus, a statutory allocation mechanism applies by default, the binding effect of which can only be overcome through an agreement between the competition authorities.[52] Although this mechanism might not prevent disputes over the allocation of cases, issues of concurrency will not arise. Either the BKartA or a *single* LKartB is competent to take enforcement action,[53] but never both and never several LKartBs.

Some tasks in relation to EU competition policy fall within the exclusive domain of the BKartA. These exclusive functions concern activities within

[46] § 49(1) GWB. The LKartB that is to be informed by the BKartA is the LKartB of the state where the undertaking has its seat.

[47] *WuW-Sonderheft* (n 45) 140. See also § 36 OWiG in conjunction with § 81(10) GWB.

[48] Becker in Loewenheim/Meessen/Riesenkampff (n 23) § 48 Rdnr 4.

[49] ibid Rdnr 5.

[50] OLG Düsseldorf WuW/E DE-R 1179 (1181ff) – *Stromcontracting*. Indications of cross-border effects suffice for the BKartA to assume competence. If the investigations then later reveal that cross-border effects have not materialised, the case is transferred to the competent LKartB. For a more nuanced description of this effect principle, see Becker in Loewenheim/Meessen/Riesenkampff (n 23) § 48 Rdnr 5.

[51] Where an LKartB requests the BKartA to hand over a case, the transfer can be blocked by another LKartB.

[52] The binding allocation mechanism of § 48 GWB creates rights for the parties involved in reparatory proceedings (*Beteiligten*). This can be concluded from § 55 GWB, which provides a means for judicial redress against decisions of the BKartA and LKartBs assuming competence. It should be noted that decisions on relative competence are not an exact science and that the courts seem to deal with this issue in a rather flexible manner. Even when cross-border effect cannot be proved indisputably, this does not necessarily lead to the annulment of the decision; see, eg, OLG Düsseldorf Aktenzeichen VI-2 Kart 10/08 – *Transportbeton*.

[53] As a result of the exclusive competence of the BKartA for anti-competitive practices with cross-border effects, allocation issues between two or more LKartB will not arise.

the ECN and follow from §§ 50 and 50a GWB.[54] All communication of the LKartBs to and from the Commission and foreign NCAs takes place centrally over the BKartA. It implicitly follows from § 50(2) GWB that the LKartBs can give instructions to the BKartA on issues (eg, viewpoints and questions) concerning them and their cases.[55] The BKartA then takes on the role of agent of the LKartB vis-a-vis the Network. This centralised communication system does not prevent the LKartBs from pursuing direct contact with the Commission or other NCAs on a more informal basis.[56] In addition to this centralised system of notification and information exchange, the BKartA alone is granted the power and duty to cooperate with investigations of other Network members taking place on German territory.[57]

Decisions by the competition authorities can be appealed in two instances. A first instance appeal lies with the Court of Appeal (*Oberlandesgericht* (OLG)). A further appeal on points of law can be lodged with the Federal Court of Justice (*Bundesgerichtshof* (BGH)). The OLG with jurisdiction over the particular competition authority is exclusively competent. Decisions of the BKartA can be appealed before the OLG in Düsseldorf. The OLGs have specialised chambers that hear competition law cases.[58] The appeal procedures differ depending on whether reparatory sanctions or punitive sanctions are concerned.

With regard to reparatory sanctions, addressees and other interested parties can apply to the OLG for 'judicial review'.[59] Before the application reaches the OLG, the competition authority re-evaluates whether it maintains its decision. This mechanism is formalised by requiring the applicant to lodge its application for review with the competition authority. If the latter decides to maintain its decision, the application is transferred to the OLG.[60] The OLG then reviews the legality of the decision. This action for review is called a *Beschwerde*. The OLG investigates the facts of the case on its own motion[61] and can base its decision on new facts and evidence.[62] Within the boundaries of the application,[63] the OLG decides the case on the basis of the conclusions that it 'freely reaches from the

[54] The BKartA seems to be the only German NCA that has signed the Statement regarding the Network Notice; see <http://ec.europa.eu/competition/antitrust/legislation/list_of_authorities_joint_statement.pdf> accessed 1 July 2013.

[55] Bechtold (n 32) § 50 Rdnr 6; C-D Bracher in Jaeger/Pohlmann/Rieger/Schroeder, *Frankfurter Kommentar zum Kartellrecht* (Stand April 2009, Verlag Dr Otto Schmidt) § 50 Tz 10.

[56] *WuW-Sonderheft* (n 45) 184.

[57] § 50(3) GWB.

[58] § 91 GWB.

[59] § 63(4) GWB.

[60] Bechtold (n 32) § 66 Rdnr 3.

[61] § 70(1) GWB.

[62] § 63(1) GWB.

[63] Bechtold (n 32) § 71 Rdnr 6.

overall results of the proceedings'.[64] This phrase should not be misinterpreted. These conclusions can basically lead to two decisions: the OLG may either uphold or annul (a part of)[65] the enforcement decision.[66] Annulment of the enforcement decision can be based on two grounds: the enforcement decision is ultra vires (*unzulässig*) or unfounded (*unbegründet*).[67] Judgments of the OLG can be appealed to the BGH.[68] The BGH will only consider the application of the law and will not re-establish the relevant facts and circumstances.[69]

In addition, penalty decisions can be appealed before the OLG.[70] Before having access to the OLG, the applicant should apply to the competition authority for administrative review (*Einspruch*).[71] The authority will then decide whether it maintains or withdraws its decision and, for this purpose, could reopen the investigation and, for instance, hear new witnesses.[72] If the authority decides to maintain its decision, it sends the case file to the public prosecutor.[73] The latter then takes over the case. The public prosecutor takes an autonomous decision on whether to pursue the case before the OLG.[74] Although the public prosecutor generally decides to continue prosecution, this decision could easily take several months and is by no means a formality. In penalty proceedings, the OLG undertakes a full merits review.[75] The decision of the competition authority has a mere guiding role and might best be described as an indictment. In accordance with the *Mündlichkeitsprinzip* (requiring all evidence to be brought in the proceedings orally) and the *Unmittelbarkeitsprinzip* (requiring the OLG to base its judgment on the findings reached in the main proceedings), all facts need to be established afresh. For this purpose, the court disposes of investigatory powers, most notably the hearing of (expert) witnesses.[76] The OLG does not give a ruling on the enforcement decision, but renders a wholly autonomous enforcement decision instead, vesting 'original' rights and obligations. The decision of the OLG may even lead to a more severe penalty than that originally imposed and thus to a *reformatio in*

[64] § 71(1) GWB ('*Das Beschwerdegericht entscheidet durch Beschluss nach seiner freien, aus dem Gesamtergebnis des Verfahrens gewonnenen Überzeugung*').

[65] Bechtold (n 32) § 71 Rdnr 6.

[66] § 71(2) GWB.

[67] ibid.

[68] §§ 74(1) and 76(2) GWB.

[69] § 76(2) and (4) GWB.

[70] § 83 GWB.

[71] § 67 OWiG.

[72] § 69(2) OWiG.

[73] §§ 69(3) OWiG and 83(1) GWB.

[74] In penalty proceedings, the initiation and continuation of proceedings fall within the *pflichtgemäßen Ermessen* of the 'prosecuting authority'. This follows from § 47 OWiG. By referring to the 'prosecuting authority' (*Verfolgungsbehörde*), the scope of § 47 OWiG covers not only the initiation of proceedings by the competition authorities but also extends to the continuation of the proceedings by the public prosecutor after an application has been made for administrative review.

[75] § 77(1) OWiG.

[76] § 71(2) OWiG. This could for instance mean that leniency applicants and authors/proprietors of incriminating documentary evidence are heard.

peius.[77] For example, in the recent *Flüssiggaskartell* case, the OLG Düsseldorf imposed fines totalling €244 million, whereas the BKartA's fine did not exceed €180 million.[78] Decisions by the OLG may be appealed on points of law to the BGH.[79]

5.2.3 Enforcement Institutions in the Netherlands

The institutional enforcement framework in the Netherlands has recently been changed. Until 1 April 2013, Articles 101 and 102 TFEU were enforced by the Netherlands Competition Authority (*Nederlandse Mededingingsautoriteit* (NMa)). The NMa was established by the introduction of the Netherlands Competition Act in 1998. At the beginning of 2011, and as part of a broader governmental cost savings and austerity plan, preparations began for institutional changes. This has resulted in the merger of the NMa with the Independent Post and Telecommunications Authority (*Onafhankelijke Post en Telecommunicatie Autoriteit*) and the Consumers Authority (*Consumenten Autoriteit*) into a single authority. This new organisation is called the Consumer and Market Authority (*Autoriteit Consument en Markt* (ACM)).[80] As of 1 April 2013, the enforcement of Articles 101 and 102 TFEU is thus in the hands of an authority responsible for competition law, sector-specific regulation and consumer protection.[81] The merger of the three authorities will have repercussions for the sanctioning powers under Articles 101 and 102 TFEU. In order to simplify and streamline the tasks of the ACM, the powers and procedures across the various fields of its activities will be harmonised.[82] The harmonisation of enforcement powers alone is expected to yield annual cost savings of as much as €2 million.[83] A 'Streamline law' is currently being prepared.[84] This book cannot anticipate all these changes, but will indicate as far as possible how the proposals will affect the current sanctioning powers.

The powers of the ACM for the enforcement of Articles 101 and 102 TFEU are laid down in three bodies of law. The Netherlands Competition Act (*Mededingingswet* (Mw)) provides specific powers for the enforcement of competition law. Pursuant to Article 89 Mw, the enforcement of Articles 101 and 102 TFEU benefits from all

[77] The possibility for a *reformatio in peius* is subject to one exception. If the main proceedings have not been opened and the OLG decides by ways of an order, the OLG cannot reach a decision that is more burdensome for the parties involved than the original enforcement decision; see § 72(3) OWiG.

[78] OLG Düsseldorf Pressemitteilung Nr 10/2013 (16 April 2013) <www.olg-duesseldorf.nrw.de> accessed 1 July 2013.

[79] § 84 GWB.

[80] *Wet van 28 februari 2013, houdende regels omtrent de instelling van de Autoriteit Consument en Markt*, Stb 21 maart 2013, nr 102.

[81] Apart from competition law and consumer protection law, the ACM will be responsible for the following sectors: energy, transport and telecoms.

[82] TK 2012–13, 33622, nr 2.

[83] TK 2012–13, 33622, nr 3.

[84] ibid.

enforcement powers available for national competition law.[85] These powers are supplemented by the Law Establishing the ACM (*Wet van 28 februari 2013, houdende regels omtrent de instelling van de Autoriteit Consument en Markt*, hereinafter the 'ACM law') and the General Act on Administrative Law (*Algemene wet bestuursrecht* (Awb)). These two framework laws extend beyond the enforcement of competition law.

Enforcement powers are vested in the Board of Directors of the ACM. The Directors are appointed by the responsible minister. The Chairperson is appointed for a period of seven years. All other Directors serve five-year terms. Directors can be reappointed only once. The minister can also terminate appointments.[86] The Directors are independent from government and private parties.[87] The authority has no legal personality and staff are provided by the responsible minister. However, in accordance with Article 16 of the Framework Act on Independent Government Agencies (*Kaderwet Zelfstandige Bestuursorganen*), staff are subordinated and accountable only to the authority. The minister may adopt guidelines on the exercise of the authority's powers[88] and it may give instructions to the competition authority to take certain action in the context of Articles 101 and 102 TFEU.[89] The ACM law emphasises that these instructions may not relate to individual cases.[90]

The administrative procedure is divided by 'Chinese walls' into an investigatory phase and an adjudicative phase.[91] Accordingly, the activities leading to the imposition of a *fine or periodic penalty* will be performed by persons who have not been involved in the collection of evidence and the drafting of the statement of objections. In *ETB Vos*, this division of tasks was not respected and this led to the exclusion of evidence collected by the adjudicative department and – consequently – in the collapse of the case.[92] The Streamline law proposes internal separation between the investigatory phase and the adjudicative phase for all ACM procedures in which a *fine* is imposed. This means that procedures resulting in a periodic penalty payment, including procedures pursuant to Articles 101 and 102 TFEU, will no longer be divided by Chinese walls.[93]

When the competition authority decides to exercise its enforcement powers and impose a sanction, further safeguards are available. Parties can make an application to the authority for administrative review (*bezwaar*). The authority then has to reassess the case.[94] If the authority maintains (part of) its decision, parties

[85] For ease of reference, Article 89 Mw will not be included in future references to enforcement powers.

[86] Article 12 *Kaderwet Zelfstandige Bestuursorganen.*

[87] Articles 9 and 13 *Kaderwet Zelfstandige Bestuursorganen.*

[88] Article 5d Mw.

[89] Article 5b Mw.

[90] Article 9 ACM law.

[91] Article 54a Mw.

[92] Rb Rotterdam *ETB Vos* LJN BI3337.

[93] TK 2012-2013, 33622, nr 3.

[94] Pursuant to Article 92 Mw, this re-assessment takes place on the basis of an opinion of the Committee of Advice, an advice committee independent of the competition authority. The Streamline law proposes to terminate this phase of the administrative review procedure.

may apply to the Rotterdam Court (Administrative Division) for judicial review.[95] Parties may also request the authority to skip the administrative review phase and make a direct application to the Rotterdam Court.[96] The Court's examination is limited to the legality of the decision, with a full review of any punitive sanction.[97] However, this full review cannot lead to a *reformatio in peius*.[98] It should be noted that the application of this domestic legal principle in the context of EU law has been accepted by the Court of Justice.[99] A further appeal may be lodged with the Appeal Tribunal for Trade and Industry (*College van Beroep voor het bedrijfsleven* (CBb)).[100] Like the Rotterdam Court,[101] the jurisdiction of the CBb is *not* limited to points of law and extends to the facts on which the decision has been based.[102]

5.2.4 Enforcement Institutions in the UK

The institutional enforcement framework in the UK has been under review. With its 2011 consultation document *A Competition Regime for Growth: A Consultation on Options for Reform*,[103] the Department for Business, Innovation & Skills (hereinafter 'BIS') started a debate on the future of competition law enforcement in the UK. From the very beginning, BIS did not shy away from suggesting far-reaching changes to the institutional framework. Meanwhile, the Enterprise and Regulatory Reform Act (ERRA) 2013 has been adopted and the UK is in the process of merging two of its competition authorities, the Office of Fair Trading (OFT) and the Competition Commission, into the newly established Competition and Markets Authority (CMA). This merger was meant to limit duplication and inefficiencies caused by the division of enforcement responsibility between two authorities.[104] Traditionally, the OFT has been responsible for the enforcement of Articles 101 and 102 TFEU and their domestic equivalents. It has shared this responsibility

[95] Article 93(1) Mw.

[96] Article 7:1a Awb.

[97] Rb Rotterdam *Fietsenkartel* LJN BB0440. See more generally S Lavrijssen, 'More Intensive Judicial Review in Competition Law and Economic Regulation in the Netherlands: Vice or Virtue?' in O Essens, A Gerbrandy and S Lavrijssen (eds), *National Courts and the Standard of Review in Competition Law and Economic Regulation* (Europa Law Publishing, 2009) 182.

[98] Rb Rotterdam *Garnalen* LJN AY4888.

[99] Case C-455/06 *Heemskerk and Schaap* [2008] ECR I-8763.

[100] *Wet bestuursrechtspraak bedrijfsorganisatie.*

[101] Article 8:69 Awb.

[102] Article 22 *Wet bestuursrechtspraak bedrijfsorganisatie.* See further A Gerbrandy, *Convergentie in het Mededingingsrecht: De Invloed van het EG-Recht op Materiële Toepassing, Toegang, Bewijs en Toetsing bij de Nederlandse Mededingingsbestuursrechter, Bezien in het Licht van Effectieve Rechtsbescherming* (Boom Juridische uitgevers, 2009) 7.

[103] Department for Business, Innovation & Skills, *A Competition Regime for Growth: A Consultation on Options for Reform* (2011) <www.bis.gov.uk/Consultations/competition-regime-for-growth> accessed 1 July 2013.

[104] Department for Business, Innovation & Skills, *Enterprise and Regulatory Reform Act 2013: Policy Paper* (2013) <www.gov.uk/government/uploads/system/uploads/attachment_data/file/209896/bis-13-905-enterprise-and-regulatory-reform-act-2013-policy.pdf> accessed 1 July 2013, para 3.1.

with various sector regulators. The remit of the Competition Commission has been more diverse, but did not include Articles 101 and 102 TFEU. The replacement of the OFT and Competition Commission by the CMA will become effective as of 1 April 2014. This book will anticipate this merger and all other changes brought about by the ERRA 2013 as much as possible.

Prior to the establishment of the CMA, the enforcement of competition law in the UK was shared by the OFT, sector regulators and the Competition Commission. Apart from its role in merger control, the Competition Commission undertook so-called market investigations upon a reference by the OFT,[105] the sector regulators[106] or the Secretary of State.[107] A reference could be made if there were reasonable grounds for suspecting that any feature, or combination of features of a UK market, prevented, restricted or distorted competition in connection with the supply or acquisition of any goods or services in (a part of) the UK.[108] The term 'feature of a market' relates to the structure of the market and the conduct by market operators.[109] Once a reference had been made, the Competition Commission examined whether any feature of a market adversely affected competition by preventing, restricting or distorting competition.[110] It further decided whether and what action should be taken to remedy, mitigate or prevent the adverse effect on competition or the detrimental consequences for customers.[111] It could either adopt remedies itself or make recommendations for others to adopt remedies. The remedies with regard to individual undertakings could include behavioural remedies (restrictions on conduct and obligations to be performed, including the supply and publication of information) and structural remedies (restrictions on acquisitions and obligations of division).[112] Irrespective of the Competition Commission's important role in the implementation of competition policy, it had not been designated as an NCA and could not apply Articles 101 and 102 TFEU. To date, market investigations can be conducted by the CMA.

Several UK authorities share responsibility for the enforcement of Articles 101 and 102 TFEU.[113] These are the following:

- the CMA;
- the Office of Communications ('Ofcom');
- the Gas and Electricity Markets Authority ('Ofgem');

[105] EA02, s 131.

[106] Communications Act 2003, s 370; Electricity Act 1989, s 43; Gas Act 1986, s 36A; Transport Act 2000, s 86; Water Industry Act 1991, s 31; Railways Act 1993, s 67; Electricity (Northern Ireland) Order 1992, s 46; Gas (Northern Ireland) Order 1996, s 23.

[107] EA02, s 132.

[108] EA02, s 131(1). Competition concerns that would otherwise have been referred to the Competition Commission for a market investigation can also be addressed by the referring authority itself by accepting undertakings in lieu of a reference; see EA02, s 154.

[109] EA02, s 131(2).

[110] EA02, s 134(1) and (2).

[111] EA02, s 134(4).

[112] EA02, sch 8.

[113] Competition Act 1998 and Other Enactments (Amendment) Regulations 2004, SI 2004/1261, reg 3.

- the Water Services Regulation Authority ('OFWAT');
- the Office of Rail Regulation (ORR);
- the Civil Aviation Authority (CAA);
- the Northern Ireland Authority for Utility Regulation ('OFREG NI').

The CMA and sector regulators are all part of the ECN.[114] These authorities will be jointly referred to as 'UK authorities', 'competition authorities' or 'authorities'. For the purposes of EU competition law, the CMA is clearly the most important UK authority.[115] The powers of the six sector regulators with regard to Articles 101 and 102 TFEU do not extend beyond their respective sectors. The CMA can apply Articles 101 and 102 TFEU to anti-competitive practices in any sector. For a limited number of sectors, the CMA thus shares its powers under Articles 101 and 102 TFEU with one of the sector regulators.[116]

Case Allocation

Rules on concurrency between the CMA and the sector regulators in relation to Articles 101 and 102 TFEU are laid down in the Competition Act 1998 (Concurrency) Regulations 2004 (hereinafter 'the Concurrency Regulations').[117] The Concurrency Regulations provide that none of the authorities is to exercise investigatory or enforcement action as long as the best placed authority is not decided on[118] or once this has been decided in favour of another authority.[119] The decision on the best placed authority is agreed upon by the authorities themselves.[120] If agreement cannot be reached, the Secretary of State determines who will handle the case.[121] Any authority that intends to undertake investigatory or enforcement action should first inform the other competent authorities.[122] During the investigation, cases

[114] OFT, *Concurrent application to regulated industries* (OFT 405 2004), para 4.12 <www.oft.gov.uk/shared_oft/business_leaflets/ca98_guidelines/oft405.pdf> accessed 1 July 2013. The OFT and sector regulators have all signed the acknowledgement statement annexed to the Network Notice; see <http://ec.europa.eu/competition/antitrust/legislation/list_of_authorities_joint_statement.pdf> accessed 1 July 2013.

[115] R Whish and D Bailey, *Competition Law* 7th edn (Oxford University Press, 2012) 438.

[116] The sector regulators are responsible for the following sectors: Ofcom for activities connected with communications matters; Ofgem for activities connected with the commercialisation of gas and commercial activities connected with the generation, transmission or supply of electricity or the use of electricity interconnectors; OFWAT for commercial activities connected with the supply of water or securing a supply of water or with the provision or securing of sewerage services; ORR for the supply of services relating to railways; CAA for the supply of air traffic services; and OFREG NI for the conveyance, storage or supply of gas and commercial activities connected with the generation, transmission or supply of electricity.

[117] Competition Act 1998 (Concurrency) Regulations 2004, SI 2004/1077.

[118] ibid reg 6(1).

[119] ibid reg 6(2).

[120] ibid reg 4(2).

[121] ibid reg 5(1).

[122] ibid reg 4(1).

can be transferred from one authority to another.[123] The Concurrency Working Party, consisting of the various authorities, has a coordinating role in this process.[124] The best placed authority is decided on the basis of factors including: the sectoral knowledge of a regulator; whether more than one regulatory sector is affected; whether there have been previous contacts between the authority and the complainants or parties; and whether any authority has recent experience with the undertakings or issues involved.[125] In March 2012, the UK government has decided to amend the Concurrency Regulations with a view to require more information sharing between the various authorities and to permit the new CMA to take over cases from the sector regulators.[126] As of 1 July 2013, no new Concurrency Regulations have been adopted, but the ERRA 2013 has formalized the UK government's intentions.[127]

In addition to the enforcement of Articles 101 and 102 TFEU and the equivalent domestic provisions, both the CMA and the sector regulators have other responsibilities. The sector regulators are first and foremost regulators of their respective sector, meaning that they monitor and determine the conditions under which goods and services are commercialised. The CMA's responsibilities extend to consumer protection, although this could change in the near future.[128]

The CMA and the sector regulators have identical powers for the enforcement of Articles 101 and 102 TFEU, but operate under distinct institutional frameworks. These institutional differences mainly concern the degree of independence to government. The CMA is a so-called non-ministerial department, giving it independence from government.[129] It consists of a Board and a Panel and is assisted by staff and a Chief Executive Officer. Board and Panel members are appointed by the Secretary of State.[130] The Board is composed of a chair and no fewer than five other members.[131] Board members serve five-year terms and can be reappointed.[132] Decisions on the basis of Articles 101 and 102 TFEU are taken by or under the authority of the CMA Board.[133] In the days of the OFT, the power to enforce Articles

[123] ibid reg 7(1). The undertaking under investigation has the opportunity to make representations on the proposed transfer unless the undertaking is still unaware of the procedures: reg 7(2)–(4).

[124] OFT (n 114) paras 3.9–3.11.

[125] ibid para 3.13.

[126] Department for Business, Innovation & Skills, *Growth, Competition and the Competition Regime: Government Response to Consultation* (2012) <www.bis.gov.uk/Consultations/competition-regime-for-growth> accessed 1 July 2013, para 8.28.

[127] ERRA 2013, ss 51–53.

[128] Department for Business, Innovation & Skills (n 126) para 10.8.

[129] Department for Business, Innovation & Skills (n 104).

[130] ERRA 2013, sch 4, para 1(1).

[131] ibid para 1(3).

[132] ibid paras 3 and 4.

[133] ibid para 28.

101 and 102 TFEU was delegated to senior officials. These officials decided whether to open an investigation, whether there was sufficient evidence to issue a statement of objections and whether there was sufficient evidence to issue an infringement decision.[134] One may expect a similar modus operandi for the CMA.[135] The CMA Panel has little relevance for the enforcement of Articles 101 and 102 TFEU. Its tasks are mainly in the area of merger control and market investigations. The CMA Panel can thus be seen as the successor of the Competition Commission (see above).

Institutional Differences

The CMA and the sector regulators have identical powers in terms of the enforcement of Articles 101 and 102 TFEU, but operate under distinct institutional frameworks. Compared to the CMA, the institutional arrangements for the CAA differ most significantly. The CAA is not a servant or agent of the Crown and does not enjoy any status, privilege or immunity of the Crown.[136] It is therefore not exempt from any tax, duty, rate, levy or other charge whatsoever, whether general or local. Its property is not to be regarded as property of, or held on behalf of, the Crown. The CAA is a public cooperation. It consists of no less than six and no more than 16 persons.[137] These persons are appointed by the Secretary of State as members of the CAA.[138] Its work is not government-funded, its costs being met entirely from the charges it imposes on those it regulates. Pursuant to section 11 of the Civil Aviation Act 1982 and subject to consultation with the Secretary of State, the CAA can impose charges in respect of the performance of its functions.

The CMA thus administers Articles 101 and 102 TFEU and their domestic equivalents, the merger regime and the market investigation regime. With regard to the enforcement of Articles 101 and 102 TFEU and the domestic equivalents, the UK government has recently proposed separating investigation from decision making.[139] This is thought to encourage independence of mind and to reduce the risk of confirmation bias. Ultimately, this is meant to achieve a greater and swifter throughput of decisions whilst reducing the frequency and success of appeals

[134] *cf* OFT, *Review of the OFT's Investigation Procedures in Competition Cases* (OFT 1263con2 2012) para 2.14 <www.oft.gov.uk/shared_oft/policy/OFT1263con2> accessed 1 July 2013.

[135] As recently as October 2012, when the establishment of the CMA was already imminent, the OFT adopted new guidance on the application of Articles 101 and 102 TFEU and the domestic equivalents. This guidance paper indicates that senior officials with delegated authority will adopt enforcement decisions. See OFT, *A Guide to the OFT's Investigation Procedures in Competition Cases* (OFT 1263rev 2012) <www.oft.gov.uk/shared_oft/policy/OFT1263rev> accessed 1 July 2013.

[136] Civil Aviation Act 1982, s 2(4).

[137] Civil Aviation Act 1982, s 2(2).

[138] ibid.

[139] Department for Business, Innovation & Skills (n 126) paras 6.25–6.26.

against those decisions.[140] The UK government has indicated that it will evaluate the efficiency gains of this enhanced administrative model with a view to deciding whether or not to stick to the model of administrative decision making.[141] In March 2012, the OFT launched a consultation on how best to organise decision making under the administrative model.[142] This has resulted in the October 2012 *A Guide to the OFT's Investigation Procedures in Competition Cases.*[143] In accordance with this guidance document, a Senior Responsible Officer will decide whether there are sufficient grounds to open a formal investigation, whether there is sufficient evidence to issue a Statement of Objections, whether to adopt interim measures, whether to adopt a commitment decision and whether to settle the case.[144] The investigation itself will be done by a case team, including this Senior Responsible Officer. Once a Statement of Objections has been issued, a three-member Case Decision Group is appointed. This Group is responsible for taking decisions on whether to issue an infringement decision (with or without directions) and on the appropriate amount of the penalty.[145] The Senior Responsible Officers will not be part of this Group.[146] The case team will remain in place to progress the investigation under the direction of the Case Decision Group.

In March 2011, the OFT started a one-year trial with a Procedural Adjudicator. Parties under investigation can ask the Procedural Adjudicator to review certain decisions on procedural issues taken during an investigation. This includes, for instance, confidentiality requests. The creation of this adjudicator was meant to improve the speed, efficiency, transparency and accountability of investigations into potential breaches of competition law. In accordance with a government request,[147] the OFT extended the trial with the Procedural Adjudicator and expanded its role.[148] The Procedural Adjudicator has been formalised with the adoption of the ERRA 2013 and will thus be maintained by the CMA.[149]

Enforcement decisions under Articles 101 and 102 TFEU can be appealed before the Competition Appeal Tribunal (CAT) or the administrative division of the High Court. The CAT is a specialised competition law tribunal established under the Enterprise Act 2002 (hereinafter 'EA02'). The jurisdiction of the CAT is limited but binding. It hears cases only when jurisdiction is expressly conferred by

[140] ibid para 6.29.

[141] ibid paras 6.29–6.30. In this respect it should be noted that the consultation document that preceded this government response contemplated both the reinforcement of the existing administrative model, in which fines can be imposed by an administrative authority, as well as a turn to a wholly prosecutorial model, in which fines can only be imposed by an independent and impartial tribunal. See *A Competition Regime For Growth* (n 103) ch 5 and 10.

[142] OFT, *Review of the OFT's Investigation Procedures in Competition Cases* (n 134).

[143] OFT (n 135).

[144] ibid para 9.10.

[145] ibid para 11.27.

[146] ibid para 11.28.

[147] Department for Business, Innovation & Skills (n 126) para 6.25.

[148] OFT (n 134) para 1.12.

[149] ERRA 2013, s 42(5) and (6).

statute.[150] Depending on the issue at hand, the CAT undertakes either a full merits review or judicial review. The difference between these two forms of judicial redress has been succinctly described by O'Neill and Sanders:

> A full merits review entails the CAT inquiring into the regulator's assessment of the facts, with a view to deciding whether the correct decision was reached on all the evidence, including new evidence that may be laid before the CAT on appeal. In challenges by way of judicial review, the question is whether the regulator erred – it is not an appeal from the decision, but a review of the soundness of the underlying decision-making process, which does not normally require a consideration of fresh evidence.[151]

In judicial review procedures, the CAT may dismiss the appeal or quash the whole or part of the decision.[152] In the latter case, it may refer the matter back to the competition authority.[153] In cases where the CAT has jurisdiction to exercise a full merits review, it may assume the role of primary decision maker. In this capacity, it may, for instance, penalise undertakings more severely than the competition authority did[154] or establish liability where the competition authority did not.[155] With the adoption of the ERRA 2013, the broad jurisdiction of the CAT under a full merits review has been circumscribed. In reviewing decisions of the CMA, the CAT has to take account of the (revised) statutory guidance on financial penalties.[156] This amendment was motivated by the desire to discourage appeals rather than to circumscribe the jurisdiction of the CAT as such.[157] However, the jurisdiction of the CAT has come under the attention of policy makers more generally and the possibility of a full merits review may be reserved to punitive sanctions.[158]

Decisions of the CAT may be appealed on points of law[159] and in relation to the amount of a penalty.[160] In Scotland, the Court of Sessions is the competent appeal court. In the rest of the UK, appeals may be lodged to the Court of Appeal.[161] It should be noted that the admissibility of these appeals is dependent on the permission of either the CAT or the competent appeal court.[162] Reportedly, the CAT grants this permission only sparingly.[163] Judgments by the Court of Appeal and

[150] With regard to the cases under Articles 101 and 102 TFEU, see Competition Act 1998 (hereinafter 'CA98'), ss 46 and 47.

[151] E O'Neill and E Sanders, *UK Competition Procedure: The Modernised Regime* (Oxford University Press, 2007) 12.12.

[152] CA98, sch 8, para 3A(3)(a).

[153] CA98, sch 8, para 3A(3)(b).

[154] *JJB Sports plc* [2005] CAT 22.

[155] *JJ Burgess & Sons* [2005] CAT 25.

[156] ERRA 2013, s 44(3).

[157] Department for Business, Innovation & Skills (n 104) para 3.5.

[158] Department for Business, Innovation & Skills, *Streamlining Regulatory and Competition Appeals: Consultation on Options for Reform* (2013) <www.gov.uk/government/uploads/system/uploads/attachment_data/file/207701/bis-13-876-regulatory-and-competition-appeals.pdf> accessed 1 July 2013.

[159] CA98, s 49(1)(c).

[160] CA98, s 49(1)(a).

[161] CA98, s 49(3).

[162] CA98, s 49(2)(b).

[163] Whish and Bailey (n 115) 449.

the Court of Sessions can be appealed before the UK Supreme Court (formerly the House of Lords). In the absence of a statutory provision to this effect, and only then,[164] judicial redress takes place before the administrative division of the High Court.[165]

Whether a full merits review or a judicial review, the appeal courts will be able to rule on the 'governing principles clause' laid down in section 60 of the Competition Act 1998 (hereinafter 'CA98'). The purpose of this clause is to ensure that questions arising under part I of the CA98 'so far as is possible' and 'having regard to any relevant differences' are dealt with in a manner which is consistent with the treatment of corresponding questions arising in EU law. Part I of the CA98 contains the UK competition law prohibitions, as well as the sanctioning powers for infringements of EU and UK competition law. Section 60 of the CA98 requires the OFT and any court, first, to secure that there is *no inconsistency* between principles applied and decisions reached under part I of the CA98 and principles laid down in the EU Treaties and relevant decisions by the Court of Justice.[166] Second, the OFT and the courts should *have regard* to any relevant decision or statement of the Commission. While the implications of section 60 of the CA98 are far more diverse,[167] it provides a *domestic* legal basis for the application of EU principles in the national orders with regard to the enforcement of Articles 101 and 102 TFEU (see above, chapter four). The CAT indeed follows EU case law on access to file,[168] burden of proof,[169] standard of proof,[170] attribution of liability[171] and the conditions of intent or negligence necessary to impose a penalty.[172] There are limits to this consistency requirement, however. The governing principles clause cannot require a *contra legem* interpretation of domestic principles and powers. For instance, a difference in the method of setting fines between the OFT and the Commission is not prohibited under section 60 of the CA98.[173]

[164] O'Neill and Sanders (n 151) 12.133: 'Where an appellant chooses to apply to the administrative court in preference to an existing statutory mechanism of appeal, it is unlikely that the administrative court would entertain the application for judicial review where there is a statutory mechanism for appeal that has not been pursued.'

[165] ibid 12.04, 12.61 and 12.133. See also R Whish, *Competition Law* 6th edn (Oxford University Press, 2009) 427: 'In so far as the Act does not provide for an appeal there remains the possibility that a claim for judicial review may be brought before the Administrative Court of the Queen's Bench Division under Part 54 of the Civil Procedure Rules in relation to perceived procedural irregularities (for example unreasonable delay) or the improper exercise of administrative discretion. It may be that permission would be refused if the Administrative Court were to consider that a particular issue can be addressed within the statutory appeal procedure' (footnotes omitted).

[166] CA98, s 60(2) and (3).

[167] Whish and Bailey (n 115) 369–73.

[168] *Napp Pharmaceutical* [2002] CAT 1 [138].

[169] ibid [110]–[112].

[170] ibid.

[171] ibid [167].

[172] ibid [455]–[458].

[173] ibid [503].

5.2.5 The Degree and Drivers of Convergence

The four jurisdictions that have been analysed above have situated the enforcement of Articles 101 and 102 TFEU in entirely different institutional regimes. At the EU level, enforcement is entrusted to a single authority: the Commission. The more practical and preparational enforcement activities have been delegated to the administrative services of the Commissioner responsible for EU competition policy. The Commission is an integrated enforcement authority, combining prosecutorial and adjudicative functions. Its decisions are subject to judicial review before the EU judiciary. The General Court has unlimited jurisdiction with regard to the severity of punitive sanctions, allowing it to even increase the amount of the penalty.

The institutional enforcement framework in the Netherlands is fairly similar, but differs in relation to some key aspects. In the Netherlands, the enforcement of Articles 101 and 102 TFEU is also entrusted to a single, integrated authority. However, with regard to the administration of Articles 101 and 102 TFEU, there is an important institutional difference between the Dutch authority and the (administrative services of the) Commission. The former is divided into an investigatory department and an adjudicative department. Finally, there are substantial differences at the judicial review stage. Unlike the General Court, the first instance Dutch appeal court does not have the jurisdiction to increase administrative penalties. Unlike the Court of Justice, the jurisdiction of the final instance Dutch appeal court is not limited to points of law.

The institutional enforcement frameworks in Germany and the UK show some more fundamental deviations from the EU model. The German legislator has created parallel procedural frameworks for reparatory sanctions and punitive sanctions, has delegated enforcement competences to a federal authority and 16 state authorities, and has allocated decision-making powers with regard to the federal authority to 12 court-like chambers. Institutional features that do appear equivalent to the institutional environment in which the Commission operates differ to a significant extent in reality. If a penalty decision of a German authority is appealed, the decision of the competition authority more or less gets demoted to an indictment. In this appeal procedure, all facts need to be established afresh. If the court is satisfied with the authority's case, it may decide to impose a lower or higher fine than that originally levied by the authority.

The UK has opted for yet another institutional design, with enforcement competences being shared between a general competition authority and various sector regulators. Another institutional feature that distinguishes the UK from the other three jurisdictions concerns the appeal procedures. Judicial protection against enforcement decisions under Article 101 and 102 TFEU is allocated to different tribunals, with different review mandates.

More than just identifying these static institutional differences, this section has also revealed tendencies of institutional convergence. With regard to the latter point, reference could be made to the Procedural Adjudicator trial in the UK. The role of this Procedural Adjudicator is comparable to the Hearing Officer in Commission proceedings. Parties under investigation can ask the Procedural Adjudicator to review certain decisions on procedural issues taken during an investigation. A more salient point of convergence relates to the allocation of decision-making powers within the various NCAs. The UK's newly established procedure for collective decision making combines features of the Dutch and the German institutional regimes. By delegating decision-making powers to three officials with no prior involvement in the investigations, the CMA separates investigation from decision making while at the same time creating ad hoc decision-making chambers. These examples can be seen as instances of convergence and indicate that convergence tendencies are inspired both by the EU model and national enforcement features.

Finally, it is worth noting that both in the Netherlands and the UK, institutional changes have been made to enhance the efficiency of enforcement. In the Netherlands, the competition authority has merged with the Independent Post and Telecommunications Authority and the Consumers Authority. In the UK, the two most important competition authorities have been merged. Both mergers were motivated by a desire to limit duplication and speed up decision making. This indicates that far-reaching changes have been made to save taxpayers money. It also indicates that the efficiency of the enforcement of Articles 101 and 102 TFEU is politically salient and may prompt changes to existing enforcement systems.

5.3 INTERIM MEASURES

The investigation of infringements of Articles 101 and 102 TFEU may take a long time. Years can separate the earliest signal of anti-competitive conduct and the adoption of a decision that censures this behaviour. The duration of enforcement procedures may last from anything from a couple months to many years. In the meantime, competition may be irreparably damaged. For example, an entrant in a market that challenges the dominance of an incumbent may have withdrawn from the market already. To prevent scenarios such as these from happening, legislators can grant their competition authorities powers to adopt so-called interim measures. Through these measures, competition authorities can protect the status quo on the market pending the investigations. Interim measures are essentially means for temporary conservation. Regulation 1/2003 explicitly provides for such measures. The Commission can adopt interim measures by virtue of Article 8 of Regulation 1/2003, while Article 5 of this Regulation allows for similar measures to be taken by the NCAs. It has been concluded in section 4.6.3 that the EU principle of effectiveness even requires Member States to accommodate interim measures. This section details the degree and drivers of convergence in this area.

5.3.1 The Powers of the Commission

Already prior to the entering into force of Regulation 1/2003, the Court of Justice concluded that the power to adopt interim measures should be seen as an essential feature in the enforcement process. Adopting interim measures could be a necessary first stage in the termination of infringements of Articles 101 and 102 TFEU.[174] Meanwhile, Regulation 1/2003 has codified and reinforced this Commission power. Breach of interim measures is threatened with fines and periodic penalty payments. The Commission may impose a periodic penalty payment of up to five per cent of the undertaking's average daily turnover per day of non-compliance.[175] Where the addressee *intentionally or negligently* contravenes an interim measures decision, the Commission may also impose a fine of up to 10 per cent of the undertaking's worldwide turnover.[176]

The Commission may order interim measures on the basis of a prima facie infringement. However, the use of this power is reserved for behaviour that poses an urgent risk of 'serious and irreparable damage to competition'. This damage relates to competition rather than competitors. While the prospect of a forced market exit due to a prima facie infringement may justify the adoption of interim measures, the interests of individual undertakings alone are not (or at least are no longer) decisive.[177] In this respect, it should be noted that victims of anti-competitive behaviour always have the possibility of starting private actions before the national courts. Within the limits of Article 16(1) of Regulation 1/2003, these courts should provide for interim relief whenever appropriate.[178] As to the point of urgency, the Commission should take into account the time it will take to reach a final decision.[179] Regulation 1/2003 does not circumscribe the type of measures that can be ordered. Interim measures can thus take the form of temporary prohibitions or requirements (eg, the termination of prima facie predatory conduct or the resumption of supplies).[180] However, the measures must be temporary or conservatory. Accordingly, interim measures may only be adopted for a limited period of time (but are renewable)[181] and will expire with the adoption of a final decision. Prior to the adoption of interim measures, the Commission should give the addressees the opportunity of being heard. For this purpose, undertakings have access to the

[174] Case 792/79 R *Camera Care* [1980] ECR 119 [17].

[175] Article 24(1) of Regulation 1/2003.

[176] Article 23(2) of Regulation 1/2003.

[177] P Roth and V Rose (eds), *Bellamy & Child: European Community Law of Competition* 6th edn (Oxford University Press, 2008) 13.119. Prior to the entering into force of Regulation 1/2003, the Commission's power to adopt interim measures was recognised by the Court in Case 792/79 R *Camera Care* [1980] ECR 119. In *Camera Care*, the Court allowed the Commission to adopt interim measures 'in order to avoid a situation likely to cause serious and irreparable damage *to the party seeking their adoption*, or which is intolerable for the public interest' ([19]) (emphasis added).

[178] Case C-213/89 *Factortame I* [1990] ECR I-2433.

[179] Roth and Rose (n 177) 13.119.

[180] ibid 13.122.

[181] Article 8(2) of Regulation 1/2003.

Commission's file. The Commission should then consult the Advisory Committee on Restrictive Practices and Dominant Positions on the draft decision. Only after these administrative stages may the Commission adopt interim measures. A decision imposing interim measures can be appealed. While this does not suspend the measures, a separate application for suspension could be made to the President of the General Court. As interim measures are adopted on the Commission's own initiative, there is no need to reject a request to adopt interim measures by third parties by ways of formal decision[182] and there are in principle no possibilities to appeal a rejection either. In practice, the Commission uses its power to adopt interim measures sparingly.[183]

5.3.2 The Powers of the German Authorities

Pursuant to § 32a GWB, the German authorities may adopt interim measures in the context of investigations into infringements of Articles 101 and 102 TFEU. This provision has been introduced with the seventh amendment to the GWB, which entered into force in 2005.[184] It has been inspired by and largely mirrors the power of the Commission under Article 8 of Regulation 1/2003.[185] Interim measures under § 32a GWB are reinforced by fines and penalty payments.[186] Breach of interim measures can attract fines of up to €1 million or – in the case of undertakings – 10 per cent of the undertaking's worldwide turnover. Penalty payments may range from €1,000 to as much as €10 million. Addressees of the interim measures may apply for judicial review. This does not suspend the authority's decision, however.[187]

Interim measures are adopted on the authority's own initiative. They may be adopted where there is a risk of serious and irreparable damage to competition. Damage to one or more undertakings is not sufficient if the anti-competitive practice does not damage competition more generally.[188] Although the text of § 32a GWB does not refer to the existence of a prima facie infringement, this is generally considered a precondition for the adoption of interim measures.[189] The competition authorities have almost full discretion as to the type of measure to

[182] J Faull and A Nikpay (eds), *The EC Law of Competition* 2nd edn (Oxford University Press, 2007) 2.111.

[183] Whish (n 165) 253.

[184] Prior to the introduction of § 32a GWB, interim measures could be adopted by virtue of the still existing § 60 GWB. The latter provision is now applicable to competition law issues falling outside the scope of Articles 101 and 102 TFEU.

[185] Deutscher Bundestag, *Gesetzentwurf der Bundesregierung: Entwurf eines Siebten Gesetzes zur Änderung des Gesetzes gegen Wettbewerbsbeschränkungen* (BT-Drucksache 15/3640) 33 <www.bundestag.de/dokumente/drucksachen/index.html> accessed 1 July 2013.

[186] § 81(2), (4) GWB (for fines); § 86a GWB (for penalty payments).

[187] J Bornkamm in Langen/Bunte (n 24) § 32a Rdnr 8.

[188] ibid Rdnr 3.

[189] T Klose in G Wiedemann, *Handbuch des Kartellrechts* (Verlag CH Beck, 2008) § 51 Rdnr 27; Bechtold (n 32) § 32a Rdnr 5; Bornkamm in Langen/Bunte (n 24) § 32a Rdnr 4.

impose, although the nature of this instrument excludes the ordering of structural measures.[190] In principle, the competition authorities should hear the parties prior to the adoption of interim measures.[191] For this purpose, parties should be granted access to the authority's file.[192] However, when the circumstances demand urgent intervention, interim measures may be adopted without hearing the parties in advance.[193] In these exceptional cases, parties should be given the possibility to be heard directly after the adoption of the interim measures.[194] This possibility of adopting interim measures instantly allows the German authorities to intervene directly upon a prima facie infringement. In any case, § 32a GWB limits the duration of the interim measures to one year.[195] Within this period, the competition authority should render a final decision. This maximum duration urges the competition authorities to speed up the decision-making process. Considering both the possibility for direct intervention and the maximum duration, the powers of the German competition authorities seem relatively well streamlined. However, this has not led to a rich practice of interim measures. As yet, the German competition authorities have not published any interim measures decisions.[196]

5.3.3 The Powers of the Dutch Authority

Pursuant to Article 83 Mw, the ACM may impose a *voorlopige last onder dwangsom*. Essentially this is an order for interim measures (*voorlopige last*) supplemented with an automatic (periodic) penalty in case of non-compliance (*dwangsom*). The penalty is automatically enforceable and can be executed by the authority.[197] This type of interim measure was and still is a unique measure in Dutch administrative law.[198] In practice, interim measures are occasionally applied for but are only exceptionally imposed.[199] The Streamline law will put an end to this 'experiment', as it intends to repeal Article 83 Mw.

Notwithstanding the measure's short life expectancy, it is worth studying the *voorlopige last onder dwangsom* in a bit more detail. Article 83 Mw allows for the adoption of interim measures on the basis of a prima facie infringement. The Dutch legislator sought to align the enforcement powers of the competition authority with

[190] Klose (n 189) § 51 Rdnr 28; Bornkamm in Langen/Bunte (n 24) § 32a Rdnr 4.
[191] Bechtold (n 32) § 32a Rdnr 11.
[192] H-H Schneider in Langen/Bunte (n 24) § 56 Rdnr 5.
[193] ibid Rdnr 4.
[194] Bechtold (n 32) § 32a Rdnr 11.
[195] § 32a(2) GWB.
[196] Bornkamm in Langen/Bunte (n 24) § 32a Rdnr 2.
[197] Article 5:33 Awb.
[198] BMJ van der Meulen, 'Bestuursrechtelijke keuzen ten aanzien van de toepassing van de Mededingingswet' (1999) *Markt & Mededinging* 19, 21.
[199] See also ibid 21–22; W VerLoren van Themaat and B Reuder (eds), *Nederlands Mededingingsrecht 2011* (Kluwer, 2011) 364.

those of the Commission.[200] However, Article 83 Mw seems more powerful than Article 8 of Regulation 1/2003. The penalty for non-compliance may either be a lump sum payment, a periodical payment or a payment for every new infringement.[201] The authority decides which type of penalty is most appropriate. While the ACM is required to indicate the maximum amount beyond which no further penalties will be levied (and obviously also the amount of the penalty that becomes periodically due), this penalty is not subject to any statutory maximum.[202] The only statutory limitation to the level of the penalty is that it should be proportionate both to the gravity of the prima facie infringement and to the purpose of the sanction.[203] The competition authority should indicate the period within which the addressee should implement the measure in order to avoid the penalty.[204]

Pursuant to Article 83 Mw, interim measures may be imposed where the behaviour is likely to qualify as an infringement and intervention is urgently necessary in view of the interests of the undertakings affected or the interests of effective competition. The interests of individual undertakings alone may thus already warrant the adoption of interim measures. In this respect, it should be noted that interim measures may be adopted not only on the authority's own initiative but also on the application of interested third parties. This combination of condition (interest of individual undertakings) and procedural right (right to apply for interim measures) suggests that third parties could try to 'force' the authority to adopt interim measures. Consequently, the position of third parties seems better protected under Dutch law than under EU law. The urgency of interim measures is considered in light of the expected duration of the adoption of a final decision. If by that time the consequences of the infringement could no longer be reversed – for instance, as a result of a forced market exit – interim measures may be taken.[205] Interim measures can require an undertaking to take or refrain from taking certain actions. These actions can be purely factual, but may also relate to legal obligations vis-a-vis third parties. The interim measures automatically lapse if the authority fails to issue a statement of objections within a period of six months. Obviously, the interim measures also lapse with the adoption of a final decision.[206] Before imposing interim measures, the authority has to communicate its plans to the undertaking concerned and allow it to make representations.[207] Interim measures are subject to judicial review, but the initiation of review procedures does not suspend the effects of the measure.[208]

With the introduction of the Streamline law, the power to adopt a *voorlopige last on dwangsom* will be repealed. However, this does not mean that the ACM is

[200] TK 1995–96, 24707, nr 3, p 97.
[201] Article 5:32b Awb.
[202] Article 5:32b(2) Awb.
[203] Article 5:32b(1) Awb.
[204] Article 5:32a(2) Awb.
[205] LEJ Korsten and M van Wanroij, *Nederlands Mededingingsrecht* (Kluwer, 2008) 287.
[206] Article 85 Mw.
[207] Article 84 Mw.
[208] Article 6:16 Awb.

barred from imposing interim measures altogether. After all, the ACM may adopt reparatory sanctions, including periodic penalty payments, in situations where an infringement is imminent (see below, section 5.6.3).

5.3.4 The Powers of the UK Authorities

The UK authorities also have the power to impose interim measures. This power is laid down in section 35 of the CA98 and originates in the 1998 reform, which was meant to align UK competition policy with EU competition policy.[209] Section 35 allows the authorities to give 'such directions as it considers appropriate for that purpose'. The temporary purpose of these measures suggests that structural measures are excluded. Interim measures cannot be enforced by the competition authorities directly. If a person fails, without reasonable excuse, to comply with these measures, the authorities may apply for a court order.[210] The court may then order the person in default to make good their failure within a given timeframe. In the case of undertakings, the court may direct this order to the undertaking itself or to any of its officers. Anyone who fails to comply with such an order will be 'in contempt of court' and can be sentenced to a term of up to two years in prison or to payment of a fine.[211]

Until recently, interim measures could be adopted when there were reasonable grounds for suspecting an infringement and when this was necessary as a matter of urgency in order to prevent *serious, irreparable damage* to a particular person or category of persons or to protect the public interest.[212] With the adoption of the ERRA 2013, 'serious, irreparable damage' has been exchanged for 'significant damage'.[213] This amendment was motivated by a 2012 observation by the UK government that interim measures are hardly ever used even though they have great value, particularly in cases of alleged predatory pricing.[214] The paucity of these measures has been explained by the fact that the conditions of 'serious, irreparable damage' constitute too high a threshold.[215] The UK government

[209] Competition HL Bill (1997–98) 140.

[210] CA98, ss 35(6), (7) and 34.

[211] UK courts are protected by the law of contempt, whether pursuant to common law or the Contempt of Court Act 1981, and hold an inherent or statutory power to punish for contempt. See Contempt of Court Act 1981, s 14. *cf* OFT, *Enforcement: Incorporating the Office of Fair Trading's Guidance as to the Circumstances in Which it May Be Appropriate to Accept Commitments* (OFT 407 2004) paras 3.16 and 2.9 <www.oft.gov.uk/shared_oft/business_leaflets/ca98_guidelines/oft407.pdf> accessed 1 July 2013.

[212] CA98, s 35(2).

[213] ERRA 2013, s 43.

[214] Department for Business, Innovation & Skills (n 126) paras 6.62–6.63.

[215] ibid para 6.64. The condition of 'serious, irreparable damage' has been interpreted by the OFT in its 2004 Enforcement Guidelines and by the CAT in its 2006 ruling in *The London Metal Exchange* [2006] CAT 19. 'Serious damage' is damage inflicting a considerable competitive disadvantage on the person(s) concerned and likely to have a lasting effect. This may be a loss of revenue or damage to goodwill or reputation. 'Irreparable damage' is damage which cannot be remedied by later intervention. The threat of insolvency of an individual undertaking will generally qualify as such.

therefore proposed the current lower threshold of 'significant damage'.[216] All other conditions from the pre-2013 era have been maintained. The condition of 'reasonable grounds for suspecting an infringement' applies to any power of investigation under the CA98 and is not particularly high.[217] The conditions of 'urgency' and 'public interest' have been interpreted by the OFT in its 2004 Enforcement Guidelines and by the CAT in its 2006 ruling in *The London Metal Exchange*.[218] It follows from *The London Metal Exchange* that urgency caused by the authority itself may not suffice for the adoption of interim measures.[219] This may be puzzling, as the authority does not have a 'personal' interest in ordering interim measures. 'Public interest' has been interpreted as the interest in preventing damage being caused to a particular industry, to consumers or to competition more generally.[220]

Interim measures can be adopted on the authority's own initiative or on a request. Before giving a direction, the authority must give written notice of its intention and allow that person to make representations.[221] This notice must indicate the nature of the proposed direction and the authority's reasons.[222] The addressee of the notice obtains access to the investigation file.[223] Before rejecting an application for interim measures, the OFT has allowed the applicant to comment and submit additional information on the provisional rejection decision.[224] Any decision by the authorities on the basis of section 35 of the CA98 whether or not to make particular directions may be appealed by the applicant before the CAT.[225] In practice, unsuccessful applicants for interim measures do appeal these decisions. This happened, for instance, in *JJ Burgess & Sons*, where a firm of funeral directors appealed against a decision of the OFT which rejected an application for interim access to its competitor's crematorium.[226] Appeals against interim measure decisions do not suspend the effect of these measures.[227] As an alternative to the adoption of an interim measure decision, the authorities may also accept informal assurances given by the undertaking in lieu of a formal decision.[228] Like interim measures, these informal assurances have also only been accepted on a few occasions.[229]

[216] Department for Business, Innovation & Skills (n 126) para 6.65.

[217] See also PJ Slot and AC Johnston, *An Introduction to Competition Law* (Hart Publishing, 2006) 227; O'Neill and Sanders (n 151) 6.62.

[218] *The London Metal Exchange* (n 215).

[219] ibid para 160. It should be noted that this ruling was given in the context of an application for costs after the OFT had withdrawn its rather frivolous interim measure decision.

[220] OFT (n 211) para 3.7. For further details, see *The London Metal Exchange* (n 215).

[221] CA98, s 35(3).

[222] CA98, s 35(4).

[223] Competition Act 1998 (Office of Fair Trading's Rules) Order 2004, SI 2004/2751, sch, r 9.

[224] OFT, *A Guide to the OFT's Investigation Procedures in Competition Cases* (OFT 1263 2011) para 8.12 <www.oft.gov.uk/shared_oft/policy/oft1263.pdf> accessed 1 July 2013.

[225] CA98, s 46.

[226] *JJ Burgess & Sons* [2005] CAT 25 [11].

[227] CA98, ss 46(4) and 47(3).

[228] OFT (n 211) para 3.17. Informal assurances are also possible before the CAT in lieu of interim relief; see *Albion Water* [2005] CAT 19 [4].

[229] Whish (n 165) 398.

5.3.5 The Degree and Drivers of Convergence

This section has demonstrated that the three Member States have sought alignment to Regulation 1/2003 with regard to interim measures. The NCAs in the investigated jurisdictions all have at their disposal the power to adopt interim measures and thereby fulfil one of their requirements under the principle of effectiveness (see above, section 4.6.3). Moreover, the conditions under which these powers may be exercised are largely identical. Yet, upon a closer examination of the various regimes, some differences emerge. First, it is worth noting that around the same time as the UK has reinforced its interim measures, the Netherlands is in the process of repealing its unused but uniquely strong interim measure powers. Going forward, the ACM will have to rely on its power to impose reparatory sanctions in situations where an infringement is imminent. Second, under UK law, interim measures may already be adopted where there are reasonable grounds for suspecting an infringement, whereas the other jurisdictions require a prima facie infringement. Third, there are differences with regard to applicable time limits and the administrative procedures. Under current Dutch law, a statement of objections in the main proceedings needs to be issued within six months of the measures having been adopted. Under German law, interim measures cannot exceed the duration of one year. More generally, it could be said that the German procedures for interim measures are relatively well streamlined. The maximum duration urges the German authorities to speed up the decision-making process in the main proceedings, while the possibility of ordering interim measures without prior hearing of the parties allows for a swift intervention. Fourth, there are differences with regard to the enforceability of interim measures. Under current Dutch law, interim measures are automatically supplemented with a periodic penalty for non-compliance. Under UK law, failure to comply can only be remedied through a separate court order, but contempt of court could result in a custodial sentence. Fifth, there are differences with regard to the role and relevance of third parties. Under both current Dutch and UK law, interim measures may be adopted in the interests of and on a request by third parties. The role of third parties before the Commission and the German authorities is less formal in this matter. These differences with regard to the powers and procedures for the adoption of interim measures should not obscure the fact that on the whole, interim measures are seldom adopted in any of the jurisdictions. There is thus only limited experience of interim measures.

5.4 EARLY RESOLUTION MEASURES

As mentioned earlier, competition law proceedings can span many years. The complexity of the applicable legislation, the confidentiality of business strategies, the secrecy of many infringements and the financial interests for the undertakings concerned all contribute to the protraction of enforcement proceedings. The administrative investigations alone can easily take a number of years, and the possibility of appeal in two or three instances may lead to a multiplication of this duration. Decades can go by before all legal remedies have been exhausted and an infringement is finally established. Apart from the legal profession and the bureaucrats involved, no one benefits from extended proceedings. Much can therefore be gained from undertakings and competition authorities finding a solution to their dispute at an early stage of the investigations, provided that this takes place in a transparent environment so as to limit the risks of maladministration and to enhance the precedent value of this solution. This section analyses the available enforcement powers and practices to reach such early resolution, as well as the degree and drivers of convergence in this area.

5.4.1 The Powers of the Commission

The Commission can steer towards the early resolution of competition law disputes in a variety of ways. Occasionally, it engages in informal resolution.[230] Undertakings then adapt their commercial practices and, in return, the Commission discontinues its investigations. The Commission's practice of informal resolution pre-dates the entering into force of Regulation 1/2003. To date, the Commission has at its disposal a formal means to reach early resolution. By virtue of Article 9 of Regulation 1/2003, it may terminate enforcement proceedings through the adoption of a so-called commitment decision. With such a decision, it makes binding the commitments offered by the investigated undertakings. Where it intends to censure anti-competitive practices and the undertakings concerned offer commitments that meet the competition-related concerns as expressed in a preliminary assessment, it may adopt a commitment decision. The adoption of a commitment decision is appropriate only in those cases where it does *not* intend to impose a fine.[231] A commitment decision does not establish the existence of an infringement, but simply concludes that there are no longer grounds for further action. While a commitment decision could be adopted for a specified period, the Commission is not required to limit the duration. The introduction of this power was motivated by considerations of procedural economy. It provides the Commission with a means to find a rapid solution to competition problems.[232]

Commitment decisions are reinforced by Articles 23 and 24 of Regulation 1/2003, allowing the Commission to impose fines and periodic penalty payments for failure to comply. Accordingly, breach of a commitment decision exposes

[230] Roth and Rose (n 177) 13.113.
[231] Recital 13 of the preamble to Regulation 1/2003.
[232] Case C-441/07 P *Alrosa* [2010] ECR I-5949 [35].

undertakings to a fine of up to 10 per cent of their worldwide turnover or a daily penalty payment of up to five per cent of their average daily turnover. Moreover, in the event of a failure to comply with a commitment decision, the Commission may reopen proceedings, either upon request or on its own initiative.[233] It may also reopen proceedings when there has been a material change in the facts on which the decision was based or where the decision was based on incomplete, incorrect or misleading information provided by the parties.[234]

Where the Commission intends to adopt a commitment decision, it has to 'market-test' the commitments by publishing a concise summary of the case and the main content of the commitments, thus allowing interested third parties to submit observations.[235] Once a commitment decision has been adopted, it may be appealed by the addressee of the decision and by interested third parties. By virtue of Article 263 TFEU, the addressee could argue, for instance, that the Commission has abused its powers and forced it to offer commitment, or that the commitments offered have not been reproduced correctly in the decision.[236] Third parties may want to challenge the proportionality of the commitment decision, for instance, when the commitments indirectly affect their commercial position. In 2006, Alrosa Company Ltd made use of this possibility when it challenged the decision that made binding the commitment offered by De Beers SA to refrain from purchasing Alrosa's raw diamonds.[237] This case shows that commitment decisions under Article 9 of Regulation 1/2003 are not subject to a comprehensive appropriateness test. The Commission should only verify:

> [T]hat the commitments in question address the concerns it expressed to the undertakings concerned and that they have not offered less onerous commitments that also address those concerns adequately.[238]

In carrying out this assessment, the Commission should take into account the interests of third parties.[239] However, the Commission is not required to seek out less onerous or more moderate solutions than the commitments offered.[240] This approach can be contrasted with the requirements of the Commission in the context of reparatory sanctions, where the proportionality requirements are more demanding (see above, section 4.6.5). In this respect, the legal safeguards for third parties affected by commitment decisions are more limited than for third parties affected by reparatory sanctions. In contrast, interested third parties have the possibility to comment on the proposed commitments, a legal safeguard they have to do without in relation to reparatory sanctions. Moreover, it should be noted that

[233] Article 9(2)(b) of Regulation 1/2003.
[234] Article 9(2) of Regulation 1/2003.
[235] Article 27(4) of Regulation 1/2003.
[236] Faull and Nikpay (n 182) 2.135.
[237] *Alrosa* (n 232).
[238] ibid [41].
[239] ibid.
[240] ibid [61].

subject to Article 16 of Regulation 1/2003,[241] a commitment decision binds neither national courts nor NCAs.[242] Therefore, a commitment decision in principle does not deprive third parties of the possibility of protecting any rights they might have vis-a-vis the addressee of this decision.[243]

The Commission regularly adopts commitment decisions. In the Commission's 2010 Report on Competition Policy, a graph indicates that in the period between 2005 and 2010, 19 commitment decisions have been adopted.[244] Practice shows that the Commission adopts commitment decisions for any type of anti-competitive behaviour except for hardcore cartels.

As commitment decisions cannot be combined with a fine for past behaviour, not every case will lend itself to this type of resolution. However, also in relation to infringements that do merit a fine, procedural economies can be sought. With regard to cartel cases, early resolution may be reached within the framework of the *Commission Notice on the conduct of settlement procedures in view of the adoption of Decisions pursuant to Article 7 and Article 23 of Council Regulation (EC) No 1/2003 in cartel cases* (hereinafter the 'Settlement Notice').[245] By virtue of Article 33 of Regulation 1/2003, the Commission has created for itself the possibility to engage in settlement discussions.[246] Settlements are meant to speed up the decision-making process once the Commission has sufficient evidence to proceed to the decision-making stage. The objective of the settlement procedure is to handle more cases with the same resources, thereby ensuring effective and timely punishment, while increasing overall deterrence.[247] Therefore, the Commission takes into account efficiency gains in terms of resources in engaging in and continuing settlement procedures.[248] In 2010, the Commission adopted its two first settlement decisions.[249] The Settlement Notice applies exclusively to cartels.

And then there is the third way for the Commission to come to an early conclusion of investigatory proceedings. The Commission can also reward the cooperation of the undertakings under investigation outside the context of the Settlement Notice. While this does not cut short the enforcement proceedings, cooperation by the undertakings can speed up these proceedings significantly. Both in terms of

[241] Article 16 of Regulation 1/2003 does not prevent national courts and NCAs from prohibiting behaviour condoned by the Commission for being contrary to Articles 101 and 102 TFEU and imposing sanctions. However, national courts and NCAs do seem precluded from adopting decisions that render the commitment decision ineffective. This point has been made earlier in MJ Frese, 'Het Toezeggingsbesluit; Kenmerken van een Nieuw Handhavingsinstrument' (2007) *Markt & Mededinging* 39, 42. See also Faull and Nikpay (n 182) 2.117.

[242] Recital 13 of the preamble to Regulation 1/2003.

[243] *Alrosa* (n 232) [49].

[244] [2011] COM 328 final 18.

[245] [2008] OJ C167/1.

[246] Commission Regulation (EC) No 773/2004 of 7 April 2004 relating to the conduct of proceedings by the Commission pursuant to Articles 81 and 82 of the EC Treaty [2004] OJ L 123/18, as amended by Regulation (EC) No 662/2008 of 30 June 2008 amending Regulation (EC) No 773/2004, as regards the conduct of settlement procedures in cartel cases [2008] OJ L 171/3.

[247] Settlement Notice, para 1.

[248] ibid para 5.

[249] Commission's Report on Competition Policy 2010 (n 244) 16.

its fining policy and its leniency policy, the Commission rewards undertakings for their cooperation in the investigations. The latter alternative is available for cartel cases only and is meant to trigger or advance an investigation by rewarding undertakings for providing incriminating evidence. While neither alternative is explicitly meant to reach early resolution,[250] both policy instruments support the Commission in achieving procedural efficiencies. In practice, virtually every cartel investigation benefits from the cooperation of the undertakings involved.

5.4.2 The Powers of the German Authorities

The early resolution of competition law disputes is also facilitated by the German enforcement framework. On the basis of § 32b GWB, the competition authorities may end their investigations into infringements of Articles 101 and 102 TFEU by declaring binding the commitments offered by the undertakings concerned. This power was introduced in 2005 with the seventh amendment to the GWB. § 32b GWB was inspired by and largely mirrors the Commission's power under Article 9 of Regulation 1/2003.[251] As with Article 9 of Regulation 1/2003, decisions on the basis of § 32b GWB refrain from any legal qualification of the alleged anti-competitive behaviour.

With regard to the feasibility of early resolution through commitment decisions, the distinction between reparatory proceedings and penalty proceedings plays an important role. Reparatory proceedings and penalty proceedings are distinct procedural trajectories that may run in parallel to each other in relation to a single infringement of Article 101 or 102 TFEU. The suggestion made by some authors that commitment decisions cannot exist alongside penalty decisions[252] can therefore be questioned. As the adoption of a commitment decision is only an alternative for infringement decisions in reparatory proceedings,[253] the offering of commitments cannot (formally) deflect penalties.[254] This could reduce the benefits for undertakings of offering commitments instead of mounting a defence against the allegations. While this circumstance seems capable of limiting the chances for early resolution, in practice, competition law disputes are frequently resolved through a commitment decision.[255] In 2008 alone, the BKartA adopted 18 commitment decisions. No examples have been found of anti-competitive practices attracting both commitment decisions and penalties.

[250] Within the framework of these policy instruments, the Commission is required to follow a full procedure, with all the regular legal safeguards.

[251] Deutscher Bundestag (n 185) 34.

[252] Bornkamm in Langen/Bunte (n 24) § 32b Rdnr 4 and 16.

[253] § 32(b) GWB.

[254] Commitment decisions cannot include any kind of financial obligation either. § 47(3) OWiG explicitly excludes this. Pursuant to this provision, the termination of penalty proceedings cannot be made conditional on the payment of a monetary amount to a '*gemeinnützige Einrichtung oder sonstige Stelle*'. This prohibition includes payments to the state or federation. See G Dannecker and J Biermann in Immenga/Mestmäcker, *GWB Kommentar* (Verlag CH Beck 2001) Vor § 81 Rdnr 162.

[255] Bornkamm in Langen/Bunte (n 24) § 32b Rdnr 2; Klose (n 189) § 51 Rdnr 31.

Commitment decisions can be enforced separately. The competition authorities may impose fines and periodic penalty payments for breach of commitments.[256] The limit of these fines is set at €1 million or 10 per cent of the undertaking's worldwide turnover. Periodic penalty payments range from €1,000 to €10 million. In addition, the competition authorities may enforce their commitment decisions by using 'administrative force' (*Verwaltungszwang*).[257] This means that the competition authority could even rely on *Ersatzvornahme* and *Unmittelbarer Zwang*, meaning that the latter could, first, require third parties to do whatever is in their power to have the commitments take effect (eg, give access to certain infrastructures) and, second, could itself take the measures that the undertaking has committed to.[258] It will depend on the nature of the commitments as to whether such direct enforcement is feasible. In any case, failure to comply with a commitment decision allows the competition authority to reopen proceedings under Articles 101 and 102 TFEU.[259] Proceedings may further be reopened when there has been a material change in the facts on which the decision was based, or the decision was based on incomplete, incorrect or misleading information provided by the parties.[260] In all other cases, the adoption of a commitment decision prevents the competition authorities from adopting cease-and-desist orders or interim measures.

Commitments can be offered only after the competition authority has notified the undertakings concerned of its preliminary concerns.[261] The commitments should be capable of dispelling these concerns. This means that they should either aim to address the authority's preliminary legal qualification or the urgency of intervention.[262] Commitments may take the form of behavioural or structural measures.[263] It falls within the discretion of the competition authority whether or not to close proceedings with a commitment decision.[264] The competition authorities have to ensure that the commitments are clear and specific enough to function as a legal basis for penalties in case of failure to comply.[265]

As a result of the consensual nature of commitment decisions, successful appeals by the addressees of the decision seems limited to situations of mistake (*Irrtum*),[266] where the decision does not coincide with the commitments offered[267] or where there is a disagreement on interpretation.[268] Commitment decisions may also be appealed by third parties provided that their commercial interests are

[256] § 81(2), (4) GWB (for fines); § 86a GWB (for periodic penalty payments).
[257] Bechtold (n 32) § 32b Rdnr 6.
[258] §§ 10 and 12 *Verwaltungs-Vollstreckungsgesetz.*
[259] § 32b(2) GWB.
[260] ibid.
[261] Bornkamm in Langen/Bunte (n 24) § 32b Rdnr 5.
[262] ibid Rdnr 7–8.
[263] ibid Rdnr 7.
[264] ibid Rdnr 16.
[265] ibid Rdnr 13.
[266] ibid Rdnr 10–11.
[267] ibid Rdnr 35–36.
[268] Bechtold (n 32) § 32b Rdnr 6a.

affected.[269] The competition authorities are not explicitly required to market-test the commitments before adopting the decision.[270] This deviation from the Commission model has some advantages in terms of procedural economy as market-testing could significantly prolong the proceedings. However, this does limit the legal safeguards of third parties. Of course, the competition authorities are not prohibited from publishing draft decisions and inviting comments.

The competition authorities may also seek early resolution in the context of penalty proceedings. These settlements are less formalised than the adoption of commitment decisions. The BKartA's settlement practice is part of its fining policy. It grants early confessing offenders a reduction of up to 10 per cent of the amount of the fine that would otherwise be imposed.[271] This practice supplements the BKartA's leniency policy, which also supports early resolution. The BKartA regularly manages to speed up penalty procedures, whether through a settlement or with the help of leniency applications.[272]

5.4.3 The Powers of the Dutch Authority

As is the case with the Commission and the German authorities, the ACM is also vested with powers to seek early resolution of competition law disputes. It may adopt a decision rendering binding the commitments offered by the undertakings involved.[273] These commitments can be offered even before a statement of objections has been issued and up to and until the moment that a final decision is adopted. If satisfied by the commitments, the authority can decide to terminate the investigations with a commitment decision. The authority then refrains from making a final decision on the nature of the behaviour and from imposing sanctions. This power was introduced in 2007[274] with the objective of aligning the domestic enforcement regime with Regulation 1/2003.[275] The authority regularly resolves competition concerns with a commitment decision.[276] Prior to the introduction of this power, the competition authority occasionally terminated

[269] ibid Rdnr 6a; Bornkamm in Langen/Bunte (n 24) § 32b Rdnr 39.

[270] Klose (n 189) § 51 Rdnr 38.

[271] Deutscher Bundestag, *Unterrichtung durch die Bundesregierung: Bericht des Bundeskartellamtes über seine Tätigkeit in den Jahren 2007-2008 sowie über die Lage und Entwicklung auf seinem Aufgabengebiet und Stellingnahme der Bundesregierung* (BT-Drucksache 16/13500) 35 <www.bundestag.de/dokumente/drucksachen/index.html> accessed 1 July 2013.

[272] ibid 35.

[273] Article 49a Mw. The Streamline law will change the legal basis for commitment decisions. In order to extend the scope of the ACM's power to adopt commitment decisions to all its fields of activity, the Streamline law amends the ACM law by providing a general power to adopt commitment decisions. Article 49a–d Mw will be repealed.

[274] *Wet van 28 juni 2007 houdende wijziging van de Mededingingswet als gevolg van de evaluatie van die wet.*

[275] TK 2005-2006, 30071, nr 19 herdruk.

[276] NMa Zaak 5709_1/242.B931 *Kinderopvang Amsterdam*; NMa Zaak 7138 *Stichting Zorggroep West- en Midden-Brabant.*

investigations informally after assurances about future conduct had been made by the undertakings concerned.[277]

Commitment decisions can be enforced separately. The Dutch authority may impose a fine of up to €450,000 or 10 per cent of the undertaking's worldwide turnover, whichever is more, for failure to comply with a commitment decision.[278] However, the authority *cannot* impose a periodic penalty payment. Breach of the commitments also allows the authority to reopen proceedings under Articles 101 and 102 TFEU.[279] Investigations may also be resumed in the event of a material change in the facts on which the commitment decision was based or in the event that the decision was based on incomplete, incorrect or misleading information provided by the parties.

The conditions under which commitment decisions can be adopted are part of the proposals to streamline the powers and procedures of the ACM across the various fields of its activity. These conditions may thus change in the near future. Currently, the conditions under which the ACM may adopt commitment decisions differ from the Commission's power under Article 9 of Regulation 1/2003, both in procedural and substantive terms. First, commitment decisions may only be adopted for a limited duration, although they can be renewed.[280] Second, and more importantly, while a commitment decision contains no judgment on the (il)legality of the undertakings' behaviour,[281] the ACM may adopt such a decision in order to 'prevent' or 'terminate' 'infringements' and provided that compliance with competition law is 'guaranteed'.[282] It follows that while the scope for commitment decisions is broader than under Article 9 of Regulation 1/2003 (termination *and prevention*), the conditions for application are more restrictive (termination and prevention *of an infringement*).[283] The conditions for the adoption of commitment decisions seem more restrictive in another sense as well. The ACM may contemplate the adoption of a commitment decision only when: (i) this *guarantees* that the undertakings concerned will indeed act in accordance with Articles 101 and 102 TFEU; (ii) it is likely that the undertakings will comply with the decision in a verifiable manner; and (iii) the adoption of a commitment decision is a more effective (*doeltreffend*) enforcement measure than a fine or a periodic penalty payment.[284] The ACM's predecessor has recognised that the text of Article 49a Mw differs from Article 9 of Regulation 1/2003, but has also indicated that it would interpret its powers in accordance with Article 9 of Regulation 1/2003.[285] The Streamline law seems

[277] See CT Dekker and AM Hoekstra-Borzymowska, 'Kroniek NMa-besluiten 2007: Mededingingsafspraken, machtsposities en procedures' (2008) *Markt & Mededinging* 46; LEJ Korsten and M van Wanroij, *Nederlands Mededingingsrecht* (Kluwer, 2008) 257.

[278] Article 76a Mw. With the adoption of the Streamline law, the legal basis for the enforcement of commitment decisions will be transferred from the Mw to the ACM law.

[279] Article 49c(1)(c) Mw.

[280] Article 49a(5) Mw.

[281] Article 49a(3) Mw.

[282] Article 49a(1)(2) Mw.

[283] This point has been made earlier in Frese (n 241) 47.

[284] Article 49a(2) Mw.

[285] NMa Zaak 6435/29 *NMa v X*, para 28.

to extend the circumstances under which commitment decisions can be adopted by applying a single condition: the adoption of a commitment decision should be more effective than any other sanction. Under this regime, the ACM may adopt a commitment decision even after an infringement has been established.[286]

The procedure that governs the adoption of commitment decisions is surrounded by various legal safeguards, both for the undertakings involved and for third parties. Currently, the preparation of commitment decisions takes place in accordance with the public preparation procedure (*uniforme openbare voorbereidingsprocedure*).[287] This is a general administrative law procedure in accordance with which draft decisions should be consulted and can be commented upon. For this purpose, the draft decision, or its most important parts, needs to be published in one or more newspapers. This ensures the transparency of the decision-making process and allows third parties to participate in the proceedings. However, it is unclear whether this public preparation procedure will be maintained once the Streamline law has entered into force.[288] What will be maintained is that commitment decisions, once adopted, can be appealed both by their addressees and by interested third parties.[289] The rejection of an application to close an investigation with a commitment decision cannot be appealed.[290]

Early resolution is also possible for cases where penalties are a more effective enforcement measure and where commitment decisions are therefore not available. The ACM rewards cooperative undertakings through the medium of penalty reductions in the context of the applicable fining guidelines and its leniency policy. Furthermore, in the context of widespread bid-rigging practices in the Dutch construction sector,[291] the ACM's predecessor has applied an ad hoc fast-track procedure in order to render the enforcement of over 1,400 cases manageable. Within the context of this unique procedure, undertakings could earn an additional discount by waiving certain procedural rights (eg, access to documents and the possibility of disputing the main findings). This has been a largely successful experiment and has supposedly attracted a lot of attention from other authorities.[292] Other examples of the authority's more general interest in early resolution are the deal it negotiated with representatives of the homecare sector, which was ultimately rejected by the homecare undertakings,[293] and the settlement it has

[286] TK 2012-2013, 33622, nr 3.

[287] Article 49b Mw.

[288] The Streamline law repeals Article 49b Mw and therefore terminates the applicability of the public preparation regime. However, the government has indicated that it expects the ACM to apply this regime on its own motion if it intends to adopt a commitment decision; see TK 2012-2013, 33622, nr 3.

[289] Article 8:1 Awb.

[290] Article 1 Annex 2 Awb.

[291] Bid-rigging could be described as agreements between undertakings on the conditions of their bids in the context of a public or private tender.

[292] The website of the ICN includes a presentation by an NMa official giving a presentation at the 2006 Cartel Workshop in The Hague on this bid-rigging investigation. See <www.internationalcompetitionnetwork.org> accessed 1 July 2013.

[293] NMa press release of 20 May 2010, available at <www.acm.nl/nl/> accessed 1 November 2013.

reached with a manager who was initially unwilling to pay a fine imposed upon him in the administrative phase.[294]

5.4.4 The Powers of the UK Authorities

The UK authorities may also seek early resolution of competition law disputes. They may, for instance, adopt commitment decisions to terminate investigations into infringements of Articles 101 and 102 TFEU. This discretionary power is laid down in section 31A of the CA98 and was introduced by the *Competition Act 1998 and Other Enactments (Amendment) Regulation 2004*.[295] This amendment was meant to align the domestic enforcement regime with Regulation 1/2003.[296] Prior to the introduction of this power, cases could be closed on the basis of informal assurances by the undertakings concerned.[297] The OFT has regularly managed to reach early resolution, whether by accepting informal assurances,[298] by adopting commitment decisions[299] or by negotiating informal settlements.[300]

Commitment decisions cannot be enforced directly. Instead, if a person fails to comply with a commitment decision, the authority may apply for a court order.[301] Application can be made for an order requiring the addressee to make good its failure within a given timeframe. In the case of undertakings, this order can be directed either to the undertaking itself or to any of its officers. Any person who fails to comply with such an order will be 'in contempt of court' and risks a custodial sentence or a fine. Alternatively, the authority could simply reinitiate enforcement proceedings under Articles 101 and 102 TFEU, possibly leading to the imposition of fines and reparatory sanctions.[302] Moreover, enforcement proceedings may be resumed where there are reasonable grounds for believing that there has been a material change of circumstances or that the commitment decision was based on incomplete, false or misleading information.[303]

Commitments can be offered in the period between the initiation of proceedings and the adoption of a final decision. However, the OFT has indicated that it will normally not make use of this instrument after the statement of objections

294 NMa press release of 11 November 2010, available through <www.acm.nl/nl/> accessed 1 November 2013. This manager reportedly paid the fine plus a part of the authority's costs for bringing the case before court.

295 SI 2004/1261.

296 Competition Act 1998 and Other Enactments (Amendment) Regulation 2004, explanatory notes.

297 *Pernod-Ricard* [2004] CAT 10.

298 ibid.

299 OFT Case CE/2479/03 *London-wide newspaper distribution.*

300 OFT Case CE/2890-03 *Independent fee-paying schools*; OFT Case CE/2596-03 *Tobacco.*

301 CA98, s 31E.

302 The OFT has indicated that it will consider a breach of commitments a strong indication that any infringement of EU competition law that derives from this breach was committed intentionally: OFT (n 211) para 5.7.

303 CA98, s 31B(4).

has been issued.[304] It has further indicated that it will accept both behavioural and structural commitments.[305] The power 'to take such action (or refrain from taking such action) as it considers appropriate' laid down in section 31A(2) of the CA98 indeed seems sufficiently unspecific to allow for both types of commitments. However, because commitment decisions will generally be adopted for a limited duration, structural commitments will be rather exceptional.[306] Once commitments have been offered, the form and content of these commitments can be subject to further negotiations between the party and the authority.[307] While a commitment decision will not include a statement on the legality of the undertaking's behaviour before or after the commitments,[308] it should state that the commitments meet the authority's concerns. Section 31B(3) of the CA98 suggests that the authorities may also adopt commitment decisions to deal with part of their concerns. Any remaining issues may then be addressed with an infringement decision. Although unlikely, this possibility has indeed been left open in the OFT's Guideline Enforcement.[309] In all likelihood, the CMA will continue the earlier practice of the OFT.

The adoption of a commitment decision is subject to various conditions. Commitment decisions can only be adopted if the salient issues are readily identifiable and the commitments can be implemented effectively.[310] Commitments that cannot be properly monitored will not be accepted and, in addition, deterrence considerations could lead to a rejection.[311] In line with the latter condition, the OFT has indicated that it will not accept commitments in cases involving secret cartels or serious abuses of dominance such as predatory pricing.[312] After a commitment decision has been adopted, the authority is no longer able to continue the investigation and to adopt other enforcement decisions.[313] Of course, this does not prevent the authority from monitoring compliance with the commitments or from re-evaluating their adequacy and effectiveness, and varying or releasing them whenever appropriate.[314] In fact, the Secretary of State may demand a report on the effectiveness of the operational commitment decisions.[315]

[304] OFT (n 211) para 4.16. See also OFT, *A Guide to the OFT's Investigation Procedures in Competition Cases* (OFT 1263rev 2012) para 10.18 <www.oft.gov.uk/shared_oft/policy/OFT1263rev> accessed 1 July 2013.

[305] ibid para 4.6.

[306] ibid para 4.8.

[307] O'Neill and Sanders (n 151) 10.33.

[308] OFT (n 211) para 4.7.

[309] ibid para 4.10. It seems rather exceptional that the OFT would accept such 'partial commitments'. In the same Guideline, the OFT has indicated that it will accept commitments only when they fully address its concerns (para 4.3).

[310] ibid.

[311] ibid para 4.5.

[312] ibid para 4.4.

[313] CA98, s 31B(2).

[314] CA98, sch 6A.

[315] CA98, s 31C.

Before a commitment decision can be adopted, the authority must market-test the draft decision by 'giving notice'.[316] The authority will give notice to 'such persons as it considers likely to be affected'. Interested third parties then have the opportunity to make representations.[317] Once adopted and in place, the addressee of the decision may always propose variations to the commitments.[318] Third parties with a sufficient interest may appeal to the CAT with regard to a decision of the authority to accept commitments, including a variation to earlier commitments, or to release commitments.[319] The addressee of a commitment decision that has unsuccessfully requested the authority to release it from the commitments may appeal to the CAT as well.[320] Moreover, the addressee may appeal against a decision that releases it from the commitments.[321] It may have an interest to do so, as the release of commitments allows the authority to resume enforcement proceedings. Notwithstanding the CAT's wide jurisdiction with regard to commitment decisions, it has *no* jurisdiction to hear appeals against a commitment decision by the addressee of such a decision. In the event of perceived maladministration in the adoption of a commitment decision, the addressee should file an appeal with the administrative division of the High Court.

Further to the adoption of commitment decisions, cases can be closed with a financial settlement.[322] Undertakings can benefit from a reduction to the amount of the fine as a quid pro quo for their admission and cooperation. The appropriateness of a settlement is decided on a case-by-case basis.[323] This reduction may be granted both within and outside the framework of the leniency programme.[324] In addition, these financial settlements could speed up procedures and lead to the early resolution of competition concerns. With the adoption of the ERRA 2013, the possibility of reaching a settlement has been formalised.[325]

5.4.5 The Degree and Drivers of Convergence

With a view to establish the degree and drivers of convergence, this section has analysed powers and practices to reach the early resolution of putative infringements of Articles 101 and 102 TFEU. There are essentially three alternatives for the early resolution of competition law disputes and these alternatives are available in all four jurisdictions. First, the authorities may agree to terminate the investigations after having reached a formal accord with the undertakings involved.

[316] CA98, sch 6A, para 2.
[317] OFT (n 211) para 4.21.
[318] CA98, s 31A(3).
[319] CA98, s 47.
[320] CA98, s 46(2)(g).
[321] CA98, s 46(2)(h).
[322] OFT (n 224) para 11.2.
[323] ibid.
[324] *cf* OFT Case CE/2890-03 *Independent fee-paying schools.*
[325] ERRA 2013, s 42(7).

For this purpose, the competition authorities can adopt so-called commitment decisions. With these decisions, the authorities can render binding the commitments offered by the undertakings under investigation. A commitment decision does not contain a statement on the legality of the commercial practices that triggered the investigation and therefore does not establish whether or not an infringement of Article 101 or 102 TFEU has been committed. As long as the undertakings comply with their commitments, the authorities will in principle refrain from reopening investigations. Breach of a commitment decision may lead to penalties, irrespective of whether this behaviour also qualifies as an infringement of Article 101 or 102 TFEU. In addition, the authorities may decide to reopen their investigations in order to censure and penalise the behaviour under Articles 101 and 102 TFEU.

The other two alternatives for the early resolution of competition law disputes are more informal or coincidental. Competition authorities may simply decide to terminate their investigations as a result of informal assurances given by the undertakings. No decision will be adopted and no fines are imposed (or looming), but investigations can be resumed at any time. Such informal accords have been practised by authorities in all four jurisdictions, but have lost much of their appeal with the introduction of commitment decisions. Procedural economies can further be obtained by rewarding the cooperation of undertakings with a reduction of the fine otherwise imposed. While this will not necessarily cut short procedures, it can speed up the procedures significantly. Mitigation as a quid pro quo for cooperation can be organised in the framework of the authority's fining policy or leniency programme, but can also be the subject of a separate settlement procedure. In the latter case, undertakings agree to a fast-track procedure in which they waive certain procedural rights in exchange for a reduction in their fine.

Strong tendencies of convergence can be observed with regard to the measures for early resolution of competition law disputes. All four jurisdictions provide for essentially the same alternatives, without any EU requirement to this effect. With regard to commitment procedures, it can be concluded that the domestic regimes have all been inspired by Regulation 1/2003. Article 5 of this Regulation explicitly allows NCAs to terminate investigations into infringements of Articles 101 and 102 TFEU with a commitment decision (see above, section 2.3). Parliamentary deliberations indicate that national legislators have sought to mirror the Commission's powers under Article 9 of Regulation 1/2003. When comparing the conditions and legal safeguards applicable to commitment decisions, it becomes clear that national legislators have largely succeeded in this objective. From a convergence perspective, it is also worth noting that the Dutch authority has shown some degree of 'administrative disobedience' with regard to its policy on commitment decisions. It has stretched its statutory powers by indicating that it will adopt commitment decisions under conditions equivalent to Article 9 of Regulation 1/2003.

However, there are also some notable differences. A first difference relates to the attractiveness for the undertakings concerned to engage in commitment procedures. The adoption of a commitment decision by the German authorities does not seem to preclude the same authority from penalising the undertakings involved for their past conduct. This is the consequence of the procedural separation of reparatory decisions and penalty decisions. In practice, the combination of a commitment decision and a penalty decision to terminate and punish a single infringement will be rather exceptional. A comparable situation occurs in the UK. The UK authorities may decide to adopt a commitment decision to deal with a part of their concerns. Any remaining concerns may then be addressed by an infringement decision and accompanying sanction. However, in the UK, partial commitments will be rather exceptional.

More substantial differences can be found in the context of the enforcement of commitment decisions. While not always feasible, the German authorities can enforce commitments even without the help of the undertaking that offered them. This possibility complements the authority's more conventional powers of enforcement through fines and periodic penalty payments. At the other end of the enforcement spectrum are the possibilities of the UK authorities, who need a court order to enforce their commitment decisions. Only a failure to comply with this court order will attract penalties. Yet, these penalties are severe. Contempt of court can attract custodial sentences alongside financial penalties. The Dutch authority and the Commission take the middle ground, but their enforcement powers differ. Whereas the Commission can enforce its commitment decisions through fines *and* periodic penalty payments, the ACM relies on fines alone.

The conditions for the adoption of commitment decisions and the role of third parties in drafting these decisions are not entirely uniform either. Unlike the other authorities, the German authorities need not to 'market-test' draft decisions. Were the German authorities indeed to refrain from consulting market parties, this would mean that third parties are in this respect worse off in Germany than in the other jurisdictions. Not having to deal with the observations of third parties of course also means that the German legal framework is better streamlined and more conducive to *early* resolution. Furthermore, there are some differences with regard to the possibility of judicial redress. Especially in UK law, detailed appeal arrangements for addressees and third parties have been put in place.

Outside the area of commitment decisions, all authorities are willing to engage in financial settlements and to reward undertakings that cooperate with the investigations. The Dutch authority in particular has built a track record of flexible financial settlements. However, in terms of detail and transparency, the Commission's settlement procedure is unprecedented.

5.5 DECLARATORY FINDINGS

With a declaratory finding, competition authorities can establish that an infringement of Articles 101 and 102 TFEU has been committed. Such a decision will normally be adopted jointly with a sanction, but may also be adopted separately in cases where a sanction would not be warranted or would no longer be allowed due to statutes of limitation. Not imposing any legal obligations, declaratory findings of past infringements cannot be considered sanctions themselves. Yet, the precedent value of such a decision may be used by the competition authority as an enforcement instrument and the exposure this will generate may feel like a sanction for the undertakings concerned.[326] In this respect, it is worth noting the intertwined systems of public enforcement and private enforcement. Pursuant to Article 16(1) of Regulation 1/2003, decisions of the Commission are binding for the national courts. The latter cannot take decisions running counter to the decisions of the Commission. This means that national civil courts should treat a declaratory finding of a past infringement by the Commission as indisputable evidence for the unlawfulness of the behaviour. Some Member States go even further. Under German law, more specifically § 33(4) GWB, civil courts are bound by the decisions of the Commission, the German competition authorities and the competition authorities of the other Member States. In addition, in the other Member States, decisions by the NCAs will always have at least some precedent value in the civil courts.[327] The binding effect (or precedent effect) of administrative decisions in private disputes facilitates victims in pursuing damages claims. The addressees of a declaratory finding might experience this as a sanction. Declaratory findings also contribute to the public enforcement of Articles 101 and 102 TFEU. The authorities may use this as an instrument to clarify the implications of Articles 101 and 102 TFEU. This limits information costs for market participants and may reduce future infringements. In this respect, declaratory findings of past infringements could be as valuable as declaratory findings of non-infringement. However, declaratory findings that Articles 101 and 102 TFEU are *not* applicable to a particular type of commercial behaviour, so-called findings of inapplicability, have been reserved for the Commission (see above, section 2.3). What remains for the NCAs are findings of applicability. This section details the degree and drivers of convergence in this area.

5.5.1 The Powers of the Commission

The Commission can adopt declaratory findings with regard to Articles 101 and 102 TFEU. Pursuant to Article 7(1) of Regulation 1/2003 and provided it has a legitimate interest in doing so, the Commission may find that an infringement has been committed in the past. It may also adopt declaratory findings in relation to persisting infringements of Articles 101 and 102 TFEU. In fact, the Commission

[326] *cf* Joined Cases T-22/02 and T-23/02 *Sumitomo* [2005] ECR II-4065, where the applicant argued (at [39]), albeit unsuccessfully, that a decision finding an infringement falls within the meaning of penalties.

[327] See also WPJ Wils, 'The Relationship between Public Antitrust Enforcement and Private Actions for Damages' (2009) 32 *World Competition* 3, 15–16.

is not even required to terminate persisting anti-competitive behaviour once it has found an infringement of Article 101 or 102 TFEU.[328] Prior to the adoption of Regulation 1/2003, the Court of Justice considered declaratory findings an implied power of the Commission.[329] More specifically, the Court found that the Commission's explicit powers to end an infringement and impose sanctions necessarily implied a power to make a finding that the infringement exists or existed.[330] Yet, the power to adopt a declaratory finding was not dependent on the use of explicit powers.[331] The termination of an infringement prior to the adoption of a decision did not in itself constitute an obstacle for the Commission to adopt such a finding.[332] However, this implied power was conditional upon the Commission having a legitimate interest in taking such a decision.[333] Article 7(1) of Regulation 1/2003 thus codifies existing practice. Further to the adoption of declaratory findings of past or persisting infringements, the Commission may also adopt findings of inapplicability. This power has been introduced by Article 10 of Regulation 1/2003. Where the EU public interest so requires, the Commission may, acting on its own initiative, adopt a decision stating that the conditions of Articles 101 and 102 TFEU are not fulfilled. As yet, the Commission has not made use of this power.

Declaratory findings of past infringements require a legitimate interest on the part of the Commission. These findings may be adopted where there is a real danger of a resumption of the anti-competitive behaviour so as to clarify that this is prohibited.[334] The General Court has further suggested that the Commission may adopt declaratory findings of past infringements in order to help injured third parties in legal proceedings before the national civil courts, provided that these proceedings are already initiated or can be envisaged.[335]

As long as there are no specific rules on the limitation period for declaratory findings, the Commission is only precluded from making such findings where it initiates these actions excessively late.[336] The procedure for the adoption of these decisions offers all regular legal safeguards. The parties involved should be given the possibility of being heard by the Commission, to comment on a statement of objections and to access the Commission's file.[337] Declaratory findings can be appealed. The General Court has demonstrated that it will seriously test the Commission interests in taking such a decision.[338]

[328] Case T-16/91 *Rendo* [1992] ECR II-2417 [98].
[329] Case 7/82 *GVL* [1983] ECR 483; *Sumitomo* (n 326).
[330] *GVL* (n 329) [23].
[331] *Sumitomo* (n 326) [63].
[332] ibid [37].
[333] ibid [24].
[334] *GVL* (n 329) [27]. *cf Thread* (Case COMP/38.337) Commission Decision of 14 September 2005, paras 407–17, available at <http://ec.europa.eu/competition/elojade/isef/case_details.cfm?proc_code=1_38337> accessed 1 July 2013.
[335] *Sumitomo* (n 326) [137]–[138]. See also Faull and Nikpay (n 182) 2.95.
[336] *Sumitomo* (n 326) [88]. See more extensively section 4.5.4.
[337] Article 27 Regulation 1/2003. See also Regulation 773/2004 (n 246).
[338] *Sumitomo* (n 326) [129]–[140].

5.5.2 The Powers of the German Authorities

Pursuant to § 32(3) GWB, the German authorities can make declaratory findings of past infringements. This power was introduced in 2005 with the seventh amendment to the GWB.[339] The German legislator drew its inspiration from Regulation 1/2003.[340] The authorities may adopt a finding of past infringements only if they have a legitimate interest. It has been suggested in the literature that this condition does *not* require a direct risk of a resumption of the anti-competitive behaviour by the undertakings concerned.[341] In fact, were such a risk to exist, the competition authorities may already adopt a cease-and-desist order.[342] In practice, the BKartA has adopted declaratory findings of past infringements with a view to clarifying the law and limiting future infringements.[343] Various authors have argued that assisting injured third parties in follow-on damages actions qualifies as a legitimate interest as well.[344] The German authorities would even be allowed to adopt declaratory findings with a view to *stimulating* damages actions.[345] It should be recalled that the German civil courts are bound by these findings.[346] The administrative procedures leading to the adoption of such a decision are surrounded by various legal safeguards. Parties participating in the procedure are offered the possibility to make representations and may challenge the findings before the court.[347]

By virtue of § 32c GWB, the authorities also have the possibility of terminating proceedings with a finding that there are no grounds for further action on their part. This power was introduced with the seventh amendment to the GWB and is meant for those cases in which the authorities conclude that the conditions of Articles 101 and 102 TFEU are *not* fulfilled.[348] Decisions on the basis of § 32c GWB fall within the discretion of the competition authorities.[349] The latter may also terminate proceedings in an informal way.[350] Occasionally, the BKartA terminates proceedings on the basis of § 32c GWB.[351] In 2009, it found that there were no grounds for further action after first having made an indepth analysis of an alleged margin squeeze strategy and finding the existence of an

[339] Deutscher Bundestag (n 185) 33.
[340] ibid.
[341] Bornkamm in Langen/Bunte (n 24) §32 Rdnr 49–50.
[342] Bechtold (n 32) § 32 Rdnr 18; Bornkamm in Langen/Bunte (n 24) §32 Rdnr 49.
[343] BKartA B9-149/04 *Bau und Hobby*.
[344] Bechtold (n 32) § 32 Rdnr 19; Bornkamm in Langen/Bunte (n 24) §32 Rdnr 51.
[345] Bechtold (n 32) § 32 Rdnr 19.
[346] § 33(4) GWB.
[347] §§ 56 and 63ff GWB.
[348] Deutscher Bundestag (n 185) 34.
[349] ibid.
[350] In fact, thus far, the competition authorities are more likely to terminate proceedings informally than through a decision on the basis of § 32c GWB. See Bornkamm in Langen/Bunte (n 24) §32c Rdnr 3.
[351] BKartA B7-73/08 *Mobilfunk – Sprachtelefonie*; BKartA B7-11/09 *Verbindungsaufbau im öffentlichen Telefonnetz zu Mehrwertdiensten und Leistungen zur Erbringung von MABEZ-Diensten gegenüber Programmanbietern.*

abuse highly unlikely.[352] Through this approach, the BKartA complied with its requirements under Regulation 1/2003 not to make findings of inapplicability (see above, section 2.3), while still clarifying the implications of the competition law prohibitions.

5.5.3 The Powers of the Dutch Authority

While the Dutch authority may give undertakings a direction to comply with Articles 101 and 102 TFEU,[353] it cannot adopt a *decision* making declaratory findings of past infringements. A 'decision' under Dutch administrative law is an administrative act which vests original rights or obligations: an act with legal effect. Declaratory findings, by definition, do not establish rights or obligations. 'Declaratory decisions' – a *contradictio in terminis* under Dutch administrative law – do exist, but seem limited to policy areas where the exercise of rights requires some form of registration (eg, voting rights).[354] A more common instrument under Dutch administrative law, albeit not an unproblematic one, is the administrative interpretation (*bestuurlijk rechtsoordeel*): an interpretation of the law by an administrative authority charged with the application of this law. The adoption of a *bestuurlijk rechtsoordeel* is mainly practised in the field of zoning law and its problematic aspects concern the available legal safeguards (only 'decisions' are subject to judicial review).[355] As the *bestuurlijk rechtsoordeel* generally relates to future situations rather than past behaviour, the transposition of this implied power to a competition law context would be somewhat unusual. Consequently, what remains is the possibility for the competition authority to issue an opinion on the nature of past behaviour. Such an opinion would have no formal authority and would not be subject to appeal.[356] Alternatively, the authority could make a finding of past infringement and impose a symbolic fine, or reduce the amount of the fine to nil. This alternative would of course be subject to the statute of limitation applicable to fines, which could limit its value.

The Dutch authority makes use of both alternatives, albeit somewhat obliviously. In a press release of 7 February 2003, the authority indicated that it would let an association of real estate agents off with a warning.[357] This action could be interpreted as an opinion in relation to past behaviour. In *ANKO*[358] and *Taxi*

[352] BKartA B7-11/09 *Verbindungsaufbau im öffenlichen Telefonnetz zu Mehrwertdiensten und Leistungen zur Erbringung von MABEZ-Diensten gegenüber Programmanbietern.*

[353] Article 56(1)(c) Mw.

[354] RJN Schlössels and SE Zijlstra, *De Haan/Drupsteen/Fernhout: Bestuursrecht in de Sociale Rechtsstaat* 6th edn (Kluwer, 2010) 245.

[355] ibid 246.

[356] *cf* ABRvS 28 juni 2006, *JB* 2006, 244.

[357] NMa press release of 7 February 2003 (*LMV*), available at <www.acm.nl/nl/> accessed 1 November 2013.

[358] NMa Zaak 2234/36 *ANKO.*

Rotterdam,[359] the authority adopted a 'decision', but refrained from imposing fines. In neither instance did it wonder whether its actions actually qualified as decisions.[360] It is submitted that these declaratory findings do not qualify as such, precisely because they had no legal effect. From a doctrinal perspective, it would have been more appropriate in these cases for the authority to impose a fine and reduce the amount to nil. Declaratory findings of past infringements, however framed, will remain a rather rare phenomenon. In *OSB*, the authority has indicated that it will refrain from imposing a fine only in the event of exceptional circumstances.[361]

Occasionally, the Dutch authority makes findings of inapplicability.[362] Both in *Shiva*[363] and more recently in *GasTerra*,[364] it concluded that the undertakings concerned did not charge excessive prices. And in *FHRS v CR Delta*, the authority reached the conclusion that there was no abuse of dominance.[365] In view of the *Tele2 Polska* ruling of the Court of Justice,[366] the Dutch authority seems prohibited from making such absolute findings with regard to practices falling within the scope of Articles 101 and 102 TFEU any longer (see above, section 2.3). In accordance with Article 5 of Regulation 1/2003, the authority should terminate investigations with a finding that there are no grounds for action on its part.

5.5.4 The Powers of the UK Authorities

The UK authorities can adopt declaratory findings with regard to past infringements of Articles 101 and 102 TFEU. Whereas an explicit power seems lacking, it follows from sections 31, 32 and 36 of the CA98 that the authorities may adopt a decision establishing that Articles 101 and 102 TFEU have been breached without imposing directions or penalties. This interpretation finds resonance in the OFT's 2011 guide for investigation procedures, which provides that the infringement decision sets out the facts on which the OFT relied and *may* also contain a fine or directions.[367] More importantly, the possibility of adopting declaratory findings is confirmed by sections 46 and 47 of the CA98, providing that a decision as to whether Articles 101 and 102 TFEU have been infringed is an appealable act. In practice, declaratory findings of past infringements are occasionally adopted. For

[359] NMa Zaak 2228 *Taxi Rotterdam*.

[360] See also NMa Zaak 2501 *Dienstapotheek Regio Assen*, where the authority imposed a periodic penalty payment for future conduct, but refrained from imposing a fine.

[361] NMa Zaak 2021/397 *OSB*, para 20.

[362] MJ Frese, 'Handhavingsautonomie bij de Decentrale Toepassing van het EU Mededingingsrecht' (2011) 17 *Nederlands Tijdschrift voor Europees Recht* 200.

[363] NMa Zaak 11 *Shiva*.

[364] NMa press release of 23 December 2008 (*NMa: Gasterra rekende geen excessieve prijzen*), available at <www.acm.nl/nl/> accessed 1 November 2013.

[365] NMa Zaak 1205-165 *FHRS v CR Delta*.

[366] Case C-375/09 *Tele2 Polska* [2011] ECR I-3055.

[367] OFT (n 224).

instance, in its *MasterCard UK Members Forum Ltd* case, the OFT found an infringement of Article 101 TFEU, but refrained from imposing directions or penalties.[368] In *Cardiff Bus*, it concluded that an infringement had been committed, but refrained from attaching legal consequences to this finding.[369] It should be noted that the latter case concerned an infringement of national competition law and that the anti-competitive behaviour originally benefited from the *de minimis* immunity for fines provided by section 40 of the CA98.[370] Not being part of a specific legal regime, a decision making declaratory findings of past infringements is subject to the regular legal safeguards. The authority has to issue a statement of objections, give access to its file and allow parties to make written and oral representations.[371] Both the addressee of a declaratory finding and interested third parties may appeal this decision before the CAT.[372]

The UK authorities also have a practice of adopting non-infringement decisions. For example, in its *Anaesthetists' group* investigation, the OFT terminated proceedings after it concluded that the anaesthetists' groups each operated as a single undertaking.[373] Therefore, agreements between the members of each group as to the levels of fees to be charged for their private professional services did not fall within the scope of the competition law prohibitions. This approach was common in the notification days, when undertakings could still notify their agreements and practices under sections 14 and 22 of the CA98. Meanwhile, these provisions have been repealed.[374] Yet, case closure through non-infringement decisions still occurs. In *EDFE*, Ofgem concluded that the conditions of Article 102 TFEU were not fulfilled, as EDF Energy plc did not hold a dominant position.[375] In *Television Access Service*, Ofcom concluded that BBC Broadcast Ltd's exclusive agreement with the Channel 4 Television Corporation to provide television access service was not in breach of Articles 101 and 102 TFEU.[376] The BBC was found not to have a dominant position in the sense of Article 102 TFEU and the agreement benefited from the Commission's Block Exemption Regulation on Vertical Agreements, while the non-compete obligation did not appreciably restrict competition in the sense of Article 101(1) TFEU. In fact, Ofcom has adopted a whole range of non-infringement decisions over the years.[377] This practice of terminating investigations with non-infringement decisions is even facilitated by legislation. Rule 9 of the OFT's Rules[378] provides pro-

[368] OFT Case CP/0090/00/S *MasterCard UK Members Forum Ltd.*

[369] OFT Case CE/5281/04 *Cardiff Bus.*

[370] Sections 39 and 40 of the CA98 provide immunity for fines in relation to anti-competitive behaviour of minor importance. These provisions do no apply to the prohibitions laid down in Articles 101 and 102 TFEU.

[371] Competition Act 1998 (Office of Fair Trading's Rules) Order 2004, rr 4 and 5.

[372] CA98, ss 46 and 47.

[373] OFT press release No 15/04/2003 <www.oft.gov.uk> accessed 1 July 2013.

[374] SI 2004/1261.

[375] Ofgem Decision of 24 January 2007, *Non-infringement EDFE* <www.ofgem.gov.uk/About%20us/enforcement/Investigations/ClosedInvest/Documents1/53.pdf> accessed 1 July 2013.

[376] Ofcom Case CW/00842/06/05 *Television Access Service.*

[377] Ofcom Decision of 7 August 2006 *Digital cordless phones*; Ofcom Decision of 1 August 2008 *BT's charges for NTS call termination*; Ofcom Case CW/00805/12/04 *Vodafone Limited.*

[378] Competition Act 1998 (Office of Fair Trading's Rules) Order 2004, sch.

cedural safeguards with regard to decisions finding that the conditions of Articles 101 and 102 TFEU are not fulfilled. Since the Court of Justice rendered its *Tele2 Polska* judgment,[379] it is highly questionable whether such findings can still be made with regard to Articles 101 and 102 TFEU (see above, section 2.3). In this respect, it is noteworthy that in the more recent *Flybe*[380] and *BT*[381] cases, the competition authorities closed the investigations with findings that there were insufficient grounds for finding an abuse.[382]

5.5.5 The Degree and Drivers of Convergence

This section has shown, first of all, that the authorities all have a practice of adopting declaratory findings. These findings are not limited to past infringements, but include findings of inapplicability. In light of the *Tele2 Polska* ruling of the Court of Justice, it can be expected that national authorities will refrain from making absolute statements on the inapplicability of Articles 101 and 102 TFEU any longer. Indeed, in the UK, a change in approach can already be observed. Apart from this limitation of domestic sanctioning powers, there are no clear tendencies of convergence. This is the second conclusion of this section. Only the German legislator has explicitly sought alignment with Regulation 1/2003 and the powers of the Commission. Yet, this alignment is not perfect. The conditions under which the German authorities may adopt declaratory findings are more generous than the conditions for the Commission. This places the German authorities in a better position to clarify the implications of Articles 101 and 102 TFEU and to decide on the legality of commercial practices. Contrary to the Commission, the German authorities may even adopt declaratory findings with a view to *stimulating* damages actions. The Netherlands even deviates from the basic features of the EU model. Declaratory findings of past infringements are legally non-existent under Dutch law. In the UK, declaratory findings of past infringements have been made, but these do not seem subject to similar conditions as the Commission's power.

5.6 REPARATORY SANCTIONS

Undertakings will generally cease their anti-competitive practices as soon as the competition authorities start their investigations. However, there are also cases in which the anti-competitive behaviour continues pending the investigation or,

[379] *Tele2 Polska* (n 366).
[380] OFT Case MPINF-PSWA001 *Flybe.*
[381] Ofcom Case CW/00613/04/03 *BT.*
[382] The ORR has recently still adopted a non-infringement decision, in which it concludes that the conditions of Article 102 TFEU were not fulfilled; see ORR Decision of 02-08-2010 *DB Schenker Rail.*

more commonly, where there are reasons to fear that the anti-competitive behaviour may be resumed after the proceedings. In these situations, the competition authorities may have to issue cease-and-desist orders or impose other remedies (hereinafter jointly referred to as 'remedies' or 'reparatory sanctions'). Unlike punitive sanctions such as fines, reparatory sanctions are not meant to punish the offender for past behaviour. These sanctions are forward-looking in that they are meant to terminate and/or prevent future offences. With a remedy, the competition authority can impose customised obligations to bring the undertakings' activities into line with Articles 101 and 102 TFEU.[383] These obligations may be enforced separately.

Anti-competitive behaviour can come in various forms and, accordingly, demands a variety of remedies. These remedies are generally divided along two lines. One line distinguishes negative orders from positive orders. The other line distinguishes behavioural remedies from structural remedies. A negative order imposes an obligation to cease or refrain from certain anti-competitive behaviour. A positive order imposes an obligation to take certain action in order to discontinue the infringement. Both types could have the form of a behavioural remedy. Behavioural remedies require the addressee to change its commercial behaviour either by refraining from certain action or by engaging in certain action. Structural remedies are positive orders without exception, as they require the addressee to divest itself of the possibility of engaging in anti-competitive behaviour, for instance, by terminating joint venture contracts or selling off assets. Structural remedies are generally perceived as the more intrusive form of intervention. In order to establish the heterogeneity of sanctioning preferences and the instances of regulatory innovation, this section analyses the degree and drivers of convergence in the area of reparatory sanctions.

5.6.1 The Powers of the Commission

Pursuant to Article 7(1) of Regulation 1/2003, the Commission may require undertakings to bring infringements of Articles 101 and 102 TFEU to an end. For this purpose, the Commission may in principle impose 'any' behavioural or struc-

[383] *cf* Case T-201/04 *Microsoft* [2007] ECR II-3601, where the General Court held: 'When the Commission finds in a decision that an undertaking has infringed Article 82 EC [now Article 102 TFEU], that undertaking is required to take, without delay, all the measures necessary to comply with that provision, even in the absence of specific measures prescribed by the Commission in that decision. Where remedies are provided for in the decision, the undertaking concerned is required to implement them – and to assume all the costs associated with their implementation – failing which it exposes itself to liability for periodic penalty payments imposed pursuant to Article 16 of Regulation No 17.' See, however, Case T-34/92 *Fiatagri* [1994] ECR II-905 [39], where the General Court held that a decision requiring the undertakings involved to refrain from entering into any information-exchange system having an object identical or similar to the agreement for which an exemption had been sought was purely declaratory.

tural remedy.[384] The Commission may order remedies even in the event that the undertakings have ceased their anti-competitive behaviour already. This is the case either when the Commission cannot tell whether the infringement has been terminated or simply in order to prevent undertakings from engaging in this behaviour in the future.[385]

Decisions on the basis of Article 7 of Regulation 1/2003 can be reinforced with a periodic penalty payment. Jointly with a decision under Article 7 of Regulation 1/2003 or by means of a later decision, the Commission can require undertakings to comply with a remedy on pain of forfeiting a periodic penalty.[386] This periodic penalty may not exceed five per cent of the average daily worldwide turnover in the preceding business year per day of non-compliance. Breach of a decision under Article 7 of Regulation 1/2003 cannot result in fines directly. However, failure to comply with such a decision will often amount to an infringement of Articles 101 and 102 TFEU and may trigger new enforcement proceedings. This could eventually lead to a fine (see below, section 5.7.1).

Regulatory Innovation by the Commission

The analysis of the development of sanctioning powers that is undertaken in this chapter is partially aimed at determining if decentralisation has led to regulatory innovation. It should be noted that regulatory innovation may of course also result from a jurisdiction's own experiences. This type of innovation is not necessarily linked to decentralisation. An example is the Commission's use of periodic penalty payments to reinforce remedies. Decisions on the basis of Article 7 of Regulation 1/2003 can be reinforced by a periodic penalty payment. The periodic penalty payment may be imposed jointly with a decision under Article 7 of Regulation 1/2003 or by means of a later decision. In *Microsoft*, the Commission opted for the multi-stage alternative.[387] The Commission's administrative services have indicated that this alternative, in which periodic penalty payments are imposed by means of a separate decision, can be relatively lengthy and cumbersome.[388] This has to do with the duplication of procedures and accompanying legal safeguards for the undertakings involved. In light of these experiences, the

[384] The power to impose positive orders was already recognised by the Court of Justice prior to the entering into force of Regulation 1/2003, when this power was not yet explicitly provided. See Joined Cases 6/73 and 7/73 *Commercial Solvents* [1974] ECR 223 [45].

[385] Roth and Rose (n 177) 13.126.

[386] Article 24 of Regulation 1/2003. For an example of a separate periodic penalty decision, see *Microsoft* (Case COMP/C-3/37.792) Commission Decision of 10 November 2005, available at <http://ec.europa.eu/competition/elojade/isef/case_details.cfm?proc_code=1_37792> accessed 1 July 2013. For an example of a single decision, including both the prohibition order and a periodic penalty payment for failure to comply, see *MasterCard* (Case COMP/34.579) Summary of Commission Decision 2009/C 264/04 [2009] OJ C264/8.

[387] *Microsoft* (n 386).

[388] Commission Staff Working Paper (n 4) para 137.

Commission decided to go with a different approach in *MasterCard*.[389] In the latter case, prohibition and periodic penalty payment were ordered in a single decision.

Irrespective of what the text of Article 7(1) of Regulation 1/2003 may suggest, the Commission cannot impose any remedy whatsoever. A first limitation follows from *Ford*, where the Court of Justice concluded that the Commission cannot adopt orders to change behaviour that is not itself contrary to Articles 101 and 102 TFEU.[390] Second, in choosing an appropriate remedy, the Commission should have regard to the principle of proportionality.[391] Remedies should be proportionate to the infringement and necessary to bring the infringement effectively to an end.[392] The proportionality of orders prohibiting (the continuation of) certain action is dependent on this action itself being contrary to Article 101 or 102 TFEU, but does not depend on the situation of the undertakings concerned at the time that the decision was adopted.[393] With regard to structural remedies, the principle of proportionality limits their use to situations where there is no equally effective behavioural remedy or where any equally effective behavioural remedy would be more burdensome for the undertaking concerned.[394] A structural remedy would be an appropriate response in cases where the risk of a lasting or repeated infringement derives from the very structure of the undertaking.[395] The implications of the principle of proportionality for the Commission's powers to impose remedies can further be demonstrated in *Automec II*.[396] In this case, the General Court assessed whether the Commission could order BMW AG to grant access to its distribution network to an independent car dealer. In response to a request for such an order, the Commission had argued that it lacked this power. The Court sided with the Commission and concluded that the latter is not allowed to order a party to enter into contractual relations where there are other suitable remedies available.[397] The potential infringement of Article 101 TFEU could also be eliminated by abandoning or amending the conditions of the distribution system. In those situations, it is not for the Commission to impose upon the parties its own choice from among all the various potential courses of action which are in conformity with the Treaty.[398] *Automec II* may also be understood as a more funda-

[389] *MasterCard* (n 386).

[390] Joined Cases 228/82 and 229/82 *Ford* [1984] ECR 1129 [21].

[391] *cf* Joined Cases C-241/91 P and C-242/91 P *Magill* [1995] ECR I-743; Case T-334/94 *Sarrió* [1998] ECR II-1446; Case T-65/98 *Van den Bergh Foods* [2003] ECR II-4653; Joined Cases T-456/05 and T-457/05 *Gütermann* [2010] ECR II-1443. See more extensively section 4.6.5.

[392] Article 7(1) of Regulation 1/2003.

[393] *Gütermann* (n 391) [66].

[394] Article 7(1) of Regulation 1/2003.

[395] Recital 12 of the preamble to Regulation 1/2003.

[396] Case T-24/90 *Automec II* [1992] ECR II-2223.

[397] ibid [51]–[52].

[398] See also Case T-167/08 *Microsoft II* [2012] OJ C243/13 [95].

mental limitation of the Commission's powers, restricting the use of compulsory supplies to infringements of Article 102 TFEU.[399] This brings us to the third limitation of the Commission's remedial powers. Some types of remedies simply seem excluded from the Commission's powers altogether. It is, for instance, questionable whether the Commission has a power to control prices.[400] This limitation is mainly relevant in the context of 'excessive pricing', 'predatory pricing' or 'margin squeezing' – three abuse strategies falling within the scope of Article 102 TFEU. Further, the Commission cannot simply delegate its supervisory duties. In its *Microsoft* decision, the Commission ordered the appointment of an independent monitoring trustee, empowered to access and have available Microsoft Corp's assistance, information, documents, premises, employees and the source code of its relevant products. At the same time, the Commission ordered Microsoft to bear all the costs of the appointment and activities of the monitoring trustee.[401] On appeal, the General Court quashed this part of the decision, holding that under these conditions, there was no legal basis for the appointment of an independent monitoring trustee.[402] This case provides another indication that the Commission cannot impose *any* remedy whatsoever.

The initiation of proceedings and the adoption of remedies fall within the discretion of the Commission. The Commission may decide not to open proceedings and refer complainants to the national courts for private actions.[403] Where the Commission decides to initiate proceedings with a view to imposing remedies, the administrative procedure offers various legal safeguards to the parties involved. Prior to adopting these remedies, the Commission should give the parties the possibility of being heard, to comment on a statement of objections and to access the Commission's file.[404]

The Commission regularly makes use of its power to impose remedies. These remedies range from the obligation to inform third parties that the infringement has been brought to an end[405] to the resumption of supplies[406], and from licencing intellectual property rights[407] to the obligation to unbundle products and offer them separately.[408] However, structural remedies under Article 7 Regulation 1/2003 remain highly unusual. The Commission's reservation with regard to structural remedies finds support in the legal literature.[409]

[399] Whish (n 165) 251.
[400] Roth and Rose (n 177) 13.129. *cf Microsoft II* (n 398) [95].
[401] See *Microsoft* (n 383) [1251]–[1279].
[402] ibid [1278].
[403] *Automec II* (n 396).
[404] Article 27 of Regulation 1/2003. See further Regulation 773/2004.
[405] *VW* (Case IV/35.733) Commission Decision 98/273/EC [1998] OJ L124/60.
[406] *cf Commercial Solvents* (n 384).
[407] *cf Magill* (n 391).
[408] *Microsoft* (Case COMP/37.792) Commission Decision 2007/53/EC [2007] OJ L32/23.
[409] See Faull and Nikpay (n 182) 2.106, where several additional conditions have been suggested before the Commission should consider structural remedies (substantial impact on competition and consumers, repeated infringements or a market structure that causes infringements, break-up does not lead to a significant loss of efficiency at the level of the undertaking).

5.6.2 The Powers of the German Authorities

By virtue of § 32(1) GWB, the German authorities may adopt decisions requiring undertakings to bring infringements of Articles 101 and 102 TFEU to an end. The authorities may also order undertakings not to engage in specific anti-competitive behaviour, provided that there is a real risk that an infringement will be committed.[410] These cease-and-desist orders could be supplemented with further obligations. The competition authorities may impose all proportionate measures that are necessary to bring the infringement to an end.[411] In accordance with this proportionality requirement, the authorities should opt for the least onerous alternative in ending an infringement.

Remedies can be enforced separately. In case of non-compliance, the authorities may use *Verwaltungszwang*.[412] This means that the competition authorities could require third parties to do whatever is in their powers to make sure that the remedies are implemented and could even themselves take the measures that the undertaking failed to take.[413] Not every remedy will be suitable for this type of direct enforcement; it will depend on the nature of the remedies whether this is feasible. Alternatively, compliance with an earlier remedy decision can be secured with the help of periodic penalty payments.[414] Breach of a remedy may also constitute an administrative offence, provided that this breach has been committed intentionally or negligently.[415] This offence can be punished separately by a fine of up to €1 million or 10 per cent of the undertaking's worldwide turnover.

Remedies may take the form of both negative and positive orders.[416] The power to give positive orders was introduced in 2005 with the seventh amendment to the GWB.[417] Prior to this amendment, the remedial powers of the competition authorities were in principle limited to negative orders.[418] This extension of the authorities' powers was meant to align their powers with those of the Commission.[419] Yet, the remedial powers of the German authorities are more extensive. The eighth amendment to the GWB has introduced a § 32(2a), which provides the competition authorities with the power to order undertakings to compensate third parties for injuries caused by the anti-competitive behaviour. It has been suggested in the literature that by virtue of § 32(2) GWB, this power to impose compensation orders already existed prior to the eighth amendment to the GWB.[420] This interpretation

410 Bornkamm in Langen/Bunte (n 24) § 32 Rdnr 18–19; Bechtold (n 32) § 32 Rdnr 10.
411 § 32(2) GWB.
412 Bechtold (n 32) § 32 Rn. 8.
413 §§ 10 and 12 *Verwantungs-Vollstreckungsgesetz.*
414 § 86a GWB. Penalty payments range from €1,000 to €10 million.
415 § 81 GWB.
416 *WuW-Sonderheft* (n 45) 130.
417 Deutscher Bundestag (n 185) 33.
418 ibid. See also Bornkamm in Langen/Bunte (n 24) § 32 Rdnr 27; Bechtold (n 32) § 32 Rdnr 14
419 Deutscher Bundestag (n 185) 33.
420 Bornkamm in Langen/Bunte (n 24) § 32 Rdnr 32–36.

has indeed found resonance with the BGH in *Stadtwerke Uelzen*.[421] Apart from the possibilities under § 32 GWB, by virtue of § 34(1) GWB, the authorities are allowed to skim off illegal gains made through an intentional or negligent infringement of Article 101 or 102 TFEU. The latter measure is aimed to supplement fines, including fines imposed by the Commission,[422] and will be discussed more extensively in section 5.7.2. Another positive order that may be imposed on the basis of § 32(2) GWB is a structural remedy, for instance, the divestiture of shares or certain assets.[423] Although initially not explicitly provided for, the parliamentary deliberations in the context of the 7th amendment to the GWB indicate that the German authorities were allowed to adopt structural remedies.[424] In addition, this power has been reinforced with the 8th amendment to the GWB, making provision for structural remedies in the text of § 32(2) GWB. Structural remedies are an *ultimum remedium*,[425] to be reserved for situations where there is no equally effective behavioural remedy or where any equally effective behavioural remedy would be more burdensome for the undertaking concerned.

The initiation of proceedings and the adoption of remedies are discretionary powers.[426] If the authorities decide to initiate proceedings with a view to impose remedies, they need to comply with the framework for reparatory proceedings. This means, for instance, that the authorities should issue a statement of objections prior to the adoption of the remedies.[427] It also means that the remedies should leave the addressee as much choice as possible in terminating the infringement.[428] Irrespective of the intended alignment to the Commission's powers, German law seems more demanding as to the specificity of the remedy.[429] In this respect, the BGH has held:

> Die vom Gericht erster Instanz der Europäischen Gemeinschaften gebilligte Praxis der Europäischen Kommission lässt sich entgegen der Auffassung der Rechtsbeschwerde für das deutsche Verfahrensrecht nicht nutzbar machen. Insbesondere kann das Bundeskartellamt nicht darauf verwiesen werden, sich bei der Formulierung der Abstellungsverfügung auf ein Verbot zu beschränken, das der Betroffenen aufgibt, „von Maßnahmen gleicher Zweckbestimmung oder Wirkung abzusehen", wie sie für die beanstandeten langfristigen Lieferverträge typisch waren (vgl. EuG, Urt. v. 23.10.2003 – T-65/98, Slg. 2003, II-4653 Tz. 205 – Van den Bergh Foods). Eine solche Tenorierung des

[421] BGH *Stadtwerke Uelzen* WuW/E DE-R 2538 Tz 16, as discussed by Bornkamm in Langen/Bunte (n 24) § 32 Rdnr 33. The BGH referred the appeal back to a lower court to render final decision, but noted that the power to impose reparatory sanctions includes the requirement to pay back illegal gains.

[422] *WuW-Sonderheft* (n 45) 134: 'Eine Vorteilsabschöpfung ist darüber hinaus bei Geldbußen der Kommission, die reinen Ahndungscharacter haben und nicht die Abschöpfung des wirtschaftlichen Vorteils bezwecken, denkbar.'

[423] The application of structural measures may not undermine undertakings' unfettered rights to organic growth; see *WuW-Sonderheft* (n 45) 130.

[424] Deutscher Bundestag (n 185) 33.

[425] Bornkamm in Langen/Bunte (n 24) § 32 Rdnr 31. See also Bechtold (n 32) § 32 Rdnr 17, who argues that structural remedies are in principle not allowed, except in very exceptional situations.

[426] Bornkamm in Langen/Bunte (n 24) § 32 Rdnr 12; Bechtold (n 32) § 32 Rdnr 4–6.

[427] Bornkamm in Langen/Bunte (n 24) § 32 Rdnr 14.

[428] ibid § 32 Rdnr 40–48. *cf* BKartA B9-188/05 *Fahrdienst*.

[429] Bornkamm in Langen/Bunte (n 24) § 32 Rdnr 48.

> Verbots würde nicht den nach deutschem Verfahrensrecht bestehenden Anforderungen an die Bestimmtheit eines strafbewehrten Verstoßes genügen.[430]

In this respect, it should be noted that unlike remedies imposed by the Commission, a breach of remedies imposed by German authorities is a separate administrative offence which directly attract fines. It seems that precisely this difference has urged the BGH to depart from EU case law as to the required specificity of the remedies.

The BKartA regularly imposes remedies. Often, these remedies are not limited to negative orders. In *Laborchemikalien*, for instance, the BKartA ordered the supply of certain goods in order to terminate behaviour that was both contrary to Article 101 TFEU and the German prohibition of discriminatory treatment laid down in § 20 GWB.[431] In *Kalksandstein*, the BKartA required one of the parties to terminate its partnership with other undertakings.[432] In *Fahrdienst*, finally, the BKartA required undertakings to enter into negotiations with regard to granting access to port facilities.[433]

5.6.3 The Powers of the Dutch Authority

The initiatives to streamline the enforcement procedures of the ACM may have repercussions for the reparatory sanctions available for the enforcement of Articles 101 and 102 TFEU. For instance, the power to adopt directions could be transferred from the Mw to the ACM law. In addition, the Streamline law may also make substantive changes. Although only the latter changes will be accounted for, the reader is warned that some of the footnote references to the Mw may not be accurate for much longer.

To remedy an infringement of Article 101 or 102 TFEU, the ACM can impose an 'order' or a 'direction'. An order (*last*) can be imposed in situations of actual or imminent infringement[434] and comes jointly with a periodic penalty payment (*dwangsom*).[435] The order should specify which measures the undertaking must take and should give the latter a period within which it can remedy the situation

[430] BGH *Gaslieferverträge* WuW/E DE-R 2679 Tz 52. The quoted text could be translated as follows: 'Contrary to the appeal, the Commission practice, which has been endorsed by the Court of First Instance of the European Communities is not applicable to German procedural law. In particular, the Bundeskartellamt cannot be asked to reduce the text of its cease and desist order to a prohibition that requires the addressees to desist "from measures with similar objectives or effects" as the long-term supply agreements that were deemed incompatible (cf CFI, Judgment of 23.10.2003 – T-65/98, ECR 2003, II-4653 para 205 – Van den Bergh Foods). Such formulation of the prohibition in the operative part of the decision would not satisfy the existing requirements under German procedural law relating to the definition of a punishable infringements.'

[431] BKartA B3-64/05 *Laborchemikalien*.

[432] BKartA B1-116/04 *Kalksandstein*.

[433] BKartA B9-188/05 *Fahrdienst*.

[434] Article 5:7 Awb.

[435] Article 56(1)(b) Mw.

without incurring a penalty.[436] The order may include a separate requirement to keep the authority informed,[437] which allows the authority to monitor compliance with the order. The periodic penalty payment that supplements the order can be levied in three ways: a single lump-sum payment for non-compliance after a certain period; a penalty that is levied periodically in accordance with a set timeframe for as long as the infringement persists; and a penalty for each time an infringement is committed.[438] Whichever alternative is chosen, the competition authority should fix a maximum amount beyond which no further penalties can be levied.[439] Although both the periodic and the maximum amount need to be proportionate to the gravity of the infringement and to the purpose of the penalty,[440] these amounts are not subject to any statutory cap. Payment is due within six weeks upon the expiration of the set period and can be summoned by the authority itself, provided that it has adopted a decision on the execution of the penalties.[441] The authority may at any time amend or withdraw the order, but not before having invited the addressee to submit observations.[442]

The ACM can order both behavioural and structural remedies.[443] Behavioural remedies can be ordered for a period of up to two years.[444] With regard to the structural remedies, the Dutch legislator has sought alignment with the powers of the Commission in the most explicit terms possible. Article 58a Mw provides that the authority may impose orders 'of the type referred to in Article 7 Regulation 1/2003 as structural remedies'.[445] The introduction of this power was motivated by the fact that the Council deemed it necessary for the Commission to have this power; the Dutch authority was therefore deemed to need this power too.[446] The conditions under which the Dutch authority may impose structural remedies for infringements of Articles 101 and 102 TFEU are identical to the conditions for the Commission: structural remedies may only be imposed where there is no equally effective behavioural remedy available or where any equally effective behavioural remedy would be more burdensome for the undertaking concerned.[447] In the parliamentary deliberations, structural remedies have been presented as an *ultimum remedium*.[448]

Alternatively, the Dutch authority may give a 'direction' to comply with Articles 101 and 102 TFEU (*bindende aanwijzing*).[449] As the legislator has not limited the

[436] 5:32a Awb.

[437] Article 58(1) Mw.

[438] Article 5:32b(1) Awb.

[439] Article 5:32b(2) Awb.

[440] Article 5:32b(3) Awb.

[441] Articles 5:33 and 5:37 Awb.

[442] Article 66 Mw.

[443] Articles 58 and 58a Mw.

[444] Article 58(2) in conjunction with Article 58a(2) Mw.

[445] The authentic Dutch translation reads 'in de vorm van een structurele maatregel als bedoeld in artikel 7 van Verordening 1/2003'.

[446] TK 2005-2006, 30071, nr 3, p 10.

[447] Article 58a(1) Mw.

[448] TK 2005–06, 30071, nr 3, p 11.

[449] Article 56(1)(c) Mw. The legal basis for a *bindende aanwijzing* will change with the adoption of the Streamline law.

type of directions that could be given, in principle both behavioural and structural directions seem possible. Breach of a direction allows the authority to adopt an order or a decision imposing a fine.[450] A direction differs from an order in that a penalty for breach of the former does not follow automatically. In fact, breach of a direction may lead to the imposition of an order, thus postponing the penalty even further. At the stage of enforcement, all the authority would seem to have to prove is that the addressee acted contrary to the direction. Whether the direction is indeed necessary for the purpose of Articles 101 and 102 TFEU no longer seems to be up for dispute. This point would have to be raised against the decision giving the direction. This interpretation finds support in the fact that a direction can only be given after an infringement of Articles 101 and 102 TFEU has been established.[451] The introduction of the power to give directions was primarily meant to involve consumer organisations in the enforcement process.[452] The latter may request the competition authority to give a direction and could thereby voice the interests of consumers in the enforcement of Articles 101 and 102 TFEU. However, directions may also be given *ex officio*, allowing the competition authority to use this power more widely.

The procedural requirements for the adoption of orders and directions have differed in the first couple of years of their joint existence. Prior to the adoption of an order, the ACM has to issue a statement of objections.[453] The scope of the requirement to issue a statement of objections is limited to situations where the competition authority has a reasonable suspicion that an infringement of Article 101 or 102 TFEU has been committed *and* a fine or order needs to be imposed. The addressee of the statement of objections obtains access to the authority's file[454] and the authority is, in principle, required to organise a hearing.[455] Within eight months after issuing the statement of objections, the competition authority should take a final decision.[456] The requirement to issue a statement of objections prior to the adoption of an order is an exception to the general administrative law regime, limiting the requirement to adopt statements of objections to fines and, to the extent provided for in specific legislation, other punitive sanctions.[457] Administrative orders, even those that come jointly with a periodic penalty payment, are considered reparatory sanctions under Dutch law.[458] The exceptional

[450] Article 56(2) Mw.

[451] Article 56(1) Mw.

[452] TK 2005–06, 30071, nr 14.

[453] Article 59 Mw.

[454] Article 59(2) Mw, in conjunction with Article 5:49 Awb.

[455] Article 4:8 Awb. There are situations in which the authority is not required to organise a hearing prior to the adoption of a decision imposing an order. This is the case when the authority relies entirely on information provided by the addressee itself, or – even more exceptionally – when the salient information does not relate to the addressee. As the exceptions to the hearing requirement follow from the general administrative law regime, these exceptions seem primarily relevant for decisions outside the remit of competition law.

[456] Article 62 Mw.

[457] Articles 5:48 and 5:54 Awb.

[458] Article 5:31d Awb.

nature of this requirement helps to explain why directions to comply with Articles 101 and 102 TFEU and/or simple findings of infringement need not be preceded by a statement of objections. It also helps to explain why the requirement to issue a statement of objections prior to the adoption of an order will be abandoned with the introduction of the Streamline law.

The ACM and its predecessor have not made frequent use of its remedial powers in the context of Articles 101 and 102 TFEU.[459] The 2011 *GasTerra* decision[460] appears to be the first time that remedies were imposed for infringements of EU competition law. This concerned a perceived infringement of Article 102 TFEU. However, this remedy was already withdrawn in the administrative review stage.[461]

5.6.4 The Powers of the UK Authorities

The UK authorities may adopt remedies in response to infringements of Articles 101 and 102 TFEU. Pursuant to sections 32 and 33 of the CA98, the authorities may give 'to such person or persons as it considers appropriate such directions as it considers appropriate' to bring infringements of Articles 101 and 102 TFEU to an end. The CAT has indicated that the power to give a direction includes the power to ensure that an infringement is not repeated.[462] Moreover, the power to bring the infringement to an end would cover conduct closely linked to, or to the like effect as, the infringement found.[463] In practice, the OFT will not give any directions in cases where it is satisfied that the infringements have ceased.[464] Where a direction is deemed necessary, the OFT will closely determine whether the burden on the undertakings is proportionate to the benefits for consumers.[465]

Before adopting an infringement decision and giving directions, the OFT should issue a statement of objections and allow the addressees to inspect the relevant documents in the OFT's case file and make written and oral representations.[466] This statement of objections should include the (reasons for the) proposed directions. However, the OFT is not obliged to give directions together with the infringement decisions; directions may be given by separate decision some time later.[467]

459 Orders for infringements of Dutch competition law have been imposed (although not necessarily maintained), for instance, in the following cases: NMa Zaak 3353–89 *CR Delta*; NMa Zaak 757 *Chilly en Basilicum v G-Star/Secon Groep*; NMa Zaak 1528/894 *Wegener*. The Dutch authority frequently gives directions in other areas of economic regulation, such as in its capacity of regulator of the energy sector.

460 NMa Zaak 4296_1/213 *GasTerra*.

461 NMa Zaak 4296_1/214 *GasTerra*.

462 *Genzyme* [2005] CAT 32.

463 ibid.

464 OFT Case CE/2464-03 *Desiccant*; OFT Case CE/3861-04 *Stock check pads*; OFT Case CE/2890-03 *Independent fee-paying schools*; OFT Case CE/2596-03 *Tobacco*.

465 OFT Case CE/8931-08 *Reckitt Benckiser*.

466 Competition Act 1998 (Office of Fair Trading's Rules) Order 2004, SI 2004/2751, r 5.

467 O'Neill and Sanders (n 151) 10.114.

Directions under sections 32 and 33 of the CA98 can be addressed to a relatively wide group of persons. 'Appropriate persons' are not necessarily the perpetrators of the infringement, but could be anyone with the ability to influence the perpetrator.[468] Directions may be addressed to legal persons and natural persons, and could thus be directed to the company or to persons in charge with the management of the undertaking.[469]

There exists some uncertainty as to the type of directions that can be given. 'Appropriate directions' could take the form of cease-and-desist orders, but may also include positive obligations (eg, reporting requirements).[470] What seems important in light of the CAT's case law is that the directions are sufficiently 'ancillary' to the authority's purpose in terminating the infringement.[471] The OFT has taken the position that its power to take 'such directions as it considers appropriate' covers directions aimed at changing the undertaking's very structure, ie, structural remedies.[472] The availability of structural remedies with regard to Articles 101 and 102 TFEU is not undisputed, however. The text of sections 32 and 33 CA98 only lists examples of behavioural remedies.[473] Moreover, the interplay between the enforcement of Articles 101 and 102 TFEU and the domestic equivalents, on the one hand, and the UK market investigation regime, on the other hand, may suggest otherwise.

Traditionally, under the market investigation regime, the UK Competition Commission (as the predecessor of the CMA Panel) was granted the explicit power to adopt structural remedies if the conduct of an undertaking restricted competition in connection with the supply or acquisition of any goods or services in the UK (see above, section 5.2.4).[474] As the OFT (as the predecessor of the CMA Board) and the sector regulators were granted the power to make references to the Competition Commission, they were never powerless when it came to anti-competitive behaviour caused by the structure of the undertaking.[475] The OFT has even indicated that it will consider making a reference in situations where individual undertakings behave anti-competitively and where the OFT was not able to take effective action.[476] Sufrin and Furse have therefore concluded that structural remedies are not available under the enforcement regime of the CA98, which also governs the enforcement of Articles 101 and 102 TFEU.[477] Similarly, Slot and Johnston have argued that compulsory divestitures or break-ups 'would not

[468] Whish (n 165) 400.
[469] OFT (n 211) para 2.2.
[470] ibid para 2.3.
[471] *Napp Pharmaceutical* (n 168) [553].
[472] OFT (n 211) para 2.3.
[473] CA98, ss 32(3) and 33(3).
[474] EA02, s 161 and sch 8.
[475] EA02, s 131.
[476] OFT, *Market Investigation References: Guidance about the Making of References under Part 4 of the Enterprise Act* (OFT 511 2002) paras 2.3 and 2.8 <www.oft.gov.uk/shared_oft/business_leaflets/enterprise_ act/oft511.pdf> accessed 1 July 2013.
[477] B Sufrin and M Furse, 'Market Investigations' [2002] *Competition Law Journal* 244, 246–47.

necessarily be an appropriate use of the power to issue directions'.[478] Whish and Bailey, on the other hand, have submitted that structural remedies would seem justified where the infringement of Article 101 or 102 TFEU is the consequence of a structural feature in the market (eg, an anti-competitive joint venture agreement), but hesitate when it comes to the use of structural remedies more generally.[479] Yet another position has been taken by O'Neill and Sanders. These authors have argued that the competition authorities may 'need' to impose structural remedies for infringements of Articles 101 and 102 TFEU. This conclusion is based on the need to provide remedies to ensure the effectiveness of EU competition law.[480] More important than any consideration of effectiveness to decide whether the competition authorities should be empowered to impose structural remedies are considerations of equivalence (see above, sections 4.6.2 and 4.6.3). If the Competition Commission or the CMA Panel can impose structural remedies for the protection of UK competition law, then the OFT or the CMA Board should be able to impose structural remedies for the protection of EU competition law as well.

Meanwhile, the need for clarification has only become more urgent. The enforcement of Articles 101 and 102 TFEU and the UK market investigation regime are both administered by the CMA. Along with this institutional change, the remedial powers under the market investigation regime have been supplemented with the adoption of the ERRA 2013. The CMA Panel will be enabled to require parties to appoint and remunerate an independent third party to monitor and/or arbitrate on the implementation of remedies.[481] In other words, the CMA will be allowed to do exactly what *Microsoft* has prohibited the Commission from doing in the context of Articles 101 and 102 TFEU (see above, section 5.6.1). The UK thus reserves some powerful measures for national competition law alone. The UK government has indicated that there is no need for further legislation to improve the interaction between market investigations and the enforcement of Articles 101 and 102 TFEU.[482] The tensions between these parallel competition regimes and the EU principle of equivalence will not be taken away.

Irrespective of the type of directions that can be imposed for infringements of Articles 101 and 102 TFEU, the authorities cannot enforce them directly. Instead, if a person fails, without reasonable excuse, to comply with a direction, the authority can apply for a court order.[483] Application can be made for an order requiring the addressee of the direction to make good its default within a given timeframe. If the direction relates to the management or administration of the undertaking, application can be made for an order requiring the undertaking or

[478] Slot and Johnston (n 217) 226.
[479] Whish and Bailey (n 115) 408.
[480] O'Neill and Sanders (n 151) 10.112.
[481] ERRA 2013, s 49. See further Department for Business, Innovation & Skills (n 126) para 4.38.
[482] Department for Business, Innovation & Skills (n 126) para 4.52.
[483] CA98, s 34.

any of its officers to comply with the direction. Any person who fails to comply with a court order will be 'in contempt of court' and risks a custodial sentence or fine.

As to the specificity of the imposed remedies, the CAT has conformed to EU practice. In *Napp Pharmaceutical*, the CAT concluded that an obligation to cease the infringements in question and refrain from conduct of the same or equivalent effect is a measure similar to orders made in decisions of the Commission and should therefore be accepted.[484] Any doubt as to the scope of that obligation would have to be resolved if and when the authorities came to enforce their directions before the court.[485]

The competition authorities occasionally give directions. In *National Grid*, Ofgem required the undertaking involved to terminate an infringement and refrain from engaging in conduct with equivalent exclusionary effects.[486] In *Napp Pharmaceutical*, the OFT gave extensive directions, requiring the addressee, amongst others, to lower the list prices of certain of its products and renegotiate existing supply contracts.[487] In addition, in *Genzyme*, the OFT imposed price-related directions.[488]

5.6.5 The Degree and Drivers of Convergence

It can be concluded from the foregoing analysis that there is a considerable degree of convergence with regard to the types of remedies that can be imposed for infringements of Articles 101 and 102 TFEU. In all four jurisdictions, the authorities may impose both negative and positive behavioural orders and most jurisdictions explicitly provide for structural remedies too. With the exception of the UK, when it comes to the principle of equivalence, the duty of sincere cooperation seems to be satisfied by all three Member States. To a large extent, Regulation 1/2003 and the powers of the Commission have functioned as a driver of convergence. Yet, upon closer inspection, some notable differences emerge. In a general sense, it seems that the Commission is less keen to impose intrusive remedies than some of the national authorities. This difference is most apparent with regard to compulsory supplies to remedy infringements of Article 101 TFEU and price intervention to remedy infringements of Article 102 TFEU. Moreover, there are some more specific differences. For instance, the German authorities are alone in their ability to skim off illegal gains and to order undertakings to pay damages to third parties that have been injured as a result of the

[484] *Napp Pharmaceutical* (n 168) [553].
[485] ibid.
[486] Ofgem 27/08 *National Grid.*
[487] OFT No CA98/2D/2001 *Napp Pharmaceutical.*
[488] OFT Case CP/0488-01 *Genzyme*. On appeal: *Genzyme* [2005] CAT 32.

anti-competitive behaviour. While Dutch law (and to a lesser extent UK law) also blends remedial intervention with some form of consumer protection, injured parties cannot rely on the ACM (or on the UK authorities) for compensation of the harm caused by the infringement of Articles 101 and 102 TFEU. Another difference relates to the group of potential addressees. No other jurisdiction than the UK so clearly allows its authorities to impose remedies on managers and other company officials.

Furthermore, the enforcement of remedies has been organised differently in the various jurisdictions. The German authorities are vested with the most extensive powers. They can require third parties to do whatever is in their power to make sure that the remedies are implemented and could even themselves take the measures that the undertaking failed to take. Furthermore, they have at their disposal the power to impose periodic penalty payments and fines. The UK authorities can be positioned at the other end of the spectrum, lacking autonomous enforcement powers. Yet, non-compliance with a remedy imposed by the UK authorities could ultimately result in a custodial sentence, making non-compliance in the UK a highly risky activity. In between these extremes are situated the Commission and the ACM. Breach of a Commission remedy may lead to periodic penalty payments, but is no ground for the imposition of a fine. The powers of the Dutch authority are more elaborate and flexible. For the purposes of remedying an infringement of Articles 101 and 102 TFEU, the ACM can choose either to issue an order with an automatic penalty payment or to proceed on the basis of a direction. Breach of a direction provides a ground for the adoption of an order or the imposition of a fine. Where the ACM chooses an order, either directly or after first having given a direction, it may supplement this order with a single lump-sum payment for non-compliance after a certain period, with a penalty that is levied periodically in accordance with a set timeframe for as long as the infringement persists, or with a penalty for each time an infringement is committed. As there is no statutory cap on the total amount of periodic penalties, the ACM should fix this amount in accordance with the principle of proportionality.

These differences in relation to the enforcement of remedies have an impact on the legal safeguards for the undertakings involved. Because a breach of a remedy imposed by the German authorities constitutes an administrative offence and may attract fines, German law deviates from Commission procedures as to the specificity of the remedy. The opposite development can be observed in the UK, where the courts have sought alignment with the criteria for the Commission. In this respect, it should be recalled that the UK authorities cannot enforce their remedies directly. The available legal safeguards with regard to remedies for infringements of Articles 101 and 102 TFEU also differ in other respects. For instance, the Dutch authority may impose remedies without having to issue a statement of objections. This is in stark contrast to the other jurisdictions, which in this respect provide better legal protection. Notwithstanding the tendencies of convergence, there thus remain considerable disparities in terms of the remedial powers of the various authorities.

5.7 PECUNIARY SANCTIONS

The most common type of pecuniary sanction for infringements of Articles 101 and 102 TFEU is the fine. A fine is a measure to punish past behaviour. However, the fact that this sanction is a response to something that happened in the past should not obscure the measure's ability to change future conduct. Fines not only have a retributive function, they may also be used to deter undertakings and individuals from engaging in anti-competitive behaviour. In fact, in the context of competition law, deterrence seems to have become the key driver in fining policy.[489] This is reflected in the Commission fines, the average amount of which has steadily increased in the last two decades.[490] This development is not so much the consequence of anti-competitive practices becoming ever more pernicious, but could rather be explained as a response to the pervasiveness of some of these practices. The adjustment of the level of fines to the deterrence effects of earlier fines could be seen as the outcome of a learning process. In accordance with what was concluded in chapter three, the decentralisation of the enforcement of Articles 101 and 102 TFEU could give a boost to these learning processes. It also allows Member States to cater for domestic preferences in the area of fines, for instance, in terms of severity and potential addressees. Whether such regulatory innovation and preference matching actually occur is largely dependent on the development of domestic fining powers. Against this background, this section will study the development in our subset of jurisdictions. More specifically, it will look for convergence and differentiation with regard to fines and other pecuniary sanctions. Additionally, this section will evaluate the compatibility of the domestic regimes with the principles set out in chapter four, as well as with the Model Leniency Programme and the Fining Principles adopted under the aegis of the ECN and the ECA.

5.7.1 The Powers of the Commission

The Commission may impose fines on undertakings that intentionally or negligently infringe Articles 101 and 102 TFEU.[491] The maximum fine that can be levied equals 10 per cent of the undertaking's worldwide turnover. Regulation 1/2003 stresses that these fines are not of a criminal law nature.[492] In principle, the Commission cannot fine individuals. Save for the highly exceptional situation that

[489] *cf* OECD Recommendation concerning Effective Action Against Hard Core Cartels C(98)35 <www.oecd.org> accessed 1 July 2013; ECA Fining Principles <www.bundeskartellamt.de/wDeutsch/download/pdf/ECA/ECA_principles_for_convergence.pdf> accessed 1 July 2013.

[490] See <http://ec.europa.eu/competition/cartels/statistics/statistics.pdf> accessed 1 July 2013.

[491] Article 23 of Regulation 1/2003.

[492] Article 23(5) of Regulation 1/2003.

an infringement is committed by an unincorporated trader, fines will always be borne by legal persons.

In contrast to reparatory sanctions, fines may only be imposed for *intentional* or *negligent* infringements. There is no clear distinction between these conditions and the Commission, although formally required to establish intent or negligence, sometimes does not characterise the nature of the infringement at all.[493] These conditions can be fulfilled even if the undertaking played only a subsidiary, accessory or passive role in the infringement.[494] Moreover, a fine may already be imposed where the undertaking cannot have been unaware of the anti-competitive nature of its conduct.[495] Whether or not it is aware that this conduct is contrary to Article 101 or 102 TFEU is irrelevant. The Court of Justice considers intentional and negligent infringements to be equally serious.[496]

Undertakings may escape liability if they erroneously assume that their agreement or practice is covered by any of the 'safe havens' provided by the Commission. This follows from the Commission's *De Minimis* Notice,[497] which lays down guidelines on how the Commission deals with the notion of 'restriction of competition' in the application of Article 101 TFEU. In this Notice, the Commission elaborates on the case law requirement that any restriction of competition in the sense of Article 101 TFEU should be appreciable.[498] The Commission qualifies this notion of appreciability with the help of market share thresholds, below which it considers the initiation of enforcement proceedings to be unwarranted. Importantly, the *De Minimis* Notice also exonerates undertakings that in good faith wrongly assumed that their agreement benefited from the safe haven.[499]

The Commission may impose fines both for past and persisting infringements. However, this power is subject to a limitation period. Past infringements cannot be fined indefinitely. Regulation 1/2003 has fixed this limitation period at five years.[500] Time begins to run the day on which the infringement is committed.[501] However, infringements of Articles 101 and 102 TFEU hardly ever come in the form of a one-off act that can be assigned to a single day.[502] Therefore, Regulation

[493] Roth and Rose (n 177) 13.137; Faull and Nikpay (n 182) 8.592.

[494] *cf* Case T-29/05 *Deltafina* [2010] ECR II-4077 [55] et seq. At [61], the General Court reiterated: 'although the limited importance, as the case may be, of the participation of the undertaking concerned cannot therefore call into question its individual liability for the infringement as a whole, it nonetheless has an influence on the assessment of the extent of that liability and thus the severity of the penalty'.

[495] Joined Cases 96–102, 104, 105, 108 and 110/82 *IAZ International Belgium* [1983] ECR 3369 [45].

[496] Case C-137/95 P *SPO* [1996] ECR I-1611 [55]. However, the Commission considers that infringements committed out of negligence are eligible for a mitigated fine; see Guidelines on the method of setting fines imposed pursuant to Article 23(2)(a) of Regulation No 1/2003 [2006] OJ C210/2.

[497] Commission Notice on agreements of minor importance which do not appreciably restrict competition under Article 81(1) of the Treaty establishing the European Community (*de minimis*) [2001] OJ C368/13.

[498] Case 5/69 *Völk v Vervaeke* [1969] ECR 295.

[499] *De Minimis* Notice (n 497), para 4.

[500] Article 25(1) of Regulation 1/2003.

[501] Article 25(2) of Regulation 1/2003.

[502] A rare example of a one-off act contrary to Article 101 TFEU can be found in Case C-8/08 *T-Mobile Netherlands* [2009] ECR I-4529, where the infringement consisted of a single anti-competitive meeting.

1/2003 provides an alternative starting date for repeated or continuous infringements: the day on which the infringement has ceased.[503] This alternative starting date for continuous infringements has led to a large body of case law on the question of when exactly various anti-competitive acts can be considered part of an SCI. If these acts are part of a single anti-competitive objective, in that they are complementary in their object or effect to restrict competition, they may be considered part of an SCI (see above, section 4.3.3). The starting date of the limitation period for anti-competitive behaviour forming part of an SCI is effectively extended to the final instance of anti-competitive conduct.

The five-year limitation period can be interrupted. Any investigatory action by the Commission or an NCA that has been notified to at least one of the undertakings interrupts the limitation period in relation to all undertakings involved.[504] With each interruption, the five-year period starts running afresh. However, interruptions may not extend the total duration between termination of the infringement and the imposition of the fine to more than two times the limitation period.[505] This means that this duration cannot exceed 10 years. Procedures before the Court of Justice, whether interim or on appeal, have no effect on the limitation period. The limitation period is suspended for as long as the decision is pending before the Court.[506]

Determining the Amount of the Fine

In fixing the appropriate amount of the fine, the Commission must take into account the gravity and duration of the infringement.[507] The gravity of the infringement is determined by reference to various factors.[508] The proportion of turnover derived from the goods in respect of which the infringement was committed has been considered a relevant factor.[509] Further, the Commission should have regard to the profit which the undertaking was able to derive from the infringement.[510] However, the fact that the undertaking did not benefit from the infringement does not preclude the imposition of a (severe) fine.[511] The Commission does not have to take account of the financial situation of the undertakings involved either.[512] In any case, the final amount may not exceed the statutory maximum of 10 per cent of the undertaking's worldwide turnover in the preceding business year.[513]

[503] Article 25(2) of Regulation 1/2003.
[504] Article 25(3) of Regulation 1/2003.
[505] Article 25(3)–(5) of Regulation 1/2003.
[506] Article 25(6) of Regulation 1/2003. See also Case T-372/10 *Bolloré II* [2012] OJ C235/13 [216].
[507] Article 23(3) of Regulation 1/2003.
[508] *cf* Case C-272/09 P *KME* [2012] OJ C32/4 [96]–[97].
[509] *cf* Case T-446/05 *Amann & Söhne* [2010] ECR II-1255 [188].
[510] *cf* Joined Cases 100–03/80 *Musique diffusion francaise* [1983] ECR 1825 [129]; Joined Cases C-189, C-202, C-205–08 and C-213/02 P *Dansk Rørindustri* [2005] ECR I-5425 [292].
[511] Case T-213/00 *CMA CGM* [2003] ECR II-913 [340]–[341].
[512] *IAZ International Belgium* (n 495) [54]–[55].
[513] Article 23(2) of Regulation 1/2003.

The wide margin of discretion enjoyed by the Commission allows it to pursue a fining policy aimed at deterrence.[514] The Commission's tasks are not limited to the enforcement of Articles 101 and 102 TFEU in individual cases. It has a broader supervisory role, which includes the duty to pursue a general policy to steer undertakings away from infringements.[515] Accordingly, the Commission's fines should not only deter the undertakings concerned from engaging in future infringements (special deterrence), they should also be able to deter potential future offenders more generally (general deterrence).[516] This requires the Commission to take into account the frequency of infringements.[517] Within the limits of Regulation 1/2003, the Commission may deviate from earlier fining practice if this is needed to implement EU competition law in an effective manner.[518] The Commission may therefore at any time, and within the boundaries of the statutory maximum, adjust the level of its fines.[519] For this purpose, it may also take into account aggravating circumstances not taken into account in earlier decisions.[520] The persistance of infringements of Articles 101 and 102 TFEU has led the Commission to increase the average amount of its fines. The 10 largest fines for individual undertakings have all been levied in the new millennium.[521] Nine-digit fines have become the rule. In 2008, Saint Gobain SA was fined a record amount of €896 million for its participation in the *Car Glass* cartel.[522]

In order to deter undertakings from engaging in infringements of Articles 101 and 102 TFEU and, at the same time, ensure the transparency and impartiality of its fining decisions, the Commission has published *Guidelines on the method of setting fines imposed pursuant to Article 23(2)(a) of Regulation No 1/2003* (hereinafter the 'Fining Guidelines').[523] In these Fining Guidelines, the Commission indicates that fines should have a deterrent effect in order to punish the undertakings involved in the infringement and to deter other undertakings from engaging in, or continuing, behaviour that is contrary to Articles 101 and 102 TFEU.[524] This has resulted in a method for setting fines in which, first, a basic amount is calculated by reference to the value of the undertaking's sales of goods or services to which the infringement relates. Depending on the nature and scope of the infringement, on whether the infringement has been implemented, and on the market share of the undertakings, the Commission will set the basic amount of the fine at a level that will generally not exceed 30 per cent of the value of sales.[525] This amount will then be multiplied by the

[514] *Musique diffusion francaise* (n 510) [105]–[106].
[515] ibid [105].
[516] Case T-13/03 *Nintendo* [2009] ECR II-975 [73].
[517] *Musique diffusion francaise* (n 510) [106]–[108].
[518] *Dansk Rørindustri* (n 510) [191]–[193].
[519] *Musique diffusion francaise* (n 510) [109].
[520] Case T-343/08 *Arkema France* [2011] ECR II-2287 [56].
[521] *cf*<http://ec.europa.eu/competition/cartels/statistics/statistics.pdf> accessed 28 October 2013.
[522] *Car Glass* (Case COMP/39.125) Summary of Commission Decision 2009/C 173/08 [2009] OJ C173/13.
[523] [2006] OJ C210/2.
[524] Fining Guidelines, para 4.
[525] ibid paras 21, 22 and 37.

number of years of participation in the infringement and topped up with an 'entrance-fee' of between 15 and 25 per cent of the value of sales, irrespective of the duration. Second, this basic amount can be increased if there are aggravating circumstances, notably in cases of recidivism, refusal to cooperate, or where the undertaking had a leading role. Third, the basic amount may be reduced if there are mitigating circumstances (swift termination, unintentional infringement, limited involvement, cooperation with the Commission, authorisation or encouragement by public authorities or legislation). Compensation of injured parties does not qualify as a mitigating circumstance.[526] Fourth, the Commission may then increase the amount again in order to ensure a sufficiently deterrent effect. This may be needed when the undertakings are large and diversified or when they have made considerable illegal overcharges. It should be noted that the calculation of the basic amount of the fine, using a percentage of the relevant turnover, seems to have been inspired by the 2001 fining guidelines of the Dutch competition authority.[527]

The Commission has supplemented its deterrence-focused fining policy with a whistleblower arrangement for the most serious infringements of Article 101 TFEU. The Commission considers that it is in the EU's interest to reward undertakings involved in covert horizontal agreements (ie, agreements between competitors) which are willing to terminate their involvement independently and assist the Commission in its investigations. This reward consists of granting immunity or a reduction in the level of fines. This leniency policy has been laid down in the *Commission Notice on Immunity from fines and reduction of fines in cartel cases* (hereinafter the 'Leniency Notice').[528] There are three general conditions for leniency: (i) genuine, full, continuous and expeditious cooperation; (ii) prompt termination of the infringement; and (iii) no tampering with the evidence or disclosure of the leniency application.[529] In addition, there are specific conditions for full and partial immunity.

The leniency applicant who is the first to submit information and evidence enabling the Commission to either carry out a targeted inspection or to prove an infringement is entitled to full immunity.[530] Immunity is conditional on the Commission not already having sufficient information itself to carry out an inspection or to establish the infringement.[531] A further condition for immunity is that the applicant undertaking did not coerce its former co-cartelists to partici-

[526] While there is no formal Commission policy to take into account compensatory payments in setting the amount of the fine, on two occasions it has done so nonetheless. See *Pre-insulated Pipes* (Case IV/35.691/E-4) Commission Decision 1999/60/EC [1999] OJ L24/1, para 172; *PO Video Games, PO Nintendo Distribution, Omega – Nintendo* (Case COMP 35.587) (Case COMP 35.706) (Case COMP 36.321) [2003] OJ L255/33, paras 440–41. However, the General Court has held that the Commission is *not* required to take into account compensation as a mitigating circumstance; see Case T-59/02 *Archer Daniels Midland* [2006] ECR II-3627 [349]–[355].

[527] *cf* WPJ Wils, 'The European Commission's 2006 Guidelines on Antitrust Fines: A Legal and Economic Analysis' (2007) 30 *World Competition* 197, 209.

[528] [2006] OJ C298/17.

[529] Leniency Notice, paras 12 and 24.

[530] ibid para 8

[531] ibid paras 10–11.

pate in the cartel.[532] The immunity applicant must provide the Commission with a corporate statement (written or oral), including a detailed description of the infringement and the participants, as well as other (contemporaneous) evidence.[533] Immunity applicants have the opportunity to apply for a so-called 'marker' before proceeding to a formal application.[534] This allows them to gather all incriminating evidence without jeopardising their position relative to other leniency applicants. If the applicant completes its application within the period set by the Commission, the evidence provided will be deemed to have been submitted on the date when the marker was registered.[535]

Undertakings that do not qualify for immunity are entitled to apply for a reduction of the fine. To qualify for such a reduction, the undertaking must provide the Commission with evidence that has significant *added* value, meaning evidence that strengthens the Commission's ability to prove the alleged cartel (eg, directly incriminating contemporaneous documentary evidence).[536] The level of reduction depends on the value of the evidence provided and the order of application. The first undertaking to provide evidence of significant added value may expect a reduction of 30–50 per cent. The second undertaking is eligible for a 20–30 per cent reduction. Subsequent applicants can earn a reduction of up to 20 per cent.[537] Incriminating facts that increase the gravity or duration of the infringement are not taken into account in relation to the applicant who furnished the evidence for these additional facts ('mini-immunity').[538]

Cooperation with the Commission's cartel investigations can also be rewarded in the context of a settlement procedure (see above, section 5.4.1). This procedure has been worked out in the Settlement Notice.[539] Like the Leniency Notice, the Settlement Notice also applies exclusively to cartels. Whereas the Leniency Notice is meant to trigger or advance an investigation by rewarding undertakings for providing incriminating evidence, the Settlement Notice is meant to speed up the decision-making process once the Commission has sufficient evidence to proceed to the decision-making stage.

Undertakings can make an application under the Settlement Notice, either subsequent to an earlier leniency application or autonomously.[540] Cooperation in the framework of the Settlement Notice may lead to an (additional) fine discount of 10 per cent.[541] During the bilateral settlement discussions, the Commission will disclose the essential elements which it intends to take into consideration in drafting its statement of objections in order to reach a common understanding.[542] The

[532] ibid para 13.
[533] ibid para 9.
[534] ibid para 14.
[535] ibid para 15.
[536] ibid paras 24–25.
[537] ibid para 26.
[538] ibid.
[539] [2008] OJ C167/1.
[540] Settlement Notice, para 1.
[541] ibid paras 32–33.
[542] ibid para 16.

undertaking may then file a settlement submission in which it, amongst others, acknowledges liability for the infringement in accordance with the common understanding and waives certain procedural rights (access to the file, oral hearing).[543] The Commission then drafts a statement of objections in accordance with the settlement submission, to which the parties may reply with a simple confirmation.[544] Finally, the Commission adopts a regular fining decision pursuant to Articles 7 and 23 of Regulation 1/2003.[545] During the whole process, the Commission retains a broad margin of discretion in determining which cases may be suitable to explore the parties' interest to engage in settlement discussions, as well as to engage in them or discontinue them or to definitely settle.[546]

Judicial Protection

A fine can be appealed in two instances. After a first instance appeal before the General Court, a further appeal may be lodged with the Court of Justice on points of law. In accordance with Article 261 TFEU, the General Court has 'unlimited jurisdiction' to review decisions whereby the Commission *has fixed a fine.*[547] This suggests that the Court has unlimited jurisdiction only with regard to the level of the fine. The finding that there has been an infringement can of course be appealed as well, but is subject to the review procedure of Article 263 TFEU.[548] The Court's unlimited jurisdiction with regard to fines allows it to reassess all matters of fact or law and to cancel, reduce *or increase* the fine. In making this assessment, the Court is not in any way bound by the Commission's Fining Guidelines and it may take into account additional information that is not part of the decision.[549] In practice, the Court tends to follow the approach of the Fining Guidelines and reserves its powers to increase the fine only in exceptional cases. It is for this reason that lodging an appeal against a Commission fine is generally worthwhile. The detailed calculation method of the Commission provides ample opportunity to convince the Court of a weak spot somewhere in the calculation. With the unparalleled amounts that the Commission levies, already the smallest reduction percentage-wise by the Court can reduce a fine by millions of euros.

Fines are generally payable within three months.[550] An appeal does not automatically suspend this requirement. However, parties may apply to the President of the General Court for interim relief. Such an interim procedure is generally not

[543] ibid para 20.

[544] ibid paras 25–26.

[545] ibid para 28.

[546] ibid paras 5–6.

[547] Article 31 of Regulation 1/2003.

[548] Under Article 263 TFEU, the Court has jurisdiction to annul a decision for lack of competence, infringement of an essential procedural requirement, infringement of the Treaty or EU legislation, or misuse of power. While it may partially annul a decision, it cannot find an infringement different from the one found by the Commission.

[549] Case C-291/98 P *Sarrió* [2000] ECR I-9991 [71].

[550] Roth and Rose (n 177) 13.248.

necessary as the Commission is willing to accept a bank guarantee pending the appeal procedures.[551]

5.7.2 The Powers of the German Authorities

Like the Commission, the German authorities can also impose fines for infringements of Articles 101 and 102 TFEU. This is the case for infringements that constitute an administrative offence (*Ordnungswidrigkeit*).[552] For this purpose, the infringement has to be committed intentionally or negligently. Both natural and legal persons can be fined for their involvement in infringements of Articles 101 and 102 TFEU. Natural persons can be punished with fines of up to €1 million.[553] Legal persons may be punished with fines up to €1 million or 10 per cent of the undertaking's worldwide turnover.[554] Pursuant to § 17(2) OWiG, infringements committed negligently cannot be punished with more than half of the maximum punishment, ie €500,000,000 or five per cent of the undertaking's worldwide turnover. Where the authorities intend to disgorge the illegal gains of the infringement rather than to punish the offender, the fine may exceed the above amounts (see below).

The general system of administrative offences has traditionally been concerned with the actions of natural persons. The administrative offence resulting from an intentional or negligent breach of Article 101 or 102 TFEU therefore focuses on the responsible natural persons. While legal persons cannot escape liability for their role in infringements of Articles 101 and 102 TFEU either, their exposure is mainly of a secondary nature, deriving from the administrative offence committed by the responsible natural persons.

Natural persons may be fined as (co-)perpetrator of the administrative offence or in their capacity of proprietor (*Inhaber*) of the undertaking. The latter possibility is rather exceptional, however. In the exceptional circumstance that an infringement of Article 101 or 102 TFEU has been committed by an unincorporated undertaking, the natural person who can be identified with the undertaking is directly liable on the basis of § 81(1) and (4) GWB, possibly in conjunction with § 130 OWiG. In the more common scenario where the natural person and the undertaking are not unified, the former may be fined as (co-)perpetrator of the infringement. Natural persons responsible for the actions of the undertakings and involved in the infringement may be fined in accordance with § 81(1) and (4) GWB in conjunction with § 9 or 14 OWiG.

In addition, legal persons can be held liable for infringements of Articles 101 and 102 TFEU. In accordance with § 30 OWiG, a company can be fined if one of

[551] ibid.
[552] § 81(1) GWB.
[553] § 81(4) GWB, § 130(3) OWiG.
[554] § 81(4) GWB.

its officers[555] has committed an administrative offence by breaching rules that are addressed to the company. This laborious approach alone shows that the liability of legal persons is somewhat atypical under German law. The possibility of fining companies for infringements of Articles 101 and 102 TFEU was mainly inspired by the powers of the Commission.[556] While the liability of a legal person for an infringement of Article 101 or 102 TFEU thus derives from the administrative offence committed by a natural person, the competition authority may decide to use its fining powers on the former alone.[557]

This derivative corporate liability has led the BKartA, the appeal courts and ultimately the German legislator to grapple with the issue of corporate restructurings. In *Industrieversicherer*, the BKartA imposed a fine on a company for its role in an anti-competitive agreement in the market for industrial insurances.[558] More specifically, the company was held responsible for the anti-competitive agreements concluded by one of the company's organs and senior officials. The infringement lasted from 1999 to 2002. The BKartA imposed a fine in 2005. In 2006, a corporate restructuring took place and one of the parent companies that owned the relevant economic unit was sold to a third party. The target and the acquiring company were then integrated through a legal merger and assets of the new entity were divested to other group companies. By 2007, only four per cent of the infringing economic unit's insurances were owned by the new entity. This amounted to 28 per cent of the new entity's business. The OLG Düsseldorf, and the ultimately the BGH, had to decide whether the new entity was liable for the infringement.[559] Both courts declared that the new entity was not liable. They concluded that under § 30 OWiG, liability did not attach to the economic unit. Instead, the administrative offence was committed by a company's organ and senior official. Only that company could be liable under § 30 OWiG. Liability could only be extended to the legal successor of that company in situations where the former was identical to the latter in an economic sense. Considering the business of the new entity, the exception could not be relied upon in this case. Needless to say, this interpretation invites companies to game the system and circumvent liability. Unsurprisingly, the German legislator reacted swiftly by amending § 30 OWiG. This amendment was part of the 8th amendment of the GWB. A subsection, § 30(2a), was introduced to ensure that legal successors can be held liable for infringements committed by organs or senior officials of their legal predecessor. In light of what has been concluded in section 4.3.2 above, one could argue that this amendment would not have been strictly necessary for the purposes of Articles 101 and 102 TFEU. After all, the economic continuity doctrine applies

555 § 30(1) OWiG limits the group of company officers whose breach of obligations could attract liability for the legal person. This group includes, among others, statutory directors and responsible managers.

556 Raum in Langen/Bunte (n 24) § 82 Rdnr 1.

557 § 30(4) OWiG.

558 The below facts can be found in BGH *Industrieversicherer* Aktenzeichen KRB 55/10.

559 In penalty proceedings, the OLG undertakes a full merits review and all facts need to be established afresh (see above, section 5.2.2).

when the legal person responsible for running the undertaking has ceased to exist in law after the infringement has been committed or when the transferring legal person remains nothing but an empty shell. In these cases, the acquirer can be held liable directly on the basis of EU competition law.

The difficulties with corporate restructurings are due to the fact that under German law, corporate liability derives from the liability of natural persons. However, there are also situations where a company can be fined more directly for practices contrary to Articles 101 and 102 TFEU. This is the case for companies engaged in criminal bid-rigging cartels. A single bid-rigging cartel may be prohibited both under Article 101 TFEU and § 298 of the German Criminal Code (*Strafgesetzbuch* (StGB')).[560] As legal persons are exonerated under German criminal law, companies that rig bids are not subject to criminal sanctions. § 30 OWiG foresees this lacuna by providing that a company can be fined *administratively* if one of its officers has committed a *criminal* offence by breaching rules that are addressed to the company, eg, the prohibition against bid-rigging. By virtue of § 82(1) GWB, the competition authorities may initiate these administrative proceedings. In other words, bid-rigging cartels could lead to two *autonomous* enforcement proceedings: criminal proceedings by the public prosecutor against the natural persons involved and administrative proceedings by the competition authorities against the responsible companies.

§ 30 OWiG thus forms the legal basis for the administrative liability of companies in situations where a company officer has either committed an administrative offence (eg, a breach of § 81(1) GWB in conjunction with Article 101 or 102 TFEU) or a criminal offence (eg, § 298 StGB). Interestingly, the magnitude of this liability may differ. Whereas the corporate fine in the event of a criminal offence can reach €10 million, the corporate fine in the event of an administrative offence is determined by the provisions for that administrative offence. A breach of § 81(1) GWB in conjunction with Article 101 or 102 TFEU may be punished with fines up to 10 per cent of the undertaking's worldwide turnover and may thus exceed €10 million. Situations like these have been found to be undesirable by the German legislator. By virtue of § 30(2) OWiG, a corporate fine for criminal bid-rigging can thus reach 10 per cent of the undertaking's worldwide turnover.

Criminal Fines

Apart from administrative fines imposed by the competition authorities, some anti-competitive practices may also attract criminal fines. This is the case for bid-rigging cartels (§ 298 StGB). Proceedings under § 298 StGB are outside the realm of the competition authorities. Only natural persons can be fined in these criminal proceedings. The amount of the fine is fixed in

[560] An important difference between illegal bid-rigging under Article 101 TFEU and illegal bid-rigging under § 298 StGB is that the latter relates to the offer based on an anti-competitive agreement rather than the underlying agreement itself.

accordance with § 40 StGB. The statutory maximum of this fine is calculated by multiplying the maximum amount of daily instalments (*Tagessätzen*) with the maximum value that an instalment could have. This could lead to a maximum amount of €1.8 million for a single offence.[561] The actual amount of the fine in individual cases is based on the personal and economic circumstances of the offender.[562]

Compared with these criminal fines, the maximum fine for administrative offences (€1 million) appears relatively modest. This may cause a rift between anti-competitive practices prohibited under § 298 StGB and all other infringements of Articles 101 and 102 TFEU, and may raise concerns in relation to the EU principle of equivalence (see above, section 4.6.2). Whatever could be said about this policy choice, it does not seem contrary to the spirit of the principle of equivalence. After all, the 'discriminatory treatment' relates more to the nature of the anti-competitive practice than to the origin of the prohibition. Bid-rigging cartels that fall within the scope of Article 101 TFEU may also fall within the scope of § 298 StGB, thus benefiting from the increased level of deterrence. In any case, the difference between the fine actually imposed by the criminal court and the fine actually imposed by the competition authority may well be more equivalent than the statutory maximum amounts suggest (and could even be in favour of the latter).[563]

A second possibility for autonomous corporate fines in the context of Articles 101 and 102 TFEU is provided by § 82 GWB and § 130 OWiG. Under the latter provision, the proprietor of an undertaking can be fined for intentionally or negligently failing to take precautionary measures necessary to prevent the undertaking from engaging in infringements of Articles 101 and 102 TFEU. The term 'proprietor' (*Inhaber*) not only relates to natural persons, but also covers legal persons. § 130 OWiG thus provides a legal basis to hold a parent company liable for infringements committed by its subsidiaries.[564] In light of what has been concluded in section 4.3.2, for the purposes of EU competition law, this explicit legal basis is mainly relevant for situations where the parent and subsidiary do not form a single economic entity in the sense of Articles 101 and 102 TFEU. In the event that

[561] A very clear description of the calculation of criminal fines can, surprisingly, be found in an OFT report: 'criminal fines are payable in daily instalments, where for each sentence the number of instalments is at least five, but cannot exceed 360. The amount payable in each instalment can range from €1 to €5,000, so that the maximum total fine for offences under the Criminal Code is 360 x €5,000 = €1.8 million' (footnotes omitted) See OFT, *An Assessment of Discretionary Penalties Regimes* (OFT 1132 2009) para A.117 <www.oft.gov.uk/shared_oft/economic_research/oft1132.pdf> accessed 1 July 2013.

[562] § 40(2) StGB.

[563] *cf* LG Düsseldorf Aktenzeichen 24b Ns 9/06, where a criminal fine of below €100 was imposed.

[564] Parent liability under § 130 OWiG does not even seem to require a 100 per cent shareholding. § 14 OWiG suggests that various shareholders could also breach § 130 OWiG jointly provided that they have a supervisory duty.

the parent and subsidiary do form a single economic entity, parent liability follows directly from the concept of undertaking laid down in Articles 101 and 102 TFEU.

Irrespective of the addressee of the decision, whether a natural or legal person, infringements of Articles 101 and 102 TFEU may no longer be fined after the expiry of the statutory limitation period. This period is five years,[565] but may be interrupted by any enforcement action listed in § 33 OWiG (eg, hearing, inspection, statement of objections). This possibility of interruption is extended to similar actions by the Commission or other NCAs.[566] With each interruption, time starts running afresh. The interruption of the limitation period is personal and only applies to those persons against whom the enforcement action is directed.[567] In any case, interruptions may not extend the total duration between the termination of the infringement and the imposition of the fine to more than two times the limitation period.[568] In this respect, it should be noted that the limitation period extends to the proceedings before the OLG.[569] The latter should therefore render a judgment imposing fines within 10 years of the termination of the infringement.

Determining the Amount of the Fine

Under the pre-2005 penalty regime, fines for infringements of competition law were capped by a relatively low fixed ceiling (€500,000) or by an amount equal to three times that of the illegal gains (*Mehrerlös*). This put the competition authorities between a rock and a hard place. They either had to content themselves with a modest fine or face the challenge of calculating the illegal gains. As a result, fines were either manifestly insufficient or fraught with contestable assumptions. To put an end to this conundrum, in 2005 the German legislator exchanged this regime for the arguably more effective method laid down in Regulation 1/2003.[570] As is clear from the report of the parliamentary committee responsible for competition matters, this amendment was considered especially urgent in light of the establishment of the ECN and the power of the Commission to take over cases from the German authorities pursuant to Article 11(6) of Regulation 1/2003.[571] Consequently, with the seventh amendment to the GWB, the German authorities saw their fining powers being aligned to those of the Commission.[572] This alignment even has a dynamic feature, as it extends to the Commission's fining guidelines, which can be amended

[565] § 81(8) GWB.
[566] § 81(9) GWB.
[567] § 33(4) OWiG. See also Raum in Langen/Bunte (n 24) § 81 Rdnr 189.
[568] § 33(3) OWiG.
[569] §§ 31–33 OWiG.
[570] *cf* Deutscher Bundestag, *Beschlussempfelung und Bericht des Auschusses für Wirtschaft und Arbeit (9. Ausschuss) zu dem Gesetzentwurf der Bundesregierung – Drucksache 15/3640 – Entwurf eines Siebten Gesetzes zür Änderung des Gesetzes gegen Wettbewerbsbeschränkungen* (BT-Drucksache 15/5049) 50 <www.bundestag.de/dokumente/drucksachen/index.html> accessed 1 July 2013.
[571] ibid.
[572] Deutscher Bundestag (n 185) 42.

at any time.[573] Accordingly, the BKartA needs to take into account the Commission's Fining Guidelines in determining the appropriate amount of the fine. As yet, it is unclear how this requirement will exactly play out in situations where there is a conflict between the administrative guidelines of the BKartA and the Commission's Fining Guidelines.

The intended alignment to the Commission model has recently been restricted by the BGH. In *Zement*, the BGH decided that, contrary to the Commission model, the 10 per cent turnover threshold should be seen as the upper boundary in determining the amount of the fine.[574] At the EU level, the 10 per cent turnover threshold functions as an absolute restriction to the discretion of the Commission is determining the amount of the fine. The difference between these two approaches is that under German law, the calculation process may never render an amount in excess of 10 per cent of the undertaking's turnover, not even at some intermediate stage. More importantly, under German law, the turnover percentage constituted by the amount of the fine needs to reflect the severity of the infringement.

Since 2005, the competition authorities may *punish* infringements of Articles 101 and 102 TFEU with fines of up to €1 million or, with regard to undertakings, 10 per cent of the undertaking's worldwide turnover.[575] In fixing the amount of the fine, the competition authorities should take into account the gravity and duration of the infringement.[576] Above and beyond the gravity and duration of the infringement, fines should be calculated in accordance with hierarchical superior general principles of domestic law (*allgemeine übergeordnete Grundsätze* and *allgemeine rechtliche Grenzen*).[577] Accordingly, market impact, affected commerce, economic conditions of the undertakings involved, the period between infringement and fine, and the implications of the *Doppelverwertungsverbot* (in accordance with this 'dual-use prohibition', the constituent elements of the prohibition may not be used as an aggravating factor for the severity of a penalty) should all be taken into account.[578] In addition, procedural delays caused by the prosecuting authorities could warrant a reduction of the fine.[579]

The possibility to impose fines with the sole aim of *punishing* is an exception to the general rules for penalty proceedings under German law. Outside the field of competition law, administrative fines are meant to exceed the illegal gains and therefore have an inherent disgorgement effect.[580] This exception for competition

[573] Deutscher Bundestag (n 570) 50: 'Im Rahmen einer teleologischen Auslegung sind daher auch die von der Europäischen Kommission praktizierten Leitlinien für das Verfahren zur Festsetzung von Geldbußen mit heranzuziehen.' See also A Mundt, 'Die Bußgeldleitlinien des Bundeskartellamtes' (2007) *Wirtschaft und Wettbewerb* 458, 465.

[574] BGH *Zement* Aktenzeichen KRB 20/12.

[575] § 81(4) GWB.

[576] ibid.

[577] Raum in Langen/Bunte (n 24) § 81 Rdnr 160–68.

[578] ibid.

[579] BGH *Zement* Aktenzeichen KRB 20/12.

[580] § 17(4) OWiG.

law purposes was motivated by the wish to follow the Commission's fining practice, which was understood to have as its sole objective punishment ('*Sanktionscharakter*').[581] Notwithstanding this aim to converge to the Commission model, § 81(5) GWB still allows the competition authorities to fix the amount of the fine with a view to disgorging the illegal gains. In other words, fines may be adopted with the sole aim of punishment, but may also be adopted with the dual aim of punishment and disgorgement.[582] Contrary to what § 81(4) GWB might suggest, the disgorgement part may bring the amount of the fine to well over 10 per cent of the undertaking's worldwide turnover, as only the punitive part (*Ahndung*) of the fine has been capped.[583] This possibility is in accordance with the ECA Fining Principles, which provide that 'the level of fines should exceed any potential gains that may be expected from the infringement'.[584]

Disgorgement of Illegal Gains

In addition to punitive fines, perpetrators of infringements of Articles 101 and 102 TFEU may also be confronted with disgorgement measures, skimming off illegal gains made with the anti-competitive practices. While this could be done through several means, illegal gains can only be skimmed off once.[585] On the basis of § 81(5) GWB, competition authorities may take into account the illegal gains in fixing the amount of the fine. This allows the authorities to disgorge illegal gains under the guise of a fine. Pursuant to § 34 GWB, disgorgement could also take place by way of a separate decision.[586] This possibility for disgorgement may be contemplated to the extent that the illegal gains have not already been redistributed as a result of fines and/or awarded damages claims and/or compensation orders.[587] This power under § 34 GWB is only available with regard to intentional or negligent infringements. A third possibility to redistribute illegal gains relies on the

[581] Deutscher Bundestag (n 185) 42.

[582] § 81(5) GWB reads as follows: 'Bei der Zumessung der Geldbuße findet § 17 Abs. 4 des Gesetzes über Ordnungswidrigkeiten mit der Maßgabe Anwendung, dass der wirtschaftliche Vorteil, der aus der Ordnungswidrigkeit gezogen wurde, durch die Geldbuße nach Absatz 4 abgeschöpft werden kann. Dient die Geldbuße allein der Ahndung, ist dies bei der Zumessung entsprechend zu berücksichtigen.'

[583] § 17(4) OWiG. See also Mundt (n 573) 463–64. The disgorgement part of the fine may be deducted from corporate income taxes; *cf WuW-Sonderheft* (n 45) 146: 'Im Falle einer reinen Ahndungsfunktion sind Geldbußen künftig nicht mehr steuerlich abzugsfähig.'

[584] ECA Fining Principles, para I.3.

[585] *WuW-Sonderheft* (n 45) 134–35.

[586] Competition authorities might indeed be tempted to use § 34 GWB instead of imposing a 'dual-objective fine'. This way they can try to disgorge illegal gains without any extra risk with regard to the legality of the punitive fine; *cf WuW-Sonderheft* (n 45) 146. Another reason could be that decisions under § 34 GWB can be adopted in reparatory proceedings.

[587] Damages claims have priority over disgorgement actions. To the extent that illegal gains have not been redistributed to the victims of anti-competitive practices, the competition authority may skim off the (remaining) illegal gains. If damages are awarded after the authority has skimmed off the illegal gains, the latter needs to transfer the corresponding amount back to the offender; see § 34(2) GWB.

initiative of trade and industry associations. Associations for the promotion of commercial interests or independent professional interests may under specific circumstances initiate proceedings to have the illegal gains flow into the public (federal) budget.[588] With the eighth amendment to the GWB, consumer organisations are also now able to initiate proceedings for the recovery of illegal gains.[589] This third option exists only in relation to infringements committed intentionally and to the extent that redistribution has not been accomplished by the earlier intervention of the authorities. In practice, none of these means to disgorge illegal gains is frequently used.[590]

In June 2013, the BKartA has revised its Fining Guidelines.[591] These Guidelines incorporate the BGH's ruling in *Zement*, where it was decided that the 10 per cent turnover threshold functions as the upper bound in determining the amount of the fine (see above). Like the 2006 Guidelines, the 2013 Guidelines apply to *punitive* fines for *undertakings* imposed by the *BKartA*. Considering the multitude of fining modalities under German law, the scope of these Guidelines is therefore limited. Apart from the similarity in scope, much has changed since the adoption of the 2013 Guidelines.

The 2006 Guidelines provided for a two-step calculation method. As a first step, a base amount was calculated. This amount was the product of a percentage of the net *domestic* turnover affected by the infringement (maximum 30 per cent) and the duration of the infringement. This percentage depended, amongst other things, on the nature and the effect of the infringement. In the second step, this base amount was adjusted on the basis of correction factors. Essentially there were three correction factors: (i) the dissuasive effect of the fine; (ii) aggravating circumstances; and (iii) mitigating circumstances. To ensure the dissuasive effect of fines, the BKartA could increase the base amount up to 100 per cent. This increase was determined on the basis of the size of the undertaking. Contrary to what one might expect, this adjustment seemed to take place before other correction factors were taken into account.[592] After the deterrence increment, the amount of the fine could be further increased so as to take into account aggravating circumstances (degree of fault,

[588] § 34a(1) GWB.

[589] § 33(2) GWB.

[590] P Pohlmann, 'Private Losses in European Competition Law: Public or Private Enforcement?' in R Schulze (ed), *Compensation of Private Losses: The Evolution of Torts in European Business Law* (Sellier European Law Publishers, 2011) 160–61.

[591] BKartA, *Leitlinien für die Bußgeldzumessung in Kartellordnungswidrigkeitsverfahren* <www.bundeskartellamt.de/wDeutsch/download/pdf/Merkblaetter/Merkblaetter_deutsch/Bekanntmachung-_Bu__geldleitlinien-Juni_2013.pdf> accessed 1 July 2013.

[592] One would expect an increase for reasons of dissuasiveness to be the final increment. After all, only this would ensure that the fine truly has a deterrent effect, as required by the EU principle of dissuasiveness (see above, section 4.6.4), without being too much of a deterrent.

recidivism,[593] role within the infringement).[594] Contrary to the increase for reasons of dissuasiveness, there was no limit as to the size of the increase prompted by aggravating circumstances other than the statutory maximum of the fine. Finally, the amount of the fine could be decreased so as to take into account mitigating circumstances (eg, compensation of injured third parties).

In order to implement *Zement*, the 2013 Guidelines have essentially reversed the calculation method. A baseline maximum amount is calculated from which deductions can be made in accordance with the particularities of the individual case. The more severe the infringement, the lower the deductions will be. The baseline maximum amount is the lower of two amounts: 10 per cent of the undertaking's worldwide turnover (or five per cent in case of infringements committed negligently) *or* an amount calculated on the basis of the 'relevant turnover'. The relevant turnover is the domestic turnover obtained with the goods and services to which the infringement relates. This alternative baseline maximum amount is calculated by first taking 10 per cent of the relevant turnover for the entire duration of the infringement. This amount is then multiplied by a number between two and six, depending on the undertaking's worldwide turnover. This number may exceed six in cases of undertakings with a worldwide turnover in excess of €100 billion. In exceptional cases, the alternative baseline maximum may be set at a higher amount. The BKartA is remarkably unspecific about the application of deductions. In a mere two sentences, it lists some infringement-specific and undertaking-specific criteria that it says should be taken into account. In a rather unhelpful comment to these sentences, the BKartA has explained:

> Es ist eine Frage des jeweiligen Einzelfalles, ob und mit welchem Gewicht und in welcher Weise sich ein bestimmtes Zumessungskriterium auf die Geldbuße im Einzelfall auswirkt.[595]

In light of the loss of transparency, it is questionable whether undertakings are better off under the 2013 Fining Guidelines than they were before. Considering that the 2013 Fining Guidelines are a direct consequence of *Zement*, this is a rather paradoxical outcome.

[593] The period within which a second infringement qualifies as recidivism is five years (§ 153(1) *Gewerbeordnung*). It follows that earlier infringements may only constitute an aggravating circumstance if they have been punished less than five years before.

[594] The far-reaching *nemo tenetur* principle under German law has limited the possibilities for treating uncooperative behaviour (eg, destruction of evidence) as an aggravating circumstance. In penalty proceedings, any form of active cooperation may be denied. Use of this right may not be used against its holder. This strict application of the *nemo tenetur* principle could be explained by the fact that suspects of the administrative offence are first and foremost natural persons who generally benefit from stronger rights of defence than legal persons. Moreover, under German law, the *nemo tenetur* principle derives from the protection of human dignity. See M Herdegen in Maunz/Dürig, *Kommentar zum Grundgesetz* (Stand April 2009, Verlag CH Beck) Art 1 Rdnr 82.

[595] This text could be translated as follows: 'It is a matter of each individual case, whether and with what weight and in what way a particular adjustment factor affects the fine in each case.'

The BKartA also operates a leniency policy known as the *Bonusregelung*.[596] The *Bonusregelung* lays down the conditions under which immunity for fines or reductions will be granted to whistleblowing cartel participants. It applies both to legal and natural persons.[597] A leniency application by an undertaking covers its (former) employees and other natural persons who participated in the cartel on behalf of that undertaking.[598] The BKartA grants markers to leniency applicants that still need to gather all incriminating evidence and it also accepts so-called summary applications in cases where a full leniency application has been submitted to the Commission.[599] Furthermore, it allows initial contacts to be made on an anonymous basis[600] and (marker)[601] applications to be made orally.[602] The BKartA has committed itself to indicate the application's success at an early stage of the procedure.[603]

Only first applicants are eligible for immunity.[604] Immunity is granted if the application allows the BKartA either to initiate investigations or, beyond this initial stage, to prove the existence of the infringement.[605] Immunity is not available for undertakings (or for the responsible natural persons) that either were the sole ringleader of the cartel or coerced others into participating.[606] The former exclusion is especially noteworthy, as this is not provided for in the ECN Model Leniency Programme. The *Bonusregelung* does not provide for a 'mini-immunity' either. As a result, there is no general assurance that incriminating evidence will not be used against the leniency applicant that furnished the evidence. Reportedly, in practice, the BKartA does grant mini-immunity.[607] Applicants not eligible for immunity may benefit from a reduction of the fine of up to 50 per cent of the original amount.[608] For this purpose, applicants should provide information that significantly contributes to proving the infringement.[609] The actual size of the reduction depends on the value of this collaboration and the order of the applications.[610]

Leniency applicants may benefit from more than immunity or a reduction of the fine alone. The BKartA will generally also renounce disgorgement actions under § 34 GWB.[611] This intention is, of course, not the same as an absolute guarantee.[612]

[596] BKartA, *Bekanntmachung Nr. 9/2006 über den Erlass und die Reduktion von Geldbußen in Kartellsachen (Bonusregelung) vom 7. März 2006* <www.bundeskartellamt.de/wDeutsch/download/pdf/Merkblaetter/Merkblaetter_deutsch/06_Bonusregelung.pdf> accessed 1 July 2013.
[597] ibid Rdnr 1.
[598] ibid Rdnr 17.
[599] ibid Rdnr 11 and 13.
[600] ibid Rdnr 2.
[601] ibid Rdnr 11.
[602] ibid Rdnr 15.
[603] ibid Rdnr 19–20.
[604] ibid Rdnr 3–4.
[605] ibid.
[606] ibid.
[607] ECN, *ECN Model Leniency Programme: Report on Assessment of the State of Convergence* (2009) <http://ec.europa.eu/competition/ecn/model_leniency_programme.pdf> accessed 1 July 2013, para 37.
[608] *Bonusregelung* (n 595) Rdnr 5.
[609] ibid.
[610] ibid.
[611] ibid Rdnr 23.
[612] *cf* Raum in Langen/Bunte (n 24) § 81 Rdnr 182.

Arguably more problematic in terms of the attractiveness of the *Bonusregelung* is that a leniency application does not release the BKartA from its obligation to refer criminal offences (most notably bid-rigging) to the public prosecutor.[613] In fact, the whole idea behind leniency is at odds with the principle of mandatory prosecution governing criminal proceedings.[614]

The adoption of a leniency policy falls within the domain of the competition authorities. As the BKartA and the LKartBs have exclusive jurisdiction, there is no single leniency policy for the whole of Germany. Some of the LKartBs apply the *Bonusregelung* of the BKartA, while other LKartBs have leniency programmes of their own,[615] which are generally closely aligned to the *Bonusregelung*. However, not all LKartBs have a publicly available leniency policy. This seems to go against the idea of the ECN Model Leniency Programme.

Further to its *Bonusregelung*, the BKartA may reward natural and legal persons with a reduction of up to 10 per cent of the fine in exchange for an early confession.[616] Until very recently, this settlement policy (*einvernehmliche Verfahrensbeendigung*) had not been formalised in any policy document. Instead, it emerged from case practice and has been communicated by the BKartA through its biannual report to Parliament.[617] To date, brief mention of its settlement policy is made in the BKartA's 2013 Fining Guidelines. In its *Kaffeeröster* decision,[618] the BKartA has elaborated on the conditions for settlements. In accordance with the procedure described in this decision, the parties concerned should first express their willingness to engage in settlement negotiations. The BKartA will then inform the parties about the results of the investigation, its preliminary objections and the maximum amount of a possible fine. The BKartA will set a deadline within which parties can make a formal settlement confession. This confession should include the prohibited conduct as well as the circumstances that are relevant for the severity of the fine. More specifically, these persons should accept both the facts on which the objections are based and the projected fine. Parties do not have to waive their right to appeal. However, they do have to waive certain administrative safeguards, as parties will only get access to key evidence and have to accept a scantily motivated decision.[619] While the BKartA's settlement practice has been developed in the context of its *Bonusregelung*, settlements do not seem excluded outside the cartel context.[620]

[613] *Bonusregelung* Rdnr 24.

[614] Ch Vollmer, 'Experience with Criminal Law Sanctions for Competition Law Infringements in Germany' in KJ Cseres, MP Schinkel and FOW Vogelaar (eds), *Criminalization of Competition Law Enforcement. Economic and Legal Implications for the Member States* (Edward Elgar, 2006) 259.

[615] See, eg, the LKartB of Nordrhein-Westfalen <www.mwme.nrw.de> accessed 1 July 2013.

[616] Deutscher Bundestag (n 271) 35.

[617] ibid. Pursuant to § 53 GWB, the BKartA should lay a biannual report before Parliament.

[618] BKartA B11-18/08 *Kaffeeröster*.

[619] Parties will generally be keen to accept a scantily motivated decision as this limits their exposure to follow-on damages claims.

[620] Deutscher Bundestag, *Unterrichtung durch die Bundesregierung: Bericht des Bundeskartellamtes über seine Tätigkeit in den Jahren 2009-2010 sowie über die Lage und Entwicklung auf seinem Aufgabengebiet und Stellingnahme der Bundesregierung* (BT-Drucksache 17/6640) 41 <www.bundestag.de/dokumente/drucksachen/index.html> accessed 1 July 2013.

Judicial Protection

Fines for infringements of Articles 101 and 102 TFEU may be appealed before the OLG, with a further appeal on points of law to the BGH. The OLG exercises a full merits appeal.[621] The decision of the competition authority has a mere guiding role and might be best described as an indictment. In accordance with the *Mündlichkeitsprinzip* (requiring all evidence to be brought in the proceedings orally) and the *Unmittelbarkeitsprinzip* (requiring the OLG to base its judgment on the findings reached in the main proceedings), all facts need to be established afresh. For this purpose, the court disposes of investigatory powers, most notably the hearing of (expert) witnesses.[622] The OLG does not rule *on* the enforcement decision, but renders a wholly autonomous enforcement decision instead, vesting 'original' rights and obligations. The decision of the OLG may even lead to a *reformatio in peius*.[623] For example, in *Flüssiggaskartell* the OLG Düsseldorf imposed fines totalling €244 million, whereas the BKartA's fine did not exceed €180 million.[624]

5.7.3 The Powers of the Dutch Authority

The ACM may impose fines on legal persons and natural persons for infringements of Articles 101 and 102 TFEU.[625] This requires that the infringement can be imputed (*verweten*) to the person in question.[626] For this purpose, fault need not be proved by the authority and will be assumed unless the offender demonstrates the contrary.[627] In light of current EU case law, this does not seem contrary to the EU principle of *nulla poena sine culpa* (see above, section 4.5.10). Where an infringement has been committed by an incorporated undertaking, as will generally be the case, a fine may be imposed on the legal person and/or those persons who ordered the infringement ('*opdrachtgevers*') or who were the de facto decision makers ('*feitelijk leidinggevenden*').[628] The distinction between these two forms of 'derived liability' is not watertight, but the latter will generally be satisfied more easily, as this covers passive modes of involvement. De facto decision making entails that a 'person' who is competent and required to take measures needed to prevent the infringement fails to take such measures, thereby consciously taking for granted the possibility of an infringement.[629]

[621] § 77(1) OWiG.

[622] § 71(2) OWiG. This could, for instance, mean that leniency applicants and authors/proprietors of incriminating documentary evidence are heard.

[623] The possibility of *reformatio in peius* is subject to one exception: if the main proceedings have not been opened and the OLG decides by ways of an order, the OLG cannot reach a decision that is more burdensome for the parties involved than the original enforcement decision; see § 72(3) OWiG.

[624] OLG Düsseldorf Pressemitteilung Nr 10/2013 (16 April 2013) <www.olg-duesseldorf.nrw.de> accessed 1 July 2013.

[625] Articles 56(1) Mw and 5:1(3) Awb.

[626] Article 5:41 Awb.

[627] *cf* Schlössels and Zijlstra (n 354) 1008.

[628] Article 5:1(3) Awb.

[629] HR 16 December 1986, *NJ* 1987, 321 and *NJ* 1987, 322.

The fines that may be imposed for infringements of Articles 101 and 102 TFEU are subject to a statutory maximum amount or percentage. With regard to the undertaking that committed the infringement, fines may not exceed €450,000 or 10 per cent of the undertaking's worldwide turnover, whichever is the greater amount.[630] Any form of derived liability is limited to an amount of €450,000. In light of this difference, it is important to consider which persons can be directly liable for an infringement of Articles 101 and 102 TFEU and which persons are caught by the forms of derived liability.

Liability which derives from the legal person is first and foremost directed at the natural persons who are responsible for the infringement: company directors and company staff.[631] The possibility of penalising de facto decision makers has been introduced precisely to hold natural persons liable for infringements of competition law. Prior to the introduction of this criminal law doctrine of derived liability in the area of competition law, natural persons could be fined for infringements of Articles 101 and 102 TFEU only if they could be identified with the 'undertaking' – a rather theoretical possibility in the context of EU competition law. However, the doctrine of derived liability for de facto decision makers does not exonerate parent companies either. After all, despite the outright rejection by its Advocate General, the Dutch Supreme Court (*Hoge Raad*) has left open the possibility that legal persons may also qualify as de facto decision maker.[632] While this decision was rendered in a criminal law context, the Supreme Court's ruling is equally valid in proceedings under competition law. In both cases, the legal basis for derived liability is the same: Article 51 of the Dutch Criminal Code (*Wetboek van Strafrecht* (WvSr)).

Were the term 'person' in Article 51 WvSr indeed to include legal persons, this would provide a specific legal basis and, more importantly, a separate regime for parent liability in the context of competition law. This would raise several questions with regard to the enforcement of Articles 101 and 102 TFEU. First, the application of this separate legal regime would entail that fines for parent companies are limited to €450,000, instead of the 10 per cent turnover cap that normally applies to undertakings. A parent company that de facto committed the infringement would then face a relatively modest fine. This approach would be difficult to reconcile with EU case law, in accordance with which parent liability is inherent in the concept of 'undertaking' (see above, section 4.3.2). Second, once it is concluded that a parent company has acted as de facto decision maker, it seems that the individuals behind the corporate veil can no longer be held liable on this ground. In this respect, it should be recalled that the objective of extending this criminal law doctrine of derived liability to competition law was precisely to

630 Article 57 Mw. This system has the remarkable consequence of allowing the competition authority to punish small undertakings (turnover figures below €4.5 million) more severely than large undertakings. This consequence has been accepted by the court, albeit implicitly, in Rb Rotterdam *Sallandse Wegenbouw BV* LJN BD8523.

631 HR 16 juni 1981, *NJ* 1981, 586. See further NMa Zaken 6494 en 6836 *Limburgse bouwzaken 1 en 2.*

632 HR 25 januari 2000, *NJ* 2000, 279.

penalise natural persons.[633] Against this background, it is suggested herewith that any form of derived liability of legal persons under Article 51 WvSr should only be used to supplement forms of parent liability inherent in Articles 101 and 102 TFEU. This could be the case where two legal persons are not part of a single economic entity. This approach would normally bring parent and subsidiary jointly under the 10 per cent turnover cap and would reserve 'derived liability' primarily for the responsible natural persons. Moreover, this would be in accordance with earlier doctrine (prior to the introduction of derived liability in the context of competition law), when EU case law on parent liability was loyally followed.[634]

Irrespective of the addressees of the decision, the power to impose fines for infringements of Articles 101 and 102 TFEU expires five years after the infringement has taken place.[635] This period of limitation is interrupted by each act of investigation by the authority, as well as by any such act by the Commission or the competition authorities of the other Member States.[636] The interruption has effect from the day on which at least one of the undertakings is informed of such an act in writing.[637] With every interruption, the period of limitation starts afresh. However, the authority's power to impose a fine expires at the latest 10 years after the infringement has taken place, extended by the period during which the decision is appealed.[638]

Even within this limitation period, the authority and the appeal courts should prevent any undue delays. The CBb has indicated that an administrative procedure of two years, a first instance appeal procedure of one-and-a-half years and a last instance appeal procedure of two years will generally form the outer limits of what still qualifies as a reasonable duration.[639] In *AUV en Aesculaap*, the CBb reduced the fine by as much as 20 per cent for undue delays in the entire enforcement chain, including delays caused by itself. In *Bongaertz Holding*, the Rotterdam Court awarded a five per cent reduction for undue delay on its part.[640] In *Erdo*, the CBb awarded a 10 per cent reduction for undue delay on its part.[641] All these cases illustrate that the protection against undue delay is taken very seriously.

Determining the Amount of the Fine

The amount of the fine is dependent on various other factors. In fixing this amount, the authority needs to take into account the seriousness of the infringe-

[633] It should be noted that a natural person employed by the parent company (rather than the parent company itself) may be seen as the responsible decision maker with regard to the infringement committed by the subsidiary. See HR 25 januari 2000, *NJ* 2000, 279.

[634] TK 1995-1996, 24707, nr 3, pp 86–87; Rb Rotterdam *Ooms Averhorn* LJN BG2730; Rb Rotterdam *Beheersmaatschappij X* LJN BD7003.

[635] Article 5:45 Awb.

[636] Article 64 Mw.

[637] Article 64(2) Mw.

[638] Article 64(3) Mw.

[639] CBb *AUV en Aesculaap* LJN BD6629.

[640] Rb Rotterdam *Bongaertz Holding* LJN BK1215.

[641] CBb *Erdo* LJN BM1588.

ment and the degree of fault (*verwijtbaarheid*) of the person concerned.[642] The duration of the infringement is not directly relevant, but can play a role in the context of the 'seriousness' of the infringement. However, the Rotterdam Court has applied a remarkable limitation with regard to the relevance of duration in fixing the amount of the fine. The competition authority may not calculate the fine on the basis of turnover generated in periods dating back more than five years from the day on which the decision has been adopted.[643] This is effectively the same as saying that a single and continuous infringement can be partially time-barred. The five-year period is equal to the statutory limitation period, beyond which the competition authority can no longer exercise its power to impose a fine (see above). The Rotterdam Court has thus used the limitation period for the authority's statutory powers to circumscribe the latter's margin of discretion in calculating the amount of the fine. This approach is not only at odds with EU case law on the SCI concept (see above, section 4.3.3), the ECA Fining Guidelines[644] and the domestic fining guidelines adopted by the minister (see below), it is also incomprehensible why a five-year period as per the date of the decision has been chosen. After all, provided that the limitation period is timely interrupted, a penalty may be adopted as much as 10 years after the termination of the infringement (see above).

Within the limits of the statutory requirements, the competition authority should exercise its discretionary fining powers in accordance with the Fining Guidelines adopted by the minister in 2009 (*Beleidsregels van de Minister van Economische Zaken voor het opleggen van bestuurlijke boetes door de NMa*).[645] As a general objective, these Guidelines require the authority to set the rate of the fines in accordance with the objectives of special and general deterrence. For corporate fines, the following calculation method applies. The authority first needs to determine a base quotient which forms the basis of the fine (*boetegrondslag*). This base quotient is 10 per cent of the 'relevant turnover', representing the value of sales of the goods or services to which the infringement related. In principle, the relevant turnover is calculated for the entire duration of the infringement. However, as was mentioned above, the Rotterdam Court has limited the possibility of taking into account turnover for periods dating back more than five years from the day on which the decision has been adopted.[646] In the second step, this base quotient is multiplied by a factor of between one and five, depending on the gravity of the infringement and the economic context (products, markets, size of the undertakings, regulatory context and impact of the infringement). For the most serious infringements, the competition authority is to add a 'fine supplement' (*basisboete-toeslag*) of up to 25 per cent of the relevant turnover in the last full year of the undertaking's involvement in the infringement. In the third and final step, the

642 Article 5:46 Awb.
643 Rb Rotterdam *Darthuizer Boomkwekerijen* LJN BM9911.
644 ECA Fining Guidelines, para III.8
645 Stcr 22 September 2009, nr 14079.
646 *Darthuizer Boomkwekerijen* (n 643).

competition authority needs to take into account aggravating and mitigating circumstances. Aggravating circumstances are recidivism, obstruction of the investigation, coercion or ringleading, and the use of monitoring and enforcement measures. Mitigating circumstances are cooperation outside the scope of the leniency programme (see below), voluntary termination of the infringement and compensation of injured third parties. It follows that deterrence alone is not decisive in calculating the fine. With regard to fines imposed on natural persons, the competition authority needs to determine a base quotient on the basis of the seriousness of the infringement and the income and capital of the individual concerned. For infringements of Articles 101 and 102 TFEU, the base quotient will range between €50,000 and €400,000. After the base quotient has been determined, the authority needs to consider the abovementioned aggravating and mitigating circumstances, as well as the role played by the individual within the infringement and his/her position within the company.

Leniency is currently available on the basis of the 2009 Leniency Guidelines adopted by the minister (*Beleidsregels van de Minister van Economische Zaken tot vermindering van bestuurlijke boetes betreffende kartels*).[647] These Guidelines cover both undertakings and individuals that are implicated in agreements and concerted practices between competitors which have the object of restricting competition (ie, cartels). The Leniency Guidelines offer three types of leniency: a reduction of 100 per cent (immunity), a reduction of between 60 and 100 per cent, and a reduction of between 10 and 40 per cent. A reduction of between 40 and 60 per cent does not seem possible. The first two types of leniency are only available to first applicants, provided they did not coerce others into joining the cartel and provided they cooperate fully in the investigations. Only when the competition authority has not yet started an investigation *and* the leniency application allows the authority to carry out targeted inspections will the applicant be granted full immunity. Where the authority has already started investigations but has not yet adopted a statement of objections, the first applicant will benefit from a 60–100 per cent reduction, provided the application has significant added value. If this application allows the authority to actually prove the infringement, a 100 per cent reduction will be granted. All other leniency applicants which provide information with significant added value and which fully cooperate in the investigations will be granted a reduction in the range of 10–40 per cent. The order and timing of the applications play an important role in the size of the reduction. Information provided in the context of a leniency application will not be used against the applicant that provided the information.

Leniency applications can be made by an undertaking, by an individual and by various individuals jointly, provided they worked for the same undertaking during the infringement. Individuals who apply for leniency may request to share in the leniency status of their undertaking. Leniency applications can be made orally and may be preceded by a discussion with the authority on an

[647] Stcr 22 September 2009, nr 14078.

anonymous basis so as to determine whether immunity is still available. A leniency application should fulfil various conditions, including a full description of the cartel and a confession. The competition authority will provide 'markers' to incomplete applications – in order to allow the applicant within a short period to supplement its application without losing its place in line – and to applications in cases where the Commission is the best-placed authority (summary applications).

An interesting development with regard to whistleblowing in the Netherlands is the parliamentary initiatives to protect individuals who bring to light corporate offences.[648] Although these initiatives are not specifically meant for competition law infringements, they do appear to cover whistleblowing in the context of Articles 101 and 102 TFEU. In accordance with the current proposals, the individuals concerned are protected in their contractual relations with their employers and may apply to a special fund for compensatory payments should they nonetheless suffer income losses.

Prior to the adoption of the 2009 ministerial Fining Guidelines and Leniency Guidelines, the predecessor of the ACM exercised its fining powers and leniency programme under policy documents of its own. In an effort to separate policy from administration, the minister has decided to assume responsibility over fining policy, while leaving the authority wide discretion in determining the amount of the fine in individual cases. Under the pre-2009 fining regime, the authority has on one occasion applied an ad hoc lenient fining scheme for widespread bid-rigging practices in the Dutch construction sector (see above, section 5.4.3). For future purposes, any such ad hoc arrangement would seem to require ministerial blessing.

Judicial Protection

Fines can be appealed before the Rotterdam Court, but in principle not before an application for administrative review has been made to the authority. A further appeal may be lodged with the CBb. The jurisdiction of the CBb is *not* limited to points of law and extends to the facts on which the decision has been based.[649] Currently the decision is suspended pending the appeal,[650] but this may change with the introduction of the Streamline law. The examination of the Rotterdam Court and the CBb is limited to the legality of the decision, with a 'full' review of the fine.[651] This review cannot lead to a *reformatio in peius*, however.[652] Accordingly, the *total* amount of the fine after appeal may not exceed the amount before the appeal.[653] Apart from incurring moratory interests, the appellant can thus appeal

[648] TK 2003-2004, 28990, nr 5; TK 2011–12, 33258, nr 2.
[649] Gerbrandy (n 102) 7.
[650] Article 63 Mw.
[651] *Fietsenkartel* (n 97).
[652] *Garnalen* (n 98).
[653] ibid.

the fine without any risks. Whatever could be said about this domestic principle, it does not seem to be contrary to EU law.[654]

5.7.4 The Powers of the UK Authorities

The UK authorities may impose fines on undertakings which have intentionally or negligently breached Article 101 or 102 TFEU.[655] These alternative conditions are interpreted by the CAT in accordance with EU case law on intent and negligence in Commission procedures. These conditions are met where the undertaking could not have been unaware (intent) or ought to have known (negligence) that its conduct would result in a restriction of competition.[656] Fines may not exceed 10 per cent of the undertaking's worldwide turnover.[657] The applicable turnover is limited to the amounts derived by the undertaking from the sale of products and the provision of services falling within the undertaking's ordinary activities after reduction of taxes and sale rebates.[658] In determining the amount of the fine, the authorities may take into account anti-competitive effects in other Member States.[659] Conversely, the UK authorities and courts need to take into account any penalty already adopted by the Commission, an NCA or a foreign court in relation to the same infringement.[660] This approach seems to be consistent with the EU principle of natural justice (see above, section 4.5.9).

In March 2012, the UK government promised to delegate powers to the Secretary of State for the introduction of a statutory time limit.[661] Section 45 of the ERRA 2013 actually confers this power onto the Secretary of State. Until this power has been exercised and a statutory time limit has been adopted, the power to impose fines for infringements of Articles 101 and 102 TFEU is *not* subject to any limitation period. Contrary to suggestions made in the legal literature,[662] the CAT has decided that a penalty imposed by the competition authorities does not fall within the scope of section 9 of the Limitation Act 1980.[663] In *Quarmby*, the CAT concluded squarely 'that the Limitation Act 1980 does not apply to the issuing by the OFT of a Statement of Objections or a penalty notice'.[664] More importantly, the CAT also rejected the argument 'that the lack of a limitation period

[654] *Heemskerk and Schaap* (n 99).

[655] CA98, s 36.

[656] *Napp Pharmaceutical* (n 168) [456]–[457].

[657] OFT (n 211) para 5.1. See further Slot and Johnston (n 217) 228; O'Neill and Sanders (n 151) 10.111.

[658] Competition Act 1998 (Determination of Turnover for Penalties) Order 2000, SI 2000/309, as amended, sch, para 3.

[659] CA98, s 38(1A).

[660] CA98, s 38(9).

[661] Department for Business, Innovation & Skills (n 126) para 6.26.

[662] O'Neill and Sanders (n 151) 10.105; Whish (n 165) 401.

[663] This section provides that 'an action to recover any sum recoverable by virtue of any enactment shall not be brought after the expiration of six years from the date on which the cause of action accrued'.

[664] *Quarmby* [2011] CAT 11 [55].

leads to any adverse position as regards legal certainty or administrative fairness'.[665] The CAT considered that Parliament did not intend to constrain the authority by any period of limitation in relation to the exercise of its powers. It therefore concluded that it would be inappropriate to read the limitation period that applies under Article 25 Regulation 1/2003 into the domestic penalties regime.[666] It is debatable whether this position can be maintained with regard to infringements of Articles 101 and 102 TFEU. In accordance with the EU principle of legal certainty, Member States cannot leave undertakings in uncertainty about their legal position indefinitely (see above, section 4.5.4).

Criminal Fines

Individuals who cannot be identified with the undertaking do not face any *administrative* fines. However, individuals implicated in cartels may face a criminal fine. Section 188 of the EA02 establishes a cartel offence. The most serious forms of collusion between competing undertakings (price fixing, output reduction, market sharing, customer sharing and bid-rigging) are covered by this provision. Although enforcement procedures under section 188 of the EA02 are distinct from those under Article 101 TFEU, both provisions could be applicable to a single set of facts. Individuals involved in infringements of Article 101 TFEU and section 188 of the EA02 may thus expect criminal fines. A person convicted by the Crown Court on indictment is liable to an unlimited fine.[667] A person found guilty by the Magistrates' Court may receive a fine of up to £5,000. The cartel offence may also result in a custodial sanction. The procedure for pecuniary sanctions and custodial sanctions is the same and will be discussed below in section 5.8.4.

Criminal fines are only available in relation to particular forms of anti-competitive behaviour. Whatever could be said about this policy choice, it is not contrary to the spirit of the EU principle of equivalence (see above, section 4.6.2). While it might 'discriminate' against certain forms of anti-competitive behaviour, it does not truly discriminate against the origin of the prohibition. After all, cartels that fall within the scope of Article 101 TFEU may also fall within the scope of section 188 of the EA02, thus benefiting from criminal fines.

Determining the Amount of the Fine

Section 38 of the CA98 requires the CMA to publish guidance as to the appropriate amount of the administrative fine. This guidance requires prior approval by

[665] ibid [48].
[666] ibid [47].
[667] EA02, s 190(1).

the Secretary of State.[668] While the obligation to publish guidance rests on the CMA alone, the sector regulators also have to exercise their powers in accordance with this guidance.[669] From 2004 until recently, the OFT, as the predecessor of the CMA, imposed fines in accordance with its *Guidance as to the appropriate amount of a penalty* (hereinafter the '2004 Penalty Guidance').[670] The 2004 Penalty Guidance was supplemented by the OFT's Enforcement Guidelines.[671] In September 2012, the OFT published a revised Guidance document (hereinafter the '2012 Penalty Guidance').[672] The 2012 Penalty Guidance deviates from the 2004 Penalty Guidance in several respects, but has not led to fundamental policy changes. More recently, the UK legislator has provided statutory guidance for the determination of the amount of the fine. Pursuant to section 44 of the ERRA 2013, a new subsection will be added to section 36 of the CA98. This subsection provides that in fixing the amount of the fine, the CMA must have regard to the seriousness of the infringement, and the desirability of deterring both the undertaking on whom the fine is imposed and others from engaging in infringements of Articles 101 and 102 TFEU and the domestic equivalents. The 2012 Penalty Guidance seems to be in conformity with this statutory requirement.[673]

As to the conditions under which a fine can be imposed, the OFT has indicated that intent and negligence do not require any knowledge on the part of the partners or principal managers of the undertaking; action by a person who can act on behalf of the undertaking suffices.[674] The OFT has further indicated that the fact that a particular type of agreement or conduct has not previously been found to be in breach of Articles 101 and 102 TFEU does not mean that the infringement cannot be committed intentionally or negligently.[675] Even where an undertaking has been pressurised to participate in the infringement, it can still be considered to have acted intentionally or negligently.[676] This approach to intent and negligence is in accordance with EU case law (see above, sections 4.5.10 and 5.7.1). In addition, UK fining policy has been inspired by EU practice in other respects. In accordance with EU case law on 'economic continuity' (see above, section 4.3.2), the OFT's Enforcement Guidelines provide that a penalty may be imposed on a company that takes over the undertaking in question.[677] Changes in the legal

[668] CA98, s 38(4).

[669] OFT (n 211) para 5.28.

[670] OFT, *Guidance as to the Appropriate Amount of a Penalty* (OFT 423 2004) <www.oft.gov.uk/shared_oft/business_leaflets/ca98_guidelines/oft423-(December-2004).pdf> accessed 1 July 2013.

[671] OFT (n 211).

[672] OFT, *Guidance as to the Appropriate Amount of a Penalty* (OFT 423 2012) <www.oft.gov.uk/shared_oft/business_leaflets/ca98_guidelines/oft423.pdf> accessed 1 July 2013.

[673] Paragraph 1.4 of the 2012 Penalty Guidance formulates the OFT's twin objectives: (i) to impose penalties which reflect the seriousness of the infringement; and (ii) to ensure that the threat of penalties will deter both the infringing undertakings and other undertakings from engaging in anti-competitive behaviour.

[674] OFT (n 211) para 5.5.

[675] ibid para 5.8.

[676] ibid para 5.13.

[677] ibid para 5.42.

identity or ownership of an undertaking will therefore not prevent it or its component parts from being penalised. Where the original undertaking has ceased to exist by the time a penalty comes to be imposed, the penalty may be imposed on the successor undertaking.[678] There is no reason to assume that the CMA will adopt a different approach.

The OFT's recent revision of its Penalty Guidance has not led to fundamental policy changes. The OFT has maintained a step-based approach and adds that this is in line with the approach taken by other competition authorities enforcing Articles 101 and 102 TFEU.[679] As a first step, the authority decides on a percentage of the turnover affected by the infringement on the basis of the seriousness of the infringement. Second, this amount is multiplied by the number of years that the infringement lasted. Third, the authority considers whether aggravating and mitigating factors should increase or decrease the amount. The admission of liability and other forms of cooperation qualify as a mitigating factor. Then, as a fourth step, the amount is adjusted for the purposes of deterrence. At this stage, the authority will also ensure that the fine is proportionate and not excessive. Fifth, the amount may be reduced to comply with the statutory maximum and to take into account penalties imposed in parallel proceedings within the EU. In its 2004 Penalty Guidance, the OFT elaborated on how it intended to take account of anticompetitive effects in other Member States. This could be done by including turnover generated in other jurisdictions in the calculation.[680] The OFT has indicated that it will proceed on this basis only when express consent is given by the relevant Member State or NCA.[681] In the sixth and final step of the fine calculation process, the authority applies a reduction to successful leniency applicants (see below). The CMA may be expected to continue with the above approach.

Although the 2012 Penalty Guidance has not led to fundamental changes, two novel features should be mentioned. The OFT followed foreign examples (notably the Commission model, the German model and an earlier version of the Dutch model) by raising the starting amount of the fine from 10 per cent of the relevant turnover to 30 per cent.[682] More generally, the OFT indicated that it has considered the ways in which other authorities calculate fines as well as the discussions within the ECN working group on sanctions.[683] It considered such 'benchmarking' an important part of reviewing its approach to setting penalties.[684] At the same time, it found it important to avoid significant inconsistency with the approach to setting penalties adopted by the Commission and other European competition authorities:

[678] ibid.

[679] OFT, *Guidance as to the Appropriate Amount of a Penalty: A Consultation on OFT Guidance* (OFT 423con 2011) <www.oft.gov.uk/shared_oft/consultations/oft423con.pdf> accessed 1 July 2013, para 5.3.

[680] 2004 Penalty Guidance, para 2.6

[681] OFT (n 211) para 5.30.

[682] 2012 Penalty Guidance, para 2.5.

[683] OFT (n 679) para 5.5.

[684] ibid annex A.

> Avoiding such divergence and inconsistency, where possible, will in the OFT's view help to ensure the effective enforcement of Articles 101 and 102 across the Member States of the European Union.[685]

While this has not resulted in an exact copy of the Commission's Fining Guidelines, it has led the OFT to draft penalty guidance with a strong emphasis on general deterrence and proportionality along the lines of the Commission's Guidelines. As a consequence, the OFT changed the order of steps two and three and applies the deterrence increment only after having assessed the aggravating or mitigating circumstances.[686] Under the 2004 Penalty Guidance, the adjustment for deterrence took place before other correction factors were taken into account. It is submitted herewith that the approach of the 2012 Penalty Guidance is indeed preferable from the perspective of the EU principle of dissuasiveness (see above, section 4.6.4).

A further novelty in UK penalty policy has been laid down in a 2012 guidance document of the OFT. In an effort to reduce appeal rates, the OFT decided to ensure that parties are provided with an opportunity to comment in writing and orally on the key elements of the draft penalty calculation (including the proposed starting point percentage, the proposed relevant turnover figure to be used, the proposed duration and, to the extent possible, the facts that may give rise to aggravating and mitigating factors) in advance of the penalty decision being taken.[687]

In 2008, the OFT adopted its *Guidance Note on the handling of applications of leniency and no-action* (hereinafter the '2008 Leniency Guidance').[688] This guidance formed the basis for rewarding 'cartel participants' in exchange for cooperation in the investigation. This reward consisted of (partial) immunity from fines. However, the OFT also offered up to £100,000 in return for information which helped it to identify and take action against cartels.[689] This financial offer was primarily meant for outside the leniency context, eg, to induce people with knowledge about but no direct involvement in the cartel to come forward. In October 2011, it published a consultation document on leniency. The OFT aimed to enhance the transparency and predictability of its leniency policy and to better align the conditions for corporate leniency with the conditions for criminal immunity.[690] In July 2013, the OFT adopted new leniency guidance, entitled *Applications for leniency and no-action in cartel cases* (hereinafter the '2013

[685] ibid para 5.6.

[686] ibid para 1.14.

[687] OFT, *A Guide to the OFT's Investigation Procedures in Competition Cases* (OFT 1263rev 2012) <www.oft.gov.uk/shared_oft/policy/OFT1263rev> accessed 1 July 2013, para 12.31.

[688] OFT, *Leniency and No-action* (OFT 803 2008) <www.oft.gov.uk/shared_oft/reports/comp_policy/oft803.pd> accessed 1 July 2012.

[689] OFT press release 31/08 (29 February 2008) <www.oft.gov.uk/news-and-updates/press/2008/31-08#.UeQii5D8LmI> accessed 1 July 2013.

[690] OFT, *Applications for Leniency and No-action in Cartel Cases: A Consultation on OFT Guidance* (OFT 803con 2011) paras 1.3 and 5.7 <www.oft.gov.uk/shared_oft/consultations/oft803con.pdf> accessed 1 July 2013.

Leniency Guidance').[691] The 2013 Leniency Guidance maintains both the (partial) immunity from fines and the financial offer.[692] The OFT reserved the right to depart from its Leniency Guidance where appropriate given the circumstances of the particular case.[693] The CMA may be expected to apply the 2013 Leniency Guidance.

The 2013 Leniency Guidance is a highly detailed document. It is very similar to the 2008 Leniency Guidance, but does contain some interesting deviations. The 2013 Leniency Guidance has maintained the wide scope of the UK leniency regime. The availability of leniency extends beyond pure cartel activity to cover agreements on resale price maintenance, as well as vertical agreements that facilitate cartel agreements.[694] This means that the scope of the UK leniency policy is wider than the ECN Model Leniency Programme. Undertakings implicated in these types of behaviour may initially approach the authority on a no-names basis to find out whether immunity is still available. The authority accepts both markers and summary applications, and all applications can be made orally.[695] Like the 2008 Leniency Guidelines, the authority grants immunity from fines to the undertaking that is the first to come forward before it has commenced an investigation (Type A leniency). This suggests that even if the authority already has sufficient evidence to launch a formal investigation, the first undertaking to come forward may still qualify for immunity provided that the authority has not yet exercised its powers of investigation.[696] However, in its 2013 Leniency Guidance, the authority has rectified this situation by emphasising that a 'pre-existing investigation' includes situations where it considers it has reasonable grounds to suspect cartel activity, such that it may conduct an investigation.[697] This rectification is consistent with the ECN Model Leniency Programme. Immunity is also available to the first applicant to approach the authority after the investigations have commenced (so-called Type B leniency). This is the case when the information provided has significant added value to the investigations. This form of immunity is discretionary.[698] Unlike its predecessor,[699] the 2013 Leniency Guidance no longer mention that Type B leniency will in principle be granted. Only undertakings that have not coerced others to participate in the cartel are eligible for immunity. The authority applies a rather restrictive 'coercer test', which means that few undertakings will

[691] OFT, *Applications for Leniency and No-action in Cartel Cases* (OFT 1495 2013) <www.oft.gov.uk/shared_oft/reports/comp_policy/OFT1495.pdf > accessed 1 July 2013.

[692] ibid para 2.37.

[693] ibid para 1.5.

[694] OFT (n 690) paras 2.2–2.3.

[695] 2013 Leniency Guidance, para 4.31.

[696] ECN (n 607) para 26.

[697] 2013 Leniency Guidance, para 2.13.

[698] ibid para 2.18. This decision depends on a balancing exercise in which the OFT assesses 'the benefits of gaining additional evidence by reason of the grant of leniency against the disbenefit of granting immunity or a reduction in penalties after an investigation has already commenced, resources have been expended and after the OFT may already have further fruitful lines of enquiry to pursue and some probative evidence already in its possession'.

[699] OFT (n 687) para 5.3.

in practice be ineligible for immunity.[700] Undertakings that are not eligible for immunity may benefit from a reduction in the amount of the fine (Type C leniency). A reduction of the fine is conditional on the information having significant added value. This can lead to a reduction of up to 50 per cent of the fine otherwise imposed. Contrary to the ECN Model Leniency Programme, the order in which applicants for Type C leniency submit their applications is not decisive for the percentage of reduction.[701] Leniency applicants may receive a further reduction of the fine when they confess a second cartel in a distinct market.[702] This 'leniency plus' requires that the undertaking is eligible for total immunity or a 100 per cent fine reduction with regard to this second cartel. In addition to the (partial) immunity from administrative fines, leniency applications may also exonerate individuals from criminal penalties and disqualification orders (see below, sections 5.8.4 and 5.9.4). The authority has indicated that it will not accept any leniency applications after it has issued a statement of objections in relation to the reported cartel activity.[703] In addition, it may conclude that it will not accept any further leniency applications in relation to a particular investigation.[704] This could be the case where it considers that no further evidence is needed to prove the infringement.

All leniency applicants should accept and admit that they have infringed Article 101 TFEU and/or the domestic equivalent and have participated in a criminal cartel offence (see below, section 5.8.4).[705] Furthermore, they should continuously, completely and in good faith cooperate in the investigations, including criminal proceedings and defending civil or criminal appeals.[706] This could mean that undertakings even need to 'allow the coming into existence of further evidence of the cartel activity' and that individuals need to act as a 'secret source'.[707] It should be noted that a failure to cooperate on the part of a current or former employee or director of an applicant undertaking will not necessarily jeopardise the undertaking's leniency application.[708] Applicants should alert the authority to any areas of doubt by differentiating between known fact supported by evidence, statements based on beliefs or best recollection of witnesses and suspicions or assumptions.[709] In addition, they need to provide both incriminating and exculpatory material.[710] The requirement to provide exculpatory material could minimise the risk of applicants overstating the nature of the reported activity and/or supporting evidence.

[700] 2013 Leniency Guidance, paras 2.50–2.54.
[701] 2013 Leniency Guidance, para 6.10.
[702] ibid ch 9.
[703] ibid para 2.41.
[704] ibid para 2.42.
[705] ibid para 2.7.
[706] ibid.
[707] ibid paras 4.46–4.48.
[708] ibid para 5.37. Failure to cooperate on the part of a current or former employee or director of an applicant undertaking will result in the loss of all protection under the leniency programme for the non-cooperating individual (para 5.39).
[709] 2013 Leniency Guidance, para 4.28.
[710] ibid para 5.15.

Outside the framework of its leniency policy, the CMA may offer a reduction of the fine in exchange for cooperation in the cartel investigations. In the past, the OFT has indicated that it will mitigate a penalty in return for an admission and cooperation.[711] The compensation of injured parties has been part of such a negotiated settlement.[712] The OFT has indicated that it will decide on the appropriateness of a settlement on a case-by-case basis.[713] In two recent consultation documents, the predecessor of the CMA has contemplated the formalisation of its settlement policy with a view to making the procedure more transparent.[714] It has indicated that parties who admit their involvement in the anti-competitive activity and cooperate in the administrative investigation can obtain a reduction of the fine in recognition of the savings in terms of resources made by the authority.[715] It has further indicated that it will invite parties to engage in settlement discussions after it has issued a statement of objections, but that the latter may always approach the authority with a view to reaching a settlement at an earlier stage.[716] As yet, there is no official settlement procedure. However, with the adoption of the ERRA 2013, the possibility of reaching a settlement has been formalised.[717]

Judicial Protection

Fines can be appealed before the CAT. The requirement to pay the fine is suspended during these proceedings.[718] With the adoption of the ERRA 2013, the CAT has to take account of the statutory guidance on financial penalties.[719] It is questionable whether this Act of Parliament will have an effect on the review practice of the CAT. Whish and Bailey have described the CAT's review practice as, first, reviewing the OFT's application of its guidance, then setting out its own views on the seriousness of the infringement and finally making its own assessment of the level of the penalty on the basis of a 'broad brush' approach.[720] As long as the authority's penalty guidance is in accordance with the statutory guidance, the CAT can continue its review practice. The CAT can impose, revoke or vary the amount of a penalty. This may result in a higher fine than was initially imposed by the competition authority.[721] Where it imposes, confirms or varies a penalty, the CAT may in addition order that interest should be payable, as from any date after the appeal was launched, at such a rate as the CAT considers appropriate.[722]

[711] OFT (n 224) para 11.2.
[712] *Independent fee-paying schools* (n 464).
[713] OFT (n 224) para 11.2.
[714] OFT (n 134), para 2.56; OFT (n 678) para 5.50.
[715] OFT (n 678) 3.22, note 24.
[716] OFT, *A Guide to the OFT's Investigation Procedures in Competition Cases* (OFT 1263 2011) para 11.2.
[717] ERRA 2013, s 42(7).
[718] CA98, s 46(4).
[719] ERRA 2013, s 44(3).
[720] Whish and Bailey (n 115) 422.
[721] *JJB Sports plc* (n 154).
[722] OFT (n 211) para 5.48.

Launching an appeal and deferring payment of the fine pending the proceedings thus carries a risk. A decision by the CAT as to the amount of the fine can be appealed with leave to the Court of Appeal in England and Wales and in Northern Ireland, and the Court of Session in Scotland. A further appeal can be brought before the UK Supreme Court.

5.7.5 The Degree and Drivers of Convergence

This whole section has shown that the fining modalities in the analysed jurisdictions share many common features, but deviate from each other in important respects. To the extent that convergence has taken place, this process has been reinforced by various coordination initiatives launched under the aegis of the ECN and the ECA. In addition, the Member States have aligned domestic fining powers with the powers of the Commission and those of their peers. These two narratives for the established convergence tendencies are of course not mutually exclusive.

Whether they are part of a deliberative coordination process or the consequence of unilateral alignment actions, clear tendencies of convergence can be reported. The competition authorities in the analysed jurisdictions have all been granted the power to impose fines on legal persons responsible for an infringement of Article 101 or 102 TFEU. This is so even for jurisdictions that traditionally did not recognise administrative fines for legal persons. Fines are subject to the alternative conditions of intent and negligence in essentially all four jurisdictions, although the criterion of '*verweten worden*' under Dutch law is arguably less demanding. Moreover, fining powers are invariably of a discretionary nature. This discretion covers the question whether a fine should be imposed in the first place, as well as the amount of the fine. In principle, fines cannot exceed 10 per cent of the undertaking's worldwide turnover in any of the jurisdictions. Within the authorities' wide statutory boundaries, administrative guidelines ensure the transparency and legal certainty in respect of the applicable calculation methods. Until very recently, when the German federal authority was forced by the BGH to change its approach, these methods were very similar.[723] Even now, all authorities included in the above analysis take into account the gravity and duration of the infringement.

Notwithstanding clear convergence tendencies, there are also notable differences in the pecuniary sanctioning powers of the various authorities. Most fundamental is probably the different approach towards natural persons. Germany and the Netherlands have made it possible to impose administrative fines on natural persons responsible for infringements of Articles 101 and 102 TFEU. In the Netherlands, natural persons face a fine of up to €450,000. In Germany, fines for natural persons are more severe and can be as high as €1 million. The UK authorities have not been granted the power to fine natural persons for infringements of

[723] See also OFT (n 561) paras 4.14–4.20.

Articles 101 and 102 TFEU. However, UK law does foresee in a criminal cartel offence that can attract unlimited fines for individuals.

But there are other differences as well. Corporate fines under German law may exceed 10 per cent of the undertaking's worldwide turnover as long as this surplus amount is meant and needed to disgorge illegal gains rather than to punish the offender. Moreover, this 10 per cent punishment boundary functions as an absolute maximum amount and thus as a focal point for fine calculation purposes. In contrast, at the EU level, in the Netherlands and the UK, this 10 per cent boundary should be seen as a cap on the authorities' fining discretion. This different view on the 10 per cent turnover boundary has resulted in distinct fine calculation methods. The Commission, the ACM and the CMA calculate the amount of the fine on the basis of a step-based approach. The first step is to determine a basic amount. This is done by taking a percentage of the turnover derived from the goods or services in respect of which the infringement was committed ('relevant turnover'). This turnover is either calculated by summing up real turnover figures for the duration of the infringement (the Netherlands) or is a fictitious amount based on the turnover in the last business year. This basic amount is then adjusted to take into account aggravating and mitigating circumstances and considerations of deterrence. The final amount is calculated by first applying the 10 per cent turnover cap and then the leniency reduction. Since June 2013, the BKartA has essentially reversed the above steps. A baseline maximum amount is calculated, from which deductions can be made in accordance with the particularities of the individual case. The more severe the infringement, the lower the deductions will be.

The order of the steps and the definition of 'relevant turnover' are not the only differences between the authorities' fine calculation methods. For instance, the far-reaching German *nemo tenetur* principle limits the possibility of treating uncooperative behaviour (eg, destruction of evidence) as an aggravating circumstance. In the Netherlands, the Rotterdam Court has limited the authority's ability to take into account the duration of the infringement. In this respect, it should be noted that under Dutch law, duration is not a statutory criterion either. At the same time, the Dutch authority may use a basic amount representing 50 per cent of the undertaking's relevant turnover to calculate the fine, where 30 per cent was becoming the 'industry standard'. The various calculation methods also display some notable differences with regard to the element of deterrence. These differences relate to the stage at which the 'deterrence increment' is applied, as well as to the magnitude of this raise. Most deterrence-focused are the guidelines of the Commission. In Commission procedures, the deterrence increment is added just before the statutory maximum is applied. Moreover, the Commission applies a so-called 'entrance fee' in relation to cartel offenders. Accordingly, the Commission will add a sum of between 15 and 25 per cent of the relevant turnover to deter undertakings from even entering into cartels. There are also differences with regard to the relevance of parallel or consecutive enforcement procedures by colleague authorities. In this respect, the UK fining regime contains a unique feature. In determining the severity of the penalty, the UK authorities *may* take into account anti-competitive effects in other Member States and *must* take into account any penalty already imposed in relation to the same infringement by a foreign competition authority. The latter requirement is in accordance with the EU principle of natural justice (see above, section 4.5.9). In addition, the differences with regard to settlements should be mentioned here. Most jurisdictions have gained some experience with rewarding undertakings for waiving certain procedural rights; however, only the Commission operates a highly detailed *cartel* settlement procedure.

Further differences between the analysed jurisdictions can be found in the area of statutory limitation periods. In the UK, the authorities' powers to impose fines have traditionally not been subject to any statutory limitation period, but this is about to change. In the other three jurisdictions, fines cannot be levied for infringements terminated more than five years before the first investigatory action or, in case of timely interruptions, more than 10 years before the adoption of the final decision. In Germany this period includes the proceedings before the first instance appeal court. Moreover, under German law, the interruption of the limitation period is personal, whereas the Commission and the ACM can interrupt this period for all parties with a single enforcement action.

Finally, there are important differences in the jurisdiction of the appeal courts. Contrary to the situation in the other jurisdictions, the Dutch appeal court does not have the ability to increase administrative fines. Hence, appellants can lodge an appeal without running the risk of seeing their liability increased.

The treatment of whistleblowers has been the subject of intensive coordination initiatives. With the publication of the ECN Model Leniency Programme, the NCAs have indicated that they will use their best efforts to grant favourable treatment to cartel participants which cooperate in the investigations. Further to their commitment to adopt a leniency programme, the NCAs have indicated that they will align their programmes to the Model.[724]

While large parts of the ECN Model Leniency Programme have found their way into the four jurisdictions, this Model has not forged a uniform leniency regime.[725] Some differences deserve to be highlighted. For instance, while three of the analysed jurisdictions award undertakings that have become second in the race for immunity a fine reduction of up to 50 per cent, in the Netherlands these undertakings can expect a reduction of no more than 40 per cent. Both approaches are in accordance with the Model, though, which proposes a reduction of the fine by a maximum of 50 per cent. Another notable difference is that only the UK has provided for 'leniency plus', which may induce leniency applicants to confess a second, undiscovered cartel. In addition, this distinct feature is in no way contrary to the ECN Model Leniency Programme. Finally, the Dutch parliamentary pro-

[724] ECN Model Leniency Programme, para 3.

[725] *cf* ECN (n 607).

posals for the protection of whistleblowing individuals should be mentioned. In accordance with these proposals, whistleblowers will be protected in their contractual relations with their employers and may apply to a special fund for compensatory payments. Protection of this kind is not contrary to the ECN Model Leniency Programme either.

There are also deviations from the Model. Under German law, for instance, a leniency application in the context of a bid-rigging cartel does not protect the applicant against criminal prosecution. In this respect, it should be recalled that the initiation of criminal proceedings is governed by the principle of mandatory prosecution. In addition, sole ring-leading cartel participants are worse off under the BKartA's *Bonusregelung* than under the Model, as they are excluded from immunity. A final source of conflict between the Model and the German leniency regime is that not every LKartB has published a leniency programme. The UK's Leniency Guidance does not incorporate the ECN Model Leniency Programme in all its respects either. Under UK law, leniency is available even outside the area of cartels, ie, in the context of resale price maintenance. Another clear deviation from the Model is that the order in which leniency applications are received is not necessarily reflected in the percentage of reduction.

5.8 CUSTODIAL SANCTIONS

Fines need not be the only punitive sanction for the enforcement of EU competition law. Infringements of Articles 101 and 102 TFEU could also be responded to with custodial sanctions. Section 4.6.3 above has shown that Member States are entirely free to experiment with custodial sanctions. Sanctions of this type are necessarily limited to natural persons and are reserved for criminal law proceedings. In accordance with the ECHR and the EU Charter, these proceedings require adjudication by an independent court or tribunal (see above, section 4.5.1). As a result, prosecution has to be separated from adjudication and a division of enforcement powers over separate institutions is needed. A single administrative enforcement system is then no longer feasible. The introduction of custodial sanctions for individuals involved in infringements of Articles 101 and 102 TFEU may therefore have considerable institutional implications. The introduction of custodial sanctions on Member State level may also have economic implications. As was already suggested in chapter three, this will come with certain costs (eg, prison facilities), but it could also satisfy domestic preferences and may elevate the state of the art in competition law enforcement to a higher level. Precisely in those areas where there is no Commission precedent, the potential for regulatory innovation is greatest. Against this background, this section details the availability, conditions and development of custodial sanctions for infringements of Articles 101 and 102 TFEU.

5.8.1 The Powers of the Commission

The Commission cannot impose custodial sentences on individuals. The EU legal framework simply does not support this. The penalties that the Commission may impose for infringements of Articles 101 and 102 TFEU are limited to fines and period penalty payments.[726] More importantly, in accordance with fundamental rights conventions, custodial sanctions are reserved for criminal law proceedings, where cases are adjudicated by an independent and impartial tribunal.[727] Regulation 1/2003 provides for an administrative enforcement system. In this system, cases are adjudicated by the Commission instead of an independent and impartial tribunal. The Court of Justice (in reality the General Court, as the competent first instance appeal court) can 'review' the decisions of the Commission, but only upon an application. In other words, the current EU enforcement system neither provides nor accommodates custodial sanctions for infringements of Articles 101 and 102 TFEU.

Notwithstanding the above conclusion, custodial sanctions are not excluded from the Commission's purview altogether. If the Commission were to find that custodial sanctions are necessary either to ensure that EU competition law is fully effective or to take away potential distortions of competition, it may submit a proposal to the EU legislator for the harmonisation of Member States' legislation and the introduction of custodial sanctions at the Member State level (see above, section 4.6.3). As yet, there are no indications that the Commission is considering any such action.

5.8.2 The Powers of the German Institutions

Under German law, infringements of Articles 101 and 102 TFEU may qualify as an administrative offence and attract administrative fines for both natural and legal persons (see above, section 5.7.2). These infringements do not qualify as criminal offences and custodial sanctions are therefore not available. However, German law does provide for a criminal offence that overlaps partially with Article 101 TFEU. This criminal offence could result in custodial sentences. Individuals participating in bid-rigging cartels may be criminally liable under § 298 StGB. This is the case where participants in a public or private tender decide beforehand which of them will submit the most attractive bid, thereby excluding competition among themselves. Releasing the bid is a necessary condition for the criminal offence; the anti-competitive negotiations alone are insufficient. Individuals implicated in an infringement of § 298 StGB could be punished with a custodial

[726] Articles 23 and 24 of Regulation 1/2003.

[727] No one may be deprived of his or her liberty by arbitrary arrest or detention. See Article 6 EU Charter and Article 5 ECHR.

sentence of up to five years. The BGH has confirmed that § 298 StGB covers particular infringements of Article 101 TFEU.[728] A single bid-rigging cartel could thus fall within the scope of Article 101 TFEU and § 298 StGB, thereby constituting an administrative offence and a criminal offence at the same time.

With the introduction of § 298 StGB in 1997, the bid-rigging offence was given a solid statutory basis. Earlier, the BGH already accepted that participation in a bid-rigging cartel could fall within the scope of the conventional criminal offence of fraud (*Betrug*) laid down in § 263 StGB.[729] While § 298 StGB was introduced in the context of a larger legislative reform to combat corruption, this provision explicitly aims to protect competition.[730] The criminalisation of bid-rigging was intended to make enforcement more effective.[731] Other infringements of Articles 101 and 102 TFEU do not benefit from this additional deterrent. Whatever could be said about this policy choice, it does not seem contrary to the spirit of the principle of equivalence (see above, section 4.6.2). After all, the 'discriminatory treatment' relates more to the nature of the anti-competitive practice than to the origin of the prohibition. Bid-rigging cartels that fall within the scope of Article 101 TFEU may also be contrary to § 298 StGB and are thus subject to the threat of custodial sanctions.

Proceedings under § 298 StGB are governed by the *Strafprozeßordnung* (StPO). This means that the enforcement of § 298 StGB takes place outside the domain of the competition authorities. Prosecution is the sole responsibility of the public prosecutor and adjudication takes place by the criminal court. However, the competition authorities could have a role in a preliminary stage of the proceedings. The public prosecutor may take over an investigation that has been initiated by a competition authority. Reportedly, investigations by the public prosecutor and the competition authorities into bid-rigging cartels are generally conducted in close cooperation.[732] For this purpose, information can be exchanged from the start of the investigations.[733] Recently, the dialogue between the public prosecutor and the BKartA assumed a more formal character when the latter invited public prosecutors from across the country to discuss experiences with the prosecution of bid-rigging cartels.[734] The competition authorities have to hand over a case to the public prosecutor whenever there are indications that a criminal offence has been committed.[735] Even a leniency application does not release the competition authority from this obligation. In fact, the whole idea behind leniency is at odds

[728] BGH 4 StR 428/03.

[729] M Klusmann in G Wiedemann, *Handbuch des Kartellrechts* (Verlag CH Beck, 2008) § 56 Rdnr 1; Bechtold (n 32) § 82 Rdnr 2.

[730] Bundesrat, *Gesetzentwurf der Bundesregierung: Entwurf eines Gesetzes zur Bekämpfung der Korruption* (BT-Drucksache 553/96) 17 <http://dip.bundestag.de> accessed 1 July 2013.

[731] ibid.

[732] Klusmann (n 729) § 56 Rdnr 9.

[733] Vollmer (n 614) 264.

[734] BKartA Pressemeldung of 10 February 2012 <www.bundeskartellamt.de> accessed 1 July 2013.

[735] Klusmann (n 729) § 56 Rdnr 7.

with the principle of mandatory prosecution governing criminal proceedings.[736] In addition, after the administrative proceedings by the competition authority have been terminated, the public prosecutor may prosecute a case under § 298 StGB. Criminal proceedings may even be initiated against natural persons already punished with an administrative fine. The EU principle of *ne bis in idem* does not seem to prohibit this form of double jeopardy, as the Court of Justice considers that national and EU competition law protect distinct legal interests (see above, section 4.5.9). If the criminal court comes to a conviction, it repeals, wholly or partially, the earlier administrative decision so as to prevent double punishment.[737] This approach is consistent with the EU principle of natural justice (see above, section 4.5.9). The criminal court may also repeal an earlier administrative decision when it decides not to convict the defendant for reasons that also invalidate the administrative decision.[738] Once criminal sanctions have been imposed for an infringement of § 298 StGB, the German competition authorities can no longer fine these persons under Article 101 TFEU.[739]

Cases are not systematically published, but there seems to be considerable practice in the field of criminal bid-rigging cartels. Wagner-Von Papp has indicated that in the years between 1998 and 2008, more than 260 persons were indicted, more than 180 of which were convicted.[740] A conviction can lead to anything from a criminal fine below €100[741] to a custodial sentence of several years.[742] It should be noted that custodial sentences for criminal bid-rigging cartels are not always served. Sometimes these sentences are on probation[743] and oftentimes prison sentences below two years are converted into probation orders.[744]

5.8.3 The Powers of the Dutch Institutions

In the Netherlands, the public enforcement of EU competition law takes place through administrative procedures alone. Therefore, custodial sanctions are not available for infringements of Articles 101 and 102 TFEU. It has been argued in the legal literature that the criminal prohibition of unfair competition, laid down in

[736] Vollmer (n 614) 259. See also F Wagner-Von Papp, 'What if All Bid Riggers Went to Prison and Nobody Noticed? Criminal Antitrust Law Enforcement in Germany' in C Beaton-Wells and A Ezrachi (eds), *Criminalising Cartels: Critical Studies of an International Regulatory Movement* (Hart Publishing, 2011) 176–77, who sees some possibility for legislative change so as to exempt leniency applicants from criminal proceedings.

[737] Klusmann (n 729) § 56 Rdnr 8.

[738] ibid.

[739] ibid Rdnr 7.

[740] Wagner-Von Papp (n 736) 157ff. See further Klusmann (n 729) § 56 Rdnr 13; Vollmer (n 614) 266; J Biermann, 'Country Analysis – Germany' in Dannecker and Jansen (n 8) 501.

[741] LG Düsseldorf Aktenzeichen 24b Ns 9/06.

[742] BGH 4 StR 428/03.

[743] BGH 1 StR 579/00. See also Wagner-Von Papp (n 736) 157ff.

[744] Vollmer (n 614) 261.

Article 328bis WvSr, captures many situations of anti-competitive behaviour.[745] The offence of unfair competition may lead to a custodial sentence of up to a year. In practice, prosecution under this provision virtually never takes place, let alone with regard to acts that also qualify as an infringement of Article 101 or 102 TFEU. Separate criminal offences committed in the process of anti-competitive behaviour (eg, fraud, extortion or forgery of documents) may attract custodial sanctions, however.[746]

Until 1998, prior to the creation of the NMa, infringements of competition law could only be prosecuted by the public prosecutor. In practice, prosecution was highly exceptional.[747] This was partly due to the fact that anti-competitive behaviour was not automatically prohibited. Commentators have questioned whether the pre-1998 regime was even worthy to bear the label of *enforcement* regime.[748] The final case possible within the statute of limitations under the pre-1998 criminal regime dealt with bid-rigging in the construction sector and resulted in an altogether disappointing outcome for the public prosecutor.[749] To the extent that individuals were convicted, the court imposed modest, non-custodial sanctions.[750] In an effort to strengthen competition policy, the limping criminal regime was exchanged for an administrative enforcement system in 1998. Since then, the NMa and more recently the ACM have enforced competition law on the basis of their administrative powers. Compared to the enforcement actions of the public prosecutor prior to 1998, the NMa has been very successful in penalising infringements of competition law.

Despite the successes of the NMa, in around 2006, the criminalisation of competition law came under renewed scrutiny. The benefits of custodial sanctions in terms of deterrence attracted the attention of academics,[751] practitioners[752] and politicians[753] alike, and for a moment the reintroduction of criminal enforcement was seriously contemplated. In 2006, the minister promised Parliament that legislation providing for the partial criminalisation of competition law and the introduction of custodial sanctions would be prepared.[754] In November 2009, the

[745] R de Bree, 'Mededingingsrecht en Strafrecht: Hernieuwde Kennismaking' (2006) *Markt & Mededinging* 205, 207.

[746] LEJ Korsten, 'Rb Rotterdam (strafkamer), 9 juni 2005, Vooroverleg bouwbedrijven' (2005) *Markt & Mededinging* 257.

[747] De Bree (n 745) 206; DR Doorenbos, 'Strafrecht Baat Niet, Schaadt Wel' (2010) *Markt & Mededinging* 167, 168.

[748] De Bree (n 745) 209.

[749] R de Bree, 'Hof Den Haag (strafkamer), 27 november 2007, Vooroverleg bouwbedrijven' (2008) *Markt & Mededinging* 19.

[750] Korsten (n 746).

[751] FOW Vogelaar, 'Criminalisering van het Mededingingsrecht: Trendy of Noodzaak' (2005) *Ars Aequi* 1015. See more generally KJ Cseres, MP Schinkel and FOW Vogelaar (eds), *Criminalization of Competition Law Enforcement. Economic and Legal Implications for the Member States* (Edward Elgar, 2006).

[752] De Bree (n 745). De Bree did not argue in favour of criminalisation, but countered some of points of critique raised against criminalisation.

[753] TK 2005–06, 30071, nr 27.

[754] ibid.

minister's resolve to introduce custodial sanctions was still very strong.[755] At that time, the minister planned to introduce a dual enforcement system of administrative and criminal enforcement, with custodial sanctions for participants in both cartels and abusive behaviour.[756] These plans were not embraced by everyone, however, and critical voices soon emerged.[757] Since then, little action followed. The plans to criminalise competition law have now been completely abandoned.[758] To facilitate the work of the newly established ACM and to economise its tasks, legislation is being prepared that provides for a single administrative enforcement system.[759]

5.8.4 The Powers of the UK Institutions

Certain infringements of Article 101 TFEU could fall within the scope of UK criminal law. Section 188 of the EA02 establishes a cartel offence. The most serious forms of collusion between competing undertakings (price fixing, output reduction, market sharing, customer sharing and bid-rigging) are covered by this provision. A breach of section 188 of the EA02 could result in a custodial sentence. While enforcement procedures under section 188 of the EA02 are distinct from those under Article 101 TFEU, both provisions could be applicable to a single set of facts. Persons involved in hard-core infringements of Article 101 TFEU may therefore face prosecution under section 188 of the EA02.[760] Therefore, the reservation of custodial sanctions for the cartel offence is not contrary to the EU principle of equivalence (see above, section 4.6.2).

At the time of its introduction in 2003, section 188 of the EA02 prohibited a person from 'dishonestly' agreeing with one or more other persons to make or implement, or to cause to be made or implemented, a hard-core cartel agreement. The dishonesty requirement derives from more conventional fraud offences and embodies a two-stage test:[761] first, whether the act was dishonest according to the standards of reasonable and honest people; and, second, whether the defendant realised that his or her act would be regarded as such. In March 2012, the UK government indicated its intention to amend section 188 of the EA02 and remove the dishonesty requirement.[762] This proposal was motivated by the conclusion

[755] TK 2009–10, 24036, nr 369.

[756] ibid.

[757] Speeches by P Kalbfleisch at the conferences *Elseviercongres Ontwikkelingen Mededingingsrecht 2009* and *Elseviercongres Ontwikkelingen Mededingingsrecht 2010.* The text of both speeches is available at <www.acm.nl/nl/> accessed 1 November 2013. See further Doorenbos (n 747).

[758] TK 2012–13, 33622, nr 3.

[759] ibid.

[760] Persons involved in hard-core infringements will only face prosecution under s 188 of the EA02 if they have a certain degree of responsibility within the undertaking. See in this respect Rodger (n 8) 127.

[761] Whish (n 165) 415–16; C Dobbin and G Peretz, 'The Cartel Offence', in T Ward and K Smith (eds), *Competition Litigation in the UK* (Sweet & Maxwell, 2005) 5-017.

[762] Department for Business, Innovation & Skills (n 126) para 7.10.

that the dishonesty requirement made the offence too hard to prosecute and that this limited the deterrent effect of the criminal prohibition.[763] The amendment has been brought about by the ERRA 2013.[764] At the same occasion, safe harbours have been introduced.[765] These are meant to provide a more objectively measurable way of proving whether the offence had been committed.[766] A new section 188A of the EA02 provides that the conditions of the offence are not fulfilled if the customers were given relevant information, whether directly or through public information, about the collusive arrangements before they entered into supply agreements. In addition, individuals are immune from criminal prosecution if they are able to show that, at the time of concluding the agreement, they did not intend to conceal the collusive nature of the arrangements from their customers or the CMA.[767] Individuals are even immune from criminal prosecution if they took reasonable steps to ensure that the nature of arrangements was disclosed to professional legal advisers for the purpose of obtaining legal advice about them before their making or implementation.[768] Interestingly, the latter exemption does not seem to be conditional on the individual acting upon this legal advice. Time will tell how this safe harbour provision is to be interpreted.

The Cartel Offence and National Competition Law

Secrecy is and will probably remain a condition for the cartel offence. The UK government has argued that precisely this element distinguishes the cartel offence from competition law.[769] Unlike Article 101 TFEU and its domestic equivalent, the cartel offence would not apply to concerted practices either.[770] In the eyes of the UK government, this divide between the cartel offence and competition law means that criminal cases could still be pursued if there were to be parallel civil proceedings at the EU level under Article 101 TFEU.[771] This divide seems rather artificial and the UK government should take into account that by maintaining this position, it will insulate proceedings under section 188 of the EA02 from the information exchange mechanisms of Regulation 1/2003 (see above, section 2.4).

Pursuant to section 190(2) of the EA02, prosecutions under the cartel offence may be brought by the Serious Fraud Office (SFO) or the OFT. In Scotland, the

763 ibid para 7.8.
764 ERRA 2013, s 47.
765 ibid.
766 Department for Business, Innovation & Skills (n 126) para 7.26.
767 EA02, s 188B.
768 ibid.
769 Department for Business, Innovation & Skills (n 126) para 7.30.
770 ibid para 7.32.
771 ibid para 7.30.

powers of the SFO are exercised by the Lord Advocate.[772] The SFO is an independent government department that investigates and prosecutes serious or complex fraud.[773] While the initial investigations are likely to be conducted by the OFT, the SFO will normally bring the case before court and lead the prosecution.[774] Where the SFO is not willing or able to deal with a cartel prosecution, the OFT may prosecute the case itself. Private prosecutions are allowed with the consent of the OFT. The OFT is the only *competition* authority that can prosecute the cartel offence.[775]

The cartel offence has to be tried before a criminal court. The offence is triable upon an indictment at the Crown Court. Trials are heard by a judge and a 12-person jury. A person convicted on indictment is liable to imprisonment for a term of up to five years.[776] Although the complexity and seriousness of cartel offences suggest that these cases will generally end before the Crown Court,[777] the offence may also be tried in the Magistrates' Court. Trials are then heard by a panel of three judges. A summary conviction by the Magistrates' Court may result in a prison sentence not exceeding six months and/or a modest fine.[778] These 'triable-either-way' offences always commence at the Magistrates' Court. Dobbin and Peretz have described how this procedure works.[779] The accused is served a short written statement of the accusation, on the basis of which he or she pleads guilty or not guilty. In the latter case, the accused may elect a trial by indictment before the Crown Court. The case may also be transferred to the Crown Court on the Magistrates' Court's own initiative if it views the case to be too complex or its own sanctioning powers to be too limited in light of the severity of the accusation. The case may also be transferred from the Magistrates' Court to the Crown Court at an earlier stage in proceedings where the prosecutor serves a notice of transfer on the Magistrates' Court. If a case reaches the Crown Court on the prosecutor's initiative, the latter may apply to the Crown Court judge for the trial to be conducted without a jury due to the case's complexity and expected duration.[780]

Immunity from prosecution may be granted in the form of a 'no-action letter' issued by the OFT under section 190(4) of the EA02. A no-action letter will prevent an individual from being prosecuted for the cartel offence in England, Wales and Northern Ireland. Alternatively, the OFT may issue a 'comfort letter' in cases where there is insufficient evidence to implicate the individual in the cartel offence. Immunity from prosecution cannot be given in relation to Scotland.

[772] Whish and Bailey (n 115) 430.

[773] O'Neill and Sanders (n 151) 2.49.

[774] OFT, *Memorandum of Understanding between the Office of Fair Trading and the Serious Fraud Office* (OFT 547 2003) paras 3-5 <www.oft.gov.uk/shared_oft/business_leaflets/enterprise_act/oft547.pdf> accessed 1 July 2013.

[775] G Peretz, 'Enforcement and Procedure Before the OFT', in Ward and Smith (n 761) 3-005.

[776] EA02, s 190(1).

[777] Dobbin and Peretz (n 761) 5-053.

[778] EA02, s 190(1).

[779] Dobbin and Peretz (n 761) 5-052–5-054.

[780] ibid 5-057.

However, cooperation by an individual will be reported to the Lord Advocate, who will take such cooperation into account.[781]

Individuals who themselves coerced others to participate in the cartel and whose undertaking is deemed a coercer too will be denied criminal immunity.[782] In all other cases, criminal immunity is available for current and former employees and directors who cooperate in the context of a corporate immunity application. Criminal immunity will be *automatic* for *all* implicated current and former employees and directors of an undertaking which is granted Type A or B immunity, provided that these individuals cooperate with the authority's investigations.[783] There is no such 'blanket immunity' for Type B and C *leniency* cases. Instead, the OFT will consider, on an case-by-case basis, whether one or more current or former employees or directors of an undertaking qualifying for Type B or C leniency should be granted individual immunity.

Individuals may also apply for criminal immunity outside the context of a corporate leniency application. If an individual applies for immunity on his or her own account before the undertaking makes its own application, immunity covering both the undertaking and all of its cooperating current and former employees and directors will become discretionary and not guaranteed.[784] This system is meant to stimulate undertakings in making prompt immunity applications rather than awaiting any investigations and applying for Type B leniency.

There has been some experience with criminal cartel proceedings. In the period between the introduction of the cartel offence in 2003 and July 2012, two cases have been prosecuted.[785] In *Marine Hose Cartel*, three men received prison sentences of between two-and-a-half and three years. These sentences were subsequently reduced on appeal to terms between 20 months and two-and-a-half years.[786] The convictions were largely due to the three-way plea agreements between the individuals involved, the OFT and the Department of Justice in the US, where the individuals were first arrested.[787] In *Fuel Surcharge Cartel*, the OFT was less successful. In May 2010, the OFT decided to withdraw criminal proceedings and the suspects were subsequently acquitted.[788] The withdrawal followed after the discovery of a substantial volume of electronic material, which neither the OFT nor the defence had previously been able to review. The adoption of the 2013 Leniency Guidance (see above, section 5.7.4), which aims to better align the conditions for corporate leniency with the conditions for criminal immunity, might lead to more successful criminal prosecutions in the future.

[781] *cf* 2013 Leniency Guidance, paras 8.21–8.22.

[782] ibid paras 2.56–2.58.

[783] ibid paras 2.38–2.39.

[784] ibid para 2.12.

[785] Department for Business, Innovation & Skills (n 126) para 7.1.

[786] OFT, *Criminal Liability in Regulatory Contexts* (OFT 1285res 2010) Annex A <www.oft.gov.uk/shared_oft/consultations/OFT1285res.pdf> accessed 1 July 2013.

[787] J Joshua, 'DOA: Can the UK Cartel Offence be Resuscitated?' in Beaton-Wells and Ezrachi (n 735) 138–39.

[788] OFT press release 47/10 (10 May 2010) <www.oft.gov.uk> accessed 1 July 2013.

5.8.5 The Degree and Drivers of Convergence

Whereas the Commission cannot impose custodial sentences upon individuals for anti-competitive behaviour, at the Member State level, such possibilities do exist. Already since 1997, German law explicitly threatens individuals implicated in bid-rigging cartels with custodial sanctions. The introduction of this criminal bid-rigging offence with accompanying sanctions was meant to enhance the level of deterrence with regard to these practices. For similar reasons, the UK legislator in 2002 introduced a cartel offence. Under this criminal law regime, the OFT may in principle seek custodial sanctions for any type of cartel agreement. In the Netherlands, custodial sanctions for infringements of competition law are not available. However, since 2006, there have been a series of parliamentary initiatives to criminalise competition law and to introduce custodial sanctions both for cartels and abusive behaviour. In addition, these initiatives were mainly motivated by considerations of deterrence. Irrespective of these motivations for the introduction of custodial sanctions in the three Member States, it would be going too far to see these initiatives as a duty under the EU principle of dissuasiveness (see above, section 4.6.4).

This brief account may be interpreted in two ways. It could suggest that custodial sanctions are in vogue. What started as an additional deterrent in Germany for a specific form of anti-competitive agreements has developed into a general cartel repellent in the UK and has almost spread to abusive behaviour in the Netherlands. However, the above developments may also be read as a story of mixed feelings. While the UK has criminalised all cartel practices for some years now, this has not found any support in Germany and the Netherlands. Moreover, in 1998, around the same time as Germany introduced its criminal bid-rigging offence, the Netherlands actually *de*criminalised competition law in an effort to align its enforcement regime with that of the Commission. The recent initiatives by the Dutch Parliament to introduce custodial sanctions for cartels and abusive behaviour have been delayed by the government since 2006 and have now been side-tracked completely. All the while, the Commission has made no moves towards the criminalisation of EU competition law either. In this respect, it should be noted that in other fields of EU law, the Commission has sought to criminalise infringements of EU law.[789]

While there have thus been clear developments in the context of custodial sanctions, it is difficult to interpret these processes in terms of convergence and divergence. What is certain is that there are some clear differences (but also some similarities) between the analysed jurisdictions with regard to custodial sanctions. It already follows from the above discussion that there are considerable disparities as to the scope of custodial sanctions, with the Commission and the Dutch institutions

[789] For an overview of the activities of the EU in the field of criminal law, see A Klip (ed), *Materials on European Criminal Law* (Intersentia, 2012).

being entirely powerless in the respect. Under German law, custodial sanctions are limited to bid-rigging cartels. More specifically, only the act of submitting a bid that has been rigged in a public or private tender falls within the scope of the criminal offence. The anti-competitive negotiations and agreements that preceded the bid are exonerated under criminal law. Under UK law, on the other hand, custodial sanctions are in principle available against any cartel agreement and, moreover, do not require the agreement actually to have been implemented. Another important difference relates to prosecutory powers. The jurisdictions that 'went criminal' exhibit institutional differences. In Germany, administrative enforcement and criminal enforcement are largely separated. This has the effect that criminal cases can even be brought against individuals that have already been treated to an administrative fine. However, if the criminal court comes to a conviction, it repeals the administrative decision. This institutional separation also means that administrative leniency does not protect individuals against criminal prosecutions; in fact, criminal proceedings are governed by the principle of mandatory prosecution and the competition authorities have to hand over bid-rigging cases to the public prosecutor. Finally, the institutional separation means that the role of competition authorities in the prosecution of the bid-rigging offence is limited to the preliminary stage of the investigation. The UK has opted for an integrated regime. The OFT may prosecute the cartel offence itself. Whether it does so, is at the discretion of the authority. This institutional arrangement has allowed the OFT to supplement its corporate leniency programme with a criminal immunity chapter. More importantly, it has allowed the OFT to play out in its favour the prisoner's dilemma that confronts any cartel participant: whether to confess or collude.[790] For example, if an individual applies for immunity on his or her own account before the undertaking makes its application, immunity covering both the undertaking and all its cooperating current and former employees and directors is discretionary and not guaranteed. This system is meant to stimulate undertakings in making prompt immunity applications rather than to await any investigations and speculate on a reduction of the fine. However, it should be noted that this sophisticated leniency regime may be hampered by the fact that guarantees of immunity from criminal prosecution cannot be given in relation to Scotland.

There are also various similarities between Germany and the UK when it comes to custodial sanctions for anti-competitive practices. Both jurisdictions have created a separate offence. The UK government even insists that its cartel offence does not qualify as competition law. This means that there are formally no custodial sanctions for infringements of Article 101 TFEU and that it is more correct to say that custodial sanctions are available for anti-competitive practices *falling within the scope* of Article 101 TFEU. Another similarity is that both regimes apply a maximum prison sentence of five years.

[790] See also WPJ Wils, 'Leniency in Antitrust Enforcement: Theory and Practice' (2007) 30 *World Competition* 25, 55–56.

5.9 DISQUALIFICATION ORDERS

Through a disqualification order, individuals can be disqualified from holding a professional function, eg, a managerial or sales position. This could either be for a limited period of time or indefinitely. The power to impose disqualification orders in the context of EU competition law may function as an additional deterrent and could inhibit individuals from engaging in infringements, but may also be costly for society as a whole (human capital is wasted and individuals may become dependent on the state). In other words, it can be a very useful sanction, but not everyone may support it and preferences may differ according to the Member State. In this respect, and in accordance with what was concluded in chapter three, a decentralised enforcement system in which Member States can choose whether or not to implement disqualification orders comes with certain economic benefits. Were Member States to experiment with disqualification orders, this would inevitably result in regulatory innovation. The Commission lacks the power to impose or seek disqualification orders and precisely for that reason the learning curve in this area will be steep. Member States which do provide for this sanction can function as an example for other jurisdictions in terms of what does or does not work. By detailing the availability and conditions for disqualification orders in the various jurisdictions, this section could assist in this learning process. More importantly, by examining the degree and drivers of convergence in this area, it may provide useful insights into the domestic sanctioning preferences and the instances of regulatory innovation, and therefore ultimately in the economic advantages and disadvantages of decentralisation.

5.9.1 The Powers of the Commission

Regulation 1/2003 does not provide for disqualification orders. As a result, the Commission cannot impose or seek such sanctions for infringements of Articles 101 and 102 TFEU. However, as the Commission is not a mere administrative authority, it does not need to accept the status quo. The Commission is a 'self-serving authority' that may try to supplement its own enforcement powers by proposing legislation to the Council. In fact, the Commission may even propose sanctioning powers for decentralised enforcement. This means that disqualification orders for infringements of Articles 101 and 102 TFEU do not fall outside the Commission's purview altogether. Were the Commission to find such orders necessary either to ensure that EU competition law is fully effective or to take away potential distortions of competition, it may propose legislation to this effect. In accordance with Article 103 TFEU, possibly in conjunction with Article 352 TFEU, the Commission could draft a proposal to have its own sanctioning powers supplemented with disqualification orders.[791] Pursuant to Articles 83 and/or 114 TFEU, the Commission may further initiate the harmonisation of national legislation and have Member States provide disqualification orders for the purpose of decentralised enforcement (see above, section 4.6.3). Finally, the Commission may assume a more coordinating role, for instance, by ensuring that disqualification orders imposed in the Member States are recognised across the EU. There has already been some activity in this area, albeit not specifically in the area of competition law. In a 2009 Communication to the European Parliament and the Council, the Commission has indicated that the EU must aim for the mutual recognition of disqualification orders.[792] This Communication complements the *Council Framework Decision 2008/947/JHA on the application of the principle of mutual recognition to judgments and probation decisions with a view to the supervision of probation measures and alternative sanctions.*[793] In accordance with Article 4(1)(d) of this Framework Decision, disqualification orders are covered by the term 'alternative sanction' and thus fall within the scope of application of this Decision. The Decision aims, amongst others, to facilitate the application of alternative sanctions in the case of offenders who do not live in the Member State in which they are convicted. For this purpose, it provides rules on the basis of which Member States should supervise alternative sanctions imposed by other Member States.

5.9.2 The Power of the German Institutions

The German competition authorities lack the power to impose or seek disqualification orders in relation to infringements of Articles 101 and 102 TFEU. Nevertheless, individuals responsible for particular anti-competitive practices *falling within the scope* of Article 101 TFEU may face such sanctions. As has been dealt with more extensively in sections 5.7.2 and 5.8.2 above, individuals participating in bid-rigging cartels are subject to the criminal law regime of § 298 StGB. The BGH has confirmed that § 298 StGB covers particular infringements of Article 101 TFEU.[794] While not primarily intended to reinforce competition policy, let alone EU competition policy, criminal courts may impose a disqualification order (*Berufsverbot*) on individuals engaged in criminal bid-rigging cartels.[795] This power has been laid down in § 70 StGB. The duration of disqualification is decided by the court. In principle, this will be somewhere between one and five years. Exceptionally, the court may also order a lifelong prohibition from

[791] See also A Khan, 'Rethinking Sanctions for Breaching EU Competition Law: Is Director Disqualification the Answer?' (2012) 35 *World Competition* 77, 97.

[792] Communication from the Commission to the European Parliament and the Council – An area of freedom, security and justice serving the citizen [2009] COM 262 final, para 3.1.

[793] [2008] OJ L 337/102.

[794] BGH 4 StR 428/03.

[795] See also Vollmer (n 614) 257.

engaging in certain professional activities.[796] Disqualification orders are regularly used in relation to other criminal offences of an economic nature,[797] but this measure does not seem to be common practice for criminal bid-rigging cartels. Similar to what was concluded in sections 5.7.2 and 5.8.2 with regard to criminal fines and custodial sanctions, the reservation of disqualification orders for infringements of § 298 StGB is not contrary to the EU principle of equivalence (see above, section 4.6.2).

A disqualification order may be imposed on individuals who have committed a criminal offence (eg, § 298 StGB) by either abusing their professional position or failing in their professional duties.[798] This condition is fulfilled when the abuse or failure was directly related to the professional duties.[799] There should be a clear danger that if the offender would continue the work or profession, he or she would relapse into illegal behaviour.[800] The aim of disqualification is therefore wholly reparatory and not punitive. This is confirmed by the fact that disqualification orders may even be imposed on individuals who have not been convicted for the sole reason that fault could not be established. Disqualification orders can be imposed with regard to *any* type of profession and – and this is relevant for competition law purposes – are therefore not limited to persons in the higher echelons of management.[801] The prohibition from engaging in certain types of work or professions needs to be specified. The wholesale prohibition of 'any management function' would appear to be too unspecific.[802] Breach of a disqualification order can amount to a prison sentence of up to a year or a fine.[803]

Under § 61 StGB, disqualification orders qualify as criminal law 'measures' (*Maßregeln*). These measures need to be distinguished from penalties, as only the latter are conditional on some form of fault. Measures may be imposed even if the infringement has not been committed negligently or intentionally. Measures may be imposed alongside penalties.[804] The imposition of a measure is subject to the principle of proportionality, which is recognised both in the German Constititution and § 62 StGB.[805] On the basis of this principle, the impact (*Bedeutung*) of both the committed and foreseen infringement and the degree of danger (*Grad der Gefahr*) should warrant the measure.[806] These general conditions with regard to criminal law measures also apply to disqualification orders for infringements of § 298 StGB. Pursuant to § 132a StPO, the criminal court may also impose disqualification orders

[796] § 70 StGB.
[797] H Tröndle and T Fisher, *Strafgesetzbuch und Nebengesetze* (53. Auflage, Verlag CH Beck, 2006) § 70 Rdnr 4 and 10.
[798] § 70 StGB.
[799] Tröndle and Fisher (n 797) § 70 Rdnr 3.
[800] ibid Rdnr 5 and 9.
[801] ibid Rdnr 5.
[802] ibid Rdnr 10.
[803] § 145c StGB.
[804] Tröndle and Fisher (n 797) Vor § 61 Rdnr 1.
[805] ibid § 62 Rdnr 1.
[806] ibid Rdnr 4–5.

by way of interim measures. This may be done if there are strong and urgent indications (*dringende Gründe für die Annahme*) that a disqualification order will be imposed at the end of the proceedings.

5.9.3 The Powers of the Dutch Institutions

In the Netherlands, disqualification orders are not available in relation to EU competition law. The enforcement actions of the competition authority cannot result in anyone being disqualified for certain professional activities. However, in the context of recent parliamentary deliberations on the criminalisation of competition law, the minister promised to prepare legislation providing for disqualification orders.[807] Orders of this kind are not uncommon under Dutch criminal law. The idea behind these plans was to deter individuals from engaging in competition law infringements. Meanwhile, the criminalisation of competition law has been abandoned and with it the plan to introduce disqualification orders (see above, section 5.8.3).

While the plans to introduce disqualification orders for infringements of Articles 101 and 102 TFEU have been abandoned, some relevant features and developments with regard to this criminal law instrument can be mentioned. Disqualification orders can be imposed only for those criminal offences for which the law specifically provides. Currently this includes fraud and economic offences. In these cases, a disqualification order may be imposed by means of a *penalty*.[808] The duration of disqualification is generally limited to a period of two to five years.[809] Breach of a disqualification order is a criminal offence and may lead to a custodial sentence.[810] In practice, disqualification orders are a fairly rare phenomenon.[811] Yet, in recent years, this penalty has gained popularity. Reportedly, many public prosecutors and judges recognise the usefulness of such orders, albeit as a measure to prevent recidivism (*maatregel*) rather than as a penalty.[812] In 2009, the scope of criminal offences for which disqualification orders can be imposed has even been enlarged.[813]

807 TK 2009-2010, 24036, nr 369.
808 Article 28 WvSr.
809 Article 31 WvSr.
810 Article 195 WvSr.
811 WODC, *Strafrechtelijke ontzetting uit beroep of ambt. Oplegging en naleving in the periode 1995-2008* (WODC, 2009) <http://wodc.nl/publicaties> accessed 1 July 2013.
812 ibid.
813 *Wet van 12 juni 2009 tot wijziging van het Wetboek van Strafrecht, Wetboek van Strafvordering en enkele aanverwante wetten in verband met de strafbaarstelling van het deelnemen en meewerken aan training voor terrorisme, uitbreiding van de mogelijkheden tot ontzetting uit het beroep als bijkomende straf en enkele andere wijzigingen.*

5.9.4 The Powers of the UK Institutions

Under UK law, directors can be banned from managerial positions for having committed an infringement of Article 101 or 102 TFEU. These director disqualifications can either be court-ordered (disqualification order) or part of a deal with the competition authorities (disqualification undertaking).[814] The legal basis for disqualification is the Company Directors Disqualification Act 1986 (hereinafter 'CDDA86'). The maximum period of disqualification is 15 years.[815] A disqualification order can be imposed by the court in the context of a cartel offence procedure under section 188 of the EA02.[816] Outside this criminal law context, the OFT may apply for disqualification orders in relation to all types of infringements of Articles 101 and 102 TFEU.[817] The OFT should then initiate proceedings before the High Court (or the Court of Session in Scotland).[818]

Disqualification has the effect that the person involved can no longer be a director of a company, act as a receiver of a company's property, be concerned or take part in the promotion, formation or management of a company, or act as an insolvency practitioner.[819] It is a criminal offence to act contrary to a disqualification order or disqualification undertaking. Tried on indictment, this offence may lead to a custodial sentence of two years and/or an unlimited fine. On summary conviction, liability is limited to a custodial sentence of no more than six months and/or a modest fine.[820] Furthermore, any person subject to a disqualification order or disqualification undertaking but nonetheless involved in the management of a company is personally liable for all the company's relevant debts.[821]

In principle, applications for a disqualification order will be made after the competition law infringement has been proved (in a separate, earlier procedure) and is no longer subject to appeal.[822] These applications could be made following proceedings by the OFT, a sector regulator or the Commission, or following procedures before the CAT, the Court of Justice or 'any other competent court'.[823] While this excludes proceedings by foreign NCAs, it seems possible that applications for disqualification orders are made following procedures before foreign courts (upholding the administrative decision of an NCA). In any case, applications will only be made in relation to infringements with an actual or potential

[814] Before making the application, the individual concerned is given notice and allowed to make representations. This is the stage where the person concerned can offer disqualification undertakings. See CDDA86, ss 9C(4) and 9B(2).

[815] CDDA86, s 9A(9).

[816] CDDA86, s 2.

[817] CDDA86, s 9A(10).

[818] Whish and Bailey (n 115) 435.

[819] CDDA86, s 1(1).

[820] CDDA86, s 13.

[821] CDDA86, s 15.

[822] OFT, *Director Disqualification Orders in Competition Cases* (OFT 510 2010) paras 4.6–4.7, 4.10 <www.oft.gov.uk/shared_oft/business_leaflets/enterprise_act/oft510.pdf> accessed 1 July 2013.

[823] ibid para 4.6.

impact in the UK.[824] The OFT has indicated that it will only seek disqualification orders for the more serious infringements, which also merits a fine for the undertakings concerned, and that the likelihood of application will increase with the contribution to the infringement by the director in question.[825] The OFT has also formulated several aggravating and mitigating circumstances, increasing and reducing the probability that disqualification will be sought.[826] The OFT will not apply for a disqualification order against any current director of a company which benefits from leniency. However, in the context of criminal proceedings under the cartel offence, the court may always impose a disqualification order on its own motion.[827] Both the availability of leniency and the fact that the OFT will only seek a disqualification order in cases that also merit a fine suggest that this penalty is perceived as a punitive sanction. This is confirmed by the fact that the OFT considers this power as a means of providing individuals with a further incentive to comply with competition law.[828]

Director disqualification can only be ordered by the court. The court *must* impose a disqualification order if the person is a director of the company that committed an infringement of Articles 101 and 102 TFEU *and* either contributed to the infringement, did not prevent the infringement or ought to have known that an infringement took place (ie, is 'unfit' for the management of a company).[829] This suggests that the individual concerned needs to be a director at the time the infringement took place.[830] It is immaterial whether or not this person still works for the undertaking at the time that the order is made.[831] While the OFT considers the term 'director' to include a de facto director,[832] staff officers, however senior, are not affected by the CDDA86.

There is still little experience with disqualification orders in the context of competition law, but the OFT is gradually recognising the potency of this power.[833] In 2009, the OFT published a consultation document with a clear ambition to use disqualification orders so as to enhance deterrence.[834] This has led to the 2010 Guidance document *Director disqualification orders in competition cases.*[835] In 2011, the OFT issued yet another Guidance document in this field.[836] According to this document, the OFT will actively consider in all its investigations whether a

[824] ibid para 4.8.

[825] ibid paras 4.11 and 4.19.

[826] ibid paras 4.24–4.26.

[827] OFT (n 690) 5.5, note 8.

[828] OFT, *Competition Disqualification Orders: A Consultation Paper* (OFT 1111con 2009) paras 1.3–1.4 <www.oft.gov.uk/shared_oft/consultations/oft1111con.pdf> accessed 1 July 2013.

[829] CDDA86, s 9A. *cf* OFT (n 822) paras 4.19–4.23.

[830] O'Neill and Sanders (n 151) 10.124.

[831] OFT (n 822) para 4.14.

[832] ibid paras 2.3 and 4.5.

[833] In *Marine Hose Cartel*, three men were disqualified from acting as company directors for a period of between five and seven years.

[834] OFT (n 828).

[835] OFT (n 822).

[836] OFT, *Company Directors and Competition Law* (OFT 1340 2011) <www.oft.gov.uk/shared_oft/ca-and-cartels/competition-awareness-compliance/oft1340.pdf> accessed 1 July 2013.

disqualification order would be appropriate.[837] Although it will look for direct management responsibility, the OFT is even leaving open the possibility of going after non-executive directors.[838]

5.9.5 The Degree and Drivers of Convergence

It can be concluded that disqualification orders are receiving increased attention in the analysed jurisdictions, albeit not necessarily or exclusively in the context of competition law. The issue of disqualification orders is probably least topical in Germany. While German law provides for disqualification orders in relation to bid-rigging cartels, this sanction is not often imposed. The possibility of imposing disqualification orders seem to have been a byproduct of rather than a reason for the criminalisation of bid-rigging. As this sanction is in any case limited to criminal law proceedings, it plays no role in the enforcement actions of the competition authorities. In the Netherlands, disqualification orders are a topical issue in several areas of the law, but this has not led to their introduction in the context of competition law. Only the UK authorities are both able and committed to use disqualification orders against infringements of Articles 101 and 102 TFEU. As to the Commission, it currently has no power to impose or seek disqualification orders itself, and it has not ventured any legislative proposals to get these powers either. However, the Commission has taken an interest in disqualification orders at the national level. As a more general EU objective, the Commission has indicated that the EU must aim for the mutual recognition of these orders. As was concluded in section 5.9.1, Framework Decision 2008/947/JHA even facilitates this mutual recognition. This seems particularly important in the field of EU competition law, where the potential addressees of disqualification orders are typically persons who will easily find a job abroad and may therefore otherwise circumvent the order.

The above analysis has revealed that there are no real tendencies of convergence in this area. Apart from the fact that disqualification orders are not available in every jurisdiction, there are substantial differences with regard to the scope and conditions of this sanction in the jurisdictions that do provide for them. While German law reserves disqualification orders for criminal bid-rigging, UK law makes provision for such orders in relation to any type of anti-competitive practice. A further difference concerns the potential addressees of these orders. Disqualification orders under German law are not limited to persons in the higher echelons of management. Under UK law, on the other hand, disqualification orders are limited to directors, excluding all staff officers. Other fundamental differences between the German and UK regimes relate to the sanction's objectives. In Germany, disqualification orders have an entirely reparatory objective and are only

[837] ibid para 2.6.
[838] ibid paras 3.9 and 5.23–5.27.

warranted in the event of a clear danger that the offender will relapse into illegal behaviour. Provided that this is necessary, the German courts may even order a lifelong prohibition from engaging in certain professional activities. Under UK law, disqualification orders are treated as a punitive sanction. This objective is reflected in the fact that the OFT will not apply for a disqualification order against any current director of a company which benefits from leniency. As could be expected from the sanction's punitive objective, the period of disqualification is limited. Under UK law, the duration of a disqualification order may not exceed 15 years.

5.10 CONCLUSION

With a view to establishing the legal and economic implications of the decentralisation of enforcement competences, this chapter has examined the degree and drivers of convergence with regard to sanctioning powers. An indepth cross-jurisdictional analysis has been conducted with regard to: (i) institutional enforcement frameworks; (ii) interim measures; (iii) early resolution measures; (iv) declaratory findings; (v) reparatory sanctions; (vi) pecuniary sanctions; (vii) custodial sanctions; and (viii) disqualification orders. More than just examining the degree and drivers of convergence, this chapter has highlighted various sanctioning alternatives, has provided a clarification and analysis of four sanctioning regimes, and has evaluated the consistency of domestic practices with the EU principles set out in chapter four. The main findings in terms of convergence tendencies are summarised below.

5.10.1 Institutional Enforcement Frameworks

Section 5.2 dealt with the institutional enforcement frameworks in which competition law sanctioning is situated. It was concluded that the various jurisdictions have placed the enforcement of Articles 101 and 102 TFEU in entirely different institutional environments. The EU model has found most resonance in the Netherlands. Both the ACM and the Commission are integrated enforcement authorities, combining prosecutorial and adjudicative functions. Yet, there are also important differences between these two regimes. The ACM is functionally divided by 'Chinese walls' in an investigatory department and an adjudicative department, and its decisions are subject to a more defendant-friendly regime of judicial review. The institutional enforcement frameworks in Germany and the UK share fewer characteristics with the EU model. The German legislator has created parallel procedural frameworks for reparatory sanctions and punitive sanctions, has allocated enforcement competences to a federal authority and 16 state authorities, and has granted decision-making powers at the federal level to 12 court-like chambers. The UK has opted for yet another institutional framework, with enforcement competences being shared by a general competition authority and various sector regulators. In addition, the appeal procedures in Germany and the UK differ significantly from the situation at the EU level, with courts generally having a broader mandate to scrutinise administrative decisions.

Section 5.2 also revealed tendencies of institutional convergence. For instance, the role of the recently established UK Procedural Adjudicator is comparable to the Hearing Officer in Commission procedures. Furthermore, the UK's newly established procedure for collective decision making combines features of the Dutch and the German institutional regimes. These examples can be seen as instances of convergence and suggest that convergence tendencies are inspired both by the EU and national enforcement models.

5.10.2 Interim Measures

With regard to interim measures, it was concluded in section 5.3 that each of the three Member States has sought alignment to Regulation 1/2003. All the NCAs have been granted the power to adopt interim measures for prima facie infringements of Articles 101 and 102 TFEU. However, the UK authorities may already adopt interim measures where there are reasonable grounds for suspecting an infringement. Other differences between the analysed jurisdictions concern duration, time limits and the enforceability of interim measures, as well as the role and relevance of third parties. In practice, the authorities hardly ever use their powers to adopt interim measures.

5.10.3 Early Resolution Measures

Section 5.4 has dealt with legal instruments for the early resolution of competition law disputes. There have been strong tendencies towards convergence in this area. The four jurisdictions provide for essentially the same alternatives, without any EU requirement to this effect. With regard to commitment decisions, it was concluded that the domestic procedures have been inspired by Regulation 1/2003. National legislators have sought to mirror the Commission's commitment powers under Article 9 of Regulation 1/2003 and have largely succeeded in this objective. The authorities can all terminate their investigations with a decision that gives binding force to the commitments offered by the undertakings. There are also some notable differences, however. These relate to the attractiveness for the undertakings concerned to offer commitments, the conditions for the adoption of commitment decisions, the role of third parties in drafting these decisions, the judicial protection of addressees and third parties against commitment decisions, and the enforcement of commitment decisions by the authorities. Early resolution can also be reached in cases that do merit a fine. The analysed jurisdictions all cater for financial settlements with a view to reducing the duration of proceedings. However, in terms of detail and transparency, the Commission's settlement procedure is unprecedented.

5.10.4 Declaratory Findings

Section 5.5 demonstrated that all the authorities have a practice of adopting declaratory findings. These findings are not limited to past infringements, but include findings of inapplicability. In light of recent EU case law, it has been stressed that national authorities should refrain from making absolute statements on the inapplicability of Articles 101 and 102 TFEU any longer. With regard to findings of past infringements, it has been concluded that there are no clear and widespread tendencies of convergence. The national regimes for declaratory findings display various differences. Only the German legislator has explicitly sought alignment with Regulation 1/2003 and the powers of the Commission. Yet, this alignment is not perfect. The Netherlands (and to a lesser extent the UK) even deviates from the basic features of the EU model.

5.10.5 Reparatory Sanctions

Reparatory sanctions were examined in section 5.6. On a very basic level, there is a considerable degree of convergence with regard to the types of remedies that can be imposed for infringements of Articles 101 and 102 TFEU. All the authorities may impose both negative and positive behavioural orders and most jurisdictions explicitly provide for structural remedies too. To a large extent, Regulation 1/2003 and the powers of the Commission have served as a source for inspiration. However, a close examination of the various remedy regimes has led to the identification of some notable differences. First, the Commission seems less keen to impose intrusive remedies than some of the national authorities. Second, the German authorities are alone in their ability to skim off illegal gains and to order undertakings to pay damages to third parties that have been injured as a result of the anti-competitive behaviour. Third, only the UK allows its authorities to impose remedies on managers and other company officials. Fourth, there are differences with regard to the conditions under which remedies can be imposed. Fifth, the enforcement of remedies has been organised differently in the various jurisdictions. Sixth, the available legal safeguards against remedies differ across jurisdictions.

5.10.6 Pecuniary Sanctions

Section 5.7 dealt with pecuniary sanctions, notably fines. It was concluded that convergence in the field of fines has taken place and that this can be attributed partly to unilateral alignment actions by the Member States. The competition authorities have all been granted the power to impose fines on legal persons responsible for infringements of Articles 101 and 102 TFEU. Even jurisdictions that traditionally did not recognise administrative fines for legal persons now provide for this sanction. Without exception, fines are subject to the alternative conditions of intent and negligence. Moreover, fining powers are invariably of a discretionary nature. This discretion covers the question of whether or not a fine should be imposed in the first place, as well as the amount of the fine. In principle, fines cannot exceed 10 per cent of an undertaking's worldwide turnover in any of the jurisdictions. Within these wide statutory boundaries, all jurisdictions rely on administrative guidelines to enhance transparency and certainty with regard to the applicable calculation methods. With the exception of Germany, even these methods are highly comparable. Finally, whistleblowing cartel participants can benefit from leniency in all four jurisdictions. This convergence process has been reinforced by coordination initiatives in the context of the ECN and the ECA.

Notwithstanding these tendencies of convergence, there are still various differences with regard to fines for infringements of Articles 101 and 102 TFEU. Probably most fundamental is the difference in approach towards natural persons. Germany and the Netherlands both provide for administrative fines for natural persons who committed an infringement of Article 101 or 102 TFEU. The Commission and the UK authorities have not been granted this power. However, UK law does provide for a criminal cartel offence, which could result in unlimited fines for the individuals involved. In addition, with regard to fines for legal persons, there are some important differences between the various jurisdictions. These differences concern the 10 per cent turnover boundary (not necessarily applicable under German law but, if applied, a more stringent limitation), the statutory limitation period (traditionally not applicable under UK law), the jurisdiction of the appeal courts (the possibility of a *reformatio in peius* in all analysed jurisdictions except for the Netherlands), the method for calculating fines, the transparency of the authorities' settlement policy, and the availability and conditions for leniency (including deviations from the ECN Model Leniency Programme in Germany and the UK).

5.10.7 Custodial Sanctions

Section 5.8 detailed the availability and conditions of custodial sanctions. There have been several developments in the context of custodial sanctions, but one cannot speak of convergence tendencies. In any case, there is no general alignment towards any EU model and policy coordination initiatives have not been undertaken in this area either. The Commission lacks the power to seek custodial sanctions itself. The institutional framework of the EU simply does not support the imposition and execution of such criminal law sanctions at the level of the EU institutions. In 1998, the Netherlands decriminalised competition law in an effort to align its enforcement regime with that of the Commission. Irrespective of recent 'flirtations' with criminalisation, the administrative enforcement model has recently been firmly embraced. Signs for the absence of convergence in the area of custodial sanctions are borne out by converse developments in Germany and the UK. In 1997, the German legislator introduced a criminal bid-rigging offence accompanied by custodial sanctions. Only the act of submitting a bid that has been rigged falls within the scope of the criminal offence. The anti-competitive negotiations and agreements that precede the bid are exonerated under criminal law. The UK has moved away from the EU model of a single administrative regime even further. Since the introduction of the cartel offence in 2003, the CMA and its predecessor may seek custodial sanctions for, in principle, any type of cartel agreement. Unlike the situation in Germany, implementation of the cartel agreement is not required. There are also some other differences between the German and UK enforcement procedures. In Germany, administrative enforcement and criminal enforcement are largely separated. The competition authorities have no formal role in the prosecution of the bid-rigging offence and their involvement is in any case limited to the preliminary stage of the investigation. The UK has opted for a more integrated regime in which the competition authority may prosecute the cartel offence itself.

5.10.8 Disqualification Orders

Finally, infringements of Articles 101 and 102 TFEU may lead to disqualification orders. This sanction was discussed in section 5.9. It was concluded that there are no real tendencies towards convergence in this area. The Commission lacks the power to impose or seek disqualification orders and developments in the Member States do not gravitate towards a single model. The UK authorities can seek disqualification orders in relation to any infringement of Articles 101 and 102 TFEU. Under Dutch law, there is no possibility of professional disqualification in relation to competition law infringements. German law does provide for disqualification orders, but only in the context of the criminal bid-rigging offence, and thus wholly outside the ambit of the competition authorities. A closer examination of the German and UK regimes revealed some further differences. Disqualification orders under German law have an entirely reparatory purpose, are not limited to persons in the higher echelons of management and may be imposed for an indefinite period of time. Under UK law, on the contrary, disqualification orders have a punitive objective, are limited to directors and may not exceed a period of 15 years.

5.10.9 The Degree and Drivers of Convergence

In sum, the analysed jurisdictions display some tendencies towards convergence with regard to sanctioning frameworks for infringements of Articles 101 and 102

TFEU. These are partially the result of Regulation 1/2003 and the powers of the Commission, which have functioned as a model for all three Member States. This is most clearly the case with regard to interim measures and early resolution measures and, to a more limited extent, reparatory sanctions and pecuniary sanctions. Another driver of the convergence of sanctioning powers are the policy coordination initiatives in the context of the ECN and the ECA. As yet, these initiatives do not extend beyond the field of pecuniary sanctions. The above observations also reveal that the convergence process has been enhanced by Member States aligning their sanctioning powers to other *domestic* regimes. This has been the case most clearly in the area of pecuniary sanctions and institutional enforcement frameworks. Notwithstanding all the convergence tendencies, there are also some fundamental differences across the four jurisdictions and even instances of divergence. This is the case most clearly in respect of the institutional enforcement frameworks, declaratory findings, reparatory sanctions, pecuniary sanctions, custodial sanctions and disqualification orders. These differences are partially due to idiosyncrasies of the various legal orders that are unrelated to competition law. Other differences are deliberate deviations from the EU model.

The next chapter will combine the conclusions of the preceding chapters and will elaborate on the economic implications of the current division of sanctioning competences between the EU and the national levels.

6

Economies and Diseconomies in the Division of Sanctioning Competences

6.1 INTRODUCTION

This chapter draws together the conclusions of the earlier chapters to discuss the economic implications of the current division of sanctioning competences in the area of EU competition law. It was concluded in chapter three that these implications are to a large extent dependent on the scope of the sanctioning autonomy and the development of the sanctioning regimes. The more extensive the sanctioning autonomy of the Member States, the better the possibilities for preference matching and regulatory innovation, but also the larger the losses in terms of transaction costs, coordination costs and duplication costs. Chapter four detailed the sanctioning autonomy of the Member States. It has been shown that contrary to what Regulation 1/2003 might suggest, the Member States are not entirely free in terms of the enforcement of Articles 101 and 102 TFEU. When the Member States act as 'agents' of EU law, enforcing Articles 101 and 102 TFEU, the domestic sanctioning powers are governed by various EU principles. Another conclusion that was drawn in chapter three is that the actual economies and diseconomies of the current EU framework are ultimately dependent on the heterogeneity of sanctioning preferences (reflected in the disparities in sanctioning regimes) and the level of 'decentralisation-induced' innovation. As earlier studies suggested that the domestic sanctioning regimes have been subject to a process of convergence, chapter five examined the degree and drivers of this process. Convergence can be seen as evidence of homogeneous sanctioning preferences. It may also be evidence of a learning process. The analysis in chapter five demonstrated that there are indeed clear tendencies of convergence. However, it was also shown that there remain some areas that are characterised by a large degree of differentiation and that there are even examples of divergence. On the basis of all of these findings, this chapter elaborates on the economies and diseconomies of the current division of competences between the EU and the Member States in the area of sanctions. This will be done by discussing the cost-reducing capacity of the EU sanctioning principles and the convergence tendencies (section 6.2), the efficiency gains of sanctioning autonomy in light of the heterogeneity (or homogeneity) of sanctioning preferences (section 6.3) and the efficiency gains of decentralisation-induced regulatory innovation (section 6.4). Conclusions are reserved for chapter seven.

6.2 COST-REDUCING SANCTIONING PRINCIPLES AND CONVERGENCE TENDENCIES

The decentralisation of EU competition law has resulted in transaction costs for the undertakings, coordination costs for the competition authorities and duplication costs for undertakings, authorities and courts alike. Ultimately, all these costs will be borne by consumers and taxpayers. To some extent, these costs derive from the fact that multiple authorities need to be staffed and funded and that some cases will be prosecuted by more than one authority. Other costs are due to the fact that sanctioning regimes may differ according to the Member State. Arguably one of the most costly features of this second category is what has been termed precedent deflation. The precedent value of cases litigated before national courts *on the basis of domestic procedural law* will be more limited than cases litigated before the Court of Justice. These domestic precedents will in principle not extend beyond the national boundaries. As a result, more litigation is needed before the conditions under which sanctioning powers may be exercised by the various authorities have been clarified. For instance, whereas in a centralised enforcement system, legal certainty can be provided with a single EU precedent on a particular issue, a decentralised enforcement system requires an additional 28 domestic precedents. This deflation of legal precedents can be seen as a diseconomy of scale which may result in significant duplication costs. In addition, the efforts that are currently devoted to the coordination of domestic sanctioning regimes could have been saved simply by maintaining (an improved version of) the pre-2004 centralised enforcement system. Many of the civil servants who are now assigned to coordination activities within the ECN could otherwise have contributed to the uncovering and prosecution of anti-competitive behaviour. With more than 29 authorities currently participating in the ECN, this would have freed up quite a lot of extra manpower. Another 'coordination cost' that has been identified is caused by the statutory restrictions to the use of information that has been exchanged between competition authorities (see above, section 2.4). Disparities in sanctioning regimes hinder the use of information exchanged under Regulation 1/2003 and will therefore result in enforcement disadvantages. Finally, disparities in the domestic sanctioning regimes may also lead to some *ex ante* transaction costs for undertakings (eg, having to organise several compliance seminars).[1] It can safely be assumed that the larger the disparities in sanctioning powers across the Member States, the higher the costs in terms of duplicative liti-

[1] The importance of these *ex ante* transaction costs for UK undertakings has been demonstrated in BJ Rodger, 'A Study of Compliance Post-OFT Infringement Action' (2009) 5 *European Competition Journal* 65.

gation, ECN coordination, enforcement disadvantages and *ex ante* legal advice. These costs are not so much the result of the system of shared administration, but are due to the sanctioning autonomy of the Member States.

Against this background, chapter four analysed the scope of the sanctioning autonomy of the Member States. This analysis showed that the domestic sanctioning powers for infringements of Articles 101 and 102 TFEU are subject to a variety of EU principles. These principles should contribute to the uniformity of enforcement procedures by centralising parts of the EU-wide sanctioning regime. These centralisation effects are capable of limiting the need for duplicative litigation, ECN coordination and *ex ante* legal advice, while at the same time enhancing the mechanisms for information exchange under Regulation 1/2003. The magnitude of these cost reductions is dependent on the degree and areas of centralisation. For example, only an EU standard (as opposed to an EU minimum requirement) for the conditions of intent and negligence in imposing penalties for infringements of Articles 101 and 102 TFEU would effectively reduce duplicative litigation before the national courts on the issue of *nulla poena sine culpa*. Similarly, coordination costs would be reduced if, for instance, the principle of effectiveness were to require Member States to recognise and match penalty reductions awarded in other jurisdictions in the context of a leniency application. After all, this would largely take away the need for coordination within the ECN in the area of leniency. Sections 4.5.10 and 4.6.3 have shown that these examples do not reflect current EU case law. More generally, several conclusions can be drawn with regard to the degree and areas of centralisation (see above, section 4.7). First, the EU sanctioning principles are hardly concerned with the type of sanctions that the Member States impose. Second – and this is in line with the first conclusion – the EU sanctioning principles are mainly concerned with the conditions under which the sanctioning powers are exercised. Third, many of the EU sanctioning principles still leave the Member States with considerable leeway to develop these conditions. Fourth, many of the more detailed EU sanctioning principles are concerned with legal safeguards for the undertakings involved rather than with performance standards for the competition authorities. Fifth, the detailed sanctioning principles deriving from the EU fundamental rights only provide a floor below which the Member States may not operate. Hence, the EU sanctioning principles are only capable of reducing some of the costs associated with decentralisation.

However, the costs of decentralisation that are related to the sanctioning autonomy of the Member States could be phased out gradually. At some stage, all the disparities that impede the effective enforcement of Articles 101 and 102 TFEU may have levelled out as a result of ECN coordination. Beyond this stage, enforcement resources that formerly were allocated to policy coordination can be redirected to investigations. Information exchange under Regulation 1/2003 will then not be hampered any longer either. Ultimately, the need for *ex ante* legal advice and duplicative litigation may also diminish. This scenario may even be precipitated by the unilateral alignment initiatives of the Member States. Chapter five demonstrated that the domestic sanctioning powers in Germany, the Netherlands and the UK have indeed been subject to such tendencies of convergence. This is most clearly the result with regard to interim measures and early resolution measures and, to a more limited extent, reparatory sanctions, pecuniary sanctions and institutional enforcement frameworks. However, chapter five also indicated that there remain some fundamental differences between the four jurisdictions and these disparities are partially the result of 'national experiments'. This is the case most clearly with regard to the institutional enforcement frameworks, declaratory findings, reparatory sanctions, pecuniary sanctions, custodial sanctions and disqualification orders. From the perspective of enforcement costs, disparities in the latter three areas could be particularly problematic. After all, to the extent that these differences relate to the treatment of natural persons, this could form an obstacle to the information-exchange mechanisms of Regulation 1/2003. With an enforcement framework that could actually encourage Member States to experiment in an effort to outcompete their peers (see above, section 3.6), inefficiencies in terms of duplicative litigation, ECN coordination and *ex ante* legal advice may never be phased out entirely.

In sum, the 2004 decentralisation process, although politically attractive, has imposed new costs on the enforcement of EU competition law. From this perspective, decentralisation appears to have been a costly way to increase enforcement capacity. Some of the inefficiencies are inherent to the allocation of enforcement competences to the Member States, while others are closely linked to the sanctioning autonomy of the Member States. The latter are only partially reduced by the EU sanctioning principles and convergence tendencies.

6.3 DOMESTIC PREFERENCES AND THE EFFICIENT USE OF ENFORCEMENT EXPENDITURES

Chapter three has also provided a more optimistic perspective on decentralisation. The decentralisation of EU competition law, with the accompanying sanctioning autonomy, has allowed each Member State to design its own sanctioning regime for the enforcement of Articles 101 and 102 TFEU. As a result, more EU citizens will end up with a sanctioning regime they desire. After all, decentralised decision makers are generally more responsive to the preferences of their citizens than a centralised decision maker, and sanctioning preferences may very well differ according to the Member State. Considering that decisions as to how a sanctioning regime is designed have a bearing on enforcement expenditures and accompanying tax rates, it will be clear that a decentralised enforcement system that is premised on sanctioning autonomy may lead to a more efficient use of enforcement expenditures and therefore to a more efficient redistribution of tax income. Based on domestic preferences, each Member State can decide on the distribution of government resources over advocacy and enforcement, or over public enforcement and private enforcement. Similarly, also within the domain of public enforcement, there are choices to be made that may impact on government resources. Some Member States will prefer penalties that are cheap to administer (eg, fines), whereas others will prefer penalties that are more costly to impose but that send out stronger signals to society (eg, custodial sanctions). Similarly, some Member States will finance monitoring costs entirely out of government resources, whereas others might want to share these costs with the undertakings concerned (eg, by requiring undertakings to remunerate an independent third party to monitor and/or arbitrate on the implementation of remedies). In a decentralised enforcement system, no Member State pays for the other one's choices and the costs of enforcement are entirely borne by domestic taxpayers. The magnitude of these efficiencies will depend on the heterogeneity of sanctioning preferences. The more heterogeneous these preferences, the larger the advantages of decentralisation will be. Sanctioning preferences may of course also differ within a single Member State, but decentralisation will probably not solve this issue: 'bundling and mobility problems' will prevent Member States from becoming more homogeneous (see above, section 3.6). The economic advantages of decentralisation are therefore dependent on the heterogeneity of sanctioning preferences *between* the Member States.

However, decentralisation will not result in a more efficient use of enforcement expenditures if heterogeneous preferences cannot be accommodated. Against this background, chapter four has studied the applicable EU framework for domestic sanctioning powers. Member States can only satisfy the preferences of their citizens within the boundaries of the EU sanctioning principles. The analysis in chapter four has shown that these principles are concerned with the conditions under which sanctions may be imposed rather than with the actual type of sanctions. But even for those areas that are covered by the EU sanctioning principles, the Member States still retain a considerable margin of discretion in organising the enforcement of Articles 101 and 102 TFEU. This means that the current system of decentralised enforcement in large part indeed accommodates heterogeneous sanctioning preferences.

Domestic sanctioning powers will generally be the reflection of domestic sanctioning preferences.[2] By examining convergence and differentiation with regard to sanctioning powers in Germany, the Netherlands and the UK, chapter five attempted to clarify the heterogeneity of sanctioning preferences between these Member States. Convergence can be seen as evidence of homogeneous sanctioning preferences. Differentiation testifies that sanctioning preferences are heterogeneous. The conclusions that were drawn in section 5.10 can be summarised as follows. On the one hand, there are clear tendencies towards convergence. This is the case with regard to interim measures and early resolution measures and, to a

[2] That this need not always be the case is explained in R Williams, 'Cartels in the Criminal Law Landscape' in C Beaton-Wells and A Ezrachi (eds), *Criminalising Cartels: Critical Studies of an International Regulatory Movement* (Hart Publishing, 2011) 289. Williams calls this the 'bootstraps' problem: 'an attempt by the law to pull itself up by its own bootstraps'.

more limited extent, reparatory sanctions, pecuniary sanctions and institutional enforcement frameworks. On the other hand, there are also some fundamental differences between the four jurisdictions. This is the case most clearly with regard to the institutional enforcement frameworks, declaratory findings, reparatory sanctions, pecuniary sanctions, custodial sanctions and disqualification orders. These differences, as described and analysed in chapter five, can be explained only partially by national traditions. Other differences are the result of more recent legal changes in one or more Member States. These more recent legal changes are particularly informative as these may truthfully reveal prevailing differences in sanctioning preferences. Especially when these 'national experiments' have a strong bearing on enforcement expenditures, this provides an economic argument in favour of decentralisation. After all, the decentralisation of enforcement competences requires each Member State to bear the costs of its own unique mix of sanctioning powers and procedures. Regardless of the enforcement expenditures, the facilitation of national experiments may be assumed to increase the utility of the average voter.

The analysis in chapter five identified various national experiments, some with clear implications for enforcement expenditures. In particular, this is the case for the experiments in the field of custodial sanctions and disqualification orders. These sanctions could deter and even prevent future infringements and therefore have beneficial welfare effects. However, these sanctions do require substantial 'investments' and amount to 'deadweight losses', as prison facilities need to be created and those that are imprisoned or disqualified cannot contribute to society any longer.[3] The UK in particular is experimenting with these types of sanctions. Not only does this suggest that the sanctioning preferences in the UK differ from those in Germany and the Netherlands,[4] it also means that UK taxpayers alone bear the costs of these expensive (yet possibly very effective) sanctioning powers. In this respect, the decentralisation of enforcement competences has efficiently matched sanctioning preferences with enforcement expenditures.

Another national experiment with a clear impact on enforcement expenditures is the decision of the Dutch legislator to supplement the authority's power to

[3] RA Posner, *Antitrust Law* 2nd edn (University of Chicago Press, 2001) 270. The creation of prison facilities and the deadweight losses are only a fraction of the costs associated with custodial sanctions and disqualification orders. See on this issue AP Reindl, 'How Strong is the Case for Criminal Sanctions in Cartel Cases?' in KJ Cseres, MP Schinkel and FOW Vogelaar (eds), *Criminalization of Competition Law Enforcement. Economic and Legal Implications for the Member States* (Edward Elgar, 2006) 121–25. See further I Simonsson, 'Criminalising Cartels in the EU: Is There a Case for Harmonisation?' in Beaton-Wells and A Ezrachi (n 2) 211–13. There are also authors who are less convinced that custodial sanctions will increase the costs of enforcement; see P Whelan, 'A Principled Argument for Personal Criminal Sanctions as Punishment under EC Cartel Law' (2007) *Competition Law Review* 7, 33–35.

[4] However, see A Stephan, 'A Principled Argument for Personal Criminal Sanctions as Punishment under EC Cartel Law' (2008) *Competition Law Review* 123, who presents a survey conducted in the UK from which it follows that only one out of 10 Britons think individuals responsible for cartels should be imprisoned. This could suggest that sanctioning preferences in the UK might not differ that much from those in Germany and the Netherlands.

impose corporate fines with fines for the responsible individuals.[5] While this could effectively deter individuals from engaging in anti-competitive practices, it will lead to additional costs in terms of administrative procedures and subsequent appeals. These costs are borne by the Dutch taxpayers alone, thereby efficiently matching sanctioning preferences with enforcement expenditures.

Also outside the field of punitive sanctions, there are several examples suggesting that decentralisation may have actually generated efficiencies of the above type. Under Dutch law, behavioural remedies may be imposed for a maximum duration of two years. While this limits the risks of overregulation, it does mean that a case has to be reassessed regularly. These costs are entirely borne by Dutch taxpayers. Under German law, declaratory findings of past infringements can be adopted with a view to assist injured third parties in follow-on damages actions. The German taxpayers are responsible for the costs associated with these administrative procedures.

But there are of course many other domestic sanctioning preferences/powers that have a clear impact on government resources. To name but a few: under German law, interim measures can be ordered without prior hearing of the parties and commitment decisions can be adopted without consulting third parties; under UK law, interim measures may be adopted in the interest and at the request of third parties; under German law, the authorities are able to skim off illegal gains and to order undertakings to pay damages to injured third parties. These national experiments provide as many examples of the efficiencies of decentralisation.

It should be clear from the above, first, that domestic sanctioning preferences differ in the analysed jurisdictions and, second, that enforcement costs differ according to the sanctioning preferences. Hence, it may be assumed that the current decentralised enforcement system, with its deference to domestic sanctioning preferences, has resulted in a more efficient redistribution of tax income. In order to fully appreciate these benefits, it should be recalled that the current EU framework provides disciplining provisions so as to overcome free-riding problems and 'race-to-the-bottom' scenarios (see above, section 3.6). In other words, Member States do not have an incentive to free-ride on the enforcement activities of other Member States. In terms of preference matching, decentralisation has thus made a valuable contribution to the enforcement of EU competition law.

6.4 INNOVATION THROUGH DECENTRALISATION

The decentralisation of enforcement competences may also create efficiencies of a dynamic nature. By allowing for experimentation and learning among the Member States (and the Commission) in terminating and punishing infringements, decen-

[5] While individuals may also be fined for their contribution to infringements of Articles 101 and 102 TFEU in Germany, this should be qualified as a national tradition rather than a national experiment.

tralisation could elevate the state of the art in competition law enforcement to a higher level. The learning effects of experiments in the area of sanctions should be sought in the type, structure, conditions and effects of a sanction. While regulatory innovation is not inherently linked to decentralisation, a decentralised enforcement system simply allows for more experiments than a centralised enforcement system. Not only can several jurisdictions experiment more than one, but the consequences of unsuccessful experiments will remain limited to the territory of a single (smaller) jurisdiction. Moreover, the disciplining effects of fine proceeds and reputation gains – which are weaker in a centralised enforcement system – can induce the Member States and the Commission to engage in innovative experiments (see above, sections 3.6 and 3.7).

This 'innovation through decentralisation' theorem hinges on the possibilities for experimentation and learning. The possibilities for experimentation are largely dependent on the autonomy of the Member States. This was analysed in chapter four, which showed that the sanctioning autonomy of the Member States is narrowed down by a variety of EU sanctioning principles. In the areas covered by these principles, national experiments are in theory excluded.[6] However, the analysis in chapter four also showed that the EU sanctioning principles are more concerned with the conditions under which sanctions may be imposed than with the actual type of sanctions. In any case, the Member States retain a considerable margin of discretion in designing their enforcement regime. This means that the current EU framework for decentralised enforcement indeed allows for national experiments. As was established in chapter two, this framework also facilitates interjurisdictional learning. It does so in two ways. First, it requires the competition authorities to consult with each other in individual cases. The Commission needs to consult with the Advisory Committee composed of representatives of the NCAs before imposing any sanction for infringements of Articles 101 and 102 TFEU. The NCAs, in turn, have to consult with the Commission before sanctions can be imposed. These consultation mechanisms have created a structural dialogue between the various authorities. As a consequence, competition authorities learn about the sanctioning possibilities and methods abroad and this may feed back into domestic policy.[7] Second, the creation of the ECN has provided a forum for policy discussions. Within this context, competition authorities discuss and

[6] While national experiments are excluded in the areas covered by the EU sanctioning principles, regulatory innovation is not. In accordance with what was concluded in section 3.7, regulatory innovation could also take place in the national courts and with regard to legal safeguards. As a result of decentralisation, EU law will be applied more frequently in the national courts: national courts will need to review the legality of domestic decisions adopted on the basis of Articles 101 and 102 TFEU. In this capacity, national courts will not only apply domestic procedural law, they will also have to apply EU legal safeguards, for example, EU fundamental rights (see above, ch 4). In the context of these procedures, national courts may refer questions to the Court of Justice for a preliminary ruling. Whether or not with the help of the Court of Justice, the application of these EU legal safeguards in domestic procedures could lead to important precedents. This may elevate the state of the art in competition law enforcement to a higher level.

[7] See also M Drahos, *Convergence of Competition Laws and Policies in the European Community: Germany, Austria, and the Netherlands* (Kluwer Law International, 2001) 434.

share experiences with sanctioning powers and procedures. In sum, the current EU framework for decentralised enforcement contains the basic ingredients for regulatory innovation.

Actual regulatory innovation should be looked for at the level of the individual sanctioning regimes. Against this background, chapter five analysed the development of sanctioning powers at the EU level and in Germany, the Netherlands and the UK. One of the conclusions that came out of chapter five is that there are clear tendencies towards convergence. These tendencies are partly the result of Regulation 1/2003 and the powers of the Commission, which have functioned as focal points for the Member States. This is most clearly the case with regard to interim measures and early resolution measures, and, to a more limited extent, reparatory sanctions and pecuniary sanctions. Another driver of convergence is the policy coordination initiatives in the context of the ECN and the ECA. As yet, these initiatives do not extend beyond the field of pecuniary sanctions. A third driver of convergence is what could be seen as 'successful' national experiments. This has been the case most clearly in the area of pecuniary sanctions and institutional enforcement frameworks.

It should be emphasised that convergence cannot be equated with a learning process or with regulatory innovation.[8] Some convergence may be due to 'simple imitation'.[9] There are indeed some instances where this process of convergence has the appearance of simple imitation. A good example of what seems like simple imitation is the power to impose structural remedies. Not long after this power was granted to the Commission pursuant to Regulation 1/2003, the NCAs in the analysed jurisdictions were granted similar powers. Yet, thus far, neither the Commission nor these NCAs have ever made use of this power.[10] This example should not obscure the fact that there is also clear evidence for convergence through learning. One example is the OFT's 2011 consultation on a proposal for a revamped version of its Penalty Guidance (see above, section 5.7.4). The OFT proposed following foreign examples (notably the Commission model and earlier

[8] Already in 1996, van den Bergh has raised the question of whether the process of voluntary convergence in the area of substantive competition law should be seen as the result of a dynamic competitive process between legal orders. His prediction was pessimistic: rather than copying EU rules because of their superior quality in terms of allocative efficiency, the main argument in favour of alignment was the strongly perceived need for legal certainty. As a result, trial-and-error processes have been inhibited in a field of law where learning-by-doing is so important. R van den Bergh, 'Economic Criteria for Applying the Subsidiarity Principle in the European Community: The Case of Competition Policy' (1996) 16 *International Review of Law and Economics* 363, 371. Parret is critical on the convergence to the Commission model too: L Parret, *Side Effects of the Modernisation of EU Competition Law* (Wolf Legal Publishers, 2011) 227.

[9] The term 'simple imitation' has been borrowed from Drahos, who uses this term for similar purposes. Drahos (n 7) 28.

[10] For the pre-2009 period, see Commission Staff Working Paper accompanying the Communication from the Commission to the European Parliament and the Council: Report on the functioning of Regulation 1/2003 [2009] COM 206 final, para 92. However, the same Staff Working Paper indicates that the Commission does occasionally adopt structural commitment decisions (para 97). It could be argued that the Commission would not have been able to secure such commitments if it did not have the power to adopt structural remedies.

versions of the German and Dutch model) and increasing the starting amount of the fine from 10 per cent of the relevant turnover to 30 per cent. This proposal was made after a detailed assessment of various penalty regimes.[11]

Apart from the fact that convergence may not always be the result of learning processes, the existence of any such processes does not necessarily argue in favour of decentralisation. In fact, to the extent that Member States only learn from the Commission model (rather than the other way around), decentralisation could be seen as an obstacle for regulatory innovation. After all, compared to a system of centralised enforcement, the implementation of these improvements is at best delayed. This will be different only in situations where developments of the Commission model are due to the competitive pressures of the NCAs. Notwithstanding the latter possibility, the clearest example of decentralisation-induced innovation is when there is convergence towards a domestic model or domestic deviation from the Commission model. While the former can be seen as proof of successful experiments (provided this is not the result of simple imitation again), the latter provides the possibility of interjurisdictional learning. Both elevate the state of the art in competition law enforcement to a higher level. There have been some examples of convergence towards a domestic model. For instance, it appears that the Commission's method for calculating the basic amount of the fine, using a percentage of the relevant turnover, has been inspired by the Dutch model (see above, section 5.7.1). Nevertheless, chapter five mainly identified convergence towards the Commission model and domestic deviations. The latter are noticeable in the institutional enforcement frameworks of the Member States and in the areas of declaratory findings, reparatory sanctions, pecuniary sanctions, custodial sanctions and disqualification orders. These domestic deviations are partly due to the idiosyncrasies of the various legal orders that are unrelated to competition law. Other deviations are deliberate and can be seen as national experiments in the area of EU competition law. While only national experiments are evidence for the 'innovation through decentralisation' theorem, national traditions may also provide valuable information on what does or does not work. These experiments and traditions can be considered 'innovative' provided that they add to earlier Commission experiences and at least have the potential to improve the enforcement of Articles 101 and 102 TFEU. It should be emphasised that they need not necessarily be successful in order to be valuable; what is important is that these experiments and traditions enhance our knowledge of competition law enforcement.

Member States operating sanctioning powers unknown to the Commission (eg, custodial sanctions, disqualification orders and pecuniary sanctions for individuals) will in any case elevate the state of the art in competition law enforcement to a higher level. Yet, even more conventional sanctions such as corporate

[11] OFT, *An Assessment of Discretionary Penalties Regimes* (OFT 1132 2009) para A.117 <www.oft.gov.uk/shared_oft/economic_research/oft1132.pdf> accessed 1 July 2013.

fines could be subject to regulatory innovation.[12] In light of the Commission's extensive experience in this area, regulatory innovation as a result of decentralisation may be less obvious, but is certainly not excluded, and in any case is no less important. Determining an appropriate fine can be a complex matter, which may profit from learning-by-doing and from experience of diverse calculation methods. Furthermore, corporate fines are probably the most important penalty for infringements of EU competition law and any innovation in this area could therefore have great value for the enforcement of EU competition law more generally. By revisiting some domestic deviations in the area of corporate fines, we can test the 'innovation through decentralisation' theorem.

The analysis in section 5.7 identified various domestic deviations in the area of corporate fines. These deviations relate to the conditions, methods and procedures for imposing a fine. Some of these may be seen as innovative deviations. This is the case, for instance, with regard to the possibility under German law of levying fines in excess of 10 per cent of the undertaking's worldwide turnover where this is needed to disgorge illegal gains. This possibility serves clear retributive and deterrence purposes without limiting the accessibility and foreseeability of the fine as required by the EU principle of legality (see above, section 4.5.4). Unfortunately, the German authorities have not run experiments with this power. This is probably due to the difficulty of establishing the magnitude of the illegal gains or maybe because the illegal gains typically do not exceed the 10 per cent boundary. In addition, the German 2013 Fining Guidelines could be seen as regulatory innovation, in that they introduce a novel method for setting fines: a baseline maximum amount is calculated from which deductions can be made in accordance with the particularities of the individual case. Time will tell as to whether this experiment will remain a learning experience or whether it will become a template for other authorities.

With other domestic deviations, there is more experience. One of these concerns the penalisation of infringements lasting more than a year. Unlike some of its colleagues abroad, the Dutch ACM has to calculate the basic amount of the fine by summing up real turnover figures for the entire duration of the infringement. The Commission model uses a fictitious amount based on the turnover in the last business year. This Dutch deviation is innovative in the sense that it allows for a better approximation of the illegal gains. The flipside of this approach is that the ACM needs more information to calculate the amount of the fine. The longer the

[12] The possibility of innovation in the field of corporate fines is confirmed by the large body of literature on the design of fining regimes. See, eg, WPJ Wils, 'Optimal Antitrust Fines: Theory and Practice' (2006) 29 *World Competition* 183; WPJ Wils, 'Leniency in Antitrust Enforcement: Theory and Practice' (2007) 30 *World Competition* 25; C Veljanovski, 'Cartel Fines in Europe: Law, Practice and Deterrence' (2007) 30 *World Competition* 65; WPJ Wils, 'The European Commission's 2006 Guidelines on Antitrust Fines: A Legal and Economic Analysis' (2007) 30 *World Competition* 197; WPJ Wils, 'The Use of Settlements in Public Antitrust Enforcement: Objectives and Principles' (2008) 31 *World Competition* 335; WPJ Wils, 'The Relationship between Public Antitrust Enforcement and Private Actions for Damages' (2009) 32 *World Competition* 3; WPJ Wils, 'Recidivism in EU Antitrust Enforcement: A Legal and Economic Analysis' (2012) 35 *World Competition* 5; A Heimler and K Mehta, 'Violations of Antitrust Provisions: The Optimal Level of Fines for Achieving Deterrence' (2012) 35 *World Competition* 103.

duration of the infringement, the more challenging it will be to obtain this information.[13]

Another deviation from the Commission model is the treatment of compensation as an explicit ground for mitigating the fine. This Dutch 'experiment'[14] attempts to deal with the interplay between public enforcement and private enforcement. The innovative features of this experiment are that it stimulates wrongdoers to compensate injured parties and takes away some of the disadvantages of the accumulation of fines and damages in relation to a single infringement.[15]

EU competition policy is also indebted to the UK. For instance, through its experimental leniency policy, the OFT has contributed to the state of the art in competition law enforcement. The experiments with 'leniency plus' and leniency in the context of resale price maintenance are capable of uncovering more anti-competitive practices.[16] The experiments with using leniency applicants as 'secret sources' and with requiring leniency applicants to provide exculpatory material and to indicate what is fact, assumption or belief are capable of enhancing the reliability of leniency applications.

Finally, national experiments with regard to the early disclosure of the severity of the fine should be mentioned. In the context of its settlement procedure, which seems available for any type of infringement, the BKartA has indicated that it will inform the undertakings involved at an early stage about the maximum amount of a possible fine. In the UK, the predecessor of the CMA has indicated that it will ensure that undertakings are provided with an opportunity to comment in writing and orally on the key elements of the draft penalty calculation in advance of the penalty decision being taken. The innovative element in these experiments is

[13] Precisely because of this difficulty in calculating the basic amount of the fine, Wils is less enthusiastic about this experiment. See Wils, 'The European Commission's 2006 Guidelines on Antitrust Fines' (n 12) 211–12.

[14] It should be noted that compensation as a ground for mitigation is in accordance with the ECA Fining Principles, para III.18. Furthermore, the German BKartA also used to take into account compensatory payments. It is unclear whether it will continue this policy under the 2013 Fining Guidelines (see above, section 5.7.2).

[15] With regard to the disadvantages of the uncoordinated accumulation of fines and damages for a single infringement, see MJ Frese, 'Fines and Damages under EU Competition Law: Implications of the Accumulation of Liability' (2011) 34 *World Competition* 393. See also Wils, 'The Relationship between Public Antitrust Enforcement and Private Actions for Damages' (n 12) 21, who warns: 'Competition authorities should thus certainly not facilitate compensation at the expense of deterrence and punishment. This implies that, if fine reductions are granted in recognition of compensation paid, any reduction should certainly stay well below the amount of the compensation paid. It also implies that the competition authority should not have to spend significant resources on assessing whether compensation is adequate . . . It may be possible to satisfy all these concerns by having a policy under which a fine reduction (of an amount well below the amount of compensation (expected to be) paid) is granted if the offender has either reached settlements with injured parties, and/or has accepted an independent arbitration system the use of which is optional and free for damage claimants. Such a policy could help victims of the antitrust violation to obtain compensation at lower costs, without undermining deterrence and without using significant public enforcement resources' (footnotes omitted).

[16] Wils seems less enthusiastic with the experiments in the area leniency plus (or amnesty plus); see Wils, 'Leniency in Antitrust Enforcement' (n 12) 60–61: 'Given this increased probability of detection of the second cartel, once the participation of a company in a first cartel has been detected, the justification for an "Amnesty Plus" policy does not appear obvious.'

that they could decrease the number of appeal procedures and could therefore result in procedural efficiencies. In sum, decentralisation has given rise to regulatory innovation in the enforcement of EU competition law.[17]

However, these benefits should not conceal that decentralisation may also have obstructed regulatory innovation on a few occasions. After all, not every domestic deviation from the Commission model may carry the label of innovation. In fact, some national traditions seem outdated or even misguided. In addition, this can be demonstrated with examples in the area of corporate fines. For example, the application of a capped deterrence multiplier at some intermediary stage of the calculation process seems inappropriate to secure deterrent fines. Even if this multiplier is initially adequate, the subsequent application of mitigating and aggravating circumstances may still result in a fine that either fails to deter or overdeters. One would therefore expect an increase for reasons of deterrence to be the final increment, just before the statutory cap and the leniency reduction are applied. Indeed, this is also the Commission's approach. Yet, NCAs in all the analysed jurisdictions either still apply or until recently applied such a (capped) deterrence multiplier at an intermediary stage.

Another domestic deviation that is unlikely to improve the enforcement of Articles 101 and 102 TFEU is the penalisation of single and continuous infringements in the Netherlands. Under current domestic case law, the ACM may not take into account periods of a single and continuous infringement dating back more than five years from the day on which the decision has been adopted in determining the amount of the fine. Not only could this limit the amount of the fine, it also has the consequence that a single and continuous infringement can be partially time-barred. This approach is at odds with EU case law on the SCI concept (see above, section 4.3.3) and the ECA Fining Guidelines,[18] and it is in any case incomprehensible why a five-year period as per the date of the decision has been chosen.

Paradoxically, the sanctioning autonomy of the Member States may thus also block innovation, whether temporarily or permanent. This observation brings us back to the theoretical underpinnings for regulatory innovation in the field of EU competition law. It has been theorised in chapter three that the dynamic efficiencies underlying the enforcement framework for EU competition law are partially due to the disciplining effects of fine proceeds and reputation gains. These effects, it was suggested, would induce Member States to engage in innovative experiments in a bid for cases and recognition from their peers. It has been shown through various examples that the 'innovation through decentralisation' theorem

[17] Apart from the experiments with custodial sanctions, disqualifications orders and pecuniary sanctions, there are some other domestic sanctioning powers and developments that could be highly informative for other jurisdictions: the UK's intention to use interim measures more often (see above, section 5.3.4); the possibility for German authorities to use administrative procedures to compensate injured parties, whether through declaratory findings or by ordering compensatory measures (see above, sections 5.5.2 and 5.6.2); and the approach of the Dutch courts in dealing with undue delays (see above, section 5.7.3).

[18] ECA Fining Guidelines, para III.8.

indeed corresponds with developments at the Member State level. Notwithstanding this conclusion, the above observation suggests that these disciplining effects are in any case not as strong as to root out every outdated or misguided approach to competition law enforcement instantly.

The 'innovation through decentralisation' theorem needs to be nuanced for a second reason. Even if Member States do engage in innovative experiments and other Member States learn from these experiences, the latter may still not embrace the successful foreign experiments for 'cultural' reasons. This has to do with the fact that some of the 'national experiments' seem to have been path-dependent rather than the outcome of experimentation, learning and evolution-to-efficiency.[19] For example, the possibilities under German law of penalising individuals and skimming off illegal gains are deeply rooted in German law. The same could be said of disqualification orders under UK law.[20] To be sure, this is not to say that these solutions are not innovative for the purposes of EU competition policy or that they cannot provide valuable information to other jurisdictions. However, it does mean that the evolution-to-efficiency paradigm fails to explain fully why these jurisdictions ended up with these sanctions[21] and, importantly, it also limits the chances that these sanctions are introduced elsewhere. Indeed, the analysis in chapter five only identified a few examples of convergence towards a domestic model.

[19] See more generally MJ Roe, 'Chaos and Evolution in Law and Economics' (1996) 109 *Harvard Law Review* 641.

[20] See also A Khan, 'Rethinking Sanctions for Breaching EU Competition Law: Is Director Disqualification the Answer?' (2012) 35 *World Competition* 77, 89.

[21] *cf* Roe (n 19) 642.

7

General Conclusions

This book has aimed to clarify some of the legal and economic implications of the decentralisation of enforcement competences in the area of EU competition law. More specifically, it has aimed to clarify the relationship between EU law and national law for the decentralised enforcement of Articles 101 and 102 TFEU and to explain how this relationship influences the costs of enforcing these competition law prohibitions. The focus of this book has been on sanctions. For this purpose, the preceding six chapters have detailed and evaluated the distribution of sanctioning competences at the EU and national levels. This final chapter provides an overview of the study's main findings and offers some reflections and recommendations.

7.1 SANCTIONING PRINCIPLES, CONVERGENCE TENDENCIES AND ENFORCEMENT COSTS

The decentralisation of enforcement competences in the area of EU competition law has various implications for the relationship between EU law and national law. Where the Member States act as 'agents' of EU law, enforcing Articles 101 and 102 TFEU, the domestic sanctioning powers and procedures are subject to various EU principles. These principles have priority over any rule of national law and therefore influence the terms and conditions of decentralised enforcement. The EU sanctioning principles derive from five different sources of law and pursue different ends. Those that derive from Regulation 1/2003, Articles 101 and 102 TFEU and the duty of sincere cooperation are mainly concerned with the uniform and effective application of EU competition law. Principles deriving from the free movement rights and the fundamental rights are meant to guarantee that the enforcement actions of the Member States do not impinge on EU entitlements for undertakings and individuals originating outside the area of competition law. Notwithstanding the variety of EU sanctioning principles, they do not form a rigid framework or straitjacket for the Member States. Several observations can be made as to the nature of these principles. First, they are more concerned with the conditions under which domestic sanctioning powers are exercised than with the actual type of sanctions. Second, Member States have maintained considerable leeway in implementing these conditions in their domestic legal systems. Third, some of these principles only provide minimum requirements (eg, the EU fundamental rights).

The decentralisation of EU competition law has also led to other developments at the Member State level. For instance, the sanctioning regimes in Germany, the Netherlands and the UK have been subject to voluntary convergence tendencies. Partially, this is the result of Regulation 1/2003 and the powers of the Commission, which have functioned as focal points for the Member States. This can be seen most clearly in the areas of interim measures and early resolution measures and, to a more limited extent, reparatory sanctions and pecuniary sanctions. Another driver of convergence is the policy coordination taking place within the ECN and the ECA. As yet, the coordination of sanctioning powers is limited to the field of pecuniary sanctions. Finally, the convergence process has been reinforced by Member States aligning their sanctioning regimes to other *domestic* regimes. This too is most prominent in the area of pecuniary sanctions, but can also be observed in relation to the institutional enforcement frameworks. Notwithstanding these convergence tendencies, there remain fundamental differences across the various jurisdictions. Differences are most clearly observable in the institutional enforcement frameworks and in the areas of declaratory findings, reparatory sanctions, pecuniary sanctions, custodial sanctions and disqualification orders. Some of these differences are due to idiosyncrasies of the various legal orders that are unrelated to competition law, while others are deliberate deviations from the EU model.

The decentralisation of EU competition law has had various implications for the costs of operating the enforcement system. Inherent to any decentralised enforcement system is that multiple authorities need to be staffed and funded. This leads to additional enforcement costs compared to a centralised system. However, decentralised authorities may also be presumed to have superior knowledge on domestic market circumstances. With this superior knowledge, enforcement can be more efficient. A specific feature of the current decentralised enforcement system for EU competition law is that there can be parallel procedures. A single cross-border infringement can be prosecuted by various authorities. This will add again to the costs of the enforcement system. The remaining costs of decentralised enforcement are a function of the scope of the sanctioning autonomy and the development of the sanctioning regimes. The larger the sanctioning autonomy of the Member States, the higher the probability that taxpayers throughout the EU will be satisfied with 'their' sanctioning regime and the better the conditions for regulatory innovation. Yet, at the same time, enforcement costs will increase with the scope of the sanctioning autonomy.

A single sanctioning regime applicable throughout the EU would lead to savings in terms of transaction costs, coordination costs and duplication costs. In practice, the domestic sanctioning powers for infringements of Articles 101 and 102 TFEU are subject to a variety of EU sanctioning principles. However, these principles fall short of anything close to a single sanctioning regime. Thus, while these principles may reduce some of the costs of decentralisation, there is still ample room and need for undertakings to obtain *ex ante* legal advice on the domestic sanctioning regimes, for competition authorities to coordinate their sanctioning policy and practice, and for undertakings and authorities to fight over unresolved procedural issues before the national courts. Moreover, the EU sanctioning principles cannot prevent the authorities from experiencing difficulties in using information that has been exchanged under Regulation 1/2003. The decentralisation of Articles 101 and 102 TFEU has therefore been accompanied by additional enforcement costs.

However, a decentralised enforcement system that is premised on sanctioning autonomy may have countervailing benefits. Provided that the sanctioning preferences in the Member States are heterogeneous, such a system may lead to a more efficient use of enforcement expenditure. The current EU framework in large part accommodates heterogeneous sanctioning preferences, and sanctioning preferences indeed differ according to the Member State. In this respect, decentralisation may be assumed to have engendered efficiencies too. The decentralisation of enforcement competences has also resulted in benefits of a different kind. The current EU framework allows, and even stimulates, national experiments in the area of sanctions. These experiments, and the lessons they teach, elevate the state of the art in competition law enforcement to a higher level. There are various examples of innovative experiments at the Member State level. However, there is also evidence that the institutional possibilities for experimentation and learning are not fully exploited and, even worse, that Commission-driven innovation has been blocked or delayed by the Member States.

7.2 REFLECTIONS AND RECOMMENDATIONS

The legal and economic insights that have been developed in this book could – and in the author's view should – inform the enforcement of EU competition law, whether through individual cases or policy debates. This final section offers some reflections, as well as some suggestions as to how authorities may develop policy and practice, courts may render judgments, and legislators may evaluate and reconsider current legislation on the basis of the foregoing analysis.

7.2.1 Prevailing Legal Issues

The analysis in chapters four and five demonstrated that the decentralisation of EU competition law has raised various questions relating to the relationship between EU law and national law, as well as the relationship between several EU interests. Gradually, issues like these start reaching the Court of Justice. In the coming years, an increase in the number of cases on the decentralised enforcement of Articles 101 and 102 TFEU may be expected. These cases could resolve the prevailing legal issues that have been identified in this study. Some of these are more pertinent than others, but it is hoped that the Court of Justice will in any case get the chance to elaborate on the following: the relationship between EU fundamental rights and the EU principle of effectiveness in the context of Articles 101 and 102 TFEU (see above, section 4.5.1); the scope of application of the principle of good administration (see above, section 4.5.6); the status of parallel proceedings under Article 101 or 102 TFEU in light of the principle of *ne bis in idem* (see above, section 4.5.9); the consequences for the cooperation mechanisms laid down in Regulation 1/2003 of domestic definitions as to what qualifies as national *competition* law (see above, sections 4.6.2 and 5.8.4).

7.2.2 The Centralisation Effect of EU Law and Practice

More than any other court within the EU, the Court of Justice plays a crucial role in the enforcement of EU competition law. This role has been enhanced by the decentralisation of enforcement competences. Its main task is no longer to review the legality of decisions adopted by the Commission. More than ever, it now also rules on the conditions for decentralised enforcement. National courts may refer questions to the Court of Justice precisely on these conditions. But also outside the preliminary reference procedure, the Court will need to consider how its rulings will impact on domestic enforcement powers and procedures. Any ruling it makes in the context of Articles 101 and 102 TFEU, whether upon a reference by a national court or in relation to a direct action against a Commission decision, can have implications for the Member States. This is the result of the centralisation effect of primary sources of EU law (see above, section 4.2). The Court of Justice and the General Court should recognise this effect in rendering judgments and should explicitly indicate (or carefully formulate) if they do not wish to give their rulings *erga omnes* effect. Certainly for the General Court, whose jurisdiction in competition matters is limited to direct actions against Commission decisions, this responsibility for the development of enforcement policy will be something novel.

7.2.3 Implementing Economic Considerations

The relationship between EU law and national law for the decentralised enforcement of Articles 101 and 102 TFEU can develop through case practice and by legislative intervention. Examples of the former are *T-Mobile Netherlands*,[1] *VEBIC*,[2]

[1] Case C-8/08 *T-Mobile Netherlands* [2009] ECR I-4529.
[2] Case C-439/08 *VEBIC* [2010] ECR I-12471.

Tele2 Polska[3] and *Bundeswettbewerbsbehörde v Schenker*,[4] where the Court of Justice shifted the balance to EU law by choosing uniformity over autonomy.[5] In the Report on the functioning of Regulation 1/2003, the Commission contemplates a further move towards EU law by harmonising domestic sanctioning powers and procedures.[6] This would be an example of redefining the relationship between EU law and national law by legislative intervention. In making these principled choices on the relationship between EU law and national law, the Court of Justice and the EU legislator should take into account the economic implications of their decisions. This follows from the principle of subsidiarity laid down in Article 5(3) TEU.[7] This means that transaction costs, (dis)economies of scale, sanctioning preferences and the possibilities for regulatory innovation should be considered and weighed. It is submitted herewith that the Court and the legislator should accord preference to autonomy over uniformity (and hence to national law over EU law) unless there are clear indications that more uniformity will engender savings on transaction costs, duplication costs and/or coordination costs. If cost reductions can be expected, then these should still be weighed against the information advantages (ie, regulatory innovation) that are foregone as a result of uniformity and the disutility suffered by individual Member States with diverging sanctioning preferences/powers. While this approach will not always lead to a clear winning outcome, it can make decision makers more conscious and accountable for the economic implications of their choices. For obvious reasons, the Court of Justice is not always in the position to rely on economic considerations in rendering judgments. Its primary task is to ensure that 'the law is observed'.[8] However, the Court of Justice is also subject to the principle of subsidiarity[9] and it is generally seized with matters where the law is unclear. In other words, the Court can often and should as much as possible take account of the economic implications of its rulings.

To illustrate what the suggested two-step test would entail, let us briefly consider some recent case practice. Having regard to the economics of the division of

[3] Case C-375/09 *Tele2 Polska* [2011] ECR I-3055.

[4] Case C-681/11 *Bundeswettbewerbsbehörde v Schenker* [2012] OJ C89/11.

[5] This point has been made earlier in MJ Frese, 'Tightening the Grip on the Application of Article 81 EC Treaty: The European Court of Justice Guards its Province' (2011) 37 *Legal Issues of Economic Integration* 87; MJ Frese, 'Case C-439/08, Vlaamse federatie van verenigingen van Brood- en Banketbakkers, IJsbereiders en Chocoladebewerkers (VEBIC), Judgment of the Court (Grand Chamber) of 7 December 2010' (2011) 48 *Common Market Law Review* 893; MJ Frese, 'Handhavingsautonomie bij de Decentrale Toepassing van het EU Mededingingsrecht' (2011) 17 *Nederlands Tijdschrift voor Europees Recht* 200.

[6] Communication from the Commission to the European Parliament and the Council: Report on the functioning of Regulation 1/2003 [2009] COM 206 final, para 33. See further Commission Staff Working Paper accompanying the Communication from the Commission to the European Parliament and the Council: Report on the functioning of Regulation 1/2003 [2009] COM 206 final, paras 206–07.

[7] *cf* R van den Bergh, 'Economic Criteria for Applying the Subsidiarity Principle in the European Community: The Case of Competition Policy' (1996) 16 *International Review of Law and Economics* 363; AG Toth, 'Is Subsidiarity Justiciable?' (1994) 19 *European Law Review* 268, 282–83.

[8] Article 19(1) TEU.

[9] In accordance with Article 5(3) TEU and the Protocol (No 2) on the application of the principles of subsidiarity and proportionality [2010] OJ C83/206, 'each [EU] institution shall ensure that the principle of subsidiarity is complied with'. This includes the Court of Justice.

enforcement competences, the rulings in *T-Mobile Netherlands* and *Bundeswettbewerbsbehörde v Schenker* seem to be better justified than the rulings in *Tele2 Polska* and *VEBIC*. After all, ignoring possible legal objections, the *T-Mobile* extension of the legal presumption of causality between 'concertation' and 'practice' in applying Article 101 TFEU (see above, section 4.3.1) reduces the need for duplicative litigation in an area where regulatory innovation and strong domestic preferences seem less likely anyway. The same could be said about *Bundeswettbewerbsbehörde v Schenker* – where the Court extended the Commission's conditions for intent and negligence to the enforcement actions by the NCAs – albeit that this judgment is more likely to frustrate domestic preferences.[10] The *Tele2 Polska* prohibition (see above, section 2.3) increases transaction costs and duplication costs, and therefore does not even get past the first part of the suggested test. After all, the prohibition to render negative decisions on the merits has for a consequence that undertakings still not know whether their commercial behaviour is in conformity with Articles 101 and 102 TFEU. Moreover, a decision that there are 'no grounds for further action' might not prevent other authorities (or private parties) from launching proceedings a second time.[11] While this does not necessarily mean that the ruling in *Tele2 Polska* is 'wrong', it does urge the Court to formulate convincing justifications for these types of principled rulings. Compared to the above three cases, the economic implications of the *VEBIC*-requirement (see above, section 2.3) are less clear. Ensuring party status for NCAs might reduce the chances of 'false negatives' and duplicative procedures, but this requirement has also terminated an institutional experiment on the basis of fears rather than facts. In light of the disciplining effects of fine proceeds and reputation gains (see above, section 3.6), the Court of Justice could have condoned the domestic peculiarity in question and could rely on the national legislator to intervene if and when this experiment would turn out to be unsuccessful after all.

Obviously, the two-step test can also be applied to legislative intervention, for instance, to the Commission's suggestion to harmonise sanctioning powers. As a preliminary matter, it should be noted that this suggestion seems mainly motivated by the objective to protect the rights of undertakings.[12] There can be no doubt that these rights deserve protection. However, one does wonder how seriously these rights are jeopardised and whether this 'problem' can be addressed with the harmonisation of sanctioning powers. The *ex ante* uncertainty for undertakings under the current regime is limited: Articles 101 and 102 TFEU need to be applied uniformly throughout the EU anyway and the number of sanctioning

[10] What is puzzling about *Bundeswettbewerbsbehörde v Schenker* is that the conditions of intent and negligence are facultative, but once adopted need to be 'at least as stringent as the condition laid down in Article 23 of Regulation No 1/2003'. One would have expected the Court to require Member States not to adopt conditions more stringent than the condition laid down in Article 23 of Regulation No 1/2003. Indeed, this is what the Court seemed to have in mind judging by the Court's subsequent application of this requirement (see above, section 2.3).

[11] However, it cannot be excluded that the NCAs will be prohibited from launching proceedings a second time on the basis of the EU principle of *ne bis in idem* (see above, section 4.5.9).

[12] Commission Staff Working Paper (n 6) para 206.

regimes that could be applicable is limited (there are 29 sanctioning regimes, but cases involving more than three Member States are typically dealt with by the Commission). This means that undertakings should normally be able to inform themselves about the consequences of their anti-competitive practices beforehand. Any concerns there might be about *ex post* erosion of legal safeguards due to the cooperation between authorities seems to have been largely addressed by Article 12 of Regulation 1/2003 and the applicability of the EU fundamental rights. The cooperation between authorities, more precisely the exchange of information, can only impinge on domestic fundamental rights for legal persons that have not been recognised (or not recognised to a similar extent) under EU law, eg, the far-reaching *nemo tenetur* principle under German law (see above, section 5.7.2). However, it may seriously be questioned whether such a far-reaching legal safeguard for legal persons in the context of EU competition law is appropriate at all. More importantly, the erosion of legal safeguards of this kind would not necessarily be addressed by the harmonisation of sanctioning powers. This would entail a far more ambitious harmonisation project, the feasibility of which is doubtful. The only concern that the harmonisation of sanctioning powers could truly address is that undertakings and individuals are no longer dependent on the 'allocative discretion' of the competition authorities for the sanctions they face. However, this problem could also be addressed by improving the rules for case allocation. In other words, from a legal perspective, there are no compelling reasons to harmonise sanctioning powers. Approached from an economic perspective, more uniformity with regard to sanctioning powers could reduce enforcement costs for all stakeholders, but will come at the expense of regulatory innovation and the efficient allocation of national enforcement expenditures. Moreover, some of these costs can be reduced without the harmonisation of sanctioning powers (see below, section 7.2.5). It is therefore suggested that harmonisation of sanctioning powers should be reserved as a means of last resort and should be contemplated only if cost savings are foreseeable.[13]

7.2.4 Possibilities for Regulatory Innovation

The decentralisation of enforcement competences in the area of EU competition law was meant to increase enforcement capacity. It was concluded in chapter six that decentralisation may not have been the most efficient way to achieve this objective and that this is partially due to the fact that the potential welfare advantages through regulatory innovation have not been fully exploited. In order to take full advantage of the current enforcement framework, the benefits of inter-jurisdictional learning should be capitalised upon. This is mainly the responsibility of the Member States, although the Commission could have a facilitating role.

[13] A similar recommendation was made in KJ Cseres, 'Comparing Laws in the Enforcement of EU and National Competition Laws' (2010) 3 *European Journal of Legal Studies* 7, 28ff

First, Member States should evaluate national feedback systems. The enforcement of Articles 101 and 102 TFEU could be improved by ensuring that experiences abroad actually feed back into domestic enforcement policy. This requires Member States to evaluate their domestic enforcement regimes regularly in light of the results and approaches in other Member States. Second, Member States should contribute to the development of EU competition policy by taking care of existing lacunae. For example, the paucity of legal safeguards at the EU level against incursions on the right to property (see above, section 4.5.2) need not be followed by the Member States. The latter may develop policy and practice on this issue. The same applies to the right to economic engagement (see above, section 4.5.3). This too could be developed in domestic proceedings under Articles 101 and 102 TFEU. Furthermore, the Member States could contribute to the development of EU competition law by making a serious attempt to take into account the degree of culpability in punishing 'object-restrictions' and the harmful effects in punishing 'effect-restrictions' (see above, section 4.6.5). Eventually, domestic precedents in these and other areas could be taken over by the Court of Justice and could become part of EU competition policy.

7.2.5 Economising Enforcement

The decentralisation of enforcement competences in the area of EU competition law comes with various costs and benefits. Some of these costs cannot be reduced without reducing the benefits at the same time. However, there are also costs that can be reduced without any sacrifice. This is certainly the case for the costs related to the restrictions on the use of exchanged information. As a result of the current rules for information exchange, Member States will experience more difficulties in successfully imposing custodial sanctions than any other sanction. This could limit the effectiveness of the domestic enforcement regimes. Moreover, it could block regulatory innovation by rendering fewer results on the merits and demerits of this sanction and by dissuading Member States from experimenting with this sanction in the first place. It is unclear what exactly this restriction is meant to protect. It should be recalled that Regulation 1/2003 in any case prohibits the use of exchanged information to penalise natural persons if this information has not been collected in accordance with equivalent legal safeguards. Why would one want to block the use of information for custodial sanctions if it has been collected in a way which respects the same level of protection of the rights of defence and, importantly, this issue can disputed by the person in question? It is submitted herewith that the limitation on the use of information in evidence for the imposition of custodial sanctions is too far-reaching and results in unnecessary costs. This concern resonates in the Commission Staff Working Paper that accompanies the Report on the functioning of Regulation 1/2003 and might therefore be addressed in due course.[14]

[14] Commission Staff Working Paper (n 6) para 245.

What remains are the difficulties of assessing the equivalence of the rights of defence and the coordination costs that come with such an assessment (see above, section 2.4). However, these costs can also be reduced, provided that the national review courts are willing to help. The latter are herewith invited to refer as much as possible to EU fundamental rights in rendering decisions under Articles 101 and 102 TFEU. The EU fundamental rights would then start to function as a common framework of reference, while ensuring that the national authorities will not operate below these legal safeguards (authorities may of course be held to higher standards). This will, in turn, assist the authorities and other courts in determining the equivalence of legal protection for the admissibility of information.

Enforcement costs may also be reduced by bringing an end to duplicative procedures. One of the clearest diseconomies of the current enforcement system is that cases can be prosecuted by various NCAs in parallel. This leads to a multiplication of enforcement costs without any benefits. These costs could be avoided by opting for a system of single authority action.[15] This would either require that the Commission assumes jurisdiction over any case that affects more than one Member State or that NCAs obtain the power to impose sanctions with cross-border effects. The first alternative has serious drawbacks. NCAs would then be stripped of virtually all their competences under Articles 101 and 102 TFEU and many domestic investigations would have to be reallocated to the Commission once the scope of the putative infringement becomes clear. The second alternative seems more worthy of exploration, but will require some legislative courage. National authorities would then need the power to terminate and punish anti-competitive practices in foreign jurisdictions. While this alternative raises important questions about state sovereignty, it seems least sensitive with regard to corporate fines. NCAs could simply take account of EU-wide turnover in meting out an appropriate fine. This approach could be modelled on the penalty regime in the UK, where fines may already reflect 'relevant turnover' earned abroad (see above, section 5.7.4). Coincidentally, corporate fines are probably also the most frequently applied type of sanction in relation to infringements of Articles 101 and 102 TFEU. Therefore, the introduction of a 'one-stop-shop' for corporate fines would not only be relatively easy to accomplish, it would also yield the largest cost reductions. From an economic perspective, enforcement policy could therefore be improved by experimenting with this alternative.[16] The most challenging aspect of this experiment is to come up with an appropriate EU mechanism to redistribute fine proceeds over the affected jurisdictions without creating a free-rider problem with respect to enforcement.[17] This is an area that is worth exploring further and that could be interesting for future research. On a lighter note, this means that more academic research could actually economise the 'enforcement industry'!

[15] Similar recommendations were made in WPJ Wils, 'The Principle of *Ne Bis in Idem* in EC Antitrust Enforcement: A Legal and Economic Analysis' (2003) 26 *World Competition* 131, 146–47; I Simonsson, *Legitimacy in EU Cartel Control* (Hart Publishing, 2010) 341.

[16] A similar recommendation was made in S Brammer, *Co-operation between National Competition Agencies in the Enforcement of EC Competition Law* (Hart Publishing, 2009) 484.

[17] A similar recommendation was made in Wils (n 15) 147.

BIBLIOGRAPHY

BOOKS

Begründung zum Regierungsentwurf der 7. GWB-Novelle vom 26. Mai 2004, *WuW-Sonderheft* (Verlagsgruppe Handelsblatt, 2005).

Bechtold, R, *Kartellgesetz* (Gesetz gegen Wettbewerbbeschränkungen, 5. Auflage, Verlag CH Beck, 2008).

Brammer, S, *Co-operation Between National Competition Agencies in the Enforcement of EC Competition Law* (Hart Publishing, 2009).

Bunte, H-J, *Kartellrecht* (Verlag CH Beck, 2008).

Craig, P and de Búrca, G, *EU Law: Text, Cases, and Materials* 5th edn (Oxford University Press, 2011).

Cseres, KJ, Schinkel, MP and Vogelaar, FOW (eds), *Criminalization of Competition Law Enforcement: Economic and Legal Implications for the Member States* (Edward Elgar, 2006).

De Moor-van Vugt, A, *Maten en Gewichten: Het evenredigheidsbeginsel in Europees perspectief* (dissertation, Schoordijk Instituut/Centrum voor wetgevingsvraagstukken, 1995).

De Visser, M, *Network-Based Governance in EC Law: The Example of EC Competition and EC Communications Law* (Hart Publishing, 2009).

Drahos, M, *Convergence of Competition Laws and Policies in the European Community. Germany, Austria, and the Netherlands* (Kluwer Law International, 2001).

Emmerich, V, *Kartellrecht* (Verlag CH Beck, 2008).

Faull, J and Nikpay, A (eds), *The EC Law of Competition* 2nd edn (Oxford University Press, 2007).

Gerbrandy, A, *Convergentie in het Mededingingsrecht: De Invloed van het EG-Recht op Materiële Toepassing, Toegang, Bewijs en Toetsing bij de Nederlandse Mededingingsbestuursrechter, Bezien in het Licht van Effectieve Rechtsbescherming* (Boom Juridische uitgevers, 2009).

Jans, JH et al, *Europeanisation of Public Law* (Europa Law Publishing, 2007).

Klip, A (ed), *Materials on European Criminal Law* (Intersentia, 2012).

Korsten, LEJ and Van Wanroij, M, *Nederlands Mededingingsrecht* (Kluwer, 2008).

Lavrijssen-Heijmans, SACM, *Onafhankelijke mededingingstoezichthouders, regulerende bevoegdheden en de waarborgen voor good governance* (Boom Juridische uitgevers, 2006).

Lenaerts, K, Arts, D and Maselis, I, *Procedural Law of the European Union* 2nd edn (Sweet & Maxwell, 2006).

Nazzini, R, *Concurrent Proceedings in Competition Law: Procedure, Evidence and Remedies* (Oxford University Press, 2004).

O'Neill, E and Sanders, E, *UK Competition Procedure: The Modernised Regime* (Oxford University Press, 2007).

Parret, L, *Side Effects of the Modernisation of EU Competition Law* (Wolf Legal Publishers, 2011).

Posner, RA, *Antitrust Law* 2nd edn (University of Chicago Press, 2001).

Roth, P and Rose, V (eds), *Bellamy & Child: European Community Law of Competition* 6th edn (Oxford University Press, 2008).

Schlössels, RJN and Zijlstra, SE, *De Haan/Drupsteen/Fernhout: Bestuursrecht in de Sociale Rechtsstaat* 6th edn (Kluwer, 2010).

Simonsson, I, *Legitimacy in EU Cartel Control* (Hart Publishing, 2010).

Slot, PJ and Johnston, AC, *An Introduction to Competition Law* (Hart Publishing, 2006).

Tridimas, T, *The General Principles of EU Law* 2nd edn (Oxford University Press, 2006).

Tröndle, H and Fisher, T, *Strafgesetzbuch und Nebengesetze* (53. Auflage, Verlag CH Beck, 2006).

Van Bockel, B, *The Ne Bis in Idem Principle in EU Law* (Wolters Kluwer, 2010)

Van den Bergh, R and Camesasca, P, *European Competition Law and Economics: A Comparative Perspective* 2nd edn (Sweet & Maxwell, 2006).

Van Harten, HJ, *Autonomie van de Nationale Rechter in het Europees Recht: Een Verkenning van de Praktijk Aan de Hand van de Nederlandse Europeesrechtelijke Rechtspraak Over de Vestigingsvrijheid en het Vrijedienstenverkeer* (Boom Juridische uitgevers, 2011).

VerLoren van Themaat, W and Reuder, B (eds), *Nederlands Mededingingsrecht 2011* (Kluwer, 2011).

Wesseling, R, *The Modernisation of EC Antitrust Law* (Hart Publishing, 2000).

Whish, R, *Competition Law* 6th edn (Oxford University Press, 2009).

Whish, R and Bailey, D, *Competition Law* 7th edn (Oxford University Press, 2012).

Wils, WPJ, *The Optimal Enforcement of EC Antitrust Law: Essays in Law & Economics* (European Monographs, Kluwer Law International, 2002).

ARTICLES AND BOOK CHAPTERS

Andreangeli, A, 'Between Economic Freedom and Effective Competition Enforcement: The Impact of the Antitrust Remedies Provided by the Modernisation Regulation on Investigated Parties' Freedom to Contract and to Enjoy Property' (2010) 6 *Competition Law Review* 225.

Arcuri, A and Dari-Mattiacci, G, 'Centralisation versus Decentralisation as a Risk-Return Trade-Off' (2010) 53 *Journal of Law and Economics* 359.

Baker, JB, 'The Case for Antitrust Enforcement' (2003) 17 *Journal of Economic Perspectives* 27.

Becker, C in Loewenheim/Meessen/Riesenkampff, *Kartellrecht* (Band 2: GWB, Verlag CH Beck, 2006).

Biermann, J, 'Country Analysis – Germany' in G Dannecker and O Jansen (eds), *Competition Law Sanctioning in the European Union: The EU-Law Influence on the National Law Systems of Sanctions in the European Area* (Kluwer Law International, 2004).

Block, MK and Sidak, JG, 'The Cost of Antitrust Deterrence: Why Not Hang a Price Fixer Now and Then?' (1979–80) 68 *Georgetown Law Journal* 1131.

Bornkamm, J in Langen/Bunte, *Kommentar zum deutschen und europaïschen Kartellrecht* (Band 1: Deutsches Kartellrecht, 11. Auflage, Carl Heymanns Verlag/Luchterhand 2011).

Bracher, C-D in Jaeger/Pohlmann/Rieger/Schroeder, *Frankfurter Kommentar zum Kartellrecht* (Stand April 2009, Verlag Dr Otto Schmidt).

Brammer, S, 'Concurrent Jurisdiction Under Regulation 1/2003 and the Issue of Case Allocation' (2005) 42 *Common Market Law Review* 1383.
Bratton, WW and McCahery, JA, 'The New Economics of Jurisdictional Competition: Devolutionary Federalism in a Second-Best World' (1997) 86 *Georgetown Law Journal* 201.
Cseres, KJ, 'The Impact of Regulation 1/2003 in the New Member States' (2010) 6 *Competition Law Review* 145.
—— 'Comparing Laws in the Enforcement of EU and National Competition Laws' (2010) 3 *European Journal of Legal Studies* 7.
Dannecker, G and Biermann, J in Immenga/Mestmäcker, *GWB Kommentar* (Verlag CH Beck, 2001).
Dari-Mattiacci, G and Deffains, B, 'Uncertainty of Law and Legal Process' (2007) 163 *Journal of Institutional and Theoretical Economics* 627.
De Bree, R, 'Mededingingsrecht en Strafrecht: Hernieuwde Kennismaking' (2006) *Markt & Mededinging* 205.
—— 'Hof Den Haag (strafkamer), 27 november 2007, Vooroverleg bouwbedrijven' (2008) *Markt & Mededinging* 19.
Dekeyser, K and Jaspers, M, 'A New Era of ECN Cooperation. Achievements and Challenges with Special Focus on Work in the Leniency Field' (2007) 30 *World Competition* 3.
Dekker, CT and Hoekstra-Borzymowska, AM, 'Kroniek NMa-besluiten 2007: Mededingingsafspraken, machtsposities en procedures' (2008) *Markt & Mededinging* 46.
Dobbin, C and Peretz, G, 'The Cartel Offence', in T Ward and K Smith (eds), *Competition Litigation in the UK* (Sweet & Maxwell, 2005).
Doorenbos, DR, 'Strafrecht Baat Niet, Schaadt Wel' (2010) *Markt & Mededinging* 167.
Dougan, M, *National Remedies Before the Court of Justice. Issues of Harmonisation and Differentation* (Hart Publishing, 2004).
Easterbrook, FH, 'Antitrust and the Economics of Federalism' (1983) 26 *Journal of Law & Economics* 23.
Ehlermann, CD, 'The Modernization of EC Antitrust Policy: A Legal and Cultural Revolution' (2000) 37 *Common Market Law Review* 537.
Epple, D and Zelenitz, A, 'The Implications of Competition Among Jurisdictions: Does Tiebout Need Politics?' (1981) 89 *Journal of Political Economy* 1197.
Esty, DC and Geradin, D, 'Regulatory Co-Opetition' in DC Esty and D Geradin (eds), *Regulatory Competition and Economic Integration: Comparative Perspectives* (Oxford University Press, 2001).
Ezrachi, A and Kindl, J, 'Cartels as Criminal? The Long Road from Unilateral Enforcement to International Consensus' in C Beaton-Wells and A Ezrachi (eds), *Criminalising Cartels: Critical Studies of an International Regulatory Movement* (Hart Publishing, 2011).
Fischel, DR and Sykes, AO, 'Corporate Crime' (1996) 25 *Journal of Legal Studies* 319.
Fox, EM, 'Antitrust Law on a Global Scale: Races Up, Down, and Sideways' in DC Esty and D Geradin (eds), *Regulatory Competition and Economic Integration: Comparative Perspectives* (Oxford University Press, 2001).
Frese, MJ, 'Het Toezeggingsbesluit; Kenmerken van een Nieuw Handhavingsinstrument' (2007) *Markt & Mededinging* 39.
—— 'Handhavingsautonomie bij de Decentrale Toepassing van het EU Mededingingsrecht' (2011) 17 *Nederlands Tijdschrift voor Europees Recht* 200.
—— 'Tightening the Grip on the Application of Article 81 EC Treaty; the European Court of Justice Guards its Province' (2011) 37 *Legal Issues of Economic Integration* 87.

Frese, MJ, 'Case C-439/08, Vlaamse federatie van verenigingen van Brood- en Banketbakkers, IJsbereiders en Chocoladebewerkers (VEBIC), Judgment of the Court (Grand Chamber) of 7 December 2010' (2011) 48 *Common Market Law Review* 893.

——'Fines and Damages Under EU Competition Law: Implications of the Accumulation of Liability' (2011) 34 *World Competition* 393.

——'De Doorwerking van Europese Rechtsbeginselen bij de Decentrale Handhaving van het EU Mededingingsrecht' (2012) 61 *Ars Aequi* 108.

Gaitanides, Ch in Von der Groeben/Schwarze, *Kommentar zum Vertrag über die Europäische Union und zur Gründung der Europäischen Gemeinschaft* (6. Auflage Nomos, 2004).

Geradin, D, 'Competition between Rules and Rules of Competition: A Legal and Economic Analysis of the Proposed Modernization of the Enforcement of EC Competition Law' (2002–03) 9 *Columbia Journal of European Law* 1.

Gerbrandy, A, 'Procedural Convergence in Competition Law: Towards a Spontaneous *Ius Commune*?' (2009) 2 *Review of European Administrative Law* 105.

Harding, Ch, 'The Anti-Cartel Enforcement Industry: Criminological Perspectives on Cartel Criminalisation' in C Beaton-Wells and A Ezrachi (eds), *Criminalising Cartels: Critical Studies of an International Regulatory Movement* (Hart Publishing, 2011).

Heimler, A and Mehta, K, 'Violations of Antitrust Provisions: The Optimal Level of Fines for Achieving Deterrence' (2012) 35 *World Competition* 103.

Herdegen, M in Maunz/Dürig, *Kommentar zum Grundgesetz* (Stand April 2009, Verlag CH Beck).

Hüschelrath, K, 'The Costs and Benefits of Antitrust Enforcement: Identification and Measurement' (2012) 35 *World Competition* 121.

Inman, RP and Rubinfeld, DL, 'Making Sense of the Antitrust State-Action Doctrine: Balancing Political Participation and Economic Efficiency in Regulatory Federalism' (1996–97) 75 *Texas Law Review* 1203.

Joshua, J, 'DOA: Can the UK Cartel Offence be Resuscitated?' in C Beaton-Wells and A Ezrachi (eds), *Criminalising Cartels: Critical Studies of an International Regulatory Movement* (Hart Publishing, 2011).

Jung, P, 'National Report for Germany' in D Cahill (ed), *The Modernisation of EU Competition Law Enforcement in the EU: FIDE 2004 National Reports* (Cambridge University Press, 2004).

Khan, A, 'Rethinking Sanctions for Breaching EU Competition Law: Is Director Disqualification the Answer?' (2012) 35 *World Competition* 77.

Klose, T in G Wiedemann, *Handbuch des Kartellrechts* (Verlag CH Beck, 2008).

Klusmann, M in G Wiedemann, *Handbuch des Kartellrechts* (Verlag CH Beck, 2008).

Korsten, LEJ, 'Rb Rotterdam (strafkamer), 9 juni 2005, Vooroverleg bouwbedrijven' (2005) *Markt & Mededinging* 257.

Landes, WM, 'Optimal Sanctions for Antitrust Violations' (1983) 50 *University Chicago Law Review* 652.

Lavrijssen, S, 'More Intensive Judicial Review in Competition Law and Economic Regulation in the Netherlands: Vice or Virtue?' in O Essens, A Gerbrandy and S Lavrijssen (eds), *National Courts and the Standard of Review in Competition Law and Economic Regulation* (Europa Law Publishing, 2009).

Lavrijssen, S and Hancher, L, 'Networks on Track: From European Regulatory Networks to European Regulatory 'Network Agencies'' (2008) 34 *Legal Issues of Economic Integration* 23.

Lemaire, Ch and Gstalter, J, 'The Silent Revolution Beyond Regulation 1/2003' (2008) 2 *GCP Online Magazine for Global Competition Policy* <www.competitionpolicyinternational.com> accessed 1 July 2013.

Lenaerts, K, 'Modernisation of the Application and Enforcement of European Competition Law – An Introductory Overview' in J Stuyck and H Gilliams (eds), *Modernisation of European Competition Law* (Intersentia Antwerp, 2002).

Lerche, P in Maunz/Dürig, *Kommentar zum Grundgesetz* (Stand April 2009, Verlag CH Beck).

Marsden, PB, 'Inducing Member State Enforcement of European Competition Law: A Competition Policy Approach to "Antitrust Federalism"' (1997) 4 *European Competition Law Review* 234.

Mundt, A, 'Die Bußgeldleitlinien des Bundeskartellamtes' (2007) *Wirtschaft und Wettbewerb* 458.

Nägele, T in Jaeger/Pohlmann/Rieger/Schroeder, *Frankfurter Kommentar zum Kartellrecht* (Stand April 2009, Verlag Dr Otto Schmidt).

Oates, WE, 'An Essay on Fiscal Federalism' (1999) 37 *Journal of Economic Literature* 1120.

Oliver, P, 'Le Règlement 1/2003 et les Principes D'Efficacité et D'Équivalence' (2005) 41 *Cahiers de droit européen* 351.

Peretz, G, 'Enforcement and Procedure Before the OFT', in T Ward and K Smith (eds), *Competition Litigation in the UK* (Sweet & Maxwell, 2005).

Pescatore, P, 'Les Droits De L'Homme et L'Integration Europeenne' [1969] *Cahiers de droit européen* 629.

Pohlmann, P, 'Auf dem Weg zur Europäisierung nationalen Kartellrechts' in CJH Jansen et al, *Europäische Dimensionen des Vertragsrechts und des Wettbewerbsrechts* (Münsterische Juristische Vorträge, Band 15, LIT Verlag, 2005).

——'Anmerkung zu EuGH, Urteil v 3.5.2011 – C-375/09 – Tele2 Polska' in *Lindenmaier-Möhring Kommentierte BGH-Rechtsprechung* 2011, 320463 (Beck-Online) <http://beck-online.beck.de> accessed 1 July 2013.

——'Private Losses in European Competition Law: Public or Private Enforcement?' in R Schulze (ed), *Compensation of Private Losses: The Evolution of Torts in European Business Law* (Sellier European Law Publishers, 2011).

Polinsky, AM and Shavell, S, 'Punitive Damages: An Economic Analysis' (1997–98) 111 *Harvard Law Review* 869.

Prechal, S, 'EC Requirements for an Effective Remedy' in J Lonbay and A Biondi (eds), *Remedies for Breach of EC Law* (John Wiley & Sons, 1997).

Raum, R in Langen/Bunte, *Kommentar zum deutschen und europaïschen Kartellrecht* (Band 1: Deutsches Kartellrecht, 11. Auflage, Carl Heymanns Verlag/Luchterhand, 2011).

Reindl, AP, 'How Strong is the Case for Criminal Sanctions in Cartel Cases?' in KJ Cseres, MP Schinkel and FOW Vogelaar (eds), *Criminalization of Competition Law Enforcement. Economic and Legal Implications for the Member States* (Edward Elgar, 2006).

Riley, A, 'EC Antitrust Modernisation: The Commission Does Very Nicely – Thank You! Part 2: between the Idea and the Reality: Decentralisation under Regulation 1' (2003) 12 *European Competition Law Review* 657.

Rodger, BJ, 'The Competition Act and the Enterprise Act Reforms: Sanctions and Deterrence in UK Competition Law' in G Dannecker and O Jansen (eds), *Competition Law Sanctioning in the European Union: The EU-Law Influence on the National Law Systems of Sanctions in the European Area* (Kluwer Law International, 2004).

Rodger, BJ, 'A Study of Compliance Post-OFT Infringement Action' (2009) 5 *European Competition Journal* 65.

Rodger, BJ and Wylie, SR, 'Taking the Community Interest Line: Decentralisation and Subsidiarity in Competition Law Enforcement' (1997) 8 *European Competition Law Review* 485.

Roe, MJ, 'Chaos and Evolution in Law and Economics' (1996) 109 *Harvard Law Review* 641.

Rose-Ackerman, S, 'Risk Taking and Reelection: Does Federalism Promote Innovation?' (1980) 9 *Journal of Legal Studies* 593.

Salmon, P, 'Decentralisation as an Incentive Scheme' (1987) 3 *Oxford Review of Economic Policy* 24.

Schneider, H-H in Langen/Bunte, *Kommentar zum deutschen und europaïschen Kartellrecht* (Band 1: Deutsches Kartellrecht, 11. Auflage, Carl Heymanns Verlag/Luchterhand, 2011).

Schwarze, J in Schwarze (Hrsg), *EU-Kommentar* (3. Auflage Nomos, 2012).

Simonsson, I, 'Criminalising Cartels in the EU: Is There a Case for Harmonisation?' in C Beaton-Wells and A Ezrachi (eds), *Criminalising Cartels: Critical Studies of an International Regulatory Movement* (Hart Publishing, 2011).

Smits, R, 'The European Competition Network: Selected Aspects' (2005) 32 *Legal Issues of Economic Integration* 175.

Stephan, A, 'A Principled Argument for Personal Criminal Sanctions as Punishment under EC Cartel Law' (2008) *Competition Law Review* 123.

Sufrin, B and Furse, M, 'Market Investigations' (2002) *Competition Law Journal* 244.

Teichman, D, 'The Market for Criminal Justice: Federalism, Crime Control, and Jurisdictional Competition' (2004–05) 103 *Michigan Law Review* 1831.

Temple Lang, J, 'Community Constitutional Law: Article 5 EEC Treaty' (1990) 27 *Common Market Law Review* 645.

——'The Implications of the Commission's Leniency Policy for National Competition Authorities' (2003) 28 *European Law Review* 430.

——'The Development by the Court of Justice of the Duties of Cooperation of National Authorities and Community Institutions under Article 10 EC' (2007–08) 31 *Fordham International Law Journal* 1482.

Tiebout, CM, 'A Pure Theory of Local Expenditures' (1956) 64 *Journal of Political Economy* 416.

Toth, AG, 'Is Subsidiarity Justiciable?' (1994) 19 *European Law Review* 268.

Van den Bergh, R, 'Economic Criteria for Applying the Subsidiarity Principle in the European Community: The Case of Competition Policy' (1996) 16 *International Review of Law and Economics* 363.

——'Towards an Institutional Legal Framework for Regulatory Competition in Europe' (2000) 53 *KYKLOS* 435.

Van der Meulen, BMJ, 'Bestuursrechtelijke keuzen ten aanzien van de toepassing van de Mededingingswet' (1999) *Markt & Mededinging* 19.

Van der Woude, M, 'Redactionele signalen' (2007) 55 *SEW Tijdschrift voor Europees en economisch recht* 176.

Vedder, H, 'Spontaneous Harmonisation of National (Competition) Laws in the Wake of the Modernisation of EC Competition Law' (2004) 1 *Competition Law Review* 5.

Veljanovski, C, 'Cartel Fines in Europe: Law, Practice and Deterrence' (2007) 30 *World Competition* 65.

Vogelaar, FOW, 'Criminalisering van het Mededingingsrecht: Trendy of Noodzaak' (2005) *Ars Aequi* 1015.

——'Interface: EC and Dutch Competition Law – In Which Fields or Areas Would the Netherlands Still Have Autonomous Regulating Powers? And Would it Be Wise to Use Those Powers?' in D Obradovic and N Lavranos (eds), *Interface between EU Law and National Law* (Europa Law Publishing, 2007).

——'The Compulsory Licence of Intellectual Property Rights under the EC Competition Rules: An Analysis of the Exception to the General Rule of Ownership Immunity from Competition Rules' (2009) 6 *Competition Law Review* 117.

Vollmer, Ch, 'Experience with Criminal Law Sanctions for Competition Law Infringements in Germany' in KJ Cseres, MP Schinkel and FOW Vogelaar (eds), *Criminalization of Competition Law Enforcement: Economic and Legal Implications for the Member States* (Edward Elgar, 2006).

Wagner-Von Papp, F, 'What if All Bid Riggers Went to Prison and Nobody Noticed? Criminal Antitrust Law Enforcement in Germany' in C Beaton-Wells and A Ezrachi (eds), *Criminalising Cartels: Critical Studies of an International Regulatory Movement* (Hart Publishing, 2011).

Wesseling, R, 'The Draft-Regulation Modernising the Competition Rules: The Commission is Married to One Idea' (2001) 26 *European Law Review* 357.

Whelan, P, 'A Principled Argument for Personal Criminal Sanctions as Punishment under EC Cartel Law' (2007) *Competition Law Review* 7.

Williams, R, 'Cartels in the Criminal Law Landscape' in C Beaton-Wells and A Ezrachi (eds), *Criminalising Cartels: Critical Studies of an International Regulatory Movement* (Hart Publishing, 2011).

Wils, WPJ, 'The Modernisation of the Enforcement of Articles 81 and 82 EC: A Legal and Economic Analysis of the Commission's Proposal for a New Council Regulation Replacing Regulation No. 17' in B Hawk (ed), *Annual Proceedings of the Fordham Corporate Law Institute on International Antitrust Law and Policy* 2000 (Juris Publishing, 2001).

——'The Principle of *Ne Bis in Idem* in EC Antitrust Enforcement: A Legal and Economic Analysis' (2003) 26 *World Competition* 131.

——'Optimal Antitrust Fines: Theory and Practice' (2006) 29 *World Competition* 183.

——'Leniency in Antitrust Enforcement: Theory and Practice' (2007) 30 *World Competition* 25.

——'The European Commission's 2006 Guidelines on Antitrust Fines: A Legal and Economic Analysis' (2007) 30 *World Competition* 197.

——'The Use of Settlements in Public Antitrust Enforcement: Objectives and Principles' (2008) 31 *World Competition* 335.

——'The Relationship between Public Antitrust Enforcement and Private Actions for Damages' (2009) 32 *World Competition* 3.

——'EU Anti-trust Enforcement Powers and Procedural Rights and Guarantees: The Interplay between EU Law, National Law, the Charter of Fundamental Rights of the EU and the European Convention on Human Rights' (2011) 34 *World Competition* 189.

——'Recidivism in EU Antitrust Enforcement: A Legal and Economic Analysis' (2012) 35 *World Competition* 5.

RESEARCH PAPERS

Bourgeois, J and Baumé, T, 'Decentralisation of EC Competition Law Enforcement and General Principles of Community law' (2004) College of Europe Research Paper 4/2004 <www.coleurope.be> accessed 1 July 2013.

EUROPEAN COUNCIL DOCUMENTS

Presidency Conclusions of the European Council of 29/30 October 2009 <http://register.consilium.europa.eu/pdf/en/09/st15/st15265-re01.en09.pdf> accessed 1 July 2013.

PARLIAMENTARY DOCUMENTS

Germany

Bundesrat, *Gesetzentwurf der Bundesregierung: Entwurf eines Gesetzes zur Bekämpfung der Korruption* (BT-Drucksache 553/96) 17 <http://dip.bundestag.de> accessed 1 July 2013.

Deutscher Bundestag, *Gesetzentwurf der Bundesregierung: Entwurf eines Siebten Gesetzes zur Änderung des Gesetzes gegen Wettbewerbsbeschränkungen* (BT-Drucksache 15/3640) <www.bundestag.de/dokumente/drucksachen/index.html> accessed 1 July 2013.

—— *Beschlussempfelung und Bericht des Auschusses für Wirtschaft und Arbeit (9. Ausschuss) zu dem Gesetzentwurf der Bundesregierung – Drucksache 15/3640 – Entwurf eines Siebten Gesetzes zür Änderung des Gesetzes gegen Wettbewerbsbeschränkungen* (BT-Drucksache 15/5049) <www.bundestag.de/dokumente/ drucksachen/index.html> accessed 1 July 2013.

—— *Unterrichtung durch die Bundesregierung: Bericht des Bundeskartellamtes über seine Tätigkeit in den Jahren 2007-2008 sowie über die Lage und Entwicklung auf seinem Aufgabengebiet und Stellingnahme der Bundesregierung* (BT-Drucksache 16/13500) <www.bundestag.de/dokumente/drucksachen/index.html> accessed 1 July 2013.

—— *Unterrichtung durch die Bundesregierung: Bericht des Bundeskartellamtes über seine Tätigkeit in den Jahren 2009-2010 sowie über die Lage und Entwicklung auf seinem Aufgabengebiet und Stellingnahme der Bundesregierung* (BT-Drucksache 17/6640) <www.bundestag.de/dokumente/drucksachen/index.html> accessed 1 July 2013.

The Netherlands

TK 1995–96, 24707, nr 3.

TK 2003–04, 28990, nr 5.

TK 2005–06, 30071, nr 3.

TK 2005–06, 30071, nr 14.
TK 2005–06, 30071, nr 19 herdruk.
TK 2005–06, 30071, nr 27.
TK 2006–07, Aanhangsel 1586.
TK 2009–10, 24036, nr 369.
TK 2011–12, 33258, nr 2.
TK 2012–13, 33622, nr 2.

UK

Competition HL Bill (1997–98) 140.

Commission Documents

Communication from the Commission to the European Parliament and the Council: Report on the functioning of Regulation 1/2003 [2009] COM 206 final.
Communication from the Commission to the European Parliament and the Council – An area of freedom, security and justice serving the citizen [2009] COM 262 final.
Report on Competition Policy 2010 [2011] COM 328 final 18.
White Paper on the Modernisation of the Rules Implementing Articles 85 and 86 of the EC Treaty COM (1999) 101.
White Paper on Damages actions for breach of the EC antitrust rules COM (2008) 165 final.
Staff Working Paper accompanying the Communication from the Commission to the European Parliament and the Council: Report on the functioning of Regulation 1/2003 [2009] COM 206 final.

NMa Documents

'Outcome van NMa-optreden: Een Beschrijving van de Berekeningsmethode' (2010) 1 NMa Working Papers <www.acm.nl/nl/publicaties/publicatie/7121/NMa-Working-Paper---Outcome-van-NMa-optreden-Een-beschrijving-van-de-berekeningsmethode> accessed 1 July 2013.

OFT Documents

An Assessment of Discretionary Penalties Regimes (OFT 1132 2009) <www.oft.gov.uk/shared_oft/economic_research/oft1132.pdf> accessed 1 July 2013.
Annual Report and Accounts 2011–12 <www.oft.gov.uk/shared_oft/annual_report/2012/OFT_Annual_Report_and_Resou1.pdf> accessed 1 July 2013.

Competition Disqualification Orders: A Consultation Paper (OFT 1111con 2009) <www.oft.gov.uk/shared_oft/consultations/oft1111con.pdf> accessed 1 July 2013.

Guidance as to the Appropriate Amount of a Penalty: A Consultation on OFT Guidance (OFT 423con 2011) <www.oft.gov.uk/shared_oft/consultations/oft423con.pdf> accessed 1 July 2013.

A Guide to the OFT's Investigation Procedures in Competition Cases (OFT1263rev 2012) <www.oft.gov.uk/shared_oft/policy/OFT1263rev> accessed 1 July 2013.

ECN Documents

ECN Model Leniency Programme <http://ec.europa.eu/competition/ecn/model_leniency_en.pdf> accessed 1 July 2013.

ECN Model Leniency Programme: 2012 revision <http://ec.europa.eu/competition/ecn/mlp_revised_2012_en.pdf > accessed 1 July 2013.

ECN Model Leniency Programme: Report on Assessment of the State of Convergence (2009) <http://ec.europa.eu/competition/ecn/model_leniency_programme.pdf> accessed 1 July 2013.

Joint Statement of the Council and the Commission on the Functioning of the Network of Competition Authorities <http://ec.europa.eu/competition/ecn/joint_statement_en.pdf> accessed 1 July 2013.

Statement regarding the Commission Notice on Co-operation within the Network of Competition Authorities <http://ec.europa.eu/competition/antitrust/legislation/list_of_authorities_joint_statement.pdf> accessed 1 July 2013.

ECA Documents

Principles for convergence of pecuniary sanctions imposed on undertakings for infringements of antitrust law <www.bundeskartellamt.de/wDeutsch/download/pdf/ECA/ECA_principles_for_convergence.pdf> accessed 1 July 2013.

OECD Documents

Recommendation concerning Effective Action Against Hard Core Cartels C(98)35 <www.oecd.org> accessed 1 July 2013.

Other Reports

Department for Business, Innovation & Skills, *A Competition Regime For Growth: A Consultation On Options For Reform* (2011) <www.bis.gov.uk/Consultations/competition-regime-for-growth> accessed 1 July 2013.

—— *Growth, Competition and the Competition Regime: Government Response to Consultation* (2012) <www.bis.gov.uk/Consultations/ competition-regime-for-growth> accessed 1 July 2013.

—— *Enterprise and Regulatory Reform Act 2013: Policy Paper* (2013) <www.gov.uk/government/uploads/system/uploads/attachment_data/file/209896/bis-13-905-enterprise-and-regulatory-reform-act-2013-policy.pdf> accessed 1 July 2013.

—— *Streamlining Regulatory and Competition Appeals: Consultation on Options for Reform* (2013) <www.gov.uk/government/uploads/system/uploads/attachment_data/file/207701/bis-13-876-regulatory-and-competition-appeals.pdf> accessed 1 July 2013.

WODC, Strafrechtelijke ontzetting uit beroep of ambt. Oplegging en naleving in the periode 1995-2008 (WODC, 2009) <http://wodc.nl/publicaties/> accessed 1 July 2013.

Speeches

Kalbfleisch, P, 'Elseviercongres Ontwikkelingen Mededingingsrecht 2009' <www.nma.nl> accessed 1 July 2012.

—— 'Elseviercongres Ontwikkelingen Mededingingsrecht 2010' <www.nma.nl> accessed 1 July 2012.

Press Releases

BKartA Pressemeldung of 10 February 2012 <www.bundeskartellamt.de> accessed 1 July 2013.

Council of Europe press release DC041 (2013) <https://wcd.coe.int> accessed 1 July 2013.

NMa press release of 07 February 2003 (*LMV*) <www.nma.nl> accessed 1 July 2012.

NMa press release of 23 December 2008 (*NMa: Gasterra rekende geen excessieve prijzen*) <www.nma.nl> accessed 1 July 2012.

NMa press release of 20 May 2010 <www.nma.nl> accessed 1 July 2012.

NMa press release of 11 November 2010 <www.nma.nl> accessed 1 July 2012.

OFT press release No 15/04/2003 <www.oft.gov.uk> accessed 1 July 2013.

OFT press release 47/10 (10 May 2010) <http://www.oft.gov.uk> accessed 1 July 2013.

OFT press release 31/08 (29 February 2008) <www.oft.gov.uk > accessed 1 July 2013.

OLG Düsseldorf Pressemitteilung Nr 10/2013 (16 April 2013) <www.olg-duesseldorf.nrw.de> accessed 1 July 2013.

Index

www.ingramcontent.com/pod-product-compliance
Ingram Content Group UK Ltd.
Pitfield, Milton Keynes, MK11 3LW, UK
UKHW020135290926
15471UKWH00003B/491

9 781509 907038